Heidegger and the Problem of Phenomena

Also Available from Bloomsbury

Heidegger's Style: On Philosophical Anthropology and Aesthetics, Markus Weidler
Heidegger's Politics of Enframing: Technology and Responsibility, Javier Cardoza-Kon
The Ethical Imagination in Shakespeare and Heidegger, Andy Amato

Heidegger and the Problem of Phenomena

Fredrik Westerlund

BLOOMSBURY ACADEMIC
LONDON • NEW YORK • OXFORD • NEW DELHI • SYDNEY

BLOOMSBURY ACADEMIC
Bloomsbury Publishing Plc
50 Bedford Square, London, WC1B 3DP, UK
1385 Broadway, New York, NY 10018, USA
29 Earlsfort Terrace, Dublin 2, Ireland

Bloomsbury, Bloomsbury Academic and the Diana logo are trademarks of
Bloomsbury Publishing Plc

First published in Great Britain 2020
This paperback edition published in 2021

Copyright © Fredrik Westerlund, 2020

Fredrik Westerlund has asserted his right under the Copyright, Designs and Patents Act,
1988, to be identified as Author of this work.

For legal purposes the Acknowledgments on p. viii constitute an extension
of this copyright page.

Cover design by Anna Hidvégi

All rights reserved. No part of this publication may be reproduced
or transmitted in any form or by any means, electronic or mechanical,
including photocopying, recording, or any information storage or retrieval
system, without prior permission in writing from the publishers.

Bloomsbury Publishing Plc does not have any control over, or responsibility for, any
third-party websites referred to or in this book. All internet addresses given in this
book were correct at the time of going to press. The author and publisher regret any
inconvenience caused if addresses have changed or sites have ceased to exist, but can
accept no responsibility for any such changes.

A catalogue record for this book is available from the British Library.

A catalog record for this book is available from the Library of Congress.

ISBN: HB: 978-1-3500-8647-0
PB: 978-1-3502-6233-1
ePDF: 978-1-3500-8648-7
eBook: 978-1-3500-8649-4

Typeset by Newgen KnowledgeWorks Pvt. Ltd., Chennai, India

To find out more about our authors and books visit www.bloomsbury.com
and sign up for our newsletters.

CONTENTS

Acknowledgments	viii
Abbreviations: Heidegger and Husserl	x
INTRODUCTION	1

Part 1
A PHENOMENOLOGY OF FACTICAL LIFE

INTRODUCTION	13
1. PHENOMENOLOGY AS PRIMORDIAL SCIENCE OF LIFE	17
Husserl and the Promise of Phenomenology	17
Phenomenology as Primordial Science	21
The Dead End of Theoretical Philosophy	24
Heidegger's First Critique of Husserl	27
2. HEIDEGGER'S PHENOMENOLOGY OF FACTICAL LIFE	35
Phenomenology or Historicism?	35
Heidegger's Nontheoretical Phenomenology	36
Destruction and Formal Indication	41
The Primordial Structure of Life	43
A Transhistorical Phenomenology of Historical Life	45
3. LIFE AND THE TASK OF PHILOSOPHY	49
The Question of the Existential Task of Philosophy	49
Fundamental or Dispensable?	52
An Unsettling Suggestion	54

Part 2
THE HISTORICAL STRUCTURE OF PHENOMENA

INTRODUCTION	57
4. TOWARD A NEW CONCEPTION OF PHENOMENA	63
The Confrontation with Aristotle	63
Heidegger's Renewed Critique of Husserl	67
The Categorial Intuition—in Heidegger	70

5. THE PROJECT OF FUNDAMENTAL ONTOLOGY — 79
The Question of Being and the Task of Fundamental Ontology — 79
Problems and Possibilities — 82

6. BEING-IN-THE-WORLD — 85
The World — 85
Three Dimensions of Understanding — 90
Interpretation and Language — 93
Reality and Truth — 96

7. PROBLEMS OF AUTHENTICITY — 103
The Challenge of Authenticity — 103
The Lacunae in Heidegger's Analysis — 106
Dasein's Self-Choice: Between Collectivism and Subjectivism — 108
The Basic Egoism of Dasein — 112

8. HEIDEGGER'S METHOD IN *BEING AND TIME* — 119
The Question of Method—the Question of Phenomenology — 119
Heidegger's Methodological Self-Understanding — 121
Phenomenology in Practice — 124

Part 3
THE OPENNESS OF BEING

INTRODUCTION — 129

9. THE QUESTION OF THE OPENNESS OF BEING — 135
The Question of the Turn — 135
The Beginning of the Turn — 136
The Turn of Heidegger's Question — 139
Heidegger's Turn Reconsidered — 142

10. THE PROMISE OF NATIONAL SOCIALISM — 145
The Superior Task of Philosophy — 145
The Basic Facts — 148
The Philosophical Roots of Heidegger's Politics — 150
The Failed Critique — 153
The Black Hole in Heidegger's Thinking — 155

11. THE EVENT THAT OPENS THE WORLD — 161
The Question of the Binding Power of the World — 161
The Task of Thinking and the Task of Poetry — 164
The Superiority of the Task of Opening a World — 166
The Strife between the World and the Earth — 167
The Thing and the Fourfold — 175

12. HEIDEGGER'S LATE HISTORICAL THINKING 179
    The Question of Phenomenology 180
    Historical Reflection and the Need to Return to the Greek Beginning 183
    The Matter of Thinking 184
    The Way of Thinking 186
    The Fate of Phenomenology 190

Epilogue
BEING OPEN TOWARD BEINGS

INTRODUCTION 193

13. THE SOURCES OF ETHICAL-EXISTENTIAL NORMATIVITY 195
    Levinas's Critique 196
    Desire for Social Affirmation versus Love for Others 197
    Heidegger and the Binding Power of the World 201

14. THE SOURCES OF TRUTH 207
    Lafont's Critique 208
    Heidegger's Arguments 210
    Our Openness to Transhistorical Realities as the Source of Truth 213

15. PHENOMENOLOGY AND HISTORICAL REFLECTION 217
    The Method of Returning to the Historical Origin 218
    The Method of Deconstruction 221
    The Challenge of Phenomenology 223

Notes 229
Bibliography 253
Index 263

ACKNOWLEDGMENTS

The roots of this book stretch back around twenty years, to when, as a philosophy student at the University of Helsinki, I first became captivated by Heidegger's thinking in the late 1990s. Later, I wrote my PhD thesis on Heidegger and the problem of phenomenality, completing and defending it in 2014. After that, I have continued my reflections on Heidegger and thoroughly reworked my dissertation into the present book.

This book is the outcome of, and gives expression to, my long critical wrestle with Heidegger—and, crucially, with myself. When as a student I started reading Heidegger, I was immediately intrigued. Heidegger's radical pursuit of the basic philosophical questions, his insistence on their existential relevance and motives, and his phenomenological hands-on approach opened up a new sense of what concrete philosophical thinking can be. I learned a lot. However, as my own phenomenological thinking developed—and as a result of my intensified reflections on the moral psychology and ethical-existential concerns of our interpersonal life—I started to grow more and more wary both of central parts of Heidegger's philosophical vision and of the ethical-existential spirit of his thinking. My doubts and my critical gaze also concerned myself and the motives that had fueled my enthusiasm for Heidegger. I started to sense that many aspects of the emotional atmosphere of Heidegger's thinking that I had been drawn to—especially, the grandiosity and superior weight that Heidegger ascribes to the ontological task of philosophy and his supreme contempt for much of contemporary philosophy and life—could, to a significant degree, be seen as expressions of an attitude characterized, not by unreserved independence and openness, but by ressentiment and by a desperate deferred desire for self-assertion. I also grew more and more suspicious of Heidegger's driving philosophical idea about the basic historicity of being and thinking, which, when radically pursued, seems to cover up both the ethical-existential significance of human beings and the possibility of truth.

My hope is that my own dual impulses toward Heidegger and my struggle to come to terms with them have helped to bring to life—and to clarity—the tension and dynamics obtaining between the genuine possibilities and insights of Heidegger's thinking and the philosophical and ethical-existential problems that haunt it.

Here, I want to thank all those who have read and commented on the manuscript, or parts of it, along the way, and those with whom I have discussed and debated the central themes of the book: Jussi Backman, Joel Backström, Jaakko Belt, Tatjana Brandt, David Cerbone, Steven Crowell, Günter Figal, Mirja Hartimo, Sara Heinämaa, Hannes Nykänen, Simo Pulkkinen, Hans Ruin, Niklas Toivakainen, Thomas Wallgren, and Bernt Österman. In addition to this, there are numerous other friends and colleagues to whom I am grateful for the philosophical discussions we have had over the years. Finally, I want to thank all the members of the Phenomenology Research Seminar in Helsinki for making possible a vital forum for discussion and debate.

I am very grateful for the funding I have received from the Kone Foundation, the Nylands Nation Student Nation, the Oskar Öflund Foundation, the Otto A. Malm Foundation, the Academy of Finland, the University of Helsinki, and the research network Subjectivity, Historicity, Communality. Without this financial support, the book would not have been possible.

ABBREVIATIONS: HEIDEGGER AND HUSSERL

References to the works of Heidegger are as a rule provided in the text by the volume of the *Gesamtausgabe* edition (Frankfurt am Main: Vittorio Klostermann, 1975–, abbreviated as GA), followed by the German pagination, a slash, and the English pagination of published translations where available. There are two exceptions to this practice. First, in the case of *Being and Time*, I use the abbreviation SZ and only provide page references to the standard German edition published by Max Niemeyer Verlag. This pagination is contained in the margin both of the *Gesamtausgabe* edition and of the English translations. Second, since Heidegger's late text "Cézanne" is not included in the *Gesamtausgabe*, I use the abbreviation CZ and provide the page numbers of the German original and the English translation listed below. References to Husserl are to the *Husserliana* series (The Hague: Martinus Nijhoff, 1950–, abbreviated as Hua), with the exception of *Experience and Judgement*, which is not included in the series and for which I use the abbreviation EU. The German pagination is given first, followed by the pagination of the English translation where available. In the list of abbreviations below, I mention the English translations that the page numbers refer to and which I have consulted. I have frequently altered the translations as I see fit, without comment.

HEIDEGGER

SZ   *Sein und Zeit*, 17th edition, Tübingen: Max Niemeyer Verlag, [1927] 1993. English translations: *Being and Time*, trans. Joan Stambaugh, rev. Dennis Schmidt, Albany: State University of New York Press, 2010; *Being and Time*, trans. John Macquarrie and Edward Robinson, New York: Harper & Row, 1962.

CZ   "Cézanne," in *Heidegger Lesebuch*, ed. Günter Figal, Frankfurt am Main: Vittorio Klostermann, 2007. English translation: "Cézanne," trans. Jerome Veith, in *The Heidegger Reader*, ed. Günter Figal, Bloomington: Indiana University Press, 2009.

GA 4   *Erläuterungen zu Hölderlins Dichtung*, ed. Friedrich-Wilhelm von Herrmann, 1981. English translation: *Elucidations of Hölderlin's Poetry*, trans. Keith Hoeller, New York: Humanity Books, 2000.

GA 5   *Holzwege*, ed. Friedrich-Wilhelm von Herrmann, 1977. English translation: *Off the Beaten Track*, ed. and trans. Julian Young and Kenneth Haynes, Cambridge: Cambridge University Press, 2002.

GA 7   *Vorträge und Aufsätze*, ed. Friedrich-Wilhelm von Herrmann, 2000. English translations of parts of this volume: "Building Dwelling Thinking," "The Thing," and "... Poetically Man Dwells ...," trans. Alfred Hofstadter, in *Poetry, Language, Thought*, New York: Harper & Row, 1971; "Science and Reflection," trans. William Lovitt, in *The Question Concerning Technology and Other Essays*, New York: Harper & Row, 1977.

GA 9   *Wegmarken*, ed. Friedrich-Wilhelm von Herrmann, 1996. English translation: *Pathmarks*, ed. William McNeill, trans. John van Buren, Frank A. Capuzzi, James G. Hart, Michael Heim, Walter Kaufmann, Ted E. Klein Jr., David Farrell Krell, John C. Maraldo, William McNeill, Robert Metcalf, William E. Pohl, John Sallis, and Thomas Sheehan, Cambridge: Cambridge University Press, 1998.

GA 11 *Identität und Differenz*, ed. Friedrich-Wilhelm von Herrmann, 2006. English translations of parts of this volume: "The Principle of Identity," trans. Jerome Veith, in *The Heidegger Reader*, ed. Günter Figal, Bloomington: Indiana University Press, 2009; "The Onto-Theo-Logical Constitution of Metaphysics," trans. Joan Stambaugh, in *Identity and Difference*, Chicago, IL: University of Chicago Press, 2002.

GA 12 *Unterwegs zur Sprache*, ed. Friedrich-Wilhelm von Herrmann, 1985. English translation of parts of this volume: *On the Way to Language*, trans. Peter D. Hertz and Joan Stambaugh, New York: Harper & Row, 1971.

GA 14 *Zur Sache des Denkens*, ed. Friedrich-Wilhelm von Herrman, 2007. English translation of parts of this volume: *On Time and Being*, trans. Joan Stambaugh, New York: Harper & Row, 1972.

GA 15 *Seminare*, ed. Curd Ochwadt, 2005. English translation of parts of this volume: *Four Seminars: Le Thor 1966, 1968, 1969, Zähringen 1973*, trans. Andrew Mitchell and François Raffoul, Bloomington: Indiana University Press, 2003.

GA 16 *Reden und andere Zeugnisse eines Lebensweges*, ed. Hermann Heidegger, 2000. English translations of parts of this volume: "The Self-Assertion of the German University," trans. William S. Lewis, and "'Only a God Can Save Us': *Der Spiegel*'s Interview with Martin Heidegger," trans. Maria P. Alter and John D. Caputo, in *The Heidegger Controversy: A Critical Reader*, ed. Richard Wolin, Cambridge, MA: MIT Press, 1993.

GA 17 *Einführung in die phänomenologische Forschung*, ed. Friedrich-Wilhelm von Herrmann, 1994. English translation: *Introduction to Phenomenological Research*, trans. Daniel O. Dahlstrom, Bloomington: Indiana University Press, 2005.

GA 20 *Prolegomena zur Geschichte des Zeitbegriffs*, ed. Petra Jaeger, 1994. English translation: *History of the Concept of Time: Prolegomena*, trans. Theodore Kisiel, Bloomington: Indiana University Press, 1985.

GA 24 *Die Grundprobleme der Phänomenologie*, ed. Friedrich-Wilhelm von Herrmann, 1975. English translation: *The Basic Problems of Phenomenology*, trans. Alfred Hofstadter, Bloomington: Indiana University Press, 1988.

GA 26 *Metaphysische Anfangsgründe der Logik im Ausgang von Leibniz*, ed. Klaus Held, 1990. English translation: *The Metaphysical Foundations of Logic*, trans. Michael Heim, Bloomington: Indiana University Press, 1984.

GA 27 *Einleitung in die Philosophie*, ed. Otto Saame and Ina Saame-Speidel, 2001.

GA 33 *Aristoteles, Metaphysik Θ 1–3. Von Wesen und Wirklichkeit der Kraft*, ed. Heinrich Hüni, 1981. English translation: *Aristotle's Metaphysics Θ 1–3: On the Essence and Actuality of Force*, trans. Walter Brogan and Peter Warnek, Bloomington: Indiana University Press, 1995.

GA 36/37 *Sein und Wahrheit*, ed. Harmut Tietjen, 2001. English translation: *Being and Truth*, trans. Gregory Fried and Richard Polt, Bloomington: Indiana University Press, 2010.

GA 40 *Einführung in die Metaphysik*, ed. Petra Jaeger, 1983. English translation: *Introduction to Metaphysics*, trans. Gregory Fried and Richard Polt, New Haven, CT: Yale University Press, 2014.

GA 45 *Grundfragen der Philosophie. Ausgewählte "Probleme" der "Logik,"* ed. Friedrich-Wilhelm von Herrmann, 1992. English translation: *Basic Questions of Philosophy: Selected "Problems" of "Logic,"* trans. Richard Rojcewicz and André Schuwer, Bloomington: Indiana University Press, 1994.

GA 56/57 *Zur Bestimmung der Philosophie*, ed. Bernd Heimbüchel, 1987. English translation: *Towards the Definition of Philosophy*, trans. Ted Sadler, London: Athlone Press, 2000.

GA 58 *Grundprobleme der Phänomenologie*, ed. Hans-Helmuth Gander, 1993. English translation: *Basic Problems of Phenomenology*, trans. Scott M. Campbell, London: Bloomsbury, 2013.

GA 59 *Phänomenologie der Anschauung und des Ausdrucks*, ed. Claudius Strube, 1993. English translation: *Phenomenology of Intuition and Expression*, trans. Tracy Colony, London: Continuum, 2010.

GA 60 *Phänomenologie des religiösen Lebens*, ed. Matthias Jung, Thomas Regehly, and Claudius Strube, 1995. English translation: *The Phenomenology of Religious Life*, trans. Matthias Fritsch and Jennifer A. Gosetti-Ferencei, Bloomington: Indiana University Press, 2004.

GA 62 *Phänomenologische Interpretationen ausgewählter Abhandlungen des Aristoteles zur Ontologie und Logik*, ed. Günther Neumann, 2005. English translation of a part of this volume: "Phenomenological Interpretations in Connection with Aristotle (An Indication of the Hermeneutical Situation)," trans. John van Buren, in *Supplements: From the Earlies Essays to* Being and Time *and Beyond*, ed. John van Buren, Albany: State University of New York Press, 2002.

GA 63   *Ontologie (Hermeneutik der Faktizität)*, ed. Käte Bröcker-Oltmanns, 1995. English translation: *Ontology—The Hermeneutics of Facticity*, trans. John van Buren, Bloomington: Indiana University Press, 1999.

GA 65   *Beiträge zur Philosophie (Vom Ereignis)*, ed. Friedrich-Wilhelm von Herrmann, 1989. English translation: *Contributions to Philosophy (Of the Event)*, trans. Richard Rojcewicz and Daniela Vallega-Neu, Bloomington: Indiana University Press, 2012.

GA 66   *Besinnung*, ed. Friedrich-Wilhelm von Herrmann, 1997. English translation: *Mindfulness*, trans. Parvis Emad and Thomas Kalary, London: Continuum, 2006.

GA 79   *Bremer und Freiburger Vorträge*, ed. Petra Jaeger, 1994. English translation: *Bremen and Freiburg Lectures: Insight into That Which Is and Basic Principles of Thinking*, trans. Andrew J. Mitchell, Bloomington: Indiana University Press, 2012.

GA 94   *Überlegungen II–VI (Schwarze Hefte 1931–1938)*, ed. Peter Trawny, 2014. English translation: *Ponderings II–VI: Black Notebooks 1931–1938*, trans. Richard Rojcewicz, Bloomington: Indiana University Press, 2016.

GA 96   *Überlegungen XII–XV (Schwarze Hefte 1939–1941)*, ed. Peter Trawny, 2014. English translation: *Ponderings XII–XV: Black Notebooks 1939–1941*, trans. Richard Rojcewicz, Bloomington: Indiana University Press, 2017.

GA 97   *Anmerkungen I–V (Schwarze Hefte 1942–1948)*, ed. P. Trawny, 2015.

HUSSERL

Hua 2   *Die Idee der Phänomenologie. Fünf Vorlesungen*, ed. Walter Biemel, 1950. English translation: *The Idea of Phenomenology*, trans. Lee Hardy, Dordrecht: Kluwer Academic, 1999.

Hua 3   *Ideen zu einer reinen Phänomenlogie und phänomenologischen Philosophie. Erstes Buch. Allgemeine Einführung in die reine Phänomenologie*, ed. Karl Schuhmann, 1976. English translation: *Ideas Pertaining to a Pure Phenomenology and to a Phenomenological Philosophy. First Book. General Introduction to a Pure Phenomenology*, trans. Fred Kersten, The Hague: Martinus Nijhoff, 1983.

Hua 4   *Ideen zu einer reinen Phänomenlogie und phänomenologischen Philosophie. Zweites Buch. Phänomenologische Untersuchungen zur Konstitution*, ed. Marly Biemel, 1952. English translation: *Ideas Pertaining to a Pure Phenomenology and to a Phenomenological Philosophy. Second Book: Studies in the Phenomenology of Constitution*, trans. Richard Rojcewicz and André Schuwer, Dordrecht: Kluwer Academic, 1989.

Hua 5	*Ideen zur einer reinen Phänomenologie und phänomenologischen Philosophie. Drittes Buch. Die Phänomenologie und die Fundamente der Wissenschaften*, ed. Marly Biemel, 1952. English translation of a part of this volume: "Epilogue" to *Ideas I*, in *Ideas Pertaining to a Pure Phenomenology and to a Phenomenological Philosophy. Second Book: Studies in the Phenomenology of Constitution*, trans. Richard Rojcewicz and André Schuwer, Dordrecht: Kluwer Academic, 1989.
Hua 6	*Die Krisis der europäischen Wissenschaften und die Transzendentale Phänomenologie. Eine Einleitung in die phänomenologische Philosophie*, ed. Walter Biemel, 1954. English translation: *The Crisis of the European Sciences and Transcendental Phenomenology: An Introduction to Phenomenological Philosophy*, trans. David Carr, Evanston, IL: Northwestern University Press, 1970.
Hua 8	*Erste Philosophie (1923/24). Zweiter Teil. Theorie der phänomenologischen Reduktion*, ed. Rudolf Boehm, 1959.
Hua 19/1	*Logische Untersuchungen. Zweiter Band. Erster Teil. Untersuchungen zur Phänomenologie und Theorie der Erkenntnis*, ed. Ulrika Panzer, 1984. English translation: *Logical Investigations*, vols. I and II, trans. J. N. Findlay, London: Routledge & Kegan Paul, 1970.
Hua 19/2	*Logische Untersuchungen. Zweiter Band. Zweiter Teil. Untersuchungen zur Phänomenologie und Theorie der Erkenntnis*, ed. Ulrika Panzer, 1984. English translation: *Logical Investigations*, vol. II, trans. J. N. Findlay, London: Routledge & Kegan Paul, 1970
Hua 25	*Aufsätze und Vorträge (1911–1921)*, ed. Thomas Nenon and Hans Rainer Sepp. English translation of a part of this volume: "Philosophy as Rigorous Science," trans. Marcus Brainard, *The New Yearbook for Phenomenology and Phenomenological Philosophy* 2 (2002).
EU	*Erfahrung und Urteil. Untersuchungen zur Genealogie der Logik*, ed. Ludwig Landgrebe, Hamburg: Felix Meiner, 1985. English translation: *Experience and Judgment: Investigations in a Genealogy of Logic*, trans. James Spencer Churchill and Karl Ameriks, Evanston, IL: Northwestern University Press, 1973.

INTRODUCTION

Heidegger and the Problem of Phenomena

For at least a century the question of phenomena has haunted philosophy as a central problem. What does it mean that something shows itself or gives itself as a meaningful phenomenon in our experience? What does it mean to see, understand, and give expression to such phenomena? Can our direct intuitive experience of the phenomenally given serve as a ground for our understanding? Or is this experience essentially determined by the historical contexts of meaning—languages, concepts, norms—in which we live, such that our critical understanding of these contexts cannot ground itself on any phenomenological description of the intuitively given, but will need to take the form of another kind of conceptual, hermeneutic, or deconstructive analysis?

At the beginning of the twentieth century Edmund Husserl launched his immense attempt at transforming philosophy into a rigorous phenomenological science. In order for philosophy not to collapse into empty and prejudiced theoretical speculation on the basis of received concepts and theories, Husserl argued, it must concentrate on strictly seeing and describing what is concretely given in our experience. At the same time, Husserl widened the notion of intuitive givenness to include not only sense perceptions or empirical data but everything that shows itself to us as identifiable unities of meaning. Phenomenology opens up the promise that intuitive phenomenal givenness may serve as an ultimate ground for our understanding of meaningful reality.

But is this possible?

The fact is that since the middle of the past century philosophy has been characterized by a strong tendency to dismiss the very idea of direct phenomenal givenness—the "Myth of the Given," as Wilfrid Sellars (1956: 267) called it. The variations of the critique of the given are of course multiple. On the continental side, we have, for example, the hermeneutics of Martin Heidegger, Hans-Georg Gadamer, and Paul Ricoeur, the structuralism of Ferdinand de Saussure and Claude Lévi-Strauss, and the poststructuralist and deconstructivist thought of Jacques Derrida, Michel Foucault, and Jacques Lacan. On the analytical side, we have, for example, the neo-Kantianism-cum-Hegelianism of Wilfrid Sellars, John McDowell, and Robert Brandom, the ordinary language philosophy of John

Austin, the thinking of the later Ludwig Wittgenstein and much of the philosophy that it has inspired, the historicist philosophy of science of Thomas Kuhn, as well as the neo-pragmatism of Richard Rorty. Notwithstanding the immense differences between these philosophers, one of the vital effects of their combined efforts has been to establish one of the leading paradigms of thought pervading contemporary philosophy: the general and more or less vague idea that our experiential access to reality is essentially governed by the historical contexts of meaning—languages, concepts, norms—in which we live, and which determine in advance what we may see and identify as meaningful phenomena. Whereas this paradigm largely dominates the field of continental philosophy, it has never achieved a governing role in the analytic tradition, where it lives in a tense relation to the fundamental inclination toward naturalist thought.

Martin Heidegger stands at the very center of the historical development sketched above. As Heidegger emerges as an autonomous philosopher in the beginning of the 1920s, he adopts Husserl's basic phenomenological demand to return to the experientially given while at the same time critically pursuing the question concerning the nature of phenomenal givenness. In contrast to Husserl, who, according to Heidegger, had largely built on the model of theoretical observation, he insists that our primary access to meaningful reality lies in our pretheoretical experience of the world. In the course of laying bare the rootedness of this experience in the historical contexts of meaning into which we always already find ourselves thrown, Heidegger gradually moves away from the intuition-based phenomenology of Husserl toward a hermeneutic reflection on how our contexts of meaning arise and concern us as a finite and groundless historical destiny. Hence, while Heidegger takes his starting point in Husserl's phenomenology, he eventually becomes the philosopher who more than anyone else contributes to establishing the dominance of radical historicism in the continental tradition.

This book is a study of Heidegger's struggle to come to terms with the question of *phenomena*, that is, of what it means for something to show or give itself as a meaningful phenomenon; as such, it is also a study of his effort to critically develop and probe the question of *phenomenology*, that is, of what it means to explicate and articulate the structure of our experience of phenomena. However, to the extent that Heidegger's struggle with these questions constitutes one of the exemplary trajectories instituting our present situation, I also hope that my study will help to open up and illuminate some of the philosophical problems, ambiguities, and blindnesses marking our present.

The Heidegger Discussion

By now the scholarly literature on Heidegger has already grown into an enormous mass of books and articles—and it is still rapidly growing. This discursive situation certainly brings with it some obvious advantages. We are now in possession of a large amount of careful historical research covering most parts of Heidegger's production and including detailed studies of the key philosophers and traditions influencing or providing background for his thought. However, there are also grounds for interpreting the discursive situation as the symptom of a philosophical crisis, a crisis that the situation is itself contributing to. On the one hand, the greater part of the literature on Heidegger is primarily exegetical in character, exhibiting little independent and systematic philosophical work. Even when the ambition to think about the matters themselves is present, it is all too often the case that Heidegger's concepts function as the horizon that guides the thinking in a dogmatic manner. On the other hand, the circumstance that Heidegger's thought constitutes a paradigm for our own thinking makes it possible to feel that in charting the conceptual networks of Heidegger's texts one is indeed tracing the ultimate perimeters of our contemporary philosophical understanding. Yet this is a delusion—for the simple reason that a purely exegetical interpretation of a philosophical text, however philosophically powerful that text may be, can never of itself effect genuine philosophical understanding. Hence, to the extent that we go on tracing the conceptual connections of Heidegger's thinking, repeating his criticisms of philosophical positions that we, strictly speaking, do not take seriously anymore, all the while believing that we are engaged in philosophy proper, his work has started to function as an invisible wall for our thinking. The sheer mass of literature supports this state of affairs by making it virtually impossible to confront the basic thoughts of Heidegger in a systematic fashion without failing the academic demand to anchor the interpretation in the relevant literature and the elaborate picture of his thought that it sustains.

Let me try to specify the distinction between exegetical and philosophical interpretations a little. By *exegetical*—or historical—interpretations I do not only denote interpretations that deliberately or unambiguously realize an exegetical purpose. I mean all interpretations that essentially move—trace, connect, map concepts and ideas—within the conceptual horizon of the interpreted text and possible intertexts, without radically probing and accounting for the philosophical force of these concepts. By *philosophical*—or systematic, or problem-oriented— interpretations I mean interpretations that explicate a text through providing some kind of independent articulation of what the text shows and fails to show. One reason why this distinction has tended to grow dim in the current discussion may be found in the sharp and widely recognized critique that Heidegger himself levels against any attempt to draw a simple distinction between historical and systematic investigations. Heidegger's central argument is that every systematic investigation is always already guided by some historical preunderstanding of the matter in question; hence, it becomes an integral part of the systematic task to engage in a critical reflection on the historical conditions determining the focus of our questioning. But the reverse is also the case, as Heidegger himself was aware: in order for an interpretation to bring the sense of a text to life and to bring it to view in its philosophical claim on us, it must itself be able to confront and give voice to that claim. Strictly speaking, understanding a philosophical text *means* understanding what the text has to say about ourselves and the world. Hence, understanding a text essentially involves independently understanding the matters that the text is about and critically discerning how the text articulates and relates to—illuminates, clarifies, distorts, represses—these matters. If an interpretation does not do this, it is philosophically empty. This, of course, does not rule out the possibility that exegetical interpretations may be valuable in different ways, providing crucial guidance for philosophical interpretations.

In so far as our research on Heidegger is still motivated by a genuine philosophical will to learn I believe it is imperative that our engagements with Heidegger are driven by the effort to independently open up and articulate the matters themselves. Such systematically oriented interpretations may of course take many shapes: they may critically rearticulate and delimit Heidegger's concepts and analyses; or they may use Heidegger's thinking as a critical starting point for philosophical inquiries in different directions. Of course, there is a risk that such a program might be exploited as an apology for producing texts that renounce serious interpretation and translate Heidegger into a strawman for the interpreter's own purposes. But this is a risk I think we have to take today; otherwise, we hazard a much greater danger: that Heidegger's work is transformed into a prison and a sanctuary instead of being freed up, critically delimited and overcome—in short, teach us what it can teach us—as the powerful, finite, and deeply problematic work that it is.

The Phenomenological versus the Hermeneutic-Deconstructive Reading

The discussion concerning the issue of phenomena/phenomenology in Heidegger's thinking has for a few decades been dominated by two diverging interpretations. On the one hand, we have the *transcendental phenomenological interpretation* defended by, for example, Steven Crowell, Daniel Dahlstrom, Søren Overgaard, Burt Hopkins, and Dermot Moran.[1] This interpretation basically reads Heidegger's philosophy as a critical yet fundamentally faithful elaboration of Husserl's transcendental phenomenology, which is conceived of as providing the key to rigorous philosophizing. Even though Heidegger criticizes Husserl for having neglected the pretheoretical and historically conditioned nature of our experience, the systematic promise of his own philosophy lies precisely in a hermeneutically sharpened intuitive reflection on the basic—necessary and universal—structures characterizing our primary experience of the meaningful world. On the other hand, we have the *hermeneutic-deconstructive interpretation* defended by, for example, Hans-Georg Gadamer, Charles Guignon, Françoise Dastur, Günter Figal, John Sallis, John van Buren, David Farrell Krell, and Hans Ruin.[2] This interpretation explicates and hails Heidegger as one of the most severe critics of the idea, still held by Husserl, that our reflective seeing of intuitively given structures of meaning could serve as a measure for our understanding. According to this interpretation, Heidegger provides a groundbreaking analysis of the radical historicity of all experience of meaning: it is only on account of our thrownness into groundless and finite historical contexts of meaning that we are able to experience objects as meaningful. Hence, philosophy cannot hope to ground itself on any direct experience of the phenomenally given but needs to take the form of a critical explication of its own historical predicament. There have been two basic ways of developing this line of interpretation, which cannot always be kept strictly apart. The hermeneutic interpretation—represented by, for example, Hans-Georg Gadamer, Françoise Dastur, and Günter Figal—tends to highlight our fundamental rootedness in our own finite tradition and inquires into the possibilities of remaining faithful to that tradition while at the same time critically reflecting upon it and opening up to other people and histories. The deconstructive interpretation—represented by, for example, John Sallis, David Farrell Krell, and Hans Ruin—tends to stress the primary task of tracing and answering to the groundless differential logic at the basis of every historical formation of meaning.

It is no surprise that the two systematic visions outlined above tend to favor different sorts of descriptions of the role of phenomenology in the history of Heidegger's thought. From the point of view of the transcendental phenomenological interpretation, Heidegger's early thinking from the early 1920s up to *Being and Time* naturally emerges as the philosophical summit of his path of thinking. The picture is this: In the early twenties Heidegger develops his hermeneutic phenomenology as a critical elaboration of Husserl's phenomenology. Even though Heidegger emphasizes the historical conditions of thinking and focuses his attention on the temporal-historical structure of our pretheoretical experience of the world, he nevertheless essentially remains faithful to Husserl's method of phenomenological reflection. Consequently, the turn that Heidegger's thinking undergoes in the middle of the 1930s is viewed as a transition from the hermeneutic phenomenology of *Being and Time* toward a historical thinking, which, although containing important elements of intuition-based phenomenological description, is more prone to give rise to speculation and metaphysical construction. From the point of view of the hermeneutic-deconstructive interpretation, the story is almost the reverse. Heidegger's exploration of his main theme—the opening up of groundless, finite being—is bound to appear as a more continuous journey from his groping and ambivalent phenomenological origins toward a historical thinking which is able to answer more consistently to its own finitude and historicity. Moreover, John van Buren has brought forth a tripartite narrative, which views Heidegger's early Freiburg-lectures—with what he claims is their strong emphasis on the elusive, theoretically ungraspable event-character of our pretheoretical experience of the world—as a promising beginning, which gets lost in the more traditional, transcendental phenomenological project of fundamental ontology of *Being and Time*, and which is then rehabilitated and radicalized in Heidegger's later thinking (van Buren 1994a; cf. also Kisiel 1993: 3, 16).

One thing that easily obscures the philosophical stakes of the difference between the two lines of interpretation is that representatives of the hermeneutic-deconstructive reading often tend to label the historical thought of Heidegger "phenomenology." For instance, Günter Figal claims that Heidegger's thinking remains "radical phenomenology … also after *Being and Time*" (2009: 37, my translation). But what does this mean? In fact, Figal maintains that Heidegger's later thinking does not rely on direct intuition of experiential structures but transpires as interpretation of received historical meanings. As Figal puts it: "What other possibilities of thinking could there be except those handed down by the tradition?" (38) To be sure, we can call such a mode of thinking "phenomenology" if we want to. However, we need to see that this is a conception of thinking that radically differs from what I will be calling "phenomenology" in this book. I have reserved this term for the kind of thinking that essentially relies on intuitive reflection on the structures of our experience, structures that transcend whatever historical preconceptions we might have of them. Hence, from our point of view, what Figal is saying, strictly speaking, is that the later Heidegger is a historicist thinker who does not do phenomenology anymore.[3]

The controversy between the two standard interpretations forms the background for my own reading of Heidegger and I will engage in more detail with representatives of each of them along the way. As will become clear, I think the controversy between the interpretations mirrors a tension that goes deep in Heidegger's thinking. On the one hand, Heidegger starts out from and for many years remains committed—at least in his practice—to Husserl's idea of phenomenology as intuitive reflection on the structures of our experiences. On the other hand, he is from the outset convinced of the historicity of our phenomenal experience. This conviction gradually leads him to believe that intuition-based phenomenology must be renounced in favor of a radically historical mode of thinking. There is thus no doubt that both interpretations are able to point to basic aspects of Heidegger's thinking. However, it seems to me that by focusing one-sidedly on either one of Heidegger's conflicting impulses, the interpretations are unable to account for how the tension between them is played out at the heart of his thinking. My contention is that by attending to and exploring the nature of this tension we can get a better grip on the motives that drive Heidegger's philosophical development. Not only are we able to follow the reasoning that makes Heidegger renounce the idea of direct intuition and insist more and more on the historicity of being and thinking, we can also appreciate how awake Heidegger is to the difficulties involved in giving up phenomenology. Granted that all our understanding is determined by our historical contexts of meaning, what is it that allows us to uphold the critical difference between prejudice and primordial understanding? In fact, much of Heidegger's later thinking is an attempt to respond to this challenge by showing how historical being can address us as binding and primordial.

Objective

This book is an extended critical study of what I claim is Heidegger's lifelong effort to come to terms with the problem of phenomena.

In the existent literature, the basic tendency has been to tell some version of the following story of Heidegger's relationship to phenomenology: Whereas the early Heidegger is more or less committed to Husserl's phenomenology, the later Heidegger to a greater or lesser degree gives up phenomenology in favor of another kind of historical reflection on the event that opens up historical being. This way of writing the history of phenomenology in Heidegger's thinking goes all the way back to William J. Richardson's pioneering book from 1963, *Heidegger: Through Phenomenology to Thought*. Richardson originally intended to use the formula "From Phenomenology to Thought" but changed the "from" to "through" on Heidegger's own suggestion.[4] Nevertheless, he portrays Heidegger's philosophical development as a trajectory which starts from a phenomenology of the human being and develops into a thinking of the event of being itself. More recently, Theodore Kisiel has called the years 1919–27 Heidegger's "phenomenological decade" (1993: 59), a description later echoed by, for example, Dermot Moran, Steven Crowell, and Edgar C. Boedeker Jr. (Moran 2000: 194; Crowell 2001: 115, 225; Boedeker 2005: 156). As a general schema, this story is obviously correct. Nevertheless, in recounting the fate of phenomenology in Heidegger's thinking in this way, there is the risk that we overlook the fact that Heidegger for all his life remained intensely engaged both by the problem of phenomena and by the problem of phenomenology.

In this study, I widen the scope of the question so that it includes both the problem of phenomena and the problem of phenomenology in Heidegger's thought. What I hope to show is that the question concerning the nature and structure of phenomena constitutes one of the core problems that Heidegger's thinking revolves around from his early Freiburg lecture courses in 1919–23 up to his late writings from the 1960s—that is, even in the long period of Heidegger's later thinking during which he largely refrains from using the word "phenomenology" as an appropriate term for his own thinking.

The book aims to demonstrate that the problem of phenomena plays a very basic role as a problem that constantly motivates Heidegger and moves his thinking forward, not only regulating his effort to critically develop and eventually abandon the phenomenological method of inquiry, but also informing his central analyses of the pretheoretical experience, the historical structure of understanding, the ontological difference, authenticity, the *Ereignis* of being, and so on. By focusing on the problem of phenomena I also think it is possible to shed new light on some of the central aspects of Heidegger's philosophical development, for example: on the shift that Heidegger's early Freiburg phenomenology of factical life undergoes in 1921 when Heidegger discovers the historical as-structure of understanding in Aristotle; on the ambivalences in his conception of phenomena/phenomenology that underlie his abandonment of the project of fundamental ontology launched in *Being and Time*; and on the so-called "turn" of Heidegger's thinking in the mid-1930s, which I interpret as a turn in his interrogation of the problem of phenomena.

As concerns the historical sources of Heidegger's thinking, I will deal in some detail only with Husserl's phenomenology. In addition to providing a short exposition of Husserl's general phenomenological program as the starting point of Heidegger's early philosophy, the book also examines the basic critical confrontations with Husserl that Heidegger undertakes during his path of thinking. Although I cannot hope to do full justice to Husserl's massive and complex philosophical work, I will nevertheless try to indicate the force and limits of Heidegger's criticisms. By contrast, the other central sources informing Heidegger's thinking of phenomena—for example, Aristotle, Dilthey, Hölderlin, the pre-Socratics—are only mentioned briefly, and they will only figure in the roles that Heidegger accords to them in his own interpretations.

Along with offering a new interpretation of Heidegger's philosophical development from the point of view of the problem of phenomena, the ambition of the book is also critical and systematic. Throughout the historical exposition I try to lay bare the inner problems and ambiguities that motivate and drive Heidegger's thinking on phenomena and phenomenology forward. In the epilogue of the book, I undertake a critical delimitation of Heidegger's radical historicization of phenomenal givenness and sketch a positive countervision of how I think we should conceive of the relation between history and direct intuition in our understanding of phenomena. Contrary to Heidegger, I will insist that our first-person experience gives us direct intuitive access to meaningful beings, which transcend our historical concepts and preunderstandings, and which constitute an irreducible source of ethical-existential normativity and truth.

Although it is impossible for me to offer anything like an ample treatment of the difficult and inflammatory question of Heidegger's relationship to National Socialism, the third part of the book nevertheless contains a chapter dealing with this issue. As will become clear, I think Heidegger's Nazi engagement and his later grave failure to respond to it are connected with some of his central philosophical convictions, and it remains a crucial responsibility to attend to and investigate the nature and depth of this connection. However, this does not free us from the autonomous philosophical task of explicating the sense of Heidegger's thinking, and critically interrogating its truth and untruth as well as its moral problems. In fact, simply denouncing Heidegger's entire philosophy as a species of Nazism is ill advised. Such an attitude not only conceals the important and highly influential philosophical work done by Heidegger, thereby forfeiting the task of understanding and learning from the insights and delusions of his thinking. It also hinders us from seeing how the philosophical and moral problems of Heidegger's thinking that are related to his plunge into Nazism still—in different ways—constitute central ethical-existential challenges to ourselves.

Structure

The book is structured as a chronological narrative. It is divided into three main parts successively investigating what I suggest are the three main phases in Heidegger's struggle with the problem of phenomena. The three parts are followed by an epilogue in which I offer a critical discussion and delimitation of Heidegger's radically historicist conception of phenomena and phenomenology.

Part One focuses on Heidegger's earliest Freiburg lectures in 1919–21, which, I argue, constitute a distinct philosophical stage in his development. The aim of these lectures is to develop Husserl's phenomenology into a "primordial science" of life.

My claim is that Heidegger in these years remains firmly committed to Husserlian phenomenology as intuitive reflection on the basic structures of experience. At the same time, he critically elaborates the sense of phenomenology by stressing the existential difficulties and challenges of philosophical understanding and by emphasizing the need to attend to and dismantle the historical prejudices that tend to guide our thinking. Against what he claims is the basic theoretical orientation of Western philosophy—the aim of which has always been to provide theoretical foundations for our supposedly naive pretheoretical experience—Heidegger insists that our primary and irreducible access to meaningful phenomena is found precisely in our pretheoretical experience of the significances of our world. Although he claims that this experience is anchored in the historical situation of the experiencing self, his analysis of its historical structure remains weak and his programmatic claims about the need for phenomenology to become a historical mode of thinking remain at the level of program. Moreover, Heidegger's emphasis on the primacy and self-sufficiency of our pretheoretical experience gives rise to problems and ambivalences since it makes it difficult for him to account for the role of philosophy in pretheoretical life.

Part Two focuses on the period commencing with Heidegger's groundbreaking confrontation with Aristotle in 1921 and culminating with the publication of *Being and Time* in 1927. What happens in the early 1920s is that Heidegger discovers what he believes is the basic historical as-structure—which a few years later he will name the "ontological difference"—of our experience of phenomena. The idea is that our experience of beings as meaningful phenomena is determined by our prior understanding of the historical contexts of meaning in which we live; moreover, he claims that this understanding is itself ultimately guided by our understanding of the sense of being. Heidegger's new conception of the historical structure of phenomena gives him a ground for arguing that philosophy cannot transpire as intuition-based phenomenology anymore but needs to take the form of a hermeneutic-destructive reflection on the historical origins of our understanding. Moreover, it allows him to conceive of philosophy in terms of the fundamental ontological task of explicating the sense of being as the hidden horizon of all experience. The bulk of this part is a critical exploration of how Heidegger articulates—and develops the consequences of—his notion of the historical structure of phenomenal experience in *Being and Time*. I argue that Heidegger's radical historicism raises the critical question of how historical meanings can show up and address us as in some sense binding or primordial and thus be distinguished from mere prejudices. However, he fails to address this question in *Being and Time* and this lacuna gives rise to deep problems and ambivalences in his project of fundamental ontology. First, it makes Heidegger unable to tell how Dasein's guiding historical life-possibilities—which, according to his analysis, is the ultimate source of normativity and significance that determines our experience of meaningful phenomena—can address it as binding beyond the collective prejudices of the They. As a result, Heidegger's conception of authenticity—and, hence, his entire conception of phenomena—remains stuck in an oscillation between collectivism and subjectivism. Second, it hinders Heidegger from implementing his program for a hermeneutic-destructive thinking and forces him to have recourse, in his concrete investigations, to the kind of intuition-based phenomenological reflection that his analysis of the historical structure of phenomena has ruled out.

Part Three focuses on how Heidegger's struggle with the problem of phenomena plays out in his later thinking. I argue that the so-called "turn" that Heidegger's thinking undergoes from the late 1920s to the mid-1930s can be understood as a turn in his interrogation of the problem of phenomena. Whereas Heidegger in *Being and Time* focused on explicating the historical structure of our experience of phenomena (the question of the sense of being) he now turns to the question that was left unasked in his magnum opus (the question of the openness or truth of being): How is historical being opened up and how can it address and give itself to us as something binding? The aim of Heidegger's entire later thinking is to explicate the event—*Ereignis*—that opens up a historical world as a groundless and finite yet binding destiny. I offer a detailed analysis of Heidegger's main effort to concretely account for the dynamics that open up a world. This is found in "The Origin of the Work of Art" where he depicts how the work of art establishes a world by enacting the "strife" between the historical "world" and the material-sensuous "earth." Furthermore, I explicate the fate of phenomenology within the framework of the later Heidegger's attempt to conceive of and implement his thinking as a form of radically historical reflection that traces and retrieves the most primordial possibilities of thinking harbored by our history, especially by its Greek beginning. The part also includes a chapter that deals with the question of the philosophical motivation and relevance of Heidegger's Nazism.

The book ends with an extended epilogue in which I endeavor to critically delimit the truth—and untruth—of some of the central aspects of Heidegger's attempt to radically historicize being and thinking. To do this, I also sketch—in a very preliminary way—my own alternative views on the matters in question. Basically, my critical delimitation of Heidegger is an elaboration of the kind of critique previously presented by Emmanuel Levinas, Ernst Tugendhat, and Cristina Lafont.

The epilogue focuses on three main issues: ethical-existential normativity, truth, and phenomenology. First, Heidegger's conception of the historical structure of phenomena implies that he conceives of the values and norms harbored by our history as our ultimate source of ethical-existential normativity. Here, I try to show that Heidegger, despite his effort to describe how our historical world can address us as binding, is unable to account for a source of ethical-existential claims beyond collective pressure and rhetorical-persuasive force. I present the suggestion that the other person, regardless of historical context, claims and concerns us as someone to love and care about as such and that the ethical relevance of historical values and norms depends on how they relate to the primary ethical claim of the other. Second, according to Heidegger, our historical contexts of meaning determine in advance what we can identify as meaningful phenomena. Hence, our historical world constitutes our primordial source of truth, which means that it cannot itself be true or false. Here, I argue that when it comes to understanding central existential realities such as the ethical claim of the other or the structures of our phenomenal experience, understanding essentially consists in openly seeing and grasping independent matters that transcend our historical concepts and preunderstandings. Finally, I discuss the possibilities and limits of the later Heidegger's attempt to abandon intuition-based phenomenology in favor of a radically historical form of reflection. I argue that this kind of historical thinking cannot replace phenomenology given that intuitive reflection constitutes our basic and irreducible access to the meaning and structure of our experience. Although severe, the point of my critique is also essentially positive: to open up the possibility of grasping and appropriating Heidegger's insights within their proper limits.

Part One

A PHENOMENOLOGY OF FACTICAL LIFE

Introduction

Heidegger's breakthrough as an independent philosopher takes place immediately after the end of the First World War. In the lecture course "The Idea of Philosophy and the Problem of Worldview,"[1] delivered at the University of Freiburg in the extraordinary war emergency semester (*Kriegsnotsemester*) in the beginning of 1919, Heidegger launches the idea that phenomenology, in order to realize its true philosophical potential, needs to develop into a "primordial science" of life: a science that leaves the traditional philosophical effort to find theoretical foundations for our naive everyday experience behind, and takes on the task of recovering and explicating our factical pretheoretical experience as our primary and irreducible access to meaningful reality.

It is no exaggeration to highlight "The Idea of Philosophy" as the decisive opening of Heidegger's philosophical authorship.[2] In his pre-war writings Heidegger still basically appears as a capable yet unexceptional philosopher on the contemporary academic scene taking his main philosophical cues from Husserlian phenomenology and neo-Kantianism.[3] Had this been all he wrote he would today at most be remembered as a typical figure of the philosophical debate of that time. In "The Idea of Philosophy," by contrast, Heidegger for the first time emerges as a distinct philosophical voice provisionally opening up many of the basic philosophical questions and motifs that will henceforth guide his thinking.

"The Idea of Philosophy" marks the beginning of an intensive period of lecturing as unsalaried lecturer—*Privatdozent*—at the University of Freiburg. The time in Freiburg continues until the autumn of 1923 when Heidegger moves away to become Professor of Philosophy in Marburg. However, in this part I am going to focus only on the *earliest* Freiburg lecture courses from 1919 to 1921. My reason for this is that—as I hope to show—these courses exhibit a quite distinct philosophical approach, especially as regards Heidegger's take on the problem of phenomena and his conception of phenomenology.[4] Although Heidegger's lectures are often wild and groping in character, unrelentingly probing new directions of questioning without establishing a fixed general conceptuality, they still constitute a unified philosophical project guided by the idea of phenomenology as a primordial science of life. Whereas "The Idea of Philosophy" opens up the idea of phenomenology as primordial science, the lecture course "Basic Problems of Phenomenology" from the winter term 1919–20 offers a more unified and detailed elaboration of this idea and the central issues contained in it. It is no coincidence that this course also contains Heidegger's first critique of Husserl's phenomenology. Other important courses from this period are "Phenomenology of Intuition and Expression" from the summer term 1920 and "Introduction to the Phenomenology of Religion" from the winter term 1920–1.

The period under consideration reaches its end around the summer of 1921 when Heidegger gives a seminar on Aristotle's *De Anima*, which opens up a new phase of concerted thinking and lecturing on Aristotle. As I will argue, Heidegger's earliest Freiburg philosophy is basically a critical continuation of Husserl's phenomenology. Although he from the outset presents claims about the historical character of phenomena and phenomenology, his analyses in this direction remain quite weak and do not unsettle his commitment to Husserlian phenomenology. Heidegger's turn to Aristotle is largely motivated by the inner problems and ambivalences of his primordial science. His readings of Aristotle result in a new conception of the historical structure of phenomena, a conception that also makes him rearticulate the task of phenomenology in terms of a historical mode of hermeneutic-destructive interrogation of the sense of being. These events, which initiate the project of fundamental ontology in *Being and Time*, will be examined in the next part.

Next to Husserl's phenomenology, the most palpable historical background to Heidegger's early thought is Wilhelm Dilthey and the hermeneutic tradition in general. Dilthey's influence is profoundly discernable in Heidegger's emphasis on the pretheoretical experience and in his effort to explicate its temporal-historical character. In his attempt to press phenomenology toward the pretheoretical sphere of dynamic individual life, Heidegger also takes his inspiration, first, from modern life-philosophers such as Nietzsche, Bergson, and Jaspers; second, from Christian thinkers such as St. Paul, Augustine, Meister Eckhart, Luther, and Kierkegaard. What is more, Heidegger's lecture courses unfold in a continuous critical dialogue with some of the main representatives of the neo-Kantian philosophy that dominated German academic philosophy at the time. Whereas Heinrich Rickert and Paul Natorp mostly figure as exemplary manifestations of the theoretical philosophy to be overcome, the writings of the younger Emil Lask—killed during the war in 1918—play an important role in Heidegger's attempts to articulate the way categorial meaning is given in the pretheoretical experience of life.[5]

The philosophical reception of the early Freiburg lectures has been shaped by the remarkable fact that Heidegger published nothing during these formative years. Indeed, the entire period between the publication of his *Habilitationsschrift* in 1916 and of *Being and Time* in 1927 is one of silence in the public domain. Hence, as *Being and Time* is published and captivates the contemporary philosophical scene it is as if it had appeared out of nowhere, leaving its readers to struggle with this pioneering and difficult text with no opportunity to consult the early Freiburg and Marburg lecture courses in which this thinking evolved. As Heidegger's early courses were successively published from the late 1980s to the early 1990s, a feverish research effort took off, driven by many ambitions: to philologically map his early development; to shed light on the problematic and conceptuality of *Being and Time*; to come across original and strong philosophical thoughts; and finally, to detect in these early lecture courses primordial problems and motifs which could corroborate one or another claim about what constitutes Heidegger's basic philosophical concern.

In this discussion, the question of Heidegger's take on the issues of phenomena and phenomenology has from the beginning been present as a central and controversial theme. On the one hand, representatives of the hermeneutic-deconstructive interpretation—among them both the major chroniclers of Heidegger's early thought, Theodore Kisiel and John van Buren—have portrayed his thinking in these years as a radical departure from the ambitions of traditional transcendental philosophy, including Husserl's phenomenology. Abandoning Husserl's belief in the possibility of describing intuitively given universal structures of sense, they claim, Heidegger here launches a hermeneutic-deconstructivist mode of thinking tracing the finite historical sense of factical life. On the other hand, representatives of the transcendental phenomenological interpretation—for example, Steven Crowell and Dan Zahavi—have read the early lectures as a critical yet basically faithful elaboration of Husserl's idea of phenomenology as intuitive reflection on the transcendental structures of our experience.

It is no surprise that the question of phenomena/phenomenology has been a central object of debate. Heidegger's early lecture courses basically unfold as a critical elaboration of Husserl and are obviously of key importance for assessing his relationship to phenomenology. Moreover, already at a quick glance it is evident that Heidegger's attitude to Husserl is ambivalent and that his lectures exhibit what seem like opposing tendencies that can be taken to lend support to both of the conflicting interpretations above.

In this part, I am going to argue that Heidegger in his earliest Freiburg lectures remains committed to Husserl's idea of phenomenology as intuitive reflection on the essential structures of our first-person experiences. What makes these lectures philosophically interesting is precisely that Heidegger, within this framework, provides a critique of the theoretical bias of Husserl's phenomenology and articulates an original vision of the task and challenges of a phenomenology that takes as its prime focus our pretheoretical experience of ethically-existentially significant phenomena. At the same time, Heidegger's investigations of the structure of our pretheoretical experience of phenomena lead him to assert that this experience is radically historical in character and that this makes it necessary to reconceive of phenomenology as a historical mode of thinking. In what follows, I will explicate the sense of these tensions in Heidegger's thinking, tensions that will eventually alienate him from his early phenomenology of life.

The part contains three chapters. In Chapter 1, I describe how Heidegger develops his idea of phenomenology as primordial science on the basis of Husserl's phenomenology. I also review Heidegger's criticism of the theoretical character of Husserl's project. In Chapter 2, I offer a detailed analysis of Heidegger's phenomenological method and of his analysis of the structure of pretheoretical life. Finally, in Chapter 3, I explicate Heidegger's view of—and problems with accounting for—the role and motivation of philosophy in our pretheoretical life-experience.

1

PHENOMENOLOGY AS PRIMORDIAL SCIENCE OF LIFE

Husserl and the Promise of Phenomenology

Before turning to Heidegger's early Freiburg lecture courses, I will give a brief outline of Husserl's phenomenological program as the critical starting point of Heidegger's philosophical endeavor.

Husserl's phenomenological breakthrough took place in his *Logical Investigations*, published in two volumes in 1900 and 1901. His conception of phenomenology as transcendental philosophy then gradually matured in the following decade. It was provisionally announced in the programmatic article "Philosophy as Rigorous Science," published in 1911 in the newly launched journal *Logos*, and it received its standard formulation in the key work *Ideas Pertaining to a Pure Phenomenology and to a Phenomenological Philosophy* from 1913.[1] The transcendental philosophical program consolidated in this period largely remained in force in Husserl's later thinking even though he never tired of rearticulating and complementing it.

In the following, I will outline what I see as the philosophical core and promise of Husserl's phenomenology. It must be kept in mind that my outline does not pretend to do justice to the complexity and development of Husserl's massive philosophical work: his recurrent efforts to rearticulate the task and method of phenomenology and his prolific work of phenomenological investigation. What is more, I will here concentrate on the philosophical potential of Husserl's phenomenology— an open potential that sets Heidegger's philosophy into motion and that has animated phenomenological thinking ever since—while initially passing over the problematic tendencies that in my view impede and distort his conception of phenomenology. Later in this chapter, I will indicate my understanding of these problems in connection with discussing Heidegger's critique of Husserl.

The heart of Husserl's phenomenology comes to expression in the famous motto "To the matters themselves!" Against what he conceives as the age-old tendency of philosophy to fall back on historical prejudices or resort to theoretical constructions, Husserl insists that philosophy must go to the matters themselves as they are concretely given as phenomena in our experience. It is precisely this demand to abide by the phenomenally given that receives its classic formulation in "the principle of all principles" in *Ideas I*:

> Enough now of absurd theories. No conceivable theory can make us err with respect to the principle of all principles: that every originarily giving intuition (*Anschauung*) is a legitimizing source of knowledge, that everything originarily (in its bodily actuality, so to speak) offered to us in "intuition" (*Intuition*), is simply to be received as what it gives itself, but also only within the limits in which it gives itself there. Every statement which does no more than confer expression on such givens by simple explication and by means of significations precisely conforming to them is … really an absolute beginning, called upon to serve as a foundation in a genuine sense, a principium. (Hua 3: 51/44)

In short, the only way to rigorously grounded knowledge consists not in arguing or inferring anything but in strictly seeing and describing what is concretely given in our de facto experiences while avoiding all conceptual and theoretical prejudices.

However, what is the philosophical import of this principle?

It is Husserl's basic assertion that our first-person experiences of meaningful phenomena constitute our basic access to intelligible reality. However, according to Husserl, it has been the decisive characteristic of the Western philosophical tradition to deny and explain away the full phenomenal content of our experience. Instead, philosophy has dogmatically limited the scope of experiential givenness to include only empirical objects and sense-data. With momentous results. Denying the phenomenal content of our experience as a measure of understanding, philosophy has set itself the task of accounting for the ontological meaning of the world and the possibility of knowledge by relying on theoretical arguments of different sorts, for example, on deductions from first principles, on inductive inferences, or on analyses of our received historical concepts. However, Husserl holds that every attempt to account for the meaning of things and the structure of our experience with reference to any other, supposedly more secure and deep-seated ground of knowledge than their phenomenal self-presentation in our experience, is bound to result in prejudiced belief and theoretical construction.

Husserl's diagnosis of this state of affairs is seductively simple: Our tendency to limit the sphere of true phenomenality to our experience of empirical objects is rooted in the "natural attitude" (Hua 3: 56/51). Our natural manner of experience is centrally characterized by its strong and exclusive directedness toward its objects. In seeing a tree, we are primarily directed toward the tree itself; in remembering a landscape, our attention dwells on the landscape itself. It is, Husserl claims, part of the intentionality of our natural experience that it presents its objects independently of our acts of experiencing them. The objects appear to us as objectual identities in the manifold of perspectival experiences without our being aware of the experiences themselves in which the objects are given and receive their sense (cf. Hua 3: §41). Hence, what Husserl calls the "general thesis of the natural attitude" emerges with a certain necessity (Hua 3: 61/57). This is the conviction that reality is essentially made up of individual objects that exist and are what they are independently of every human subject and experience.

According to Husserl, the reliance of traditional philosophy on the natural attitude fatally hampers its ability to clarify and answer what he takes to be the central problems of philosophy. As concerns the epistemological problem, philosophy has been unable to explain how our subjective acts of knowledge may arrive at act-transcendent objects at all. As regards the ontological problem, it has been incapable of accounting for the ontological sense of beings as essentially phenomenal objects of different possible experiences. As the philosopher of the natural attitude tries to account for the relationship between our experiences and their objects, she is forced to construe this relation in terms of some kind of interaction between different sorts of objects, thereby inescapably engendering reductionist and incoherent constructions.

Husserl's insistence on the primacy and irreducibility of our first-person experience of phenomena goes hand in hand with his claim that philosophy primarily needs to take the form of phenomenological reflection on the essential structures of this experience. Husserl names the central maneuver of his transcendental phenomenology the "phenomenological reduction." The reduction comprises two central components, which are described in the following way in the later epilogue to *Ideas I* published in 1930:

> On the one hand, certain judgments are excluded, all those that, resting on natural experience, are about this world constantly and altogether unquestionably pregiven as existing. On the other hand, by means of this epoché the regard is freed for the universal phenomenon, "the world of consciousness purely as such," the world purely *as* given in the manifold flux of conscious life. (Hua 5: 145/412)

On the one hand, the phenomenologist suspends the general thesis of the natural attitude concerning the metaphysical status of reality, seeing that every such thesis based on the natural direction of experience necessarily lacks a sufficient phenomenal basis and is thus prejudiced. On the other hand, the phenomenologist frees herself from the object-directed movement of our natural experience, and instead carries out a reflective turn, which allows her to observe the objects of experience strictly as they are given in corresponding acts of consciousness.

How should this be understood?

Husserl describes the phenomenological reduction as a reflective turn in which we free ourselves from our normal directedness at the objects of our experience and instead reflect on these objects as they are given in our experiences. This does not—as, for example, Dan Zahavi (2003a: 44–6) has pointed out—imply that we turn our attention from the objects of the outer world toward the inner acts of the experiencing subject; rather, it means that we expand our attention so that we shift from the one-sided object-directedness of our natural attitude toward a synoptic reflection on the objects in correlation with the specific acts of consciousness in which they are given. Husserl makes it very clear that the reduction does not entail a "restriction of the investigation to the sphere of real immanence," but signifies a "limitation to the sphere of *pure self-givenness*" (Hua 2: 60/45).

Indeed, Husserl claims, the reflective study opened by the reduction reveals precisely that our human consciousness essentially exhibits an intentional structure: our seeing is always a seeing of something, our brooding is always a brooding over something. It belongs to the very sense of our acts of consciousness that they are directed, not at inner representations or sense-data that would mediate our relation to outer reality, but at the things themselves that they intend. Conversely, the world is only available as concretely given unities of meaning in correlation with particular acts of experience. Husserl's concept of intentionality thus effects a dissolution both of the traditional idea of consciousness as an inner sphere that has to be transcended in order to attain true knowledge of the outer world and of the idea of reality as basically mind-independent. Just as it is impossible to understand the meaning of things in isolation from the experiences in which they are given as meaningful, it is impossible to understand the acts of the subject in abstraction from the matters and things with which they are concerned. As a result, Husserl states that the word "phenomenon" is itself "twofold by virtue of the essential correlation between *appearing* (*Erscheinen*) and *that which appears* (*Erscheinendem*)" (Hua 2: 14/69).

The reflective turn of the phenomenological reduction should thus not be understood as a turn to a self-contained subject, but to our experience as a whole in its intentional correlation between our acts of consciousness and the objects as they are given in these acts, between *noesis* and *noema*. Whereas in the natural attitude we pass through our intentional experiences as in a tunnel, directed straightly and exclusively at the particular objects of these experiences, in the reduction we reflect on the pure and full sphere of experiential givenness, in which the objects appear in their concretion as noematic identities in correlative noetic acts of consciousness.

Finally, it is crucial to note that Husserl's phenomenology is a "science of essences" or an "eidetic science" (Hua 3: 6/XXII). The point of phenomenology is not to register and describe the individual contents and traits of any particular experiences. Rather, the task of phenomenology is to make out and describe the structural elements that are essential and necessary constituents of the experiences under investigation. Explicating essential structures basically means understanding the elements and structures that make our experiences what they are and give them the character and significance they have for us. The essential structures include whatever is essential for understanding a certain kind of experience: our ways of perceiving and relating to people and things, the ethical-existential motives and concerns that fuel our experiences, the key roles played by intersubjectivity, time, history, language, our bodily nature, and so on.[2] Here are two examples. In analyzing visual perception, we may—following Husserl—describe how in perceiving an object we are at each moment presented with only one side of the object and how, on account of our previous sedimented understandings, we nevertheless experience our present perceptions as moving within a horizon of possible perceptions of the same unified object. Or, in analyzing shame, it can be argued—as I have done elsewhere (Westerlund 2019a)—that experiencing shame essentially involves seeing oneself as one thinks one appears to others, and that the negative perception of oneself as worthless and despicable is motivated by our urge for social affirmation.

In the end, the phenomenological and the eidetic reductions open up the possibility of implementing Husserl's guiding idea of the philosophical task of phenomenology as transcendental constitutional research: to investigate, through strict phenomenological reflection, how different kinds of objects are given and constituted in different kinds of experiences. Led by this idea, Husserl is during his whole career ceaselessly occupied with carrying out concrete phenomenological descriptions of different experiences, his themes including, for example, intentionality, time-consciousness, the unthematic horizons of intentional experience, the lived body, passive synthesis, the life-world, and intersubjectivity.

As stated above, my intention here has been to sketch the basics of Husserl's phenomenology in view of its open philosophical potential. The promise of phenomenology has sparked a rich and vital tradition of thinking that includes thinkers like Heidegger, Max Scheler, Edith Stein, Alfred Schutz, Jean-Paul Sartre, Maurice Merleau-Ponty, Emmanuel Levinas, and many more. In addition to producing a wealth of phenomenological analyses, the tradition has involved multiple efforts to articulate the task and identity of phenomenology. Then again, the very idea of phenomenology—especially the idea that intuitive reflection on first-person experiences can ground understanding of essential structures of meaning—has persistently been questioned by historicists and naturalists alike. Even today, the question of the character, potential, and scope of phenomenology is far from settled. This book is another intervention in the ongoing debate. By tracing and analyzing Heidegger's highly ambivalent relationship to phenomenology, I both try to take stock of his positive efforts to develop Husserlian phenomenology and to assess and delimit the force of his criticisms of the phenomenological project. In the epilogue, I offer a brief outline of my own view of the possibilities and challenges of phenomenological philosophy.

Phenomenology as Primordial Science

Heidegger opens his 1919 breakthrough course "The Idea of Philosophy" by questioning what he claims to be the traditional conception of the task of philosophy that has tended to guide philosophy in a more or less habitual and inarticulate way. It has, he suggests, always been the aim of philosophy to theoretically establish a philosophical "worldview" (*Weltanschauung*), by which he means "a basic conception of the world" on the basis of which we can attain well-founded knowledge of the "meaning and purpose of human existence" (GA 56/57: 8/7).[3]

And yet, Heidegger asks, what if "there is no connection at all" between philosophy and worldview? What if the traditional conception of philosophy as theoretical worldview-formation is essentially deluded and misleading?

Heidegger's questioning of the traditional theoretical conception of philosophy is driven by his conviction that the idea of phenomenology launched by Husserl implies a radical challenge to the customary self-understanding of philosophy. The two core ideas that motivate Heidegger's critique are the following. First, Heidegger insists that our primary and irreducible access to meaningful reality is found in our first-person experience of meaningful phenomena, more precisely—as he is keen to stress in contrast to Husserl—in our pretheoretical experience of significances. Second, he insists that philosophy must take the form of phenomenological reflection on the essential structures of this pretheoretical experience.

According to Heidegger, the entire tradition of Western philosophy has been built on a denial of this central insight of phenomenology. Suppressing the primacy of our pretheoretical experience of phenomena, philosophy has given itself the task of providing theoretical foundations for this supposedly naive experience.

In radical opposition to this, Heidegger presents phenomenology as "primordial science" (*Urwissenshaft* or *Ursprungswissenschaft*) of life (GA 56/57: 12/10; GA 58: 2/2). In contrast to theoretical philosophy, phenomenology as primordial science proceeds from the acknowledgment that our pretheoretical experience—which Heidegger also calls "life" or "factical life" (*das faktische Leben*) (GA 58: 29/24, 37/30)—is our basic access to meaningful being. Heidegger defines his primordial phenomenological science as a science of the "origin"—that is, of the "primordial structure" and "primordial sense"—of life (GA 58: 1/2, 259/195, 167/127). In short, the task of the primordial science is none other than to phenomenologically explicate the basic sense and structure of our pretheoretical experience of significant phenomena.

Heidegger's entire conception of the task of philosophy is centered on the problem of givenness or phenomenality:[4] What is the primary experiential domain where matters are given as meaningful phenomena? What is the sense and structure of this domain? The difference between theoretical philosophy and phenomenology turns precisely on how they conceive of givenness. Whereas theoretical philosophy explains away our pretheoretical experience of phenomena as ancillary and naive, Heidegger insists that this pretheoretical experience constitutes our irreducible source for understanding the significances that things have for us. Indeed, the key question of phenomenology concerns givenness itself: "What does 'given' mean? 'Givenness'? This magic word of phenomenology and the 'stumbling block' for others" (GA 58: 5/4). As Hans Ruin aptly notes: "the nature of the given is here addressed as a problem in its own right. ... givenness is precisely the problem" (1994: 55).

Heidegger from the outset of his philosophical trajectory identifies phenomenal givenness with meaningful being. Raising the question of how it is possible for theoretical philosophy to account for anything meaningful at all in so far as it only acknowledges and deals with theoretical objects—while denying phenomenal givenness as its source of understanding—Heidegger writes:

> Is even a single thing given if only things are given (*Gibt es überhaupt eine einzige Sache, wenn es nur Sachen gibt*)? In that case, nothing would be given; not even *nothing*, because with the sole supremacy of the sphere of things not even the "is

given" would be given (*weil es bei einer Allherrschaft der Sachsphäre auch kein 'es gibt' gibt*). Is the "is given" given? (GA 56/57: 62/52)

And he immediately answers:

> Already in the opening of the question "Is something given …?" something is given. Our *entire* problematic has arrived at a decisive point, which, however, makes a meager impression. We are standing at the methodical crossroads which decides on the very life or death of philosophy. We stand at an abyss: either into the nothing, that is, the nothing of absolute thingness, or we manage for the first time to make the leap into *another world*, or, more precisely, into the world as such. (GA 56/57: 63/53)

According to Heidegger, the domain of pretheoretical givenness constitutes nothing less than the basic domain of given meaningful being. To deny this and reach for grounds and objects beyond the given—as theoretical philosophy does—is to reach out into nothingness.

So how does Heidegger conceive of the primary domain of pretheoretical experience?

In "The Idea of Philosophy," he offers the following, by now classic, phenomenological description of what happens as he enters the lecture hall and sees the lectern at which he is to speak: "What do 'I' see? Brown surfaces, at right angles to one another? … A large box with another smaller one set upon it? Not at all. I see the lectern at which I am to speak." There is, he writes, no "order of foundation" (*Fundierungszusammenhang*) in the pure experience, so that he would first see brown surfaces, which would then present themselves as a wooden box, in order then, finally, to come forth as a lectern in the university lecture hall. Not at all, he sees the lectern "in one fell swoop, so to speak" as it appears as significant within the context of the academic world and the present situation of lecturing (GA 56/57: 71/60):

> In the experience of seeing the lectern something is given *to me* from out of an immediate surrounding world (*Umwelt*). What surrounds us (lectern, book, blackboard, notebook, fountain pen, caretaker, student fraternity, tram car, motor car, etc.) does not consist of things with a certain character of significance, of objects, which are then conceived as signifying this and that; rather, the significant is primary and immediately given to me without any mental detours across an apprehension of things. Living in a surrounding world, it signifies to me everywhere and always, everything is worldly, "*it worlds*" (*es weltet*), which is something different from "it values" (*es wertet*). (GA 56/57: 72-3/61)

According to Heidegger, what is primarily given in our pretheoretical experience is not sense-data but significances that immediately appear to us and engage us without any active effort of interpretation or judgment. The experience in question cannot be understood in terms of a distanced observation in which the perceiving subject looks at isolated objects parading before its gaze: "The lived experience does not pass in front of me like a thing"; rather, it is a unitary "event" (*Ereignis*) in which the experiencing self "swings along" (GA 56/57: 75/63).

To grasp the philosophical import of Heidegger's insistence on the primacy of the pretheoretical, we need to see that for Heidegger our pretheoretical experience is the experience where beings show up as ethically-existentially significant and important to us—where they concern and matter to us. The priority of the pretheoretical in relation to the theoretical is not a matter of how we first or normally experience things. What gives to our pretheoretical experience its philosophical priority and irreducibility is the fact that here matters are concretely given with the significance and import that they have for us. For Heidegger, the pretheoretical experience of ethical-existential significance is ontologically fundamental. The ethical-existential significance of beings defines what they are for us and it is within the horizon of such significant being that all kinds of being and knowledge have whatever meanings and functions they have. This is why Heidegger can claim that by acknowledging and explicating the sense and structure of pretheoretical life, his primordial science will be able to uncover the "basic sense of '*existence*'" as the ground for understanding "the sense of *reality* in all layers of life" (GA 58: 261/197).

In addition to the above, there is one further motif that prompts Heidegger's critique of theoretical philosophy and vision of phenomenology as primordial science. In these early years, Heidegger is strongly drawn to the idea that pretheoretical life constitutes a self-sufficient domain of understanding and is in no need of philosophical grounding or explication. Hence, he is inclined to think that, ultimately, the task of phenomenological philosophy is to allow us to renounce philosophy as superfluous and to enact life as the self-sufficient sphere of significance that it is. This idea gives rise to a deep tension in Heidegger's early thought—a tension between his inclination to view his primordial science as fundamental and necessary for a clear understanding of life, and his propensity to view it as dispensable—that I will deal with in the last chapter of this part.

The Dead End of Theoretical Philosophy

Throughout his early Freiburg lectures Heidegger emphasizes the primacy of our pretheoretical experience of significance and the impossibility of the traditional philosophical dream of a more basic theoretical knowledge of the world.

According to the historical diagnosis offered by Heidegger in these years, the entire tradition of Western philosophy since Plato and Aristotle has been characterized by the "general domination of the *theoretical*" (GA 56/57: 87/73). This means, first, that philosophy has tended to deny and explain away the phenomenal substance and primacy of our pretheoretical experience. What, according to theoretical philosophy, is strictly speaking given in our pretheoretical experience is only rudimentary sensory data. Second, it means that philosophy has set up theoretical knowledge—of the kind pursued in mathematics and the natural sciences—as the paradigm of rigorous knowledge in general. Heidegger's characterization of the ideal of theoretical knowledge is quite open and formal in order to be able to accommodate the varying strategies of the philosophical tradition. Basically, theoretical knowledge as defined by Heidegger is a knowledge that is not grounded on the phenomenal significances given in pretheoretical life, and that is able to establish a "pure ... objectified context" (GA 58: 126/99) that can be accessed and assessed objectively by anyone at any time (GA 58: 141–4/108–11). Ultimately, Heidegger believes there are strong ethical-existential motivations behind the ideal of theoretical philosophy. Above all, there is the impulse to flee from and cover up the weight and finitude of factical life by fostering the dream of attaining the kind of secure and universal theoretical knowledge that would allow us to survey and control life without having to actually live it.

Heidegger maintains that theoretical philosophy lives on a denial of the phenomenal substance of pretheoretical life and is motivated by the task of grounding and critically justifying it on a theoretical basis. If, as theoretical philosophy claims, what is strictly speaking given in our pretheoretical experience is only unstructured sensory data, this implies that the phenomena we experience receive their meaning and organization from somewhere else, namely, from theoretical-conceptual structures that are *not* given in our experience. Heidegger takes Paul Natorp's conception of the given to be exemplary. According to Natorp, we are never in a position to speak of an object being given to us. Since the sensory content of our sense perception can only be experienced as a given object in so far as it is determined by the conceptual laws and structures of objectifying thought, it strictly speaking amounts to no more than a pure undetermined X. As Heidegger puts it: "The sensation is ... only the X of the equation, and only receives its meaning in and *through* the context of theoretical objectivation" (GA 56/57: 87/73). As a result, our pretheoretical experience emerges as essentially naive and prejudiced. Since in enacting this experience we only have access to primitive sensory data and lack every measure for examining the truth of the concepts that determine our sight, we are necessarily guided by these concepts in a prejudiced manner. Hence, the task of theoretical philosophy ensues: "The justification of naive consciousness and its elevation to the scientific and critical level" (GA 56/57: 84/71).

This is not the place to gauge Heidegger's early historical diagnosis of the theoretical bias of Western philosophy. Suffice it to say that I believe there is much truth in the claim that philosophy since its Greek beginning has been characterized by a strong inclination to deny and downgrade the phenomena given in our first-person pretheoretical experience. Denying the epistemic value of our pretheoretical experience of significances, philosophy has tended to understand its task as that of elaborating a qualified theoretical method promising to lead us out of our everyday imprisonment in the world of mere appearances and allowing us to find a deeper and more secure ground—*archē, principium*—on the basis of which it would become possible to attain well-founded knowledge of all beings. Of course, the ideas concerning what constitutes the qualified method of philosophy and the fundamental domain of being-knowledge have varied a lot. For example, we may think of deduction from first principles, generalization and abstraction from empirical data, inference of the basic features of the transcendental subject, and dialectical analysis of the historical concepts supposedly determining our understanding of the world.

According to Heidegger, the traditional endeavor of philosophy to theoretically ground and justify our factical pretheoretical experience is bound to fail. Why? The theoretical attitude of philosophy, he argues, essentially emerges as an estrangement from our pretheoretical experience. Suppressing our pretheoretical experience, philosophy only recognizes theoretically purified experiences, such as observation of objects or intake of sense-data. Heidegger says of this kind of experience that it is "a rudiment of lived experience (*Er-leben*) ... a de-living (*Ent-leben*)" (GA 56/57: 73–4/62). By this, he means that these theoreticized experiences and objects have been detached from our everyday pretheoretical experience and do not give us access to the significances that different experiences and matters have in our lives. Hence, Heidegger describes the basic deficit of theoretical philosophy as follows:

> I cannot explain these meaningful phenomena of the experience of the surrounding world (*Umwelterlebnis*) by destroying their essential character, by abolishing their sense, and advancing a theory. Explanation through dismemberment, i.e., destruction: one wants to explain something which one no longer has as such, which one will not and cannot recognize as such in its validity. (GA 56/57: 86/72–3)

The central thrust of this argument is that the effort of philosophy to theoretically ground the phenomena of our pretheoretical experience is predicated on its having blinded itself to the very experiences in which the phenomena are given and understandable to us in the first place. To understand the meanings that things have in our lives, the only possible way is to look at the experiences and situations in which these meanings manifest themselves. If, given a certain question or problem, we want to understand what "love," "knowledge," "greed," or "car" is, we need to attend to the experiences and phenomena in question and try to explicate their meaning. If we turn away from our de facto experiences and instead attempt to infer these meanings from some other source—for example, our historical concepts and preunderstandings, universal ideas and principles, historical origins, or empirical data of some sort—we will inevitably be examining *something else* than the experiences and significances in question. These other things may, of course, by way of likeness or contrast or supplementary information, shed light on the significances that we want to understand, yet in order to pursue this comparison we would essentially need to draw on the primary experiences that we left behind.

The central point of Heidegger's argument is not that the theoretical stance would be intrinsically misguided and deceptive. Clearly, theoretical investigations and practices may have important roles to play within our pretheoretically given contexts of significance. It is only when philosophy attempts to reduce the pretheoretical to the theoretical that the theoretical starts to function as an illusionary false ground.

The consequence of all this, Heidegger claims, is that to the extent that theoretical philosophy neglects the primary pretheoretical givenness of significances it is bound to give rise to prejudice and construction. To be sure, theoretical philosophy is for the most part not purely theoretical in that it unwittingly tends to develop its thinking by drawing on pretheoretical experiences as its hidden and suppressed ground. Indeed, a purely theoretical philosophy would necessarily materialize as an endless circular construction. As Heidegger writes: "Precisely that which first is to be *posited* (*gesetzt*) must be *presupposed* (*vorausgesezt*)" (GA 56/57: 95/80). That is, in order to make one single motivated conceptual move, theoretical philosophy would have to presuppose earlier, more basic concepts; to account for these basic concepts it would have to presuppose even more basic concepts, and so on ad infinitum. Hence, in so far as theoretical philosophy attempts to say anything at all about our meaningful world it is bound to be ambivalent and self-deceptive. Imagining itself to be engaged in some sort of theoretical reasoning from concepts and principles, it cannot but be guided and motivated by pretheoretical experiences and meanings that give it its sense but which it is unable—and unwilling—to acknowledge.

Heidegger's First Critique of Husserl

Heidegger's early Freiburg lecture courses unfold as an attempt to develop Husserl's phenomenology into a primordial science of life. However, although Heidegger credits Husserl with opening up the possibility of phenomenology, he believes Husserl was never able to free himself from the paradigm of theoretical philosophy.

Heidegger's first sustained critique of Husserl takes place in the final part of "Basic Problems of Phenomenology" (1919–20) where Heidegger interrupts the earlier path of the lecture course to take up *"the problem of givenness"* (GA 58: 127/100). In the final hours of the course he makes an intense effort to push forward and articulate the sense and method of his phenomenological science of origin. In so doing, he also carries out a critical delimitation of Husserl's phenomenology in a series of comments, sketchy and at the same time overburdened.[5] Heidegger's remarks may at first blush seem quite fragmentary and disjointed. However, I hope to show that when read against the backdrop of Heidegger's positive vision of phenomenology and his general critique of theoretical philosophy, they in fact fashion a distinct and philosophically illuminating critique of the theoretical bias of Husserl's phenomenology.

As is well known, Heidegger's major critical confrontations with Husserl take place in the Marburg lecture courses "Introduction to Phenomenological Research" (1923–4) and "History of the Concept of Time: Prolegomena" (1925). However, in that period, Heidegger's critical perspective on Husserl is strongly determined by his view of philosophy as guided by the question of being and by his conception of the radically historical, hermeneutic-destructive character of philosophical understanding. This means that his critique of Husserl is centrally directed at the very idea of intuition-based phenomenology and does not have so much to offer as a critical contribution to such phenomenology. By contrast, in his early Freiburg lecture courses, Heidegger is—or so I will argue—still basically committed to Husserl's idea of phenomenology as intuitive reflection on the structures of our first-person experience of phenomena. This means that both his effort to open up phenomenology to the task of understanding our pretheoretical experience of significance and his critical perspective on Husserl can be seen as internal critical contributions—in my view, philosophically vital contributions—to understanding and elaborating the project of intuitive-reflective phenomenology.

I will begin by going over the main points of Heidegger's critique. After that, I will indicate how I see the philosophical substance and force of the critique. In the next chapter—the results of which are already anticipated here—I will turn to explicating Heidegger's own articulation of the phenomenological method.

Heidegger's basic assessment is that Husserl, despite the revolutionary potential of his call to return to the given, never radically questions but uncritically takes over the traditional theoretical conception of philosophy. Referring to Husserl, Heidegger writes that phenomenology cannot put itself forward as the "fundamental science for philosophy" without having a "radical concept of philosophy" (GA 59: 31/22). According to Heidegger, Husserl's phenomenology basically exhibits the same schema and problems as all brands of theoretical philosophy. That is to say, it starts from a denial of the primacy of our pretheoretical experience of significance, and led by the ideal of certain and objectively verifiable theoretical knowledge, it takes on the task of theoretically grounding our understanding of the significances of life. In Husserl's case, however, the domination of the theoretical does not take the form of a downright rejection of the given in favor of theoretical-conceptual construction but is instead manifest in the way Husserl articulates the task and method of his transcendental phenomenology.

Heidegger's first and decisive charge against Husserl is precisely that he fails to acknowledge and heed our pretheoretical experience of ethical-existential significance as our irreducible access to significant being. Instead, Husserl is said to take his phenomenological starting point in "thing-comprehending experiences (e.g. perceptions)" (GA 58: 254/192). Moreover, Heidegger claims that Husserl conceives of the natural attitude in which we normally live as one in which we are exclusively directed at the intentional objects of our experience: "It is said (i.e. Husserl): in the 'natural attitude' I never arrive at experiences. Only in the act of reflection on my experiencing do I direct myself toward my experiences" (GA 58: 251/189). In short, Husserl takes as his paradigmatic starting point theoretically reduced perceptual experiences that have been abstracted from their original pretheoretical contexts of significance and that only give us access to meaningless objects.

Furthermore, Heidegger claims that Husserl's transcendental phenomenology repeats the traditional effort to theoretically ground our understanding of significant being. Having first interpreted our primary experience of phenomena in terms of object-perceptions, Husserl proposes the phenomenological reduction as the methodological maneuver that allows us to reflect on the act-structures of transcendental subjectivity as the fundamental experiential domain in which the full senses of the objects present themselves:

> One must observe ... all the contents of intuition or comprehension, all *presentative contents* (*darstellende Gehalte*); these are governed (*durchherrscht*) by specific *forms* of comprehension ... Now, if the idea of constitution of objectivities through contents is transferred to *all* sciences, then a noetic-noematic content goes along, which one may observe *reflexively*. This mode of observation is provided by "*transcendental phenomenology.*" (GA 58: 229–30/173)

The central argument of this dense passage is that Husserl's phenomenological reduction acquires its transcendental force from the assumption that the act-structures of the subject somehow "govern" the contents of the objects experienced in these acts. Hence, the phenomenological reduction is supposed to give us access to the acts of transcendental subjectivity as the fundamental domain from which all objects receive their full sense.

However, according to Heidegger, Husserl's transcendental phenomenology, like all manifestations of theoretical philosophy, is doomed to failure. Having denied the primacy of our pretheoretical experience of significance, Husserl's reflections on the act-structures of theoretically reduced object-perceptions cannot give access to the significances that were initially denied and blocked out. In so far as Husserl nevertheless pretends to ground our understanding of significant being, he cannot but resort to prejudice and construction.

What is the philosophical insight to be gained from Heidegger's critique? Does it shed light on problems and deficits in Husserl's phenomenological approach? Here, I will be content with pointing to some basic problematic tendencies in Husserl's approach indicated by Heidegger's critique. It is important to keep in mind that Husserl throughout his life continuously rearticulates and complements his phenomenological approach, but also that in his extensive work of phenomenological analysis he often transcends the guidelines of his phenomenological program.

To get a sense of the extent to which Husserl is captivated by the theoretical ideal of philosophy as defined by Heidegger, let us begin by citing the introductory passages of Husserl's programmatic article "Philosophy as Rigorous Science," which obviously is one of the central texts that Heidegger has in mind in his critique. In the classic opening of the article, Husserl states that philosophy has always claimed to be a rigorous science "that satisfies the highest theoretical needs and enables, in an ethico-religious respect, a life governed by pure norms of reason" (Hua 25: 3/249). To realize this goal, philosophy must take the form of a "philosophical system of doctrine (*Lehrsystem*) that ... actually begins from below with an indubitable foundation and rises up like any sound edifice, wherein stone is set upon stone, each as solid as the other, in accordance with guiding insights" (Hua 25: 6/251). Although these statements should be read as a preliminary and formal articulation of the task of phenomenology, they are a straightforward expression of how Husserl conceives of the philosophical ambition and scientific spirit of his phenomenology.

What I want to draw attention to here is the characteristic telos and configuration of Husserl's philosophical endeavor. First, Husserl is driven by the ambition to ultimately make possible a transparent understanding of the ethical-religious issues of life.[6] Second, he is convinced that such an understanding can only be achieved through establishing a system of doctrine that satisfies the typical demands of scientific-theoretical knowledge. That is, the knowledge to be achieved by phenomenology must form a rigorously grounded and objectively verifiable system that rests on indubitable foundational insights. In what follows, I will argue that this ideal of theoretical knowledge primarily manifests itself in Husserl's tendency to conceive of the perceptual and cognitive layers of our experience as ontologically basic and make them the paradigmatic focus of his phenomenological project. As concerns the ideals of certainty and systematicity, we need to note that although Husserl is certainly influenced by such ideals, he is also very well aware of the fact that different kinds of knowledge and understanding have different kinds of certainty and allow for different kinds of conceptual ordering.

So what is the substance of Heidegger's central charge that Husserl denies the primacy of our pretheoretical experience of significance and seeks to establish a theoretical foundation for our understanding of significant being?

To start with, it needs to be emphasized that Husserl clearly recognized the fact that in our everyday life we experience things as significant in different ways—as belonging to and playing different roles in our historical "lifeworld." According to Husserl, our everyday experience does not consist of perceptions of sensory objects. First and foremost, we tend to be practically engaged with things that have different functions, meanings, and values for us: useful tools, works of art, morally relevant character traits and actions (cf. Hua 3: §27; Hua 4: 26–7/28–9; Hua 8: 151). However, as opposed to Heidegger, Husserl does not single out the domain of pretheoretical experience of significance as the basic and irreducible domain for understanding significant being. Nor does he see it as the primary and decisive task of his phenomenology to explicate the structures and motives of this experience as our only concrete access to phenomenal significance.

Husserl's theoretical bias is manifest in the characteristic ontological presuppositions and methodological focus of his transcendental phenomenology. Husserl throughout his career subscribes to a layer-ontology, according to which the basic layer of all experiences of phenomena consists of perceptions of sensory objects: every phenomenon is "always given, at bottom, as a natural body, endowed with natural properties accessible to simple experience" (EU: 54/54; cf. Hua 3: 354/365). Although Husserl recognizes that we normally experience meaningful phenomena of various kinds—for example, practical, aesthetic, and moral phenomena—he nevertheless conceives of these phenomena as supplementary layers of meaning founded upon and presupposing a more fundamental layer of sensory object-perception.[7] Furthermore, Husserl sees it as the central task of his transcendental phenomenology to investigate how objects are "constituted" in the acts of transcendental consciousness; that is, to investigate the act-structures that allow the objects to be given and manifest to us in different ways. Taking the object types and ontologies available in the natural attitude as its "guideline," transcendental phenomenology sets out to reflectively study "the multiplicities of manners of appearing and their intentional structures" (Hua 6: 175/172). What this means is that Husserl does not—as Heidegger does—see it as the crucial task of his transcendental phenomenology to use phenomenological reflection on the full noetic-noematic structures of experience as a means for critically inquiring into the ethical-existential significance and ontological sense of whatever we experience. Instead, he accepts the object domains available in the natural attitude as his starting point and turns to reflecting on the act-systems that allow the objects to be perceptually-cognitively given to us in different manners.

From Heidegger's perspective, it is clear that in articulating the task of phenomenology in this way, Husserl sidesteps the decisive questions of philosophy. Heidegger remarks that phenomenology as primordial science "needs no 'transcendental guiding clues,' no 'ontology'" (GA 58: 239/181) and that "ontology and the research into consciousness 'correlative' to it, do not form a true unity" (GA 58: 240/181). I take this as expressive of his sense that Husserl's research into transcendental constitution, by dodging the question of the significance and being of what we experience and accepting the object ontologies of the natural attitude as its guideline, is limited to explicating structures of givenness within unclarified and prejudiced ontological horizons.

To sum up, Husserl in his articulation and practical enactment of his phenomenological program takes our perceptual object-experiences—or the perceptual-cognitive dimension of the experiences under investigation—as the paradigmatic domain of his phenomenology. In this, the central goal of his phenomenological research is to reflect on and describe the act-structures of transcendental consciousness that allow objects to be perceptually-cognitively given to us in various ways. It is no exaggeration to say that Husserl's concrete phenomenological work is steadily focused on analyzing the perceptual-cognitive experiences and layers of phenomenal givenness, such that this focus determines the bulk of his analyses of perception, knowledge, understanding of types and essences, time-consciousness, the lived body, intersubjectivity, the life-world, and so on.

The theoretical orientation of Husserl's phenomenology as described above gives rise to some characteristic deficits and problem that I believe in general hamper Husserl's phenomenological project and practice.

First, it must be said that Husserl's will and ability to take on and analyze our central existential experiences and concerns always remain weak. Considering the immensity of Husserl's phenomenological oeuvre, it is striking how little attention he pays to the emotionally charged existential experiences and issues that determine our understanding of ethical-existential significance: goodness, evil, love, hatred, shame, guilt, repression, social affirmation, self-esteem, anxiety, depression, sexual desire, and so on. Not only do such experiences receive little attention, but even when Husserl does touch on these kinds of experiences, his analyses tend to be rather traditionalist and unoriginal, mainly focusing on the cognitive aspects of the matter. Hence, as a rule, they do not offer much insight into the motivating sources and dynamics of our experiences of ethical-existential significance.

Second, it is part of the above deficit that Husserl generally fails to recognize and take seriously the ethical-existential challenges of understanding and knowledge. Heidegger, as we shall see shortly, insists that phenomenology as primordial science of life must be animated by a basic attitude of love and sympathy toward life. This insistence bears witness to his awareness of the fact that our understanding is always conditioned by our will and ability to acknowledge and openly encounter the matters in question. There are very strong motives in us—for example, our desire for social affirmation and self-esteem and our fear of shame and disesteem—that make us want to see things in certain ways and repress and explain away other things. Generally, we also have the ability to repress and misinterpret whatever we do not want to see. Hence, I think Heidegger is right to claim that phenomenological seeing and understanding can only be genuinely free and unprejudiced if it is led by a willingness and readiness to openly acknowledge the ethical-existential issues at stake. Husserl, by contrast, tends to conceive of the difficulties of phenomenological understanding as cognitive in nature, the basic challenge being to rigorously attend to and only allow oneself to be led by what is given as phenomenally evident. In this, he is largely oblivious to the existential motives and concerns that may guide our sense of what is interesting or uninteresting, relevant or irrelevant, clear or unclear, evident or not so evident, and so on.

Third, there is the question of whether Heidegger is right in asserting that Husserl is led by the goal to theoretically ground our understanding of significant being and that this makes his phenomenology fundamentally constructive and prejudiced.

As we saw above, Husserl's ultimate philosophical ambition is indeed to lay the foundations for a rigorous understanding of the ethical-existential concerns of life. And, indeed, to the extent that Husserl's phenomenological analyses of the perceptual-cognitive dimension of givenness are taken to ground our understanding of the significance beings have for us, the philosophical claims are bound to be constructive and prejudiced if they do not arise from open phenomenological reflection on the relevant experiences.

However, this problematic tendency in Husserl's overall project does not imply that Husserl's method and work of phenomenological description would be inherently prejudiced. All depends on the philosophical claims that we attach to the work. There is no doubt that Husserl has provided a wealth of groundbreaking and insightful phenomenological analyses of the perceptual and cognitive aspects of our experience of the world. If the analyses are conceived within their proper limits, there is no reason to think of them as prejudiced. In so far as we think of philosophy as centrally concerned with the ethical-existential significance of life and the world—as Heidegger does—much of Husserl's work is of course bound to appear insufficient or marginal, but this is not the same as saying that it is essentially flawed and prejudiced.

Still, even when the limits of Husserl's phenomenology are respected, the theoretical orientation of his analyses gives rise to some characteristic risks of ambiguity and distortion. The risks arise from the fact that Husserl's analyses tend to focus on the perceptual-cognitive givenness-dimension of experience while abstracting from the existentially and practically concerned experiences that make up our everyday life. In this, the connection between the former and the latter tends to remain more or less unclarified. As a result, Husserl's analyses often leave it unclear what role the perceptual-cognitive operations that they describe play in different everyday experiences. Furthermore, in our everyday life the existential and cognitive aspects of our experience are often closely connected. When this is the case, it is difficult to focus abstractly on the purely perceptual and cognitive aspects without presupposing and drawing on some particular existential setting that remains unclarified. Take, as an example, the problem of understanding other persons. In our everyday life, the cognitive difficulties of understanding are tightly bound up with the ethical-existential difficulties of relating to others. Are we open toward the other or are we merely interested in the other from the point of view of some self-concerned motive? What do we want to see in the other? How do we want to be seen? Clearly, the task of abstractly analyzing the purely perceptual-cognitive aspects of the experience of understanding others is an awkward one where it will always tend to remain more or less unclear what we have actually understood. Not only will it remain an open question what the exact role and meaning of the cognitive acts investigated is in any particular existentially charged interpersonal situation. It will also be hard to explicate the cognitive dimension without drawing on some specific existential motives that make the cognitive aspects and difficulties appear in certain ways. Just as an open and loving relationship will tend to make understanding each other appear quite unproblematic, a closed and guarded relationship will tend to make it seem cognitively demanding or even quite impossible.

Let me end by saying that even though the above criticisms illuminate some of the central problems and limitations of Husserl's phenomenology, none of them cast any doubt on the open possibility and potential of phenomenology to intuitively reflect on and explicate the structures that make our experiences of phenomena what they are.

2

HEIDEGGER'S PHENOMENOLOGY OF FACTICAL LIFE

Phenomenology or Historicism?

The driving ambition of Heidegger's early Freiburg lecture courses is to critically elaborate Husserl's phenomenological imperative into a primordial science of factical life. But how is this nontheoretical phenomenological science to be effected? And how does Heidegger conceive of the primordial structure of life? In short, how should we understand Heidegger's take on phenomenology and the structure of phenomena?

Since the publication of Heidegger's early Freiburg lecture courses was completed in the early 1990s, the debate between the transcendental phenomenological and the hermeneutic-deconstructive readings has structured the discussion regarding Heidegger's conception of phenomena/phenomenology. Both Theodore Kisiel and John van Buren, in their pioneering studies, portray Heidegger's thinking in these years as a radical departure from Husserl's intuition-based transcendental phenomenology. According to van Buren, Heidegger considered Husserl an exemplary representative of modern "ego-metaphysics" (1994a: 203). Far from employing Husserl's method of intuitive reflection on the universal structures of transcendental subjectivity, Heidegger is said to rely on a "hermeneutical intuition" (211) that "explicates the factical preconception of being that belongs to factical life" (216). Hence, the fact that Heidegger calls his thinking "phenomenological" does not imply any reliance on direct intuition but signifies that he studies "being as it *appears* historically" (245). Heidegger's central theme, van Buren claims, is the "anarchic temporalizing of being" (39). This groundless temporal event withdraws from all seeing and determination, and only intimates itself through the differentiated manifold of finite historical epochs and worlds that it produces as its effect. The task of Heidegger's postmetaphysical thinking thus consists in tracing and indicating, again and again, out of ever new historical situations, the groundless event of being. In a similar fashion, Kisiel argues that Heidegger's main theme in his early lectures is the "primary but mystical 'something'" (1993: 24) that "contextualizes (Es weltet) and temporalizes (Es er-eignet sich) each of us" (9). To access and articulate this self-withdrawing source of historical-temporal being Heidegger is said to replace Husserl's objectifying intuitive reflection with a "non-intuitive form of access which hermeneutics calls understanding, a certain familiarity which life already has of itself and which phenomenology needs only to repeat" (48).[1]

On the other hand, interpreters such as Steven Crowell and Dan Zahavi have defended a transcendental phenomenological reading of Heidegger's early Freiburg lectures. According to Crowell, Heidegger's philosophy contains "two voices," one of which is committed to Husserl's phenomenological research program and one of which succumbs to the anti-philosophical temptation of trying to appropriate being as an "ultimately mystical 'sending'" (2001: 7). Crowell for his part insists that the "philosophical relevance" of Heidegger's thinking depends on "our being able to recollect the Husserlian infrastructure of his work" (4). Heidegger's primordial science of life is said to be nothing but a continuation of Husserl's effort to investigate the transcendental conditions and structures of our experience. Although Heidegger disapproves of Husserl's concept of reflection, Crowell argues that Heidegger's own method is essentially one of intuitive reflection: "The method of formal indication ... is an explicitly cognitive-illuminative self-recollection (reflection)" (127) that moves along with life in order to explicate its basic structures of sense.

Much like Crowell, Dan Zahavi maintains that Heidegger does not give up Husserl's reflective method but elaborates it in the direction of a "non-objectifying and merely accentuating type" of reflection (2003b: 170). Furthermore, he argues that Heidegger's goal is to examine the "transcendental structures of life" (160) that we "normally live through but fail to notice due to our absorption in the surrounding world" (170).

What should we think about these opposing interpretations? In what follows, I will try to show that they in fact answer to ambivalent tendencies in Heidegger's early thinking. On the one hand, I will argue that Heidegger basically remains committed to Husserl's phenomenological method of intuitive reflection, although he critically develops it in important respects. On the other hand, Heidegger's phenomenological investigations make him conceive of our pretheoretical experience of phenomena as fundamentally historical, as situated in and determined by the historical worlds in which we happen to live. Heidegger's analysis of the historicity of pretheoretical life leads him to assert that phenomenology itself needs to be reconceived as a historical mode of thinking. However, in these years Heidegger's thesis about the historicity of thinking remains at the level of a programmatic declaration and does not unsettle his basic Husserlian phenomenological orientation.

Heidegger's Nontheoretical Phenomenology

Heidegger's task is to show how a primordial phenomenological science of life is achievable. Such a science must, in his words, be "pretheoretical" or "nontheoretical" (GA 56/57: 96/81) and avoid the theoretical tendency to deny and ground what is given in pretheoretical life. Instead, the aim must be to recover and acknowledge our full pretheoretical experience of significance in order to articulate its basic structure.

In "The Idea of Philosophy," Heidegger opens the question of the method of his primordial science by returning to Husserl's "principle of all principles," that is, the basic methodological principle that phenomenology must only receive and describe what is originarily offered to us in intuition. According to Heidegger, the very name of the principle—the *principle* of *all* principles—indicates that it cannot be understood as a theoretical principle among others but needs to be conceived as the "primordial attitude" (*Urhaltung*) or "primordial habitus" (*Urhabitus*) of phenomenology (GA 56/57: 110/92–3). However, in articulating Husserl's principle in this direction Heidegger bestows it with a new sense:

> It is the primordial intention of genuine life, the primordial attitude of lived experience and life as such, the absolute *sympathy with life* (*Lebenssympathie*) that is identical with the lived experience. The *"rigor" (Strenge)* of the scientificity awakened in phenomenology gains its primordial sense from this basic attitude and is incomparable with the "rigor" of derivative non-primordial sciences. (GA 56/57: 110/92–3)

In the next winter Heidegger rearticulates the same theme by stating that the basic attitude of philosophy consists in "*erōs*" or a "love of wisdom, of life": "*Erōs* is not only a motivational ground (*Motivgrund*) for philosophy. Rather, the philosophical activity itself requires that one lets oneself loose into the ultimate tendencies of life and returns to its ultimate motives" (GA 58: 23/17, 263/198).

What happens here?

Husserl's principle of all principles amounts to the methodological demand that we rigorously abide by and describe what is given to us in intuition. By contrast, Heidegger tells us that something like "love" or "sympathy" belongs to the core of the phenomenological attitude itself, and that it is essential to the motivation and method of phenomenology. Although Heidegger never specifies what he means by "love" and "sympathy," I think that his move is of key importance since it points to the deep interconnection between philosophical and ethical-existential problems that is crucial for how we understand phenomenology.

According to Heidegger, the task of phenomenology is no other than to acknowledge and understand our pretheoretical life with significances and this can only be done if we are guided by love and sympathy toward life. As Heidegger sees it, the failure of theoretical philosophy is fundamentally ethical-existential, not just cognitive. Unable or unwilling to bear the weight and finitude of our pretheoretical experience, theoretical philosophy denies the substance of this experience and convinces itself of the need to ground it on a more fundamental and secure level of theoretical knowledge. This means that the problems of theoretical philosophy cannot be overcome through purely intellectual seeing and thinking—however sharp and disciplined—but only through a loving and acknowledging attitude toward pretheoretical life.

Heidegger's thesis that philosophy needs to be guided by love and sympathy suggests that our philosophical understanding of the structures of our experience is dependent on our personal ability and will to openly acknowledge what we experience. The thesis points to the fact that understanding the things in life that are important to us and concern us is always an ethical-existential challenge and not just a cognitive one. We generally have strong motives working in us that make us want to see things in certain ways—ways that confirm our ideal identity, our self-esteem, our convictions—and that make us want to repress and explain away what we experience as intolerably painful or demanding, for example, our ethical responsibility to others, our mortality and vulnerability, threats to our self-esteem, and so on. Indeed, we are as a rule capable of repressing and covering up those aspects of life that we cannot bear to acknowledge. Heidegger's central point—which in my view is of crucial importance and which is independent of his specific diagnosis of the motives and problems of theoretical philosophy—is that we can only hope to understand what we are willing to face and admit. Our personal willingness and ability to open up to and acknowledge the ethical-existential challenges and significance of life thus emerge as a condition for phenomenologically elucidating our pretheoretical experiences of significance.

But how is Heidegger's phenomenological science of life to proceed concretely?

Heidegger maintains that we first and foremost live immersed in the specific situations and contexts we experience without reflecting on the primordial structures of life. How, then, is it possible to access and articulate such structures? At the end of "The Idea of Philosophy" he suggests that the phenomenological science must take the form of an "understanding, *hermeneutic intuition*" which is able to explicate life without objectifying it. But what is this hermeneutic intuition and how is it executed?

In "Basic Problems of Phenomenology" Heidegger offers a detailed account of the methodological route of phenomenological understanding. He divides the "phenomenological method" into six main steps: (1) The first step consists simply in a preliminary "pointing to" (*Hinweisen*) a particular sphere of factical life (GA 58: 254/191). (2) The second step consists in "gaining a foothold in" (*Fußfassen*) and "going along with" (*Mitgehen*) the primary movement of life "with the greatest vitality and interiority" (254/191–2) in order to see what we normally experience and understand "without any kind of reflection" (255/193). (3) Then follows what Heidegger describes as the "*the foreseeing, the leaping ahead (Vorschauen, Vorausspringen*) of the phenomenological intuition into the horizons that are given in the life experience itself, into the tendencies and motives that lie in the life experience" (254–5/192). (4–6) The fourth, fifth, and sixth steps consist in articulating, interpreting, and giving form to the dominant structural elements of the experience in their unity and reciprocity. Moreover, Heidegger maintains that during the whole course of the phenomenological explication, the phenomenologist needs to carry out a continuous "critical destruction" (*Destruktion*) of the objectivations and prejudices that tend to attach themselves to and cover up the phenomena (255/192).

Let me try to illuminate the main aspects of Heidegger's method. As the first and second steps make clear, everything depends on our first going along with and acknowledging—with sympathy and without reservations—whatever meets us and concerns us in the experience we want to understand. After this follows the central third step, which articulates what it means to phenomenologically explicate the structures of our experience. As Crowell and Zahavi have argued before me, I basically think that Heidegger adopts Husserl's method of intuitive reflection, albeit with some critical qualifications.

To begin with, Heidegger presents his phenomenological method as essentially relying on *intuition*. The phenomenological explication is described as a "seeing ahead" of the "phenomenological intuition" into the tendencies and horizons of the experience in question, that is to say, as an intuitive access to the basic structures of the experience which it only thus becomes possible to describe and articulate. There is—as opposed to what van Buren and Kisiel maintain— nothing that indicates that Heidegger would as yet envisage the phenomenological understanding as an explication of the "factual preconception of being" (van Buren 1994a: 216) that we always already live in, such that the structures he describes—for example, significance, self-world, historicity—would belong to that specific historical preconception.

Indeed, during these years Heidegger does not hesitate to describe his phenomenological mode of understanding in terms of "intuition" and "seeing." Although he stresses that the phenomenological intuition cannot be understood as a pure intellectual seeing but centrally involves a love or sympathy which allows it to acknowledge and understand the significances of life, he maintains that we have direct intuitive access to the experientially given which is not determined by our historical preconceptions. Rather, our intuition provides the measure for critically examining all such preconceptions. It is precisely the notion of a transhistorical intuition that sustains Heidegger's ambition to explicate the basic universal structures of our pretheoretical experience irrespective of our historical preconceptions. In connection with his classic description of his experience of entering the lecture hall at the University of Freiburg, Heidegger considers the possibility of a Senegalese—he uses the racially prejudiced word "Senegalneger"— doing the same thing. Coming from a nonscientific culture, and not being familiar with universities and lecterns, the Senegalese would probably first experience the lectern as "a something, 'which he does not know what to make of'" (GA 56/57: 72/61). Nevertheless, Heidegger claims, the experience of the Senegalese would be characterized by exactly the same sense-structure as his own experience: "The significant character of the 'equipmental strangeness,' and the significant character of the 'lectern,' are in their essence absolutely identical" (GA 56/57: 72/61). That is to say, the aim of Heidegger's phenomenological descriptions is not to explicate the sense manifested by some specific historical context of understanding but to describe, on the basis of intuition, the basic structures of pretheoretical life as such.

Furthermore, Heidegger characterizes his phenomenological method as *reflective*. As we have seen, he levels hard criticism at Husserl's conception of the phenomenological reduction as a reflective turn from the objects of our natural experience to the correlative acts of consciousness. Nonetheless, his own phenomenological method involves an essential element of reflection. Even if he insists that we must first "go along with" our pretheoretical experience with "the greatest vitality and interiority" (GA 58: 254/192), the idea is not just to plunge into and repeat this experience but to describe its structures. To be able to do this, we need to detach ourselves to some degree from our immersion in the experience under consideration in order to become aware of and explicate its structures: "The phenomenological reduction is a going-along-with (*Mitmachen*)—as one in which I do not become absorbed" (GA 58: 162/218).

In appropriating the reflective method Heidegger is keen to free it from what he conceives of as problematic tendencies in Husserl's notion of reduction. Husserl, remember, tends to picture the reduction as a reflective move that does not acknowledge the primacy of our pretheoretical experience of ethical-existential significance; instead, it takes its paradigmatic starting point in the realm of perceptual object-experiences in order to reflect on the act-structures of the subject that allow objects to be perceptually-cognitively given. In so far as we dogmatically take such act-structures as fundamental for understanding pretheoretical significance, we are resorting to construction and prejudice. Rejecting the above tendencies, Heidegger makes two points about the philosophical meaning and character of reflection. First, he stresses that the phenomenological reflection is guided by the aim of explicating what is given as significant in our pretheoretical experience. Its goal is the "attainment of the pure, objectification-free life out of significances. All that is without significance, all that is not intelligible is *disabled* or absorbed [phenomenological reduction!!]" (GA 58: 156/120). That is, the aim of phenomenological reflection is not to investigate the structures of perceptual-cognitive givenness but to explicate the structures of our experience of significant being as the horizon within which all kinds of knowledge and being are "absorbed" and receive their places. Second, Heidegger wants to avoid beforehand defining reflection as a turn to the acts of the subject. Instead, he emphasizes that the point of reflecting is to trace the driving "tendencies and motives" (GA 58: 255/192) that are essential for understanding the significant experience in question. In this, it must initially be an open question which aspects of our experience—historical meanings and values, drives and motives of the subject, interpersonal relations, language, acts of perception and cognition—that will turn out to be fundamental for grasping the experience in question. So, while rejecting Husserl's notion of the phenomenological reduction as a turn to the transcendental subject, Heidegger appropriates the method of reflection as a pure shift from our primary immersion in particular experiences to a reflection on the sense-structures constituting these experiences.[2]

The methodological self-understanding of Heidegger outlined here also answers well to the methodological mode of the concrete phenomenological descriptions that he provides throughout his earliest Freiburg period. Taking his starting point in our de facto pretheoretical experiences, he persistently attempts to point to and describe the basic structures that manifest themselves as constitutive of these experiences.

Destruction and Formal Indication

There are two more aspects to Heidegger's phenomenological method: first, the critical destruction of the received theoretical concepts and prejudices; second, the task of articulating and conceptualizing the structures that show up as basic to our experience.

Heidegger's emphasis on the need for a "critical destruction" is rooted in his acute awareness of the fact that we always already live in a tradition of historical concepts and preunderstandings that tend to guide our understanding in a prejudiced fashion, and thus distort and cover up the phenomena. Hence, it becomes a crucial part of the phenomenological method to attend to and critically delimit these concepts in order to free up our attention for the sense of what is concretely given in our experience. Here, it is important to note that Heidegger's early notion of "destruction" differs from the concept of "destruction" that plays a central role in the methodological program of *Being and Time*. In contrast to the latter, Heidegger's early notion of "destruction" does not involve the idea that our intuitive understanding is fundamentally determined by our historical understanding of being, and that we need to return to the historical origins of our traditional concepts as the ultimate source of understanding. Indeed, the "critical destruction" that Heidegger has in mind in his early lectures in no way undermines but rather presupposes his commitment to direct intuition. The function of the destruction is precisely to fend off and dismantle the received concepts and prejudices that threaten to obstruct and distort our intuitive understanding and explication of the phenomena.

But how should the structures of life be described and articulated? Heidegger's answer to this question is found in his notion of "formal indication" (*formale Anzeige*).[3]

In recent years, Heidegger's notion of "formal indication" has received much attention in the secondary literature.[4] It has also been central to the discussion of the problem of phenomena/phenomenology. For example, van Buren in defending his hermeneutic-deconstructive reading has argued that Heidegger's formal indication is part of his rejection of Husserlian phenomenology. Given that Heidegger's theme—the "anarchic temporalizing of being" (1994a: 39)—cannot be intuited as a universal structure but is always differentiated into different historical situations, the function of formal indication is to indicate, always from a certain situation, the non-present differential logic determining all such epochs: "formal indication ... indicates the matter of thinking in its non-presence und unsurveyable difference," so that it "remains open for being kairologically fulfilled and differentiated into an alterity of worldviews, principles, historical ages, philosophies, societies, institutions, and personal selfworlds" (van Buren 1995: 158, 165; cf. Kisiel 1993: 376). Against this, representatives of the transcendental phenomenological reading have argued that the idea of formal indication does not upset but is part of Heidegger's commitment to intuition-based phenomenology (cf. Dahlstrom 1994; Crowell 2001: 137–44).

In "Basic Problems of Phenomenology" Heidegger introduces the term "formal indication" to indicate the special character of phenomenological expressions: "The meanings of the words are all still completely formal, *prejudicing nothing*, only sounding a direction—without any definite commitment to it—perhaps, so that is only serves the purpose of letting us return on its path to the primordial motives of life" (GA 58: 3/3). In contrast to theoretical concepts, whose meaning is determined by certain defining features and by their place in a conceptual network, the formal indications of phenomenology function by pointing to the experiences and situations in which the meanings that they express are concretely given as what they are. It belongs to their very way of signifying that we cannot understand them with reference to some preconceived theoretical or historical concepts, but rather need to follow in the direction they indicate in order to experience and see for ourselves the phenomena in question.

To think of philosophical concepts as formal indications involves both a negative and a positive aspect. On the one hand, to call attention to the formally indicative character of the phenomenological concepts means to ward off all the traditional meanings that may suggest themselves in a prejudiced dogmatic way. Instead, we leave the meaning of our concepts open and undetermined—"held in abeyance" (*in der Schwebe gehalten*) (GA 60: 64/44)—until we access the experiences whose sense is at stake. On the other hand, to make use of formal indications means pointing to the concrete personal experiences in which the signified meaning is given and evident (cf. GA 58: 248/187; GA 59: 85/65; GA 9: 9–11/8–10). As Daniel Dahlstrom puts it, "[Heidegger] regards the 'formal indication' as a revisable way of pointing to some phenomenon, fixing its preliminary sense and the corresponding manner of unpacking it, while at the same time deflecting any 'uncritical lapse' into some specific conception that would foreclose pursuit of 'a genuine sense' of the phenomenon" (1994: 780).

All things considered, I think there can be no doubt that Heidegger's notion of formal indication is an integral part of his intuitive phenomenology. It belongs to the very nature of such indications that their meaning cannot be determined by any theoretical or historical concepts we might have but can only be grasped through direct intuitive reflection on the experiences to which they refer. Moreover, Heidegger emphatically underscores that the phenomenological intuition precedes and conditions every linguistic articulation of the given: "I can indeed only describe, when I have already seen" (GA 56/57: 217/184).[5]

Although Heidegger's notions of "destruction" and "formal indication" do not break with Husserl's intuition-based phenomenology, they both point to an important challenge that phenomenology is always faced with. In contrast to Husserl, Heidegger is extremely sensitive to our strong tendency to let ourselves be guided by our received concepts and preunderstandings on account of their normality and social acceptedness. Phenomenology is in no way exempt from the danger that its alleged intuitive descriptions of the given may in fact be conducted by concepts that determine what we attend to and what we see in a prejudiced way. This danger not only pertains to traditional and other preestablished concepts, but also to the phenomenologist's own concepts, which may easily stiffen into deceptive prejudices. Hence, being continuously awake to this challenge is a prerequisite for an open and unimpeded phenomenological understanding. Although Husserl is certainly not unaware of these matters, he is more naive and vulnerable than Heidegger on this point.

The Primordial Structure of Life

The aim of Heidegger's primordial science is to explicate the primordial structure of "pretheoretical experience" or "factical life." Since for Heidegger this experience constitutes the primary domain of givenness, its structure is also the basic structure of phenomena.

What is the structure of life?

In "The Idea of Philosophy" Heidegger describes our primary pretheoretical experience as a unified experience of significance where the experiencing I is no mere spectator but is essentially an engaged and concerned agent. Toward the end of the course, he characterizes the primordial structure of life—which he here calls the "primordial something" (*Ur-etwas*) of life—as follows: "Life is in itself motivated and tendential; motivating tendency, tending motivation. The basic character of life is to live *toward* something, to world out (*auswelten*) into determinate experiential worlds" (GA 56/57: 218/186). How should this preliminary projection of the basic structure of life be understood concretely?

In subsequent lectures course Heidegger goes on to offer a phenomenological analysis of the basic structure of factical life in terms of three sense-directions: "content-sense" (*Gehaltssinn*), "relation-sense" (*Bezugssinn*), and "enactment-sense" (*Vollzugssinn*) (GA 58: 261/196). In "Introduction to the Phenomenology of Religion" he spells out this structure as the totality of sense constituting every "phenomenon":

> What is phenomenology? What is phenomenon? Here this can be itself indicated only formally. Each experience—as experien*cing* and as experien*ced*—can "be taken in the phenomenon" (*ins Phänomen genommen werden*), that is to say, one can ask: 1. After the primordial "*what*," that is experienced therein (*content*). 2. After the primordial "*how*," in which it is experienced (*relation*). 3. After the primordial "*how*," in which the relation-sense is *enacted* (*enactment*). But these three directions of sense (content-, relation-, enactment-sense) do not simply coexist. "Phenomenon" is the totality of sense in these three directions. "Phenomenology" is the explication of this totality of sense; it gives the "*logos*" of the phenomena. (GA 60: 63/43)

Let us try to clarify the three aspects of this structure one by one.

First, "content-sense" denotes the "what" or "content" of our experience, that is, the significances that we experience: other people, cars, trees, dogs, lecterns, houses, universities, concerts, states, and so on. According to Heidegger, we primarily experience and live in a world of significances: "I live factically always *caught in significances,* and every significance has its surrounding of new significances: horizons of engagement, involvement, utilization, destiny" (GA 58: 104/83). We do not first perceive some kind of sensory data, which we would actively have to interpret and furnish with sense. What we experience—whether trivial or worthless or strange—essentially presents itself as significant within the context of our world. There is, moreover, no meaningful reality to be posited or discovered beyond the significant world we experience: "The *experience of existence* terminates in and is satisfied in the *characterization of significance*" (GA 58: 106/84).

Second, "relation-sense" denotes the "how" of our experience, the different ways in which the significances of the world are given and experienced. For example, the significances can present themselves and concern us in experiences such as direct encounter, memory, and imagination. So far, Heidegger's description of the interplay between content- and relation-sense can be understood as a rearticulation of Husserl's conception of the intentional correlation between *noema* and *noesis*.

Third, "enactment-sense" refers to the way in which the particular self enacts its pretheoretical experiences. According to Heidegger, our experience of significance is ultimately anchored in the particular self or "self-world" (GA 58: 59/46) which constitutes the specific temporal-historical setting of every experience. The pretheoretical experience of the world is thus always the experience of a historically situated particular self.

However, how should we understand Heidegger's critical claim that our pretheoretical experience of significance is anchored in the self who enacts the experience—a self that is said to be always particular and historical?

In "Basic Problems of Phenomenology" Heidegger makes an attempt to explicate how the experiencing self "has" or "enacts" its life. As we go along with our pretheoretical experience, he maintains, we find that we primarily enact our experiences without any awareness of an I-subject. Still, before any reflection on the subject of the experiences has taken place, we already "have ourselves" in a peculiar way. What Heidegger here has in mind is the "character of familiarity" (GA 58: 157/121) which, he claims, essentially characterizes the significances that we experience:

> I live in contexts of significance that are self-sufficient in scope. What is experienced addresses us (*spricht an*), but in a way that is always somehow familiar to us. It is itself such that it also always concerns me somehow, that I am present there (*daß ich dabei bin*). Somehow, I have myself there. (GA 58: 157/121)

According to Heidegger, it is a basic structural feature of our factical experience that the significances address and concern me *as familiar*. They are familiar not only in the sense that I am in some sense always already acquainted with them; they are also familiar in the sense that they belong to me and "express" who I am (GA 58: 158/122). Just as the world that we experience is always our own familiar world, the experiencing self is always what it is as the subject of this historical world.

As Heidegger puts it: "'I myself' am a context of significance, in which I myself live" (GA 58: 248/187). Whereas we do not normally recognize this familiarity as such, Heidegger maintains that it becomes conspicuous in situations where it is disrupted. For example, when I am surprised by something new or unknown I experience a disruption of my normal familiarity with my world, whereby this familiarity becomes striking to me in its very removal (GA 58: 251/189). In short, what Heidegger is saying is that the significances we experience essentially belong to a particular historical world—a particular context of historical significance— that always already addresses us as familiar, as our own. This world determines and delimits what we can experience as significant in the first place. As such, it also contains and circumscribes the significances and roles that determine who we can be—our possible identities in this world of ours. This is the sense of Heidegger's proclamation that it is the basic character of life to "world out" into a particular historical world (GA 56/57: 218/186).

We can now see—and on this point van Buren and Kisiel are clearly on the right track—that Heidegger's examination of the primordial structure of life culminates in his articulation of the radical historicity of our experience of phenomena. Heidegger's anchoring of our experience of significance in the historical self-world accounts for his claim that life is "historical—in an absolute sense" (GA 56/57: 21/18). Granted that my familiar historical world always already determines and delimits my possibilities of experiencing things as intelligible and important at all, this implies that it addresses me as my historical destiny: "an originary circle of familiarity [grace, calling, destiny]" (GA 58: 167/127). Our life in the world is thus essentially a life in a finite historical context of significance that cannot be founded on some supposedly deeper or more secure theoretical ground.

A Transhistorical Phenomenology of Historical Life

Heidegger's conception of the phenomenological method and his view of the structure of phenomena go in opposite directions as regards the question of whether direct intuition or history is at the basis of our understanding.

In critically elaborating Husserl's phenomenology, Heidegger retains the idea of direct intuitive reflection as a decisive aspect of his method. His phenomenological method thus basically consists in acknowledging and intuitively reflecting on our pretheoretical experiences in order to bring out the basic structural elements that constitute them and make them what they are. In this, everything he has to say about the primordial structure of life—including its historicity and finitude— emerges as universal structural features of life as such. On the other hand, Heidegger's phenomenological analyses of the primordial structure of life result in the claim that our pretheoretical experience is fundamentally historical in that the phenomenal significances we experience are essentially given as our finite historical destiny. Whereas the transcendental phenomenological interpretation defended by Crowell and Zahavi basically captures the methodological character of Heidegger's phenomenology, the hermeneutic-deconstructive reading represented by van Buren and Kisiel is right concerning his view of the radical historicity of life.

However, Heidegger does not rest content with this constellation. Rather, he believes that his analysis of the historicity of factical life implies that his phenomenological science of origin itself needs to become radically historical.

For Heidegger, the question of the relationship between phenomenology and history is from the outset a central theme. In the preceding decades, the dichotomy between systematic philosophy and historicism had surfaced as an acute problem in the philosophical debate, where prominent philosophers such as Rickert and Husserl had defended the systematic ambition of philosophy to attain true and universal knowledge against the threat of "historicism." In his *Logos* article Husserl famously argued that philosophy must reject historicism and worldview philosophy in order to become a rigorous science, and that this can only be done by means of phenomenological research into the essential structures of experience.[6] Whereas Heidegger embraces Husserl's phenomenological demand to abide by the given, he does not follow Husserl in opposing the systematic ambition of phenomenology to historicism. Instead, he proclaims that the very distinction between systematics and history is misleading and needs to be overcome: "For our purposes, however, it suffices to refer to the close connection between historical and 'systematic' examination—both are to be overcome!" (GA 56/57: 132/112). By this, however, Heidegger in no way means to collapse the distinction between philosophical investigations directed at the matters themselves and historical investigations only concerned with mapping historical standpoints. His central claim is rather that the systematic investigations of phenomenology are themselves intrinsically historical: "*Phenomenology and historical method*; their absolute unity in the purity of the understanding of life in and for itself" (GA 56/57: 125/106; cf. GA 58: 256/193).

Heidegger grounds his programmatic assertation about the historicity of phenomenology by referring to the basic historicity of life. Explicating the "familiarity" that is said to characterize our pretheoretical experience and signal its historical nature, he writes: "These characters of familiarity that express me … also designate the unaccented place of motivation (*Motivstelle*) in factical life, which motivates how all comprehension of the life-relations of life must let itself be addressed from out of life itself, and its fullness, from out of its *history*" (GA 58: 159/122; cf. GA 56/57: 21/18). Heidegger thus thinks that because our pretheoretical experience of significance is historically determined, the phenomenological comprehension of the structure of this experience must itself be such.

However, Heidegger leaves it at this and offers no explanation of why phenomenological reflection on the structures of experience would be essentially historical or of how such a historical thinking would transpire.

As such, the argument that the historicity of our experience of phenomenal significances implies that the phenomenological explication of the structure of this experience is itself historical is simply invalid. This is because we are here dealing with two different matters that may very well differ from each other as regards how we understand them. Heidegger's analysis of the structure of life focuses on our pretheoretical experience of significances such as cars, trees, animals, and churches. The claim is that these matters are what they are and concern us as parts of our finite historical world of significances. Our understanding of these matters is thus essentially an understanding of the historical contexts we live in and cannot take the form of a direct transhistorical intuition.

However, even if this were true—which is, for our part, still an open question—this would not imply that our phenomenological understanding of the historical structure of experience would itself be historically determined. In contrast to our experience of worldly significances, the phenomenological analysis focuses on the constitutive structures of basic human experiences such as handling tools, encountering persons, perceiving objects, fearing death, and feeling shame. Clearly, the values, norms, practices, and institutions that in different ways and on different levels determine or influence our experiences of different phenomena vary historically. However, it does not follow from this that basic structures of sense perception or feeling shame—structures such as the bodily and perspectival character of perception, the ability to see oneself as seen by others, the urge for social affirmation—would also be determined by historically changeable meanings and concepts and that understanding these structures would be tantamount to understanding such historical meanings. Taken radically, such a thesis would in fact be hard to make sense of and defend. It would amount to the claim that our basic humanity—the basic structures of our experience and perception, our basic human motives and desires—would be subject to historical change and that people from different cultures would be more or less alien creatures with whom we would not necessarily have any experiences in common.

We can now see that there is no contradiction in the notion of a transhistorical phenomenology that claims to discover the radical historicity of our experience of phenomena and that such a discovery would not imply that phenomenology itself would have to become historical.[7]

In order to make plausible his thesis about the historicity of phenomenology Heidegger would have to offer additional arguments for this claim. However, he does not do this.

The fact of the matter is that Heidegger's analysis of the historicity of life remains quite weak and undeveloped and does not support his thesis about the historical character of phenomenology. In the end, Heidegger's argument for the historicity of life amounts to the thesis that the self experiences the significances it encounters as always already familiar parts of its own historical world. However, he offers almost no analysis of why—no account of the structure due to which—such familiarity would constitute a necessary condition for experiencing things as meaningful. His argument that the basic familiarity of our world shows up when it is disrupted does not come close to establishing this familiarity as a necessary condition for experiencing phenomena. To be sure, in encountering unfamiliar things—such as persons or habits of an alien culture—these might first appear bewildering and not readily intelligible. Still, this in no way proves that my familiar significances would determine what I can experience as meaningful. Does not the other person address me as ethically significant regardless of my familiar understandings? Could not the unfamiliar customs and concepts be perceived as a challenge to transcend and critically question my familiar world, instead of falling back upon it as my given destiny?

Heidegger has not yet developed—as van Buren and Kisiel erroneously think he has—his analysis of the historical as-structure of understanding, which will be the corner stone of his thinking from the early 1920s onwards and which will allow him to rethink phenomenology in terms of hermeneutic-destructive interpretation of our guiding historical preunderstanding of being. Since he is unable to substantiate and develop his idea about the historical character of phenomenology, his statements about the radical historicity of phenomenology still remain programmatic assertions with little substance. Indeed, contrary to his assertions, Heidegger both articulates and practices phenomenology as direct intuitive reflection on the constitutive structures of our experience.[8]

3

LIFE AND THE TASK OF PHILOSOPHY

The Question of the Existential Task of Philosophy

Throughout his life, Heidegger is centrally concerned with the question of the existential role and relevance of philosophy in our personal everyday life. In the early Freiburg lecture courses, the question arises in the following form: If, as Heidegger claims, our factical pretheoretical experience of phenomena constitutes our primary and self-sufficient access to the realm of significance—and neither needs to nor can be theoretically grounded by philosophy—what existential task, if any, remains for philosophy as a primordial science of life?

In view of Heidegger's intense questioning of the traditional aim of philosophy to overcome and ground our naive experience by explicating the basic structures of life and being, it is striking that most commentators tend to see his primordial science as a straightforward continuation and radicalization of precisely that tradition. For instance, although offering almost diametrically opposed interpretations of the theme and method of Heidegger's early Freiburg thinking, Steven Crowell and John van Buren agree that he unproblematically continues the traditional quest for the basic structures of meaningful being—be it in the form of a phenomenological explication of the transcendental structures of experience or in the form of a historical reflection on the groundless event that opens up being.

According to Crowell, Heidegger is wholeheartedly guided by the traditional goal of philosophy to carry out "categorial research" (2001: 125). Giving little weight to Heidegger's accentuation of the self-sufficiency of pretheoretical life or to his questioning of the existential motives of philosophy, Crowell argues that the "'existential' issues" surfacing in Heidegger's lecture courses gain their "systematic sense" from the methodological notion that only phenomenological reflection on our concrete experiences can provide access to the space of meaning (131). Instead, Crowell claims that Heidegger, just like Husserl, believes that the motivation of philosophy lies in the tendency toward "genuine seeing" that characterizes our intentional experience (136). The task of philosophy is none other than to realize our inborn aspiration to evidentially grounded knowledge by overcoming the limited perspective of "naive life"—in which we are oriented "towards entities *through* meaning"—and reflectively clarifying the structures of meaning that always already organize our primarily naive experience (146). In similar fashion, van Buren presents the young Heidegger as an "heir to the Greek *prote philosophia*," an heir which turns the traditional quest for the ground or *arche* of being into a quest for its "anarchic *arche*" (1994a: 243), that is, the "*a priori* of temporality, difference, finitude" (219). Even if van Buren never tires of stressing the groundlessness and finitude of being, he endorses the view that the task of philosophy is to reach a qualified—though finite, differential—understanding of the fundamental anarchic event of being.

In contrast to Crowell and van Buren, Theodore Kisiel is more attentive to Heidegger's questioning of the existential motivation of philosophy. Highlighting Heidegger's emphasis on the primacy of our pretheoretical experience and his critique of the traditional effort of philosophy to ground it theoretically, Kisiel argues that Heidegger's sense of philosophy is essentially "phronetic" (1993: 270). Since the goal of the philosophical science of origin is none other than to "serve life" (59), the purpose of its understanding and formal indications is not to achieve a science of life for its own sake, but to "smooth the way toward intensifying the sense of the immediate in which we find ourselves" (59). Hence, what Kisiel seems to propose is that Heidegger's rejection of the possibility of philosophy to ground our factical pretheoretical understanding of life makes him think that the existential function of philosophy ultimately consists in its phronetic ability to thwart our theoretical alienation and lead us back to a primordial enactment of our pretheoretical experience.

What are the relative truths of the above interpretations? Again, I want to suggest that the discrepancy between the interpretations mirror Heidegger's own difficulty and ambivalence in grappling with the issue of the existential task of philosophy.

Heidegger from the outset launches his early Freiburg philosophy as a phenomenological science of the origin of life. In so doing, he uncritically and without further question adopts the traditional idea that the task of philosophy is, in some sense, to learn to know the basic structure and sense of meaningful reality (cf. GA 58: 1–2/2–3). This hasty appropriation of the idea of a primordial science can, in retrospect, be seen as an indication of the fact that during these years he will be unable to offer a convincing account of how the problem of origin is encountered in life as a decisive existential problem. Nevertheless, as he develops his primordial science, the question of the motivation of philosophy soon emerges as an urgent and uncircumventable question—a question that will prove hard to answer.

In his first lecture courses, Heidegger again and again stresses the primacy and irreducibility of our pretheoretical experience of phenomena. To bring out this point, he characterizes factical life as "self-sufficient" (*selbstgenügsam*). Life does not, he writes, need to "twist itself out of itself" in order to understand and accomplish its own possibilities (GA 58: 31/25): the dominion of the factical experience is "boundless"; since "it is not 'fitted' to anything, all and everything can become accessible to it" (GA 58: 217/164). Hence, to say that life is self-sufficient is to say that our pretheoretical experience constitutes our primary and full access to the realm of significant phenomena, such that these phenomena cannot and need not be grounded on some supposedly deeper or more secure ground.

Heidegger also underscores that pretheoretical life possesses its own possibilities of judging, clarifying, and communicating its experience of the world, which he sums up under the title "taking-notice" (*Kenntnisnahme*) (GA 58: 112/88): "Factically experienced contexts of significance will indeed be explicated, but still left in their vital facticity. The explication takes-notice and narrates, but in the basic style of factical experiencing, of fully going-along with life" (GA 58: 111/88). In contrast to theoretical knowledge, in which objects are viewed in detachment from their primary context of significance, pretheoretical consideration relies on the "experiential certainty" (*Erfahrungsgewißheit*) (GA 58: 113/89) of our experience, attending to and articulating the significances given here. In pretheoretically considering something, our attitude to what we experience undergoes a certain "modification" (GA 58: 116/91): we to some extent detach ourselves from our primary absorption in the experience in question in order to overview and articulate its different aspects from the point of view of the guiding question or interest of the current situation (GA 58: 112/88). According to Heidegger, the pretheoretical consideration can take many forms—deliberation, recollection, narration, report, discussion—and it makes use of the factical everyday language at our disposal. However, even though its linguistic expressions are often incomplete and conceptually floating this in no way implies that they could not be clear and fully adequate.

Heidegger's insistence on the primacy and self-sufficiency of our pretheoretical experience is at the root of his drastic questioning of the traditional aim of philosophy to theoretically ground life. In rejecting this ambition, he deprives philosophy of its standard way of understanding its own motivation. From the viewpoint of theoretical philosophy, pretheoretical life appears as a naive form of theoretical knowledge dominated by concepts that it lacks the means to verify. Hence, theoretical philosophy emerges as the much-needed task of grounding the concepts that normally guide our understanding in a prejudiced way. If, however, our pretheoretical experience provides access to the realm of significance and contains its own measures for understanding and judging the significances we experience, then philosophy can no longer uphold its central promise of critically justifying factical life on the basis of a privileged understanding of its ground or origin. The outcome of Heidegger's critique is that philosophy, as traditionally understood, "would be deprived of its most ancestral entitlements—of its regal, superior calling. What value at all could it have if it should lose this role?" (GA 56/57: 11/10).

Heidegger's emphasis on the self-sufficiency of factical life and his critique of theoretical philosophy makes the question of the existential motivation and value of philosophy urgent: "For philosophy, the philosophical experience of life itself is motivated out of life itself. We need to take seriously the motivation of the philosophical method of understanding in general from out of life itself" (GA 58: 253–4/191). The challenge facing Heidegger is, then, to show how the philosophical task of understanding the origin of life is motivated by life itself.

Fundamental or Dispensable?

Heidegger's response to the question of the motivation of philosophy is bifurcated. On the one hand, he presents a fairly traditional argument for why a philosophical understanding of the origin of life is necessary for a transparent enactment of life. On the other hand, he pursues reflections that undercut this argument and lead him to suggest that the existential task of philosophy is entirely negative and phronetic. Let us look at the two strategies in turn.

According to Heidegger, philosophy cannot hope to attain a better—deeper or more secure—understanding of the particular significances of our world than that provided by our pretheoretical experience. However, he maintains that there is one crucial matter concerning which life is not self-sufficient: "The phenomenon of 'self-sufficiency' itself cannot be seen within life in itself, when we remain therein" (GA 58: 41/33). That is to say, as long as we enact our pretheoretical experiences in a straightforward manner we lack access to the basic character of life as self-sufficient, as our primary domain of significance. This means that in so far as we are confronted with the aspiration of theoretical philosophy to establish a universal and objective theoretical ground for our factical life, we are in principle unable to reject this aspiration since we have no insight into the self-sufficiency of life. As a result of this phenomenal deficit of factical life, Heidegger argues that a primordial science is necessary in order to overrule all theoretical-philosophical prejudices about life and so make possible a transparent enactment of life as the self-sufficient finite destiny it is. Hence, Heidegger's conception of the aim of his primordial science both continues and critically transforms the traditional theoretical conception of the task of philosophy. While rejecting the ambition of philosophy to theoretically ground life Heidegger holds on to the idea that the task of philosophy is to offer an ultimate understanding of life *qua* life, which is not given in our pretheoretical experience, but which conditions a clear-sighted enactment of this experience. As Heidegger puts it in a key passage in "The Idea of Philosophy": "But genuine naivety—this is the paradox—can only be achieved through the innermost philosophical intuition!!" (GA 56/57: 92/78).

However, Heidegger has great difficulties in bearing out his thesis that a primordial science is needed to make possible transparent genuine life.

Heidegger's description of the existential task of philosophy rests on the presupposition that our everyday pretheoretical experience is centrally concerned with the question of the ontological sense—origin—of life and being, as a question the understanding of which conditions our ability to relate to the significances we encounter. Still, in these early lecture courses he provides no account of how the philosophical question of origin would meet us as a fundamental and decisive question. He does not yet entertain the idea—so central to *Being and Time*—that we always already live in a more or less prejudiced understanding of being that guides our experience of beings. To the contrary, he maintains that it belongs to the self-sufficiency of life that we experience the significances of our world without being touched by—understanding or misunderstanding—the question of the origin of life. In fact, he pictures the way in which philosophy addresses life as pure seduction. It is only, as he ironically puts it, theoretical philosophy that "awakens" life from its "slumber" and "reveals problems." To see these problems "the naive person, who knows nothing of philosophical criticism" must free herself from her pretheoretical experience and enter the theoretical perspective: "In this way one enters a new dimension, the philosophical" (GA 56/57: 79–80/67). Hence, it is only in so far as theoretical philosophy presents its promise of a theoretical grounding of life that the problem of origin starts to address us as a seductive pseudo-problem.

Heidegger's failure to account for how the philosophical problem of origin addresses us as a basic problem destabilizes his thesis that a primordial science of life is necessary for a transparent enactment of life. This shortcoming pushes him toward the conclusion that the task of philosophy is entirely negative and therapeutic. In "Phenomenology of Intuition and Expression" Heidegger thus suggests that the edifying work of philosophy is realized through self-destruction. Having reviewed some of the contemporary strategies for salvaging an autonomous task for philosophy, he concludes that none of these strategies dares touch upon the possibility that "philosophy is only seemingly a necessary good of mankind and that philosophy has the task of making itself look ridiculous with all rigor and of annihilating itself and furthermore of preventing itself from ever reoccurring" (GA 59: 189/146). That this is exactly the purpose of his own primordial science quickly becomes clear: "We do not philosophize in order to show that we need a philosophy but exactly in order to show that we do not need any" (GA 59: 191/147). If philosophy besets life in the form of distortive theoretical constructions, and life has no need of a positive understanding of the origin, then the only task that remains for philosophy is to dismantle the philosophical theories and, by so doing, guide us back to our primary enactment of life.[1]

In summary, Heidegger's inability to account for how the question of the primordial sense of life concerns us as a decisive question gives rise to a vacillation between two diverging perspectives on the existential task of philosophy. On the one hand, Heidegger projects his primordial science as a basic and necessary path to a transparent enactment of factical life as a self-sufficient historical destiny. On the other hand, he is led to the notion that the sole existential function of philosophy lies in its negative-phronetic ability to destruct theoretical philosophy and guide us back to our factical experience of our world. By exclusively focusing on either of these tendencies Heidegger's commentators have developed their conflicting readings of his view of the task of philosophy.

Heidegger's problems with accounting for the role of philosophy in life mirror, and are to some extent induced by, his historical orientation in the first Freiburg years. In this period, Heidegger is convinced that the entire tradition of philosophy—from Plato and Aristotle up to Husserl and the Neo-Kantians—is governed by the idea about the primacy of the theoretical. His own effort to reform Husserl's phenomenology into a science of pretheoretical life is influenced, first, by contemporary life-philosophers such as Dilthey, Nietzsche, Bergson, and Simmel, and, second, by Christian thinkers such as St. Paul, Augustine, Meister

Eckhart, Luther, and Kierkegaard. According to Heidegger, it has hitherto been the exclusive privilege of primal Christianity—especially Paul—to emphasize and articulate the finite temporality of factical life. However, none of these historical paradigms provides a model for a new understanding of the role of philosophy in life. Whereas the life-philosophers tend to fluctuate between an urge to keep up the traditional task of philosophy and an impulse to dissolve it into psychology or historicism, the Christian thinking of Paul et al. essentially transpires in a pretheoretical discourse that is not concerned with the philosophical question of the primordial structure of life. Hence, in launching his primordial science as a strict phenomenological realization of the traditional task of philosophy while rebutting the whole philosophical tradition as theoretical, Heidegger has no historical model for understanding how the philosophical endeavor is motivated out of life itself.

The tension in Heidegger's early lectures diagnosed above reflects the dual impulses that from the very beginning drive his thinking. First, there is the desire to critically regenerate—in the form of a phenomenology of factical life—the age-old ambition of philosophy to explicate the basic sense of life and being. Second, there is the sense that philosophy must be directly relevant to the challenge of facing and understanding the acute ethical-existential problems of our personal life. In these years Heidegger is still unable to bring these impulses together into a unified vision of the task of philosophy. A few years later he will resolve the issue by inscribing the philosophical question of being into the heart of our existential struggle and insisting that our stance toward this question conditions our ability to transparently encounter and take in the meaningful phenomena central to our lives.

An Unsettling Suggestion

In his early Freiburg lecture courses, Heidegger does not only fail to account for how the question of origin concerns us in life. The lectures also contain a suggestion that positively challenges the very idea that a philosophical-ontological understanding of the basic structures and sense of life—or of being—would be needed in order to transparently encounter and grasp the central ethical-existential significances of life.

In Heidegger's analysis of our capacity for pretheoretical "taking-notice," we find the following remarkable passage:

> The experiential character of the factical experiential certainty (*Erfahrungsgewißheit*) is an absolute one, it is unshakeable, often bracing and asserting itself stubbornly against every theoretical line of argument that is brought on. This it does as living conviction, growing within factical experience. The conviction does not simply and in general stand there as a theoretical formation. Rather, it is real in the form of significance. (GA 58: 113/89)

What Heidegger suggests here is that our pretheoretical taking-notice—relying on the "factical experiential certainty" of our experience—has the capacity of asserting itself against the theories and claims of theoretical philosophy. That is to say, even in want of any clear philosophical understanding of the primordial sense of life, which would allow us to critically discuss and delimit the claims set forth by theoretical philosophy, it is nevertheless possible for us to reject philosophical theories as unintelligible or distortive in relation to our primary direct experience of particular phenomenal significances.

To take an example, I suppose such a rejection could take the following form. Someone is presented with the idea—more or less loosely based on Richard Dawkins's theory about the selfish gene (cf. Dawkins 1989)—that man is fundamentally an egoistic creature. To this, she responds: "I am not sure that I understand the claim that we are basically selfish creatures, but it cannot make me doubt that my friend is a generous and loving person." It seems that in order to reject Dawkins's theory on this point, we do not need to understand its meaning and delimit its truth by developing a better ontological explication of the being of biological life and of the human being. What happens in the example above is that the person rejects the claim that man is a selfish creature, while leaving open the further question concerning the meaning and truth of Dawkins's general theory. The crucial thing is that, on the basis of our experience of others and ourselves, we can see the possibility of a love that differs from and is not reducible to our various egoistic motives. Certainly, this prephilosophical way of responding to philosophical theories might—due to its lack of philosophical argument and clarity—appear naive and unwarranted from a theoretical perspective, and thus be socially and intellectually hard to abide by. Even so, it might be entirely to the point in so far as it relies on our experience of the matters at issue.

Heidegger does not elaborate the idea of prephilosophical insight opened up here, and he will never return to it later. However, it seems that his suggestion not only undercuts the idea that philosophical reflection on the ontological sense of life is needed in order to reject philosophical theories on phenomenological grounds. It is also unsettling to his later paradigmatic conception of the task of philosophy in terms of the ontological difference: the idea that since we always already live in an unthematic and prejudiced understanding of being that guides our understanding of beings, a philosophical explication of the sense of being is necessary in order to attain an open and transparent understanding of beings.

Heidegger's suggestion implies that our pretheoretical experience gives us open access to the particular significances of life, an access that is not hierarchically determined by our possible philosophical-ontological understandings and theories.

To be sure, we tend to entertain different ontological conceptions—philosophical or religious—about the nature of reality and the human being, which may influence how we think about, categorize, and investigate different phenomena. However, our ontological understandings do not *determine*—they do not decide and delimit in advance, as a cognitive necessity—our experience of phenomena. Rather, the more or less strong influence that our ontological conceptions exert on us is due, first, to their often habitual and undisputed status in our understanding; second, to whatever existential motives—collective pressure, fear of shame, and so on—we may have for wanting to cling to these understandings.

The primacy and independence of our pretheoretical experience of particular phenomena show themselves in the fact that it is perfectly possible to experience and understand particular significances while simultaneously entertaining views about the ontological makeup of reality that conflict with this experience. Often, this happens without much friction. Say, for example, that I have a reductive materialist worldview according to which the conscious life of human beings is causally determined by whatever happens in their brains. Nevertheless, I normally experience and relate to the persons I encounter as free and responsible moral subjects. This is possible as long as I do not seriously apply my materialist worldview to my experience of others. However, if I were faced with the contradiction between my personal phenomenal experience of others and my materialist worldview this would be, precisely, an experience of conflict. Faced with this conflict, I could do many things: I could give up or alter my worldview; I could try to argue that materialism is compatible with free will and morality; or I could choose to repress and deny the freedom and moral responsibility of human beings. The point is that whatever I do, the entire dynamic of the situation presupposes that I do have independent experiential access to others as free and responsible subjects that is not determined by my ontological worldview.

The upshot of Heidegger's suggestion is that—contrary to his later view on the matter—philosophical ontology is not a necessary condition for achieving an open and transparent relationship to beings. This, however, does not mean that it would be meaningless or futile to inquire about different kinds of being or about being as such. Rather, it means that ontological understanding of being does not have any priority in relation to our understanding of meaningful beings. To reflect on the structures and characters of different kinds of being is simply to reflect, on a more or less general ontological level, on the meaning-structures of our different experiences of particular phenomena. This also means that ontological thinking always runs the risk of presenting general structures of being—for example, the being of tools, the being of language, the being of emotions—while leaving unclarified the particular paradigmatic experiences that they are rooted in and covering up other types of experience that do not fit the structures.

Part Two

THE HISTORICAL STRUCTURE OF PHENOMENA

Introduction

In the summer of 1921, Heidegger, still *Privatdozent* at the University of Freiburg and working as Husserl's assistant, decides to give a seminar on Aristotle's *De Anima*. The seminar initiates a period of concentrated explication of Aristotle that in important respects refurbishes his philosophical stance and culminates with the publication of his early magnum opus *Being and Time* in 1927.

Heidegger's philosophical interest in Aristotle is deeply motivated by his struggle with the problem of phenomena/phenomenology. In the first Freiburg lecture courses Heidegger set out to elaborate Husserl's phenomenology into a primordial science of life. He insisted on the primacy and self-sufficiency of our pretheoretical experience as our basic access to the domain of significant phenomena. What we here experience, he claimed, is always the factical historical world of the particular experiencing self. However, Heidegger's philosophical journey into pretheoretical life led him into fundamental aporias that he was unable to resolve. Although he stressed the need to reconceive phenomenology as a radically historical form of thinking, he basically articulated and practiced phenomenology as direct intuitive reflection on the necessary and universal structures of our experience. Furthermore, his emphasis on the self-sufficiency of pretheoretical life made him unable to bear out his vision of the fundamental role of philosophy of life.

In these early lectures, Heidegger held the conviction that the entire tradition of Western philosophy was rooted in the theoretical attitude, and that the most qualified historical paradigm for understanding the dynamics of factical life was found in primal Christianity. In this setting, Aristotle chiefly figured as the Greek originator of theoretical philosophy. Given his view that since the Middle Ages philosophy and theology had been steeped in the conceptuality of Aristotle, covering up and distorting the original Christian experience, Heidegger believed it was crucial for phenomenology to "radically break away" from the Aristotelian heritage (GA 58: 61/47).

However, when Heidegger turns to reading Aristotle in 1921 he soon comes to believe that Aristotle's texts contain nothing less than an unsurpassed model for conceiving of the historical structure of phenomena. Roughly, the idea is that our intuitive experience as significant phenomena is determined by our prior understanding of the historical contexts of meaning in which we live; moreover, that this prior understanding is itself guided by our understanding of the different senses of being and by the sense of being as such. It seems to Heidegger that this new powerful conception of the historical structure of phenomena makes it possible for him to overcome the aporias of his first lectures. First, it allows him to rethink the phenomenological method in terms of a hermeneutic-destructive explication and retrieval of our received preunderstanding of being. Second, it allows him to account for the task of philosophy in terms of the question of being, conceived as the normally hidden horizon of all our experience and understanding.

Heidegger's seminar on Aristotle's *De Anima* in 1921 is the first of a series of courses and seminars on Aristotle's texts that would continue uninterruptedly until the end of 1924. In the summer of 1922, he delivers his first full-scale course on Aristotle, consisting of detailed translations and interpretations of selected parts of the *Metaphysics* and *Physics*. At the time, Heidegger is also planning a book on Aristotle. In the autumn of 1922, he composes an introduction to the book project, intended to serve as textual support for his twin applications for professorships in Marburg and Göttingen. The book was never written, but the introduction to the project, named "Phenomenological Interpretations of Aristotle (Indication of the Hermeneutic Situation)," constitutes Heidegger's first compressed articulation of his new philosophical stance. Eventually, "Indication of the Hermeneutic Situation" also served its worldly purpose. First turned down in Göttingen, Heidegger is elected Professor of Philosophy in Marburg in the summer of 1923. In Marburg Heidegger continues and expands his conception of the structure of phenomena by further developing his analyses of the human being, *Dasein*, as temporal-historical "being-in-the-world." The period also contains two extensive critical engagements with Husserl's phenomenology. In his first Marburg lecture course "Introduction to Phenomenological Research" from the winter of 1923–4, he interprets Husserl's modern phenomenology as an alienation from Aristotle's originary phenomenology. After a few semesters of Aristotle-courses, he offers his most extensive treatment of Husserl ever in the lecture course "History of the Concept of Time: Prolegomena" from the summer of 1925. In these years, Heidegger thus works on two fronts simultaneously: while he lets his new conception of phenomena grow forth through his readings of Aristotle, he is at the same time eager to sharpen his vision by critically contrasting it to Husserl's phenomenological program.

The philosophical development initiated in 1921 culminates and receives its final systematic expression as Heidegger publishes *Being and Time* in 1927. The aim of the book is to carry out a fundamental ontology, that is to say, an investigation of the sense of being on the basis of an existential analytic of Dasein. Originally, the treatise was meant to consist of two main parts, each containing three divisions, but Heidegger never published more than the two first divisions of the first part. During the years following the publication of *Being and Time* Heidegger continues probing new strategies for realizing his project of fundamental ontology but eventually gives up the idea on account of the deep inner problems of the project. In the lecture course "The Metaphysical Foundations of Logic" from the summer of 1928, we can see the start of a new effort to critically reorient his thinking and his guiding question. I will deal with these events in the next part, which focuses on Heidegger's later thinking.

Although Heidegger mainly works out his new historical conception of phenomena and phenomenology in his lectures, courses, and texts on Aristotle, I will argue that Husserl's phenomenology continues to exercise a decisive influence on his thought. Furthermore, the influence of Dilthey—and of the hermeneutic tradition more generally—on Heidegger's attempt to work out the temporality and historicity of Dasein remains strong and constant, although it is often hidden behind Heidegger's ambition to stage his new thinking as a reappropriation of Aristotle. An important event in these years was Heidegger's reading of the correspondence between Dilthey and Count Yorck, which provided vital incentives for his thinking of historicity.

When *Being and Time* was published, it rapidly brought Heidegger fame and massive attention on the larger philosophical scene. From that moment, the book for many decades functioned as the principal hermeneutic point of focus for interpreting and discussing Heidegger's philosophical thinking in its entirety.

Although the question of phenomena/phenomenology has always been present in the discussion of *Being and Time*, it is only in recent decades that it has surfaced as one of the most central and contentious themes of the Heidegger discussion. The most obvious reason why this question remained in the background for so long is that for many years the reception was dominated by interpretations that largely ignored or downplayed the influence of Husserl's phenomenology on Heidegger's thinking. Instead, Heidegger was commonly regarded as the definitive critic of the supposed Cartesianism and belief in direct intuitive givenness still characterizing Husserl's transcendental phenomenology. The interpretation presented by Gadamer in *Truth and Method* is paradigmatic. Hailing Heidegger as the decisive stimulus for his own attempt to develop a philosophical hermeneutics, Gadamer describes how Heidegger abandons the idea of the "self-givenness of experience," which still functioned as the "methodological basis" of Husserl's phenomenology: "Under the rubric of a 'hermeneutics of facticity,' Heidegger confronted Husserl's eidetic phenomenology … with a paradoxical demand. Phenomenology should be ontologically based on the facticity of Dasein, existence, which cannot be based or derived from anything else, and not on the pure cogito as the essential constitution of typical universality—a bold idea, but difficult to carry through" ([1960] 2004: 245). This picture of Heidegger is reproduced—albeit in a critical vein—in the interpretations of Ernst Tugendhat, Karl-Otto Apel, and Jürgen Habermas. Likewise, the first two full-scale philosophical biographies of Heidegger—*Martin Heidegger's Path of Thinking* (*Der Denkweg Martin Heideggers*) (1963) by Otto Pöggeler and *Heidegger: Through Phenomenology to Thought* (1963) by William J. Richardson—both largely play down the Husserlian origins and character of Heidegger's early thinking. Moreover, in his role as a major influence on the poststructuralist and deconstructivist thought of Michel Foucault, Jacques Derrida, Jacques Lacan, and others, Heidegger is also greeted as a severe critic of the ideal of direct "presence" and "self-givenness," and as a thinker of the historicity and finitude of thought. The reception of Heidegger in the Anglo-Saxon world has also been dominated by interpretations that view Heidegger as a thinker who overcomes the theoretical-epistemological framework of Husserl's phenomenology as well as its supposed subjectivism and intuitionism. This is true of the different pragmatist readings put forward by Hubert Dreyfus, Richard Rorty, and Mark Okrent, and it is also true of the hermeneutic-deconstructive readings developed by people like John Sallis, Thomas Sheehan, John van Buren, Theodore Kisiel, Charles Guignon, and many others.

We have to wait until the 1990s for the emergence of a strong phenomenological interpretation—elaborated by, for example, Steven Crowell, Daniel Dahlstrom, and Søren Overgaard—of Heidegger's work.[1] There are many reasons for this delay. Although Heidegger pays homage to Husserl in *Being and Time* and calls the method of his fundamental ontology "phenomenology," the concrete influence of Husserl largely remains implicit. Instead, Heidegger's explicit program for a hermeneutic-destructive explication of Dasein as being-in-the-world can easily be read as a rejection of Husserl's phenomenology in favor of a radically historical thinking. When Heidegger's early Freiburg and Marburg lecture courses— in which the strong influence of Husserl is much more conspicuous—were published in the 1980s and 1990s, it became easier to get a grip on the phenomenological character of Heidegger's early thinking. Another reason—perhaps the philosophically most decisive reason—for the late birth of the phenomenological Heidegger is found in the fact that it is only in the 1990s that a new wave of intensive research on Husserl was able to bring about a more nuanced and philosophically potent picture of Husserl's phenomenology. Indeed, only when we learn to see that Husserl cannot simply be dismissed as a traditional Cartesian epistemologist but opens up a powerful and open-ended idea of philosophy as strict intuitive description of the meaning-structures of our concrete experiences—only then does it become possible to interpret Heidegger's thinking as an elaboration of Husserl's phenomenological program.

For some years now, the discussion of the problem of phenomena/phenomenology in *Being and Time* has been characterized by the antagonism between the transcendental phenomenological reading and the hermeneutic-deconstructive reading. In this, proponents of the hermeneutic-deconstructive reading have emphasized Heidegger's analysis of the temporal-historical structure of understanding and his programmatic exposition of the historical character of his phenomenology as an essentially hermeneutic and destructive endeavor. By contrast, proponents of the transcendental phenomenological reading have concentrated on bringing out the phenomenological—that is, intuitive and reflective—character of Heidegger's method, often seeking additional evidence for their claims in his earlier lecture courses. The representatives of the phenomenological reading tend to accept Heidegger's analysis of the historical structure of our everyday experience of phenomena but do not conclude from this—as do Heidegger and the representatives of the hermeneutic-deconstructive reading—that the phenomenological method of inquiry must itself become radically historical.

In what follows, I am going to develop my own interpretation on the backdrop of these opposed readings. After an introductory chapter on how Heidegger elaborates his new view of the structure of phenomena through confrontations with Aristotle and Husserl, my main focus will be on how Heidegger's struggle with the problems of phenomena and phenomenology is played out in *Being and Time*.

As concerns the question of phenomena, my view of Heidegger's analysis of the historical structure of phenomenal experience is in many ways in line with previous interpretations. Still, most commentators tend to be satisfied with explicating this structure in terms of the thesis that our access to phenomena is determined by our preunderstanding of the historical world of instrumental relations and significances in which we live. I am going to argue that Heidegger's analysis of phenomena refers to and hinges on his analysis of authenticity. According to Heidegger, the instrumental networks of meaning constituting our world are anchored in and gain their significance from the life-possibilities and ideals that we are committed to. The task of the analysis of authenticity is precisely to shed light on what an authentic understanding of our guiding life-possibilities and ideals—conceived as our ultimate sources of ethical-existential normativity and significance—amounts to. However, my critical thesis is that Heidegger in *Being and Time* fails to account for the question, raised by his radical historicism, of how historical meanings can be given as something distinct from the collective prejudices of the They—as in some sense binding or primordial. This failure, I argue, undercuts his analysis of authenticity and leaves it trapped in an oscillation between collectivism and subjectivism. Moreover, it hinders him from implementing his idea of phenomenology as a hermeneutic-destructive form of thinking. As concerns the question of phenomenology, I will argue that Heidegger's methodological self-understanding stands in an ambivalent relation to his concrete practice of thinking. While it is true that Heidegger primarily articulates his method in terms of a historical thinking that explicates and destructs our received preunderstanding of being in order to appropriate more primordial historical possibilities of understanding, I will suggest that he is not able to put this thinking into practice in *Being and Time*. Instead, I maintain that Heidegger's concrete investigations basically transpire in the mode of intuitive phenomenological reflection on the basic and necessary structures of our experience.

Eventually, these problems with realizing his vision of the historical nature of phenomena and phenomenology lead Heidegger to abandon the project of fundamental ontology and give up his plans of completing *Being and Time*.

I will proceed as follows: In Chapter 4, I review how Heidegger develops his new conception of the historical structure of phenomena through his readings of Aristotle and how this transforms his critical stance toward Husserl. In Chapter 5, I analyze Heidegger's project of fundamental ontology and the question of the sense of being as the framework for his analyses in *Being and Time*. After that, I go on to explicate those parts of Heidegger's analytic that in my view are essential to his understanding of phenomena and phenomenology. In Chapter 6, I offer a thorough analysis of Heidegger's analysis of the structure of our experience of phenomena in terms of "being-in-the-world." In Chapter 7, I examine Heidegger's attempt, in his analysis of authenticity, to account for Dasein's understanding of its guiding life-possibilities, which form the teleological horizon of its experience of phenomena. In Chapter 8, I explicate Heidegger's method and the fate of phenomenology in *Being and Time*. In my treatment, I will bypass Heidegger's analysis of temporality—except for the sections on "historicity"—since I believe it does not contribute much to the philosophical substance of his analysis of the basic structure of phenomena.[2]

4

TOWARD A NEW CONCEPTION OF PHENOMENA

The Confrontation with Aristotle

The philosophical center of Heidegger's intense interpretations of Aristotle from 1921 onward lies in his effort to work out a new analysis of the historical structure of our experience of phenomena. This analysis, he believes, provides the basis for rethinking the method and task of phenomenological philosophy in terms of a historical hermeneutic-destructive interrogation of the question of the sense of being.

Heidegger's explication of Aristotle is sensitive and violent at the same time, and the phenomenological structures that he discovers do not always have the same emphasis, precision, or ontological sense in their original context. However, here I will leave the question of the exegetic accuracy of Heidegger's reading aside and focus on the systematic role that Aristotle's concepts acquire in his own philosophical endeavor.[1]

The philosophical import of Heidegger's confrontation with Aristotle comes to a first dense expression in "Indication of the Hermeneutic Situation," the introduction he wrote in 1922 to his planned book on Aristotle. In the first part of the text, Heidegger articulates the philosophical stakes and methodological necessity of returning to Aristotle. Contemporary philosophy, he claims, still for the most part "moves inauthentically within the *Greek* conceptuality" (GA 62: 367/123). This means that our understanding of life is determined by concepts that have "lost their original expressive functions," such that the experiences that they stem from and articulate are not available to us anymore (GA 62: 367/123). It is Aristotle, Heidegger claims, who shapes and conceptualizes the basic understanding of life and being that will henceforth govern the Western tradition of philosophy. Hence, in order to be able to critically explicate our received central concepts we need to undertake a "destruction" (*Destruktion*) of these concepts, a "dismantling return" to their origin in Aristotle:

> Thus the phenomenological hermeneutic of facticity ... sees itself directed to the task of loosening up the reigning state of traditional interpretation today with respect to its hidden motives and its unexpressed tendencies and modes of interpreting so that it can, by way of a *dismantling return*, push forward

toward the original motive sources of explication. *The hermeneutic carries out its task only on the path of destruction.* In philosophical research, this destructive confrontation with its own history is not merely a supplement for illustrating how things stood in earlier times. Rather, the destruction is the authentic path upon which the present must encounter itself in its own basic movements. (GA 62: 368/124)

Heidegger's insistence on the necessity of destructing our received concepts is an expression of the transformation that his conception of phenomena and phenomenology is undergoing at this time. Already in his earliest Freiburg lectures, he had emphasized the need to attend to and critically destruct our prejudiced concepts. At that time, however, he still believed that emancipation and primordial understanding could be achieved through intuitive phenomenological reflection on the structures of life. Now he closes this possibility. Given that hermeneutic phenomenology can gain access to its matter "only on the path of destruction," this implies that our intuitive experience of meaning is fundamentally determined by our historical preunderstanding and that this preunderstanding cannot be critically examined through an intuition-based explication of the experiential matters in question but only through a destructive return to its historical sources.

For Heidegger, the historical interpretation of Aristotle thus constitutes the central methodological vehicle of his systematic philosophical endeavor. It is only by returning to Aristotle that it becomes possible to dismantle the prejudiced philosophical tradition and trace it back to the sources out of which its central conceptuality has grown forth. Moreover, by critically delimiting the meaning of its traditional concepts, philosophy is opened up to the possibility of finding, in Aristotle's texts, a new and more primordial explication of life.

So what does Heidegger find in Aristotle?

Aristotle is—to use Günter Figal's expression—for Heidegger a "Janus-headed thinker" (2007: 61, my translation). On the one hand, Heidegger claims that Aristotle ultimately determines being as *ousia*—as pure and constant presence—on the basis of the experiential paradigm of theoretical observation, *sofia*. It is this conception of being that constitutes the ontological horizon of all of Aristotle's thinking, and that will henceforth dominate the history of philosophy. On the other hand, Heidegger believes that Aristotle's analysis of *phronēsis* in the *Nicomachean Ethics* provides an unsurpassed model for thinking the historical structure of our pretheoretical experience of phenomena. Since Aristotle's articulation of life is shadowed and hampered by his conception of being as *ousia*, presence, the task Heidegger sets himself is to explicate and radicalize this embryonic articulation of life.

According to Heidegger, Aristotle's concept of *phronēsis* signifies the circumspection that guides life's practical coping with its world. This circumspection is no simple sense perception but exhibits a synthetic structure: "a going-toward beings from the 'point of view' of another being-meant" (*ein Zugehen auf das Seiende in der 'Hinsicht' eines anderen Vermeintseins*) (GA 62: 378/131). It is only to the extent that we intend particular beings on the basis of a preceding concern and understanding that these beings may show up *as* something significant: as a tree, as a house, as a human being. This synthetic as-structure is the condition for both truth and untruth. I can only perceive a horse on a field or mistake a donkey for a horse on the backdrop of a certain understanding of horses. Aristotle calls the preceding understanding guiding all our phenomenal experience "*nous*": "*Nous* is *aisthēsis tis*, a perceiving which always simply pregives the look (*Aussehen*) of the objects" (GA 62: 381/133). *Nous* thus has the character of an understanding that, prior to every possibility of truth or mistake, presents the *eidē*—the meaningful looks or essences, the "as-what-determinations" (GA 62: 379/132)—in the light of which beings can show up as one thing or the other. Given that *nous* constitutes the light conditioning all possible seeing and experience of beings, it cannot itself have the character of seeing, but must rather be understood as the primary unthematic "*doxa*" or "primordial belief" (*Urglaube*) (GA 62: 405) preceding all such seeing. Heidegger ultimately interprets *nous* in terms of the preunderstanding of historical meaning that determines our possibilities of apprehending beings as meaningful phenomena.

Nous does not only present the meaningful looks or essences that determine as what beings can show up. This understanding-of-*eidē* is, in its turn, guided by an understanding of the *archai*: the ultimate "from-out-of-which" that we always already "keep in sight" and which determine the "regions of being" of different beings (GA 62: 382/133–4).

In short, what Heidegger claims to find in Aristotle is nothing less than a qualified analysis of the basic historical as-structure of phenomenal experience, to the effect that we can only experience particular beings as meaningful phenomena on the basis of a preceding understanding of our historical contexts of meaning. This historical understanding is, in its turn, guided by an understanding of the different modes of being and, ultimately, of the sense of being as such. Five years later Heidegger will name this hierarchical structure of phenomenality the "ontological difference" (cf. GA 24: 22/17).[2] This new conception of phenomena is at the basis of Heidegger's rearticulation of the method and task of philosophy as historical interrogation of the sense of being. First, if our direct intuitive experience of phenomena is determined by our preunderstanding of historical meanings and being, then a critical explication of being cannot rely on intuition but must take the form of hermeneutic-destructive reflection of the historical meanings harbored by our tradition. Second, if our experience of phenomena is always guided by our understanding of being, then the philosophical task of critically clarifying the sense of being as such emerges as the fundamental condition for achieving a transparent understanding of all the central ethical-existential phenomena of life.

However, Heidegger claims that at the end of the day Aristotle fails to achieve a positive ontological characterization of the temporal-historical sense of life, but rather defines life negatively as a deviation from the primordial sense of being as *ousia*. Aristotle's conception of being as *ousia* arises from an explication not of *phronēsis* but of *sofia*. Terrified by its own finitude, life has a basic tendency to give up its pretheoretical concern with the world and instead engage in *sofia*: a pure perception of the *eidē* determining what particular beings are. However, by focusing strictly on the *eidē*, the pure perception of *sofia* loses sight of the pretheoretical movement of life in its temporality and historicity, thereby also covering up its own origin in factical life. As a result, it becomes possible to enact *sofia* as a pure theoretical observation of the *eidē* as a steady and constant possession. According to Heidegger, Aristotle's suppression of *phronēsis* and elevation of *sofia*—the theoretical attitude—makes him conceive of being in terms of *ousia*: constant presence. This understanding of being will determine the horizon and course of the philosophical tradition.

Heidegger's new quasi-Aristotelian conception of the structure of factical life also leads him to appropriate the word "phenomenon" as a key concept of his own thinking. In his earliest Freiburg lectures, he had primarily preferred to talk about the "givenness" or "manifestation" of the matters in our pretheoretical experience. The term "phenomenon" first surfaces in Heidegger's last Freiburg lecture course "Ontology—The Hermeneutics of Facticity" from the summer of 1923 (cf. GA 63: 67/53). In the autumn of that same year, he begins his first Marburg lecture course, "Introduction to Phenomenological Research," by offering an explication of the word "phenomenology" in which he traces it back to what he claims are its Greek roots in Aristotle's analysis of factical life.

The expression "phenomenology," Heidegger notes, is composed of the two Greek words "*phainomenon*" and "*logos*." *Phainomenon* means "something that shows itself" and constitutes a nominalization of the verbs "*phainomai*," to show itself, and "*phainō*," to bring something to the light of day (GA 17: 6–7/4). For Aristotle, Heidegger argues, the word *phainomenon* does not refer to the data of simple sense perceptions, but to the significant things we encounter in the world (GA 17: 11/8). The possibility of experiencing entities as significant phenomena depends on the structural fact that our perception essentially involves a "*logos tis*," a kind of speech. This *logos* does not primarily take the form of explicit utterances but rather has the character of an implicit speech which, like the light, illuminates and lets us see the beings we experience: "*Aisthēsis* is present in the sort of being that has *language*. Whether or not it is vocalized, it is always in some way speaking. Language speaks not only in the course of the perceiving, but even *guides* it; we see *through* language" (GA 17: 30/22). *Logos* here shoulders the role that *nous* had in "Indication of the Hermeneutic Situation," both terms designating the preceding understanding of the *eidē*—the ideas or looks—which we do "not obtain purely from" the thing, but which we "already know" (GA 17: 33/25), and which allow us to experience particular beings as meaningful phenomena in the first place.

Heidegger's appropriation of the notion of "phenomenon" and his explication of the conceptual pair phenomenon-phenomenology by reference to its Greek roots is not philosophically innocent. It is a token of his belief that he has achieved a new understanding of phenomena that fundamentally challenges Husserl's as well as his own earlier conception of the nature of self-showing. Furthermore, it opens up the strategic possibility of construing Husserl's phenomenology as a fall away from the more primordial Greek understanding of phenomena that Heidegger himself wants to retrieve and radicalize.

Heidegger's Renewed Critique of Husserl

Heidegger dedicates *Being and Time* to Husserl. In a footnote he states that in so far as the investigations of his book are able to make some headway toward elucidating the "matters themselves," this is thanks to the "personal guidance" (SZ: 38) into phenomenology that he received from his former teacher. However, notwithstanding these gestures of thanks, there is no doubt that Heidegger's attitude to Husserl's phenomenology in *Being and Time* is extremely ambivalent. Toward the end of his introductory treatment of the phenomenological method of his investigations, in which Husserl's name is not mentioned at all, Heidegger sums up the ambivalence in the following dense passage:

> The following investigations have become possible only on the basis prepared by Edmund Husserl, with whose *Logical Investigations* phenomenology achieved a breakthrough. Our elucidations of the preliminary concept of phenomenology show that what is essential in it does not lie in its *actuality* as a philosophical "movement" (*Richtung*). Higher than actuality stands *possibility*. We can understand phenomenology only by seizing upon it as a possibility. (SZ: 38)

The passage contains two claims. First, it states that Heidegger's philosophical project has become possible only "on the basis" of Husserl's phenomenology. Second, it asserts that phenomenology here has to be understood not as an "actuality" but as a pure "possibility." That is to say, in so far as Husserl's phenomenology constitutes the basis of Heidegger's thinking it does so in the form of a possibility that Husserl opens up but which he, due to his basic theoretical orientation, fails to bring to fruition in a radical manner. Heidegger thus understands his own thinking as an attempt to seize upon and develop the latent and thus far distorted potential of Husserl's phenomenology.

It is plain from the biographical record that Heidegger's explication of Aristotle in the early 1920s goes hand in hand with a renewed effort to critically distance himself from Husserl. Having just completed a seminar on Husserl's *Ideas I* in the winter semester of 1922–3, Heidegger writes the following lines to his student Karl Löwith:

> In the final hour of the seminar, I publicly burned and destroyed the *Ideas* to such an extent that I dare say that the essential foundations for the whole [of my work] are now cleanly laid out. Looking back from this vantage to the *Logical Investigations*, I am now convinced that Husserl was never a philosopher, not even for one second in his life. He becomes ever more ludicrous. (Kisiel and Sheehan 2007: 372)

Hard words indeed. Taken at face value, they hardly convey much more than Heidegger's profound ambition to dethrone his living philosophical mentor— whose influence is thus confirmed—and assert himself as an independent philosopher under the banner of the long dead and, hence, liberating father figure of Aristotle. However, what is the philosophical sense of Heidegger's harsh denunciation of Husserl?

In *Being and Time* Heidegger's relationship to Husserl largely remains implicit, although it can to some extent be glimpsed indirectly through his discussions of other thinkers of the theoretical tradition, in particular Descartes and Kant. However, in the preceding Marburg-lecture courses "Introduction to Phenomenological Research" and "History of the Concept of Time: Prolegomena," Heidegger provides thorough critical discussions of Husserl's phenomenology. Let us take a look at the main thrust of his critique.

Heidegger credits Husserl with three "fundamental discoveries" (GA 20: 34/27): intentionality, the categorial intuition, and the sense of the *a priori*. As we shall see, these concepts play very different roles in Heidegger's critical appropriation of Husserl. In explicating the concept of "intentionality," Heidegger stays close to and quite faithfully elucidates Husserl's original concept. By contrast, Heidegger's treatment of the "categorial intuition"—and also of the "*a priori*"—takes the form of a critical-transformative appropriation, such that he stresses certain aspects of this concept to articulate his own vision of the historical character of phenomena and phenomenology.[3] I will begin by elucidating Heidegger's treatment of Husserl's concept of intentionality and his basic critique of Husserl's theoretical orientation. In the next section, I will discuss Heidegger's appropriation of Husserl's notions of categorial intuition and *a priori*.

According to Heidegger, Husserl opens up the possibility of phenomenological philosophy by insisting on the need for philosophy to strictly attend to the matters themselves as they are concretely given in our intentional experience:

> The intentionality itself of consciousness is not some sort of condition of the ego; rather, in this "directing itself-at" (*Sichrichten-auf*) that at which it is directed (*das Worauf des Gerichtetsein*) is also given. Intentionality is not to be construed as a peculiarity of mental processes; instead it is to be given as a manner in which something is encountered, in such a way that what is encountered comes into view along with the encountering: the directing-itself-at in unison with its specific at-which (*Worauf*). *With this discovery of intentionality, for the first time in the entire history of philosophy, the way is explicitly given for a radical ontological research.* (GA 17: 260/200)

Husserl's discovery of intentionality, Heidegger contends, consists in the insight that our acts of consciousness are fundamentally directed toward the intended matters themselves—not toward some kind of inner representations or sense-data—and, conversely, that these matters are concretely given and intelligible as what they are only in our correlative experiences of them. Husserl's concept of intentionality thus for the first time opens the way to "radical ontological research": it is only through strict reflective explication of "the object in the manner of its being meant" (GA 17: 263/202) that it becomes possible to phenomenologically investigate the being-senses that beings show up for us without falling back either into constructive metaphysical idealism or realism.

Nevertheless, Heidegger's central critical thesis is that Husserl, despite his phenomenological breakthrough, repeats the basic theoretical orientation that has dominated the history of Western philosophy since Aristotle, something that leads him to squander and misconstrue the possibility of phenomenology that he opens up. Like his precursors, Husserl is said to be driven by an "anxiety in the face of existence" (GA 17: 97/70) and by a "care about knowledge known" (*Sorge um erkannte Erkenntnis*) (GA 17: 101/73). That is, anxiously repressing the temporal-historical finitude of life, Husserl sets his hope on achieving an absolutely justified and universally binding knowledge of life. Instead of radically posing the question of the sense of being as such—or the question of the being of the human being—Husserl is said to uncritically adopt the traditional prejudiced understanding of being as "presence-at-hand" for theoretical observation and of the human being as a theoretically knowing subject (GA 20: 178/128–9). Indeed, Heidegger claims, Husserl's determination of the basic character of phenomenal givenness as "bodily presence" (*Leibhaftigkeit*) is nothing but a rearticulation of the traditional understanding of being as presence-at-hand: "Bodily presence is a character of encounter of world-things, in so far as the world is still encountered solely in a pure apprehension, a pure perception" (GA 20: 265/195).

According to Heidegger, Husserl's adoption of the traditional conception of being as presence-at-hand comes to expression in his layer-ontology (see GA 63: 88–92/67–70; GA 17: 271–2/209; GA 20: 171–4/123–6). Although Husserl recognizes that we normally experience the meaningful objects of our life-world in terms of their use, value, aesthetic qualities, and so on, he nevertheless contends that our pure perception of sensory objects constitutes the basic layer upon which all other layers of phenomenal experience are founded. Ultimately, Heidegger claims, Husserl's privileging of the experience of theoretical observation leads him to conceive of phenomenology as reflection on the consciousness of the transcendental subject as the basic and absolutely given domain where it is possible to detect the constitutive structures and being-senses of all objects: "Consciousness, immanent and absolutely given being, is that in which every other possible entity is constituted, in which it truly 'is' what it is" (GA 20: 144/105).

As Heidegger sees it, Husserl's theoretical bias is one with—it both follows from and motivates—his failure to raise and clarify the question of the sense of being on the basis of an analysis of the human being. This means that Husserl does not take our primary pretheoretical experience of meaningful phenomena as his absolute starting point for investigating the structure and sense of meaningful being. Only within the framework of such a fundamental ontology, Heidegger insists, does it become possible to explicate the various meanings and roles that different kinds of being and different paradigms of experience—for example, theoretical observation—have in our human existence.

Husserl's neglect of the question of the sense of being, Heidegger claims, makes his transcendental phenomenology "unphenomenological" (GA 20: 178/128). In repressing the question of the sense of being, Husserl takes over the traditional conception of being as presence-at-hand in a prejudiced way. Moreover, Husserl's entire phenomenology is focused on investigating transcendental consciousness as the certain and fundamental domain where beings are constituted and receive their sense. Given Husserl's neglect of our primary experience of significant phenomena as the framework for understanding meaningful being, his investigations of transcendental subjectivity as the fundamental domain of givenness are bound to produce construction and prejudice.

Thus far, Heidegger's critical assessment of Husserl is basically the same as in his early Freiburg lecture courses. Now as then he praises Husserl for opening up the possibility of reflectively describing the objects of our experience according to how they are given in particular acts; now as then he criticizes Husserl for neglecting and theoretically distorting the being of our pretheoretical experience of the world, and for grounding the being-senses of beings in transcendental subjectivity.

In the first part, I offered a critical discussion of the force and limits of the above criticisms. However, as we shall see, the critical edge and positive direction of Heidegger's critique of Husserl have changed significantly. Heidegger's early Freiburg critique took the form of an immanent critical elaboration of Husserl's phenomenological project. While dismissing Husserl's theoretical conception of phenomenology, Heidegger accepted the key idea that phenomenology must proceed by way of intuitive reflection. On this basis, he rearticulated phenomenology in terms of intuitive reflective explication—guided by love and sympathy, and attentive to the risk of reproducing the prejudices of the tradition—of the primordial structures of our primary pretheoretical experience. Now, by contrast, the main thrust of Heidegger's critique is directed precisely at the idea of direct intuitive givenness which he previously accepted. Heidegger maintains that the very idea of intuitive givenness governing Husserl's phenomenology is a symptom of his basic inability to account for the temporal-historical being of Dasein and, hence, for the historical nature of phenomenology. Whereas Heidegger earlier endeavored to critically deepen Husserl's intuitive phenomenology, he now wants to replace it with a radically historical thinking, relying not on direct intuition but on interpretation and destructive retrieval of our historical tradition.

The Categorial Intuition—in Heidegger

In appropriating Husserl's notion of categorial intuition, Heidegger mobilizes it as an argument for his own thesis about the radical historicity of phenomena and phenomenology.

As Heidegger several decades later accounts for the role of Husserl in his philosophical development, he highlights Husserl's analysis of the categorial intuition in the *Logical Investigations* as crucial for his effort to articulate his guiding question concerning the sense of being: "Husserl touches or brushes the question of being in the sixth chapter of the sixth logical investigation, with the concept of 'categorial intuition'" (GA 15: 373/65; cf. GA 14: 86/78). Following Heidegger's own retrospective remarks, many commentators have stressed Husserl's notion of categorial intuition as the most important influence of Husserl on the development of Heidegger's thought. As it happens, these same commentators generally tend to read Heidegger as a hermeneutic-deconstructive thinker of finitude and historicity, downplaying any possible reliance of his on Husserl's phenomenological method of intuitive reflection. Conversely, those commentators favoring a phenomenological reading have tended to give little or no attention to Husserl's idea of categorial intuition.[4] This organization of the debate is no coincidence, since what is at stake in Heidegger's explication of this notion is precisely the question to what extent our understanding of categorial meaning can be based on direct intuition and to what extent it is determined by our historical conceptuality. What makes Heidegger's discussion of Husserl's notion of the categorial intuition somewhat bewildering is that he uses this notion as an argument against the very idea of direct intuition so central to Husserl.

Husserl's treatment of the categorial intuition in the sixth investigation of the *Logical Investigations* takes its starting point in the distinction between signifying acts—primarily acts of linguistic expression—in which we merely signify or intend a matter, and fulfilling acts in which the matter is intuitively given in the way we intended it, and which thus constitute the source of truth of all our intentional comportments (Hua 19/1: 44/192). According to Husserl, those parts of our signifying acts that merely signify sensory "material" can find evident fulfillment in simple sense perceptions. But what about the categorial "form" of these acts, what about the categorial elements that structure our expressions, for example, the copula, the conjunctions and disjunctions, the articles, and the terms designating general classes or universals? These categorial forms cannot, Husserl claims, be given in sense perceptions: we can perceive, with our eyes, the color "green," but there is nothing in this perception corresponding to the different categorial elements of sentences such as "the tree is green" or "flamingos are pink birds." Hence, as concerns the categorial elements of our intentions "a surplus (*Überschuß*) of meaning remains over, a form which finds nothing in the appearance itself to confirm it" (Hua 19/2: 660/273).

The consequence of this is that the question of the possibility of a categorial intuition emerges as a central challenge to Husserl's phenomenology: Are there categorial acts of fulfillment that in some sense give us direct intuitive access to categorial meanings, acts that thus transcend and provide the ground for our categorially formed intentions? Or does the categorial form of our signifying acts determine our intuitive experience of things to such a degree that our direct intuitions can do nothing more than confirm or not-confirm, but never ground and critically modify the categorial form of our intentions? The aim of Husserl's investigation is to show that there indeed is a categorial intuition which constitutes "an *analogue of common sensuous intuition*" (Hua 19/2: 670/280). Although the categorially fulfilling act is no simple sense perception, Husserl maintains that it nevertheless deserves the name "intuition," since in it the categorial is given and appears as "real" and "self-given" (Hua 19/2: 672/281). But how?

Husserl distinguishes between two kinds of categorial intuition: categorial acts of synthesis and categorial acts of ideation. The function of acts of synthesis is to bring out and explicate the logical-semantic relations between different sensuously perceived objects—the relations corresponding to terms such as "is" (in the sense of the copula), "all," "some," "and," "or," "not," "the," and "if–so." By contrast, the function of the "ideation" or "general intuition" is to grasp the general "ideas," the essences or concepts, which the particular objects instantiate (Hua 19/2: 690/292). Of these two kinds of categorial act, the general intuition is of particular philosophical importance. Since phenomenology for Husserl has the character of a science of essences, the question of how we understand general ideas and essences is decisive for how we conceive of the phenomenological method. Heidegger also stresses the crucial role of Husserl's notion of ideation both for clarifying the "genuine sense of intentionality" and for opening up the possibility of phenomenology as an ontological investigation of the sense of being (GA 20: 103/75; 98/72).

In *Logical Investigations*, Husserl's conception of the general intuition still remains quite undeveloped and ambivalent. Husserl maintains that the object of a sensuous intuition is "*immediately given*," by which he means that it is given "*at a single act-level*" (Hua 19/2: 674/282): it appears directly as a unified object and is not in need of further higher-level acts in order to appear as itself. The categorial intuition is founded on the sensuous intuition. Through various "relating, connecting acts" (Hua 19/2: 674/282), it constitutes a new kind of categorial objectivity that was not previously given in the sensuous intuition but which is nevertheless "based on" the objects given in sensuous intuition: "Acts arise in which something *appears as real* and as *self-given*, which was not given, and could not have been given, as what it now appears, in the foundational acts alone. *On the other hand, the new objects are based on the old ones, they are related to what appears in the basic acts*" (Hua 19/2: 675/282–3).

Yet how should we understand the acts of relating and connecting which, on the basis of sense perceptions, make categorial meanings appear?

In fact, Husserl's brief outline of the process of "ideation" does not clarify or bear out the idea that the general intuition would be based on—and receive its possible truth from—our direct intuitive experience of sensuous objects. He describes the general intuition as follows: "We must presuppose such an act in order that, as against the manifold single moments of one and the same kind, this *very kind* may come before us precisely *as one and the same*. For we become aware of the identity of the universal through the repeated enactment of such acts on the basis of several individual intuitions, and we plainly do so in an overreaching act of identification which brings all such single acts of abstraction into one synthesis" (Hua 19/2: 690–1/292). That is to say, we enact the ideation by moving through a manifold of individual intuitions with the aim of identifying—in a way that still remains quite obscure—the general idea that the intuited objects exemplify. Husserl says nothing that indicates how we, by intuiting particular objects or experiences, could discover their general essences or structures, such that these essences would be independent of our factical concepts and serve as their source of truth. Instead, it seems that the very possibility of going through a manifold of examples of the general idea that we want to investigate presupposes that we already possess the idea in question. This, however, suggests that the ideation is basically a procedure that relies on and explicates—but is unable to transcend or question the truth of—the factical concepts we happen to possess.

This tendency is even more palpable when Husserl later goes on to elaborate his idea of general intuition in terms of the method of "eidetic variation." Let me quote the central passage from *Experience and Judgment* where he describes the core of the method:

> [The essential seeing] is based on the modification of an experienced or imagined objectivity, turning it into an arbitrary example which, at the same time, receives the character of a guiding "model" (*Vorbild*), a point of departure for the production of an infinitely open multiplicity of variants. It is based, therefore, on a *variation*. In other words, for its modification in pure imagination, we let ourselves be guided by the fact taken as a *model*. For this it is necessary that ever new similar images be obtained as copies, as images of the imagination, which are all concretely similar to the original image. Thus, by an act of volition we produce free variants, each of which, just like the total process of variation itself, occurs in the subjective mode of the "arbitrary." It then becomes evident that a unity runs through this multiplicity of successive figures, that in such free variations of an original image, e.g., of a thing, an *invariant* is necessarily retained as the *necessary general form*, without which an object such as this thing, as an example of its kind, would not be thinkable at all. While what differentiates the variants remains indifferent to us, this form stands out in the practice of voluntary variation, and as an absolutely identical content, an invariable What, according to which all the variants coincide: a *general essence*. (EU: 410–11/340–1)

In short, we start with an—actual or imagined—arbitrary example of the general type under investigation and let it serve as the guiding model. We then go on to produce, through imagination, an open multiplicity of variants that are similar to the original model. By enacting this variation, it becomes possible to see and determine the invariant necessary form without which the arbitrarily chosen example would not be thinkable as an example of the sort under investigation. For example, we could grasp the essence of the concept of "animal" by imagining a multiplicity of arbitrary animals and related beings, thus assessing what must and what need not belong to an animal in order for it to remain an animal. By so doing, we are supposed to be able to grasp the general essence of "animal."

Now, in Husserl's description the eidetic variation basically emerges as a kind of conceptual analysis. The very possibility of producing variants of the general type under investigation, and of determining which variants count as examples of the type and which do not, presupposes that we already have an implicit grasp of the type. Whereas our factical preunderstanding of the type provides our sole measure for distinguishing between proper and improper examples, the function of the examples is none other than to bring out the essential features of this preunderstanding. This, however, implies that the method of free variation is unable to account for the possibility of phenomenologically seeing and describing the necessary structures of our experience as something that is independent of and constitutes the source of our de facto concepts. Instead, the eidetic variation amounts to a method for explicating the factual conceptual preunderstanding we happen to live.[5] As a result, it is doomed to confirm our factual concepts, dogmatically postulating the basic traits of these concepts—with all their possible flaws and imperfections—as the necessary framework organizing our experience of particular entities.

What sparks Heidegger's interest in Husserl's analysis of categorial intuition is precisely its tendency to make the phenomenological understanding of essences dependent on our factical historical contexts of meaning. According to Heidegger, Husserl's discovery of the categorial intuition "for the first time" opens "the concrete way for a genuine categorial research proceeding by way of demonstration" (GA 20: 97-8/71). The philosophical import of the discovery is twofold.

First, Heidegger underscores that Husserl's discovery "that there is a simple apprehension of the categorial" (GA 20: 64/48) allows us to overcome the traditional idealist tendency to infer the categorial form of the objects of our experience from the structures of the transcendental subject. Since the categorial form does not reside in the objects of our sense perception, such has been the standard argument, it must originate in the subject and its ways of perceiving the objects. Against this, Heidegger claims that we cannot grasp categorial forms either through sense perception or through reflection on our inner acts of consciousness. Rather, the categorial is essentially given as the object of specific acts of categorial perception.

However, how does the categorial intuition transpire?

Heidegger's second and main thesis is that Husserl's discovery "above all" lies in the insight that the categorial intuition is "invested in the most everyday of perceptions and in every experience." Here is his depiction of the general intuition:

> The acts of general intuition give what we first and simply see in the matters. When I perceive simply, moving about in my surrounding world, when I see houses, for example, I do not first see houses primarily and expressly in their individuation, in their differentiation. Rather, I first see generally: this is a house. This as-what, the general character of house, is itself not expressly apprehended in what it is, but is already coapprehended in simple intuition as that which here, as it were, illuminates what is given. (GA 20: 91/66-7)

In short, it is only because we always already live in an understanding of general ideas or meanings that we can experience particular objects as unified meaningful phenomena. Hereby Heidegger stresses the linguistic and unthematic character of this understanding. To begin with, the preceding general understanding is constituted by the way in which we always already—implicitly or explicitly—talk about things:

> It is also a matter of fact that our simplest perceptions and constitutive states are already *expressed*, even more, are *interpreted* in a certain way. It is not so much

that we see the objects and things but rather that we first talk about them. To put it more precisely: we do not say what we see, but rather the reverse, we see what one says about the matter. (GA 20: 75/56)

What is more, the categorial understanding guides our primary experience of meaning in an unthematic manner (GA 20: 65/48): as we see a house, we see it appear as a house on the basis of our unthematic understanding of what a house is without being thematically conscious of the general essence of house.

Heidegger interprets Husserl's notion of the categorial intuition in terms of our unthematic preunderstanding of our historical contexts of meaning. It is this understanding that always already determines our sensuous intuition and allows us to grasp beings as meaningful phenomena. This insight is taken by Heidegger to undermine Husserl's belief that the basic layer of our phenomenal experience is found in pure sense perceptions. Heidegger thus claims that the bodily presence of sensory objects is a "founded presence" (GA 20: 264/195) and that our pre-understanding of our historical world constitutes the "primary presence" (GA 20: 268/197) that allows us to experience beings as phenomena.

Heidegger contends that the notion of categorial intuition points to the need to reconceive of phenomenology as a historical form of thinking, more precisely, as a thematizing explication of our historical preunderstanding: "The ideal unity of the species is thus also already there in each concrete apprehending, although not expressly as that toward which the regard of comparative consideration looks. That toward which I look in comparing, the regard (*Hinsicht*) of the comparable, can in its own right be isolated in its pure state of affairs. I thus acquire the idea" (GA 20: 91–2/67). For Heidegger, our preceding unthematic understanding of our historical contexts of meaning constitutes the basis both for our immediate experience of meaningful phenomena as well as for the thematic investigations of philosophy. Hence, to carry out a phenomenological explication is essentially to critically explicate and dismantle our implicit historical understanding of being without relying on any direct transhistorical intuition.

At this point, Heidegger also submits that the a priori investigated by philosophy—Husserl's third discovery—is neither something immanent, belonging to the sphere of the subject, nor something transcendent, belonging to the objects that we experience. Instead, the *a priori* should be understood as "*a feature of the structural progression (Aufbaufolge) in the being of beings, in the being-structure of being*" (GA 20: 102/74). According to Heidegger, the a priori must be sought in the hierarchical structure of our understanding, in the fact that our understanding of beings and of our world is ultimately guided by our understanding of the sense of being. The fundamental task of philosophy is none other than to historically explicate the basic sense of being as such.

According to Heidegger, Husserl was never able to recognize the radically historical character of phenomenological thinking, properly understood:

> It hardly suffices, even within phenomenology, to appeal to merely looking at and devoting oneself to the matters. It could be that all that is burdened down

by a plethora of prejudices. In order to get *at the matters themselves*, they must be freed up and the very process of freeing them up is not one of a momentary exuberance, but of fundamental research. *The seeing must be educated* and this is a task so difficult that it is hard for it to be overemphasized since we are, like no other time, saturated by history and are even aware of the manifoldness of history. (GA 17: 275/211–12)

That is to say, since Husserl conceives of phenomenology in terms of intuitive seeing he is unable to recognize the way in which his own, supposedly direct phenomenological seeing, is mediated by the historical tradition of philosophy in a prejudiced manner. Since our direct seeing is fundamentally determined by the historical patterns of meaning we live in, the only way for phenomenology to attain an unprejudiced grasp of its matters is through a critical retrieval of the historical sources of our factical understanding.

What is the exegetical force of Heidegger's historicist critique of Husserl? Here, I can do no more than indicate the outline of an answer.

As concerns the question of phenomena, Heidegger's critique is primarily directed at Husserl's layer-ontology. I think this critique is basically on target and that Heidegger manages to show that Husserl's interrogation of how the categorial elements of our intentions are intuitively fulfilled works against his tendency to think of pure sense perception as the basic layer of phenomenal experience.

Although Husserl will always tend to conceive of sense perception as the fundamental layer of phenomenal experience, it must be remembered that in his mature and later thinking, he clearly recognizes and devotes thorough analyses to the historical dimension of experience.[6] Husserl maintains that our experience of the meaningful phenomena of our historical life-world—such as dogs, bikes, paintings—is always guided by our understanding of general "types." This understanding of types makes it possible for us to identity beings as this or that and it guides our expectations about the beings in question. Furthermore, Husserl holds that these types evolve historically and that it is possible to genetically trace their historical origins and transformations.

However, Husserl was never willing to absolutize—like Heidegger—our historically received types and meanings as the ungroundable ground determining what we can experience as phenomena.

Here, suffice it to mention Husserl's analysis of "empirical types." Although Husserl maintains that our understanding of empirical types always guides our experience of beings, he nevertheless insists that the empirical types are ultimately founded on the basis of and refer to our primary sensory experience of objects and our association of the similarities that obtain between them. This means that the general empirical types basically have the character of presumptive concepts that are open to further determination by our future experience: "Thus ... a *presumptive idea* arises, the *idea of a universal*, to which belongs, in addition to the attributes already acquired, a horizon, indeterminate and open, of unknown attributes (conceptual determinations)" (EU: 401/333). Moreover, the empirical types are essentially fallible classifications and characterizations of the objects in question.

In so far as we classify entities in accordance with superficial characteristics, which cover up the inner characteristics and relations of the objects, Husserl speaks of "nonessential types" (*außerwesentliche Typen*) (EU: 402/334). For example, the fact that the whale belongs to the class of mammals may be obscured by the exterior analogy to the way of life whales share with fish. By contrast, in so far as the empirical types express genuine empirical knowledge of the inner characteristics of the objects, Husserl uses the term "essential types" (*wesentliche Typen*) (EU: 402/334). In short, although our historically mediated understanding of empirical types guides our intuitive experience of phenomena, the types do not determine what we can experience. Rather, our preunderstanding of types amounts to a presumptive and fallible understanding that is justified by our intuitive experience of beings and whose truth or untruth is determined by the properties of the intuited beings themselves.

As concerns the question of phenomenology, Heidegger's critique is directed at Husserl's central idea of phenomenology as direct intuitive reflection on our experience. Against Husserl, he asserts that phenomenology must take the form of hermeneutic-destructive explication of our historical understanding of being.

Husserl, as we have seen, tends to articulate his method of general intuition or eidetic variation in terms of a kind of conceptual analysis that remains bound by and explicates the meanings of our factical historical concepts. However, this description of the phenomenological method fails to account either for Husserl's phenomenological program or for his phenomenological praxis. Throughout his life, Husserl leaves no doubt that the ambition of his phenomenology is to intuitively describe the basic structures that constitute our experiences and make them what they are. In so far as the description is correct, these structures—intentionality, time-consciousness, passive synthesis, and so on—pertain necessarily and universally to the experiences in question and are not relative to the de facto concepts we happen to possess. Furthermore, it is clear that the central method of Husserl's concrete investigations consists in reflecting on and describing our de facto experience with a view to their essential structures. Although such intuitive reflection takes its starting point in our factical concepts, it is not dependent on these concepts but attempts to grasp the experiences that are the source of truth of the concepts.

All in all, Husserl—in contrast to Heidegger—in many ways remains fundamentally committed to the idea of direct transhistorical intuition as a way of access to the experienced matters themselves.[7]

What about the systematic force of Heidegger's critique of Husserl? What about the truth of Heidegger's charge that Husserl's belief in direct intuition covers up the radical historicity pertaining to all understanding of phenomena? We are not yet in a position to take a stand on this decisive issue. Much of the remainder of this book will be devoted to explicating and critically questioning Heidegger's struggle to articulate and implement his vision of a radically historical thinking.

5

THE PROJECT OF FUNDAMENTAL ONTOLOGY

The Question of Being and the Task of Fundamental Ontology

Heidegger's thinking in the Marburg-years culminates with the publication of *Being and Time* in 1927. Here Heidegger articulates the task of philosophy as fundamental ontology, that is, as the task of investigating the sense of being through an analysis of the being of the human being, Dasein. Within this framework, he provides his most ambitious and detailed account of the historical structure of phenomena that he had been exploring throughout the 1920s. Indeed, as noted, this account of phenomena from the outset grounds and motivates his vision of the fundamental ontological task of philosophy.

Heidegger begins *Being and Time* by stating that the aim of the book is "to work out the question of the sense of '*being*' and to do so concretely" (SZ: 1). He claims that the question of being is nothing but the fundamental question that originally put Greek philosophy into motion, only to fall into a deep, more than two thousand years long forgetfulness that still prevails today. On Heidegger's view, the Greek philosophers became aware of the ontological difference between beings and their being, such that Aristotle was able to articulate the basic question of his *Metaphysics* as the question concerning beings *as* beings. However, although the Greeks opened up the possibility of investigating the ontological categories of all beings, they were never able to radically pose the question of the sense of being, a task which would have required an exploration of the temporal-historical structure of Dasein. Instead, Greek philosophy—paradigmatically Aristotle—basically determined being as presence-at-hand for theoretical seeing. This determination was not only biased; it also made philosophy lose sight of the question of being as a thematic question. This was because, in conceiving of being as presence-at-hand, the question of how all understanding of being is rooted in the different experiences and attitudes of the human being, is covered up. As a result, the entire tradition of philosophy has been governed by the Greek understanding of being as presence-at-hand in a prejudiced and blindfold manner.

Heidegger's conception of the task of philosophy in terms of the question of the sense of being is a rearticulation of the basic direction of questioning characterizing his thinking from the outset. When Heidegger in his first Freiburg lecture courses presents phenomenology as a primordial science of life, he does not articulate his project as an "ontology" concerned with "being." In fact, he mainly uses "ontology" as a derisive designation of the traditional bent of philosophy to examine theoretical objects detached from our pretheoretical experience. Nevertheless, it is clear that already in these years Heidegger's ambition comes very close to what he will later call "fundamental ontology." Ultimately, the aim of his primordial science is none other than to discover "the basic sense of *'existence'*" on the basis of which "the sense of *reality* in all layers of life" (GA 58: 261/197) becomes intelligible. From here there is but a small step to articulating the task of thinking as fundamental ontology.

In his earliest Freiburg lectures, Heidegger equated the question of the origin of life with the question of givenness or phenomena. In *Being and Time,* the question of being is likewise identified with the question of phenomena. Having just defined the phenomenon as *"that which shows itself in itself,"* Heidegger writes: "The *phainomena,* 'phenomena,' are thus the totality of what lies in the light of day or can be brought to light—what the Greeks sometimes identified simply with *ta onta* (beings)" (SZ: 28; cf. GA 17: 14/10). In fact, the Greek philosophers did not—as Günter Figal has pointed out (2006: 145–7)—equate *ta phainomena* with *ta onta* in any straightforward way, since they primarily used the word *phainomenon* to refer to how things merely appear to us in contrast to how they really are. However, the philological violence of the passage only underscores its importance for Heidegger himself. What it says is, in essence, that the phenomena that show—or can show—themselves as themselves are the true beings themselves. This does not of course mean that whatever appears true or real to us is always such. It means that our experience of phenomena constitutes our basic access to meaningful beings and that it is pointless to search for a ground for these phenomena by inquiring into what beings might be irrespective of how we experience them. This does not exclude the possibility that we can cover up and distort the phenomena that we encounter: "'Behind' the phenomena of phenomenology there is essentially nothing else. Nevertheless, what is to become a phenomenon can be concealed" (SZ: 36). For Heidegger, then, the question of being is essentially a question of phenomena, of what it means to show up as a meaningful phenomenon.[1] The entire fundamental ontological investigation of the sense of being through the analytic of Dasein can thus be read as one long exploration of the basic structure and sense of phenomenal givenness.

However, why is it important to ask the question of being? Why is it—as Heidegger claims it is—an existentially fundamental task?

As I argued in the first part, Heidegger's early Freiburg lectures suffered from a basic inability to account for why a primordial science of life is needed. As Heidegger now takes on the question of being as the long-forgotten fundamental question of philosophy, he is faced with the challenge of showing how this dangerously elusive question addresses us as a decisive issue in life. In this, his conception of the hierarchical structure of phenomena provides him with a new way of responding to this challenge.

Heidegger maintains that we always make use of an understanding of being in our experience and understanding of particular beings. In order to relate to an entity at all we need to have some understanding of what the entity in question "is." However, our factical understanding of being, which always already orients our experience of beings, is primarily unthematic and nebulous. This, Heidegger claims, demonstrates the necessity and import of explicating the question of being: "in every comportment and being toward beings as beings there lies *a priori* an enigma. The fact that we in each case already live in an understanding of being and that the sense of being is at the same time shrouded in darkness, proves the fundamental necessity of repeating the question of the sense of 'being'" (SZ: 4). In the lecture course "Basic Problems of Phenomenology" from the summer of 1927 Heidegger would name this hierarchical structure of phenomena the "ontological difference": "A being can be uncovered, whether by way of perception or some other mode of access, only if the being of this being is already disclosed—only if I already understand it" (GA 24: 102/72).

How should this be understood more precisely?

In *Being and Time* Heidegger argues that all our experience of particular beings as meaningful phenomena is determined by our prior understanding of the historical contexts of significance that we live in: our world. However, he also claims that our experience of beings is essentially guided by our prior understanding of the different being-modes of beings, including an understanding of being as such. The idea is that we always already have a certain understanding of the possible kinds and modes of being to which different beings may belong, such that we always understand the beings we encounter in terms of their mode of being: my next-door neighbor as a human being; my anger as a human emotion; this tree as a plant—as nature; this hammer as a tool. Our understanding of being, Heidegger claims, determines how we relate to and investigate beings. This also means that in so far as our understanding of being is prejudiced and distortive, it covers up and makes us explain away the significant phenomena that we experience in the world. For example, we can understand the human being as the egoistic end product of Darwinian evolution, or we can understand nature as the nexus of entities and forces studied by physics. In such cases, we will be apt to interpret our feelings of love, compassion, and moral obligation as expressions of our egoistic nature, or we may think that in order to achieve rigorous knowledge of humans and animals as parts of nature we have to turn to physics. Our understanding of the different modes of being is in its turn linked and organized by our understanding of what being in general is. As Heidegger has it, the Western tradition understands being as presence-at-hand: to be is, at bottom, to be an object for a theoretically observing gaze. From the point of view of this understanding, our first-person experience of meaningful phenomena will inevitably show up as a stratum of mere appearances in need of theoretical grounding.

According to Heidegger, the transparency and truthfulness of our understanding of being ultimately depend on our stance toward the question of the *sense* of being. The received understanding of being as presence-at-hand is, he maintains, the result of a dogmatic prioritizing of theoretical observation as the prime experiential paradigm for determining being as such. In this, one does not ask what role this kind of experience plays in the life of Dasein and one does not investigate the being of Dasein as the framework for answering this question. To ask about the "sense" (*Sinn*) of being is for Heidegger precisely to ask about the basic "structure" or "framework" (*Gerüst*) that characterizes Dasein's experience and understanding of meaningful matters: "Sense is that wherein the intelligibility of something maintains itself. The *concept of sense* comprises the formal framework (*formale Gerüst*) of what necessarily belongs to that which an understanding interpretation articulates" (SZ: 151). Since Dasein's experience is the domain in which matters show up as meaningful and intelligible to us, the basic structure of this experience constitutes the ultimate horizon for understanding what being is. To explicate the sense of being is to attend to our experience of phenomena in order to explicate the central structural features characterizing this experience and bring out the ultimate horizons that give to these phenomena the significance they have for us. It is only in so far as we come to understand the structures that constitute Dasein's experience of phenomena that it becomes possible to clearly grasp and delimit the senses of the different modes and domains of being within the overall context of meaningful being. It is only thus that we are in a position to clarify the senses and roles that experiential paradigms such as theoretical observation, practical coping, art, and love have in our lives.

We can now see how Heidegger's picture of the hierarchical structure of phenomenal understanding assigns a decisive role to the question of being in human life. Given that our understanding of ourselves and our world is conducted by our understanding of being, and given that this understanding in the first place remains obscure and prejudiced, such that it covers up the sense of the phenomena we encounter—then explicating the sense of being becomes a requirement for attaining an open and transparent relationship to beings in general, including the central ethical-existential issues of life.

Problems and Possibilities

Heidegger's conception of the ontological difference is undoubtedly one of the most ambitious attempts to demonstrate the primacy and necessity of philosophy—as fundamental ontology—for achieving clarity about ourselves and the world. This is not the place for a detailed assessment of the problems and possibilities of this conception. Still, let me briefly indicate my perspective on the issue.

As I see it, Heidegger's notion of the primacy of our understanding of being as a conditioning and necessary guide for our understanding of beings is fundamentally problematic. As argued in the first part, it seems that even if it is true that we always already tend to entertain different understandings of the ontological makeup of the world, these understandings do not necessarily determine how we can experience and relate to beings. Regardless of our understanding of being, we are open to the possibility of taking in and understanding the meaningful phenomena we encounter: the ethical claim of the other person, the practice of riding a bicycle, the nature that surrounds us. There is of course the possibility that we let ourselves be led by prejudiced ontological concepts that cover up the meaning of the phenomena. However, such dissimulation is not a cognitive necessity, it is something that happens due to the grip of our habits of thought and due to the different existential motives—collective pressure, fear of shame, and so on—that make us want to see certain things and repress others. For the same reason, we do not need a clear and worked-out understanding of the sense of being in order to access the phenomena. Rather, the ontological thinking of philosophy should be seen as a form of reflection that articulates the central structures of experiences and phenomena that we already have access to, and that ponders the relationship between different kinds of being on a more or less general ontological level. Ontological thinking of this kind can certainly be of help in—and is an integral part of—our effort to think clearly about the phenomena we encounter in our lives, but it is nothing that stands above and conditions this effort. Hence, the question of being is not the fundamental existential question of life. In so far as pondering this question is important, it is as a way of clarifying the central ethical-existential issues of life that meet us prior to the question of being: How should we relate to the claim of the other, to love and conscience, to shame and collective pressure, to death and pain, to evil and injustice?

Heidegger's idea of philosophy as fundamental ontology also bears within itself the problematic assumption that there is *one* fundamental structure of Dasein to be found that constitutes the sense of being as such. This assumption guides his analysis of Dasein as temporally structured being-in-the-world, whereby all possible modes of experience and being are interpreted as modifications of this structure. To be sure, there are experiential structures and existential trials that are decisive for how we understand and relate to life in general. However, it seems prejudiced to assume in advance that these experiences can be understood as modifications or variations of one fundamental structure. It must be said that Heidegger is more sensitive than most philosophers to how the general and abstract concepts of philosophy are rooted in particular experiential paradigms. Nevertheless, I think that his drive toward one basic structure makes him prone to cover up the manifold and distinctiveness of our existentially vital experiences, and to refrain from engaging in a deep and radical enough questioning of the particular existential attitudes and experiences informing his own fundamental ontology.

What is more, Heidegger's elevation of the question of being as the central question of life and philosophy leads him to interpret the entire history of philosophy as a monolithic narrative centered on this single issue. Because of this, he is disposed to disregard and cover up all the directions of interrogation and investigation that divert from or perhaps question the fundamentality of this question.

However, the problems shadowing Heidegger's project of fundamental ontology do not simply nullify its philosophical potential or necessarily lead all the investigations done within this project astray. Although Heidegger's articulation of the question of being is misleading, in *Being and Time* it basically functions as a framework for a set of phenomenological analyses whose truth and clarificatory force is independent of that framework. Moreover, the question of being harbors significant critical potential. Heidegger's asking of this question is an expression of his effort to phenomenologically explicate the structures of our experiences while critically attending to and dismantling the traditional ontological concepts that tend to organize the systematic projections of philosophy in a hidden and prejudiced manner.

6

BEING-IN-THE-WORLD

Heidegger's existential analytic in *Being and Time* is his most ambitious attempt to work out and articulate the basic structure of phenomena. It is meant to provide answers to the following questions: How do beings primarily show up as meaningful phenomena? What structure characterizes our experience of such phenomena? What are the ultimate teleological horizons or sources that give to the phenomena the significances they have for us? How do we understand and explicate the phenomena?

"Being-in-the-world" is Heidegger's title for the basic structure of our primary experience of beings as meaningful phenomena that concern and touch us in various ways. The structure of being-in-the-world comprises three aspects: (1) "world"—designating the context of significance toward which Dasein is open and on the basis of which it experiences things; (2) "being-in"—designating the different ways in which Dasein is in and understands its world; and (3) "who"—signifying the being who understands itself and its world in a more or less authentic way (SZ: 53). Heidegger emphasizes that being-in-the-world should be understood as a unitary structure consisting of interdependent "equiprimordial" aspects (SZ: 131). This, however, does not rule out the possibility of focusing on one aspect at a time as long as we remember to co-understand the other aspects.

I begin this chapter by examining Heidegger's account of how we primarily encounter beings as "tools" within a particular historical context of significance—a "world"—and how he conceives of the structure of such a world. After that, I explicate two of the main aspects of "being-in": understanding and interpretation. I end the chapter by considering what happens to the notions of "reality" and "truth" in Heidegger's historicized conception of phenomena.

The World

The "world" (*Welt*), Heidegger writes in a formal definition, is "that '*in which*' a factical Dasein as such 'lives'" (SZ: 65). However, the purpose of his analysis is not to describe the different contexts in which Dasein might live, but to explicate the ontological structure characterizing all such worlds, that is, the "worldliness" (*Weltlichkeit*) of the world (SZ: 65).

Heidegger's analysis of the worldliness of the world takes its point of departure in Dasein's everyday "concern" with its "surrounding world" (*Umwelt*), by which he means our everyday concerned dealings with the different significant beings and tasks of our lives. He asks: What is it that is primarily given to us in our everyday concern? How should we understand the sense-structure of this given?

The philosophical tradition, Heidegger claims, has always tended to conceive of the primarily given in terms of isolated objects or things parading for a theoretical gaze. However, when we turn to look at our everyday pretheoretical experience we see that the phenomena we primarily encounter have the character of "tools" or "equipment" (*Zeug*):

> Strictly speaking, there "is" no such thing as *an* equipment. To the being of any equipment there always belongs a totality of equipment, in which it can be this equipment that it is. Equipment is essentially "something in order to …" The different kinds of "in order to," such as serviceability, conduciveness, usability, handiness, constitute a totality of equipment. In the "in order to" as a structure there lies a *reference* of something to something. Equipment—in accordance with its equipmentality—always is in terms of its belonging to other equipment: writing utensils, pen, ink, paper, desk blotter, table, lamp, furniture, windows, doors, room. (SZ: 68)

That is to say, to be given as a piece of equipment is to be given as part of a totality of equipment. As such, a piece of equipment has the structure of "something in order to … " It is essentially constituted by its instrumental role or function within a certain context of purposes, tasks, and other tools. It is only on the basis of a prior understanding of this context that we can encounter a being as a tool for a purpose: a hammer to build a shelf with, a knife to cut bread with, a tree to seek shelter under. Hence, in our everyday concern we do not experience isolated objects or some kind of sense-data possessing these or those traits; rather, the phenomena we primarily encounter have the character of equipment that gain their very identity and significance within particular contexts of equipment. As Heidegger puts it, all the "properties" of the equipment are "bound up" in the ways in which it is "appropriate or inappropriate" in relation to some task or purpose (SZ: 83). For example, given the task of getting to the summer cottage in the countryside, a car might appear as suitable tool for this purpose. Here, the car is what it is for us on account of its instrumental function, such that this function determines which of its features count as relevant and which do not. Whereas it may be vital that the car is working and is sufficiently safe and trustworthy, such things as brand, maximum speed, and design may not be important. From the viewpoint of some other task—such as boosting one's social persona with an impressive car—the latter aspects may of course be highly significant.

Heidegger maintains that our everyday coping with tools does not transpire as a thematic grasp or seeing of the tools in question. Instead, the tools are primarily there for us as tools in our practical skillful handling of them: "the less we just stare at the hammer-thing, and the more we seize hold of it and use it, the more primordial does our relationship to it become, and the more unveiledly is it encountered as that which it is—as equipment" (SZ: 69). Our practical skillfulness involves a kind of understanding that Heidegger calls "circumspection" (*Umsicht*) a practical understanding that is unthematic and remains absorbed in the context of equipment that we are dealing with (SZ: 69). It consists in a sensitivity to the guiding instrumental relations of the context of equipment and to the specific function and handiness of the tools. According to Heidegger, the unthematic and absorbed character of our coping conditions our ability to handle tools in a smooth and skillful way. If we would lack this kind of practical—unthematic and habituated—skillfulness, such that we would have to think thematically about what we are doing, we would have great problems performing everyday tasks such as riding a bicycle, reading a book, or cooking a pasta dish.

Heidegger calls the mode of being of tools "readiness-to-hand" (*Zuhandenheit*) in contrast to the "presence-at-hand" (*Vorhandenheit*) of objects of theoretical observation. In the introduction to *Being and Time* he identified "phenomena" (*ta phainomena*) with "beings" (*ta onta*) through a doubtful philological reference to the Greeks. Now he claims that "the Greeks had an appropriate term for 'things': *pragmata*, that is, that with which one has to do in one's concernful dealings (*praxis*)" (SZ: 68). Whereas *ta onta* were first identified as *ta phainomena*, both are now—through this quasi-philological linkage—determined as *pragmata*. The analysis of the pragmatic character of being as readiness-to-hand should thus not only be read as a determination of the being of a certain sort of entities, namely tools and other kinds of artifacts, but rather concerns the primary mode of being of all non-human beings. Even nature, Heidegger claims, originally presents itself to us with reference to its instrumental relevance—usefulness, support, resistance—for the purposes of the human being: "The wood is a forest of timber, the mountain a quarry of rock; the river is water power, the wind is wind 'in the sails'" (SZ: 70). Hence, for Heidegger, readiness-to-hand constitutes the basic mode of being characterizing all non-human entities such as they show themselves for the primary concern of the human being: "*Readiness-to-hand is the ontological categorial definition of beings as they are 'in themselves'*" (SZ: 71).[1]

Whereas Heidegger maintains that the beings we primarily experience in our pretheoretical concern have the character of equipment, he names the context of reference on the basis of which such concern takes place the "world." However, he argues that in so far as Dasein is engaged in its absorbed everyday coping with tools, it cannot perceive and grasp the world that conditions this coping. Hence, he suggests that the world only becomes conspicuous and discernible when we experience some kind of disturbance of our coping. For instance, a piece of equipment might be broken or lacking. As a result, the totality of reference constituting the tool in question shines forth as the familiar context in which our absorbed coping has been taking place all along: "The context of equipment is lit up, not as something never seen before, but as a totality constantly sighted beforehand in circumspection. With this totality, however, the world announces itself" (SZ: 75).

Heidegger's argument has generally been accepted by his interpreters as an accurate phenomenological description.[2] However, I do not find it very convincing. Although Heidegger is clearly right in claiming that our handling of tools generally presupposes a kind of habituated unreflective practical skill in order to be performed in a smooth and optimal manner, it is not clear why this unreflective handling would not allow us to simultaneously survey or reflect on our situation. Indeed, it seems that the acquisition of habituated skills tends to free up our attention. We do not need to think about what we are doing but are free to let our attention wander: survey the context of work, reflect on its goals, think about the structure of the world—or perhaps about something else. Hence, the unthematic practical handiness described by Heidegger does not in any way cancel out, but rather facilitates the possibility of thematically attending to different things. Moreover, it seems to me that we are in any case free to disrupt our practical coping and reflect on the context of relations and purposes we are moving in—if that is what we want to do. As a result, the experience of disturbance becomes methodologically superfluous. In fact, it could even be argued that such experiences counteract the purpose ascribed to them by Heidegger. To be sure, in encountering a broken or missing tool the tool in question—as well as the immediate context of coping—may become conspicuous in a certain sense. However, in disrupting our current activity the disturbance does not by itself disrupt our interest in that activity, which means that in so far as the interest persists the disturbance will—just like a demanding task—tend to intensify our absorption in the work.

What is the ontological structure—the worldliness—of the world?

Heidegger introduces the term "relevance" (*Bewandtnis*) as a designation for the basic character of the references constituting the world: "Beings are uncovered with regard to the fact that they are referred, as those beings which they are, to something. They are relevant *for* something. The character of being of the ready-to-hand is *relevance*" (SZ: 84). "Relevance" is thus Heidegger's general term for designating the way in which tools can appear as relevant or important—useful or beneficial, or perhaps useless or obstructive—on account of their role in a specific context of tasks and tools. For example, the hammer may be relevant for hammering, the hammering may be relevant for building a house, and the house may be relevant as a sheltered place to live in. However, the instrumental references obtaining between different tools and tasks—this in order to that—are ultimately anchored in Dasein and its possibilities to be:

> The totality of relevance itself, however, ultimately goes back to a what-for (*Wozu*), which *no longer* has relevance, which itself is not a being with the kind of being of the ready-to-hand within a world, but is a being whose being is defined as being-in-the-world, to whose constitution of being worldliness itself belongs. This primary what-for is not just another for-that as a possible factor in relevance. The primary "what-for" is a for-the-sake-of-which (*Worum-willen*). But the for-the-sake-of-which always pertains to the being of Dasein, which, in its being, is essentially concerned *about* this being itself. (SZ: 84)

Whereas tools always refer to other tools and tasks in relation to which they are relevant, the possibilities of Dasein constitute the "for-the-sake-of-which" of all relevances: the ultimate horizon of purposes which determines all instrumental references and which cannot be reduced to any further purpose. It is for the sake of realizing Dasein's possibilities that we do what we do, and it is on the backdrop of these possibilities that tasks and tools may show up as relevant and important in the first place.

In characterizing Dasein as the ultimate "for-the-sake-of-which," Heidegger does not give voice to the universalist moral thesis that the human person would be an end in herself and possess absolute worth. The idea is rather that Dasein's understanding of what is valuable and significant is determined by the historical "possibilities" that it has appropriated. What Heidegger has in mind here are not our possibilities of engaging in particular activities such as hammering, cooking, drinking beer, or practicing yoga. After all, the point of the argument is precisely to account for the ultimate purposes that make such activities appear meaningful to us in the first place. In a telling passage, Heidegger writes that in authentically appropriating a historical "possibility," Dasein "chooses its hero" (SZ: 385). I think the most compelling and illuminating way of interpreting this is to conceive of the "possibilities" or "heroes" in terms of the concrete historical paradigms of a meaningful and valuable life available to us in our historical situation. Such paradigms may, I gather, take the form of historical or mythical role figures (such as Ulysses, Jesus, or Gandhi) or of anonymous roles and vocations (such as philosopher, parent, or professional athlete) that harbor and give expression to the values and ideals endorsed by a given historical society. To choose one's hero means to appropriate one such paradigm—or perhaps an amalgam of several paradigms and values—as the constitutive horizon of one's identity. To do something for the sake of a certain possibility of life means to do it in order to live up to—and avoid failing to realize—the ideals and values that one is committed to and that constitute one's identity. Dasein's guiding life-possibilities should thus be understood as the historically received paradigms and ideals that determine our conception of who we are as well as our possibilities of experiencing other beings as meaningful and relevant.

In his analysis of *historicity* (*Geschichtlichkeit*) in division two of *Being and Time* Heidegger accentuates and specifies the historical character of Dasein's factical possibilities. Answering the question "whence, *in general*, Dasein can draw those possibilities upon which it factically projects itself" (SZ: 383) he writes:

> The resoluteness in which Dasein comes back to itself discloses the current factical possibilities of authentic existing *out of the heritage* (*aus dem Erbe*), which resoluteness, as thrown, *takes over*. Resolute coming back to thrownness involves *delivering oneself over* (*Sichüberliefern*) to possibilities that have come down to one, although not necessarily *as* having thus come down. (SZ: 383)

According to Heidegger, Dasein thus essentially draws its possibilities from the historical heritage into which it has always already been thrown. Although it is the task of the individual Dasein to choose its own possibilities, it cannot of its own accord create or give meaning to its possibilities. Rather, the "repeatable possibilities" provided by the heritage constitute the "sole authority that a free existing can have" (SZ: 391). As we shall see, the challenge of authenticity is the challenge of Dasein to acknowledge the groundless and finite historical possibilities of its heritage as its lot, and to find and choose its own possibilities from the possibilities available in the heritage.

Three Dimensions of Understanding

Heidegger formally characterizes Dasein's openness toward its world as an interplay between "disposition" (*Befindlichkeit*) and "understanding" (*Verstehen*).

By "disposition," Heidegger refers to the way Dasein always already, through its moods, finds itself thrown into a particular historical world—a world which constitutes its historically given field of significances and life-possibilities. By contrast, "understanding" is Heidegger's name for the way in which Dasein sees and is these possibilities in a more or less transparent manner. Heidegger describes "understanding" as a "throw" or "projection" (*Entwurf*): "As projecting, understanding is the mode of being of Dasein in which it *is* its possibilities as possibilities" (SZ: 145). The essential interplay between disposition and understanding, between passive thrownness and active projection, makes Heidegger characterize Dasein as "thrown projection" (SZ: 148).

Here I want to distinguish between the different dimensions of understanding that figure in Heidegger's existential analytic. Since the concept of "understanding" in *Being and Time* is extremely formal, encompassing all the ways in which we may comport ourselves understandingly toward the world, it is easy to confuse the different dimensions and kinds of understanding that appear in his analysis. Indeed, I will argue that two influential readings of Heidegger—the reading developed by Hubert Dreyfus and the pragmatist reading—largely build on such confusion.

Heidegger's analysis in *Being and Time* refers to three different dimensions of understanding that need to be kept apart. First, we have the understanding which Heidegger calls "circumspection," and which discloses the relations between different tasks and tools as well as the functions and instrumental properties of those tools. Second, we have Dasein's understanding of the life-possibilities that constitute the teleological horizon of and that give significance to all the tasks that it undertakes and all the tools that it encounters. Third, we have Dasein's understanding of being, which guides and links all its other understandings. Here, I will look more closely at the first of these. The second will be dealt with at greater length in the next chapter on authenticity whereas the third will be examined in the final chapter on Heidegger's method in *Being and Time*.

In his analysis of Dasein's circumspective understanding of the tools and tasks of its world Heidegger emphasizes two main aspects of such understanding. To begin with, he emphasizes the *pragmatic meaning* of such understanding. Whereas the traditional understanding of being as presence-at-hand conceives of beings as abstract objects removed from all particular contexts of significance, Heidegger claims that beings from the outset show themselves as useful or relevant from the viewpoint of some task. Indeed, it is our tasks and purposes that allow us to identify particular beings as meaningful phenomena in the first place. Just as beings are what they are for us on account of their instrumental roles and functions, the point and motivation of all understanding and knowledge of such beings consist in the ability it gives us to perform the tasks that we want to perform.

Furthermore, Heidegger claims that our understanding of tools and tasks primarily has the character of *unthematic skillful coping*—in contrast to distanced thematic observation. He argues that it is our ability at unthematic coping that allows us to handle tools in a smooth and efficient way. In learning practical skills and appropriating different kinds of knowledge so that they take the form of a complex habituated intuition, we become able to cope with different tools and tasks in an effortless and efficient manner—something that would have been quite impossible had we been required to think about what we do all the time. Moreover, he maintains that our unthematic understanding of the tools and equipmental networks of the world functions as the necessary background for all our thematic attention and reflection. To be able to engage in some particular activity or focus on some specific matter, we already need to possess and draw on an unthematic background understanding of the world. It is only in virtue of the unthematic background character of our understanding that we can orient ourselves in the world and cope with tools the way we do, including thematically attending to and thinking about tools and other matters.³

So, whereas the pragmatic point of understanding beings as tools consists in mastering the practices and tasks of our world, the basic character of such understanding lies in our unthematic skillful handling of the tools and tasks in question.

Now, Dasein's pragmatic understanding of tools must be sharply distinguished from the two other central dimensions of understanding that figure in *Being and Time*: first, Dasein's understanding of its life-possibilities; second, its understanding of being. The understanding of tools and tasks described above consists in and is limited to excelling in practical tasks that are simply there as parts of our historical world: riding bicycles, playing chess, handling money, cooking pasta, building bridges. The understanding or know-how is successful if it allows us to excel in the task at hand and it does not as such involve asking about the truth or meaningfulness of the tasks to be performed.

By contrast, it belongs to the very meaning of understanding our guiding life-possibilities and understanding the sense of being that such an understanding can be better or worse in a way that is not reducible to pragmatic success or failure. What is at stake here is understanding and judging the ethical-existential substance of our life-possibilities and understanding the structures of phenomenal being. It makes no sense to say, as it does in the case of practical know-how, that understanding here would consist in our ability to handle some given practical tasks. Moreover, Heidegger stresses that both our understanding of our life-possibilities and our understanding of being is normally inauthentic and prejudiced, and guided by the collective conceptions of the tradition. This means that both these tasks of understanding—the task of authenticity and the philosophical task of fundamental ontology—raise the question of what good or true understanding amounts to and how it differs from prejudiced opinion.

It bears noting that two of the main Anglo-American interpretations of Heidegger have been characterized by a strong propensity to focus almost exclusively on Heidegger's account of pragmatic understanding while playing down or reducing the question of what it means to understand our guiding life-possibilities.

In his classic 1991 book *Being-in-the-World* Hubert Dreyfus highlights Dasein's practical unthematic skills—which he calls "background coping" (1991: 105)—as the fundamental dimension of our understanding of the world, which conditions and constitutes the background for all thematic understanding and knowledge. In so doing, Dreyfus largely neglects that Dasein's unthematic coping with the tasks and tools making up our world gets its direction and significance from our understanding of our guiding life-possibilities—an understanding that is not reducible to such coping. This is why Dreyfus can remove the entire discussion of authenticity to an appendix. Dreyfus's emphasis on background coping as the paradigmatic form of understanding also gives rise to a problematic interpretation of the problem of authenticity. The background coping that he explores is characterized as an unthematic skillful know-how of the tools and practices of a given historical context. To understand these practices is basically to learn to know their internal norms for success or failure and be able to engage in them. In addition to this ability to handle the practices and tools of a historical community, there is no meaningful question to be asked concerning the truth and meaningfulness of these practices: they are what they are and understanding them consists in being able to enact them. This is certainly in line with much of what Heidegger says about our unthematic circumspective coping with tools. However, understanding and choosing our possibilities of a meaningful life is an entirely different matter and Heidegger stresses that we normally tend to understand these possibilities in terms of the prejudiced opinions of the They. This means that the question of how we can disclose and choose our own possibilities truthfully or primordially, in contrast to the prejudices of the They, becomes vital and uncircumventable. Dreyfus's approach closes him to this challenge. If, as he sees it, understanding essentially consists in learning and handling the norms and practices of a given community, then choosing our guiding paradigms of life must also be a matter of simply appropriating the factical values and norms that happen to prevail. Hence, Dreyfus is able to conclude without much hesitation that the collective They constitutes our ultimate "source of significance and intelligibility" (1991: 161).

The pragmatist reading of Heidegger—chiefly developed by Carl-Friedrich Gethmann and Mark Okrent—suffers from problems very much akin to those of Dreyfus. The pragmatist interpretation basically construes Dasein's understanding in terms of our practical skills in handling tools and carrying out tasks within the purposeful contexts we are involved in. The truth of our understanding is defined in terms of its success or failure in allowing us to carry out these tasks and activities. As Okrent puts it: "For Heidegger the fundamental notion of evidence is tied to the way in which purposeful, practical activity must be recognizable as successful or unsuccessful if the activity is to count as purposeful at all. From this basic pragmatism follow his idiosyncratic notions of truth and meaning" (1988: 128; cf. also Gethmann 1989: 115–18). However, even though this reading captures an important aspect of Heidegger's analysis of circumspective concern it ignores and thus in the end misconstrues what for Heidegger constitutes the ultimate teleological horizon of understanding: Dasein's understanding of its guiding life-possibilities, which allow tools and practices to appear as significant in the first place, and the truth—and ethical-existential meaning—of which cannot be determined on the basis of any pragmatic criteria.[4]

Interpretation and Language

Heidegger calls Dasein's possibility of developing and thematically appropriating its understanding of the world "interpretation" (*Auslegung, Interpretation*). The main function of his account of interpretation is to bring out the historical predicament of all thinking. Let us take a look at what Heidegger has to say about this and at the same time briefly indicate how he conceives of language in *Being and Time*.

Heidegger's central thesis is that our experience of meaningful phenomena is from the outset characterized by understanding and interpretation and that interpretation is grounded in and thematically appropriates what we have already understood. He articulates the historical character of our phenomenal experience in terms of the "as-structure" of understanding and interpretation:

> The circumspectively interpretative answer to the circumspective question of what this particular being that is ready-to-hand is runs: it is for … Saying what it is for is not simply naming something, but what is named is understood *as* that *as* which what is in question is to be taken. What is disclosed in understanding, what is understood, is always already accessible in such a way that its "as what" can be explicitly delineated. (SZ: 149)

That is to say, we always already experience beings as this or that on the backdrop of our understanding of the historical world of significances that we live in and the projects that we are engaged in: this as a bicycle to ride on; that as a fruit to eat; this as a pen to write with. The task of the interpretation is to thematically articulate the "as what" in terms of which we have always already understood beings.

Heidegger especially emphasizes two basic aspects of Dasein's understanding and interpretation. To begin with, he maintains that "any simple prepredicative seeing of the ready-to-hand is in itself already understanding and interpreting" (SZ: 149). Our experience of beings does not primarily transpire without as-structure, so that we would first experience pure sense perceptions, which we would then actively interpret and furnish with significance. From the outset, we see this as a tree and that as a door, just as we hear this as a car starting and that as the wind blowing. Our perception is always determined by our preceding understanding of the instrumental networks of our world and by our guiding life-possibilities. It is this understanding that allows particular beings to show up with reference to their roles and functions within our historical world. Experiencing something like a pure as-free perception would require that our understanding would somehow be put out of play with the result that we would not be able to make sense of the experience at all: "When we just stare at something, our just-having-it-before-us lies before us *as a failure to understand it anymore*" (SZ: 149). Furthermore, Heidegger stresses that interpretation is "grounded in" and only appropriates and develops what we have already understood (SZ: 148). That is, interpretation does not give us access to any new or deeper ground for understanding phenomena. Rather, it always relies on our understanding of our historical world as its ultimate ground and essentially transpires as thematizing articulation of what is already there and accessible in this understanding.

The analysis of the as-structure of interpretation is followed up by an account of what Heidegger calls its "fore-structure" (*Vor-struktur*) (SZ: 151). The structural fact that we primarily experience beings as meaningful phenomena on the basis of a preceding understanding of the world implies, he claims, that all interpretation is also essentially characterized by a fore-structure. The fore-structure includes three aspects. Firstly, the interpretation is always grounded in a "fore-having" (*Vorhabe*), that is, in the factical unthematic understanding of the world in which Dasein always already lives. Secondly, the interpretation is grounded in a "fore-sight" (*Vorsicht*), that is, in a preceding grasp of the guiding "regard" (*Hinsicht*)—the problem- and being-horizon—in terms of which the phenomenon in question is to be interpreted. Thirdly, the interpretation is always grounded in a "fore-conception" (*Vorgriff*), which is to say that it always moves within a certain conceptuality that links its articulation of the matter (SZ: 150).

Heidegger's account of the fore-structure is intended to spell out the hermeneutic situation regulating all interpretation. As we attempt to interpret some phenomenon we always do this on the basis of a certain understanding of the world, a certain grasp of the problem- and being-horizon of the phenomenon in question, and a certain conceptuality—all of which we have primarily slid into and uncritically taken over as our factical historical tradition. This means that interpretation is never a "presuppositionless grasping of something pregiven" (SZ: 150); rather, what we directly see is primarily "nothing other than the self-evident, undiscussed assumption of the interpreter" (SZ: 150).

This raises the critical question: How are we to free ourselves from our initial uncritical and prejudiced preunderstanding and acquire an independent critical interpretation of the matters in question?

According to Heidegger, we need to give up the idea of direct intuitive and transhistorical access to the matters and recognize that all seeing of something as something is always already determined and guided by our historical understanding of the world and of being as such. This also means that any effort at independent interpretation is fundamentally referred to and needs to take the form of a critical explication of the factical historical understanding that we always already live in. Heidegger's central challenge is to show how independent interpretation is possible when it comes to Dasein's understanding of its life-possibilities and its understanding of being—both of which are said to be initially inauthentic and prejudiced. Whereas Heidegger's analysis of authenticity is meant to demonstrate the possibility of authentically grasping one's life-possibilities, he tries to account for the possibility of an independent primordial understanding of being—the task of *Being and Time*—in terms of a critical destruction of the history of philosophy.

Although Heidegger stresses the historical character of our understanding and interpretation of the world, he conceives of both understanding and interpretation as primarily prelinguistic in character.

Heidegger maintains that Dasein's interpretation is first and foremost implicit and does not need to take the form of explicit statements: "The articulation of what is understood … lies *before* the thematic statement about it. The 'as' does not first show up in the statement, but is only first expressed, which is possible only because it already lies before us as something expressible" (SZ: 149). For us to be able to utter explicit statements about things, the world already has to be there and open for us as a context of significance that allows of being linguistically expressed. We already need to have an understanding of chairs, dogs, and churches in order to be able to speak meaningfully about such matters. According to Heidegger, the explicit utterance is "no free-floating comportment which could of itself disclose beings in general in a primary way" (SZ: 156) but rather has to be understood as a "*derivative* mode" (SZ: 157) of interpretation which rests on our primary implicit understanding and interpretation and modifies it in a certain sense.

Heidegger makes a sharp distinction between the "existential-*hermeneutic* 'as'" characterizing Dasein's primary concerned interpretation of the world and the "*apophantical* 'as'" characterizing theoretical statements (SZ: 158). Whereas Dasein's primary interpretation articulates the tool with reference to its roles in the referential context of the world, the theoretical statement focuses exclusively on the tool as a present-at-hand object with the aim of determining its objective traits. Hence, the theoretical statement passes over the historical context that gives significance to all tools.

Although Heidegger is very sensitive to how our language—words, grammar, ways of speaking—tends to link our understanding of things, he basically conceives of language as a medium of communication that does not constitute but builds on and expresses our primary prelinguistic understanding of the world. He articulates his general view of language in terms of the somewhat puzzling distinction between "discourse" (*Rede*) and "language" (*Sprache*). "Discourse" is defined as the "articulation" or "arrangement" (*Artikulation*) of the "intelligibility" (*Verständlichkeit*) of being-in-the-world (SZ: 161). By this, Heidegger means the way in which the context we live in is always already structured as a "totality of significations" (SZ: 161). As such, discourse is the "existential-ontological foundation" of "language" (SZ: 160). By contrast, "language" designates the factical "totality of words" (*Wortganzheit*) in and through which discourse expresses itself: "The intelligibility of being-in-the-world ... *expresses itself as discourse.* The totality of significations of intelligibility is *put into words.* To significations, words accrue. But word-things do not get supplied with significations. The way in which discourse gets expressed is language" (SZ: 161). That is to say, our words and linguistic conventions do not shape or create their significances out of nothing but rather "accrue to"—that is, express and mediate—historical significances that we are always already open to and understand in a prelinguistic manner.

Heidegger's account of language in *Being and Time* remains quite rudimentary and he does not work out the distinction between "discourse" and "language" in any detail. Later, in the beginning of the 1930s, he will give up this distinction in favor of a new conception of language as the constitutive element of our historical world.

However, I think it is worth noting that there are in fact good philosophical reasons for making a distinction between the prelinguistic meanings and concepts we live in and our linguistic means of communicating them. It is clearly possible to identify and communicate different meanings and concepts without using words of one-to-one correspondence ("football" for football, "love" for love, "dog" for dog, and so on). It also seems clear that we may understand and communicate concepts and meanings for which we have no particular linguistic expression. Consider, for example, the situation of entering a bus and looking around for a free seat. In modern urban societies, this is a typical situation for many people, involving typical features and possibilities, a situation of which we have a general conception that can be identified and communicated. Yet we have no word for it— although we could have one. In fact, it seems that our understanding of the world is permeated by such prelinguistic general concepts and typifications that orient our lives. Still, the basic point of this argument is not that in addition to our linguistic concepts we also have prelinguistic concepts. Rather, it is that our understanding of concepts and meanings is primarily prelinguistic in character although it is always already linguistically codified and mediated to a greater or lesser extent. I think it is phenomenologically accurate to assert that our understanding of prelinguistic meanings and concepts grounds our possibilities of meaningful linguistic expression and communications. If we did not have an understanding of football, love, or what it means to make a promise—an understanding which is not equal to the linguistic ability to talk about these matters, although it conditions and goes hand in hand with the latter—it is hard to see how we could ever talk about or give expression to such meanings.

Reality and Truth

Heidegger's analysis of being-in-the-world in the first division of *Being and Time* ends with two paragraphs—§43 and §44—that deal with the notions of "reality" (*Realität*) and "truth" (*Wahrheit*). In fact, the entire phenomenological analysis of the structure of phenomena can be seen as an intervention in the age-old philosophical discussion of these notions. Hence, it seems that briefly explicating

Heidegger's take on "reality" and "truth" is a good way of summing up and making conspicuous the philosophical sense of his historical conception of phenomena.

The Question of Reality. Heidegger's approach to the question of reality is determined by his basic phenomenological orientation. He takes his starting point in the conviction that our phenomenal experience constitutes our very access to meaningful reality. For Heidegger, this means that the ready-to-hand tools that Dasein encounters within the horizon of its world *are* the beings themselves in the meaning they have for us.

However, according to Heidegger, the whole tradition of philosophy has been governed by the understanding of being as presence-at-hand. Being has been understood in terms of entities that are what they are irrespective of the experiential context in which they occur. Since Descartes, the question of reality has taken the form of a question concerning the existence of the outer world: Is it possible for the inner acts of subjective consciousness to reach out and establish knowledge of outer reality—a reality that transcends and is independent of human consciousness? The standard strategies of modern philosophy to answer this question have been those of realism and idealism. Whereas realism tries to prove— in the face of skeptical doubt— that the world really exists by demonstrating some connection between our experience and the outer reality that it targets, idealism maintains that "being and reality are only 'in consciousness'" (SZ: 207).

Heidegger contends that the entire traditional debate between realism and idealism is misguided and confused because it presupposes an understanding of the human being as a self-contained subject that only has access to its inner experiences and sensations. This understanding then gives rise to the unclear question of whether our inner experience is connected to and gives us knowledge of an outer reality that is supposedly completely independent of this experience.

Heidegger criticism is primarily directed at the realist effort to prove that the world exists: "The 'scandal of philosophy' does not consist in the fact that this proof is still lacking, but *in the fact that such proofs are expected and attempted again and again*" (SZ: 205). The problem of realism is that it flouts the basic phenomenological insight that Dasein's experience gives it open access to beings in the phenomenal meaning they have for us. If we want to understand some matter—what a house is, what a dog is, what courage is—we can only do this by attending to our relevant experiences of the matter in question. By contrast, the question of whether we can reach and have knowledge of outer reality—which the skeptic answers negatively and the realist positively—is misguided and senseless:[5] It is to ask whether our experience of phenomena is able to attain and establish knowledge of beings that are what they are beyond and independently of our experience of them as meaningful; it is to want to ground our understanding of meaning in a domain of objects that lacks any meaning.

In Heidegger's view, idealism is superior to realism since the basic idea of idealism, namely that being resides in consciousness, gives expression to the more or less vague insight that "being cannot be explained through beings" (SZ: 207). The insight is that it is impossible to make sense of our experience of beings as meaningful and as having this or that being-character with reference to how beings are irrespectively of our experience of them. Our experience of phenomena is the very ground for understanding what beings are for us. Nevertheless, Heidegger believes that traditional idealism is badly flawed to the extent that it holds on to the notion of a self-contained subject that in some sense constitutes or produces the world that it experiences.

Heidegger's notion that our experience of phenomena is our access to meaningful being is only his starting point. Within this framework he then sets out to answer the question of the sense of being by elaborating his analysis of the historical structure of phenomena that we have elucidated in some detail above.

Heidegger spells out the relations pertaining between Dasein, beings, and historical being—here signifying the entire historical context of meaning that determines its experience—in the following dense passage:

> The fact that reality is ontologically grounded in the being of Dasein cannot mean that something real can only be what it is in itself when and as long as Dasein exists. To be sure, only as long as Dasein *is,* that is, only as long as there is the ontic possibility of an understanding of being, "is there" being (*"gibt es" Sein*). If Dasein does not exist, then there "is" no "independence" either, nor "is" there an "in-itself." Such matters are then neither comprehensible nor incomprehensible. If Dasein does not exist, then innerworldly beings, too, can neither be uncovered, nor can they lie in concealment. *Then* it can neither be said that beings are, nor that they are not. It can *now* indeed be said that as long as there is an understanding of being and thus an understanding of presence-at-hand, that *then* beings will still continue to be. Only if an understanding of being *is*, do beings as beings become accessible; only if beings are of Dasein's kind of being, is an understanding of being possible as a being. (SZ: 211–12)

Let us take hold of the three main points of Heidegger's argument:

1. Only when Dasein exists and has an understanding of being are beings accessible "as beings." It is Dasein's understanding of historical being that conditions and determines its experience of beings as meaningful phenomena.

2. This, however, does not mean that particular real beings "can only be" what they are in themselves "when and as long as Dasein exists." That is to say, Dasein's experience does not somehow produce the beings that it experiences. Even if humans became extinct, this would not imply that the particular entities populating the universe would vanish or that their material traits would change. However, this point in no way unsettles the first point. Heidegger holds that in experiencing beings as ready-to-hand phenomena these phenomena get their significance and identity as this or that from our prior understanding of our historical world. Although the material traits of beings are what they are regardless of our experience, these traits get whatever relevance they have for us on the basis of our experience of the phenomena of our historical world.

3. The third point concerns the relationship between Dasein and being: "only as long as Dasein *is,* that is, only as long as there is the ontic possibility of an understanding of being, 'is there' being (*'gibt es' Sein*)." Given that being

determines what beings can be and given that being does not exist as a sphere of ideal universal meanings that Dasein could detect, it is in some sense dependent on Dasein; it is in some sense something that Dasein brings with itself to beings. However, Heidegger stresses that being is not a product or a feature of human consciousness, but something that Dasein is open toward. The double relationship of dependence and independence between Dasein and being is indicated when Heidegger writes that it is only as long as Dasein is that "*es gibt' Sein*." This should be taken literally: only as long as Dasein is, does "it give" being. Being is thus nothing that Dasein produces, but, as soon as Dasein exists, being is given to Dasein as the groundless dimension of historical meaning into which it has always already been thrown.

Although Heidegger rejects the idea that being is produced or constituted by the human subject, his insistence on the ontological difference between beings and being continues and reformulates one basic aspect of idealist thought. Whereas idealism holds that beings receive their identity and meaning from the forms and functions of human subjectivity, Heidegger maintains that they receive their identity and meaning from the historical world to which we belong. Here, the possibility is ruled out that beings could possess meaning in themselves apart from our historical contexts, and that that we could have direct and intuitive transhistorical access to such beings. Instead, Heidegger elevates our historical contexts of world and being as the historical *a priori* that determines in advance the possible significances that beings can have for us.

The Question of Truth. Heidegger's account of truth—just like his discussion of reality—is based on and spells out the sense and consequences of his analysis of the historical structure of phenomena.

According to Heidegger, the traditional conception of truth dominating the history of philosophy is condensed in the Latin formula: *adaequatio intellectus et rei*. Truth is thus conceived in terms of the agreement or correspondence of our propositions with the objects that they are about. However, how should we conceive of such correspondence and how is it possible? It is important to see that the point of Heidegger's discussion of truth is not to dismiss the traditional notion of truth as correspondence. Rather, what Heidegger sets out to do is to give a phenomenological account of how our beliefs and propositions may be said to correspond—or not correspond—with the beings and states of affairs that they intend. Moreover, he wants to show that truth as correspondence is only possible on the basis of Dasein's constitution as being-in-the-world.

Heidegger begins by describing what happens when our knowledge of beings demonstrates itself as true. He asks us to consider a situation where someone with her back turned to the wall makes the true statement "the picture on the wall is hanging askew" (SZ: 217). The statement demonstrates itself as true when the person in question turns around and perceives the picture hanging crookedly on the wall. What happens here? First off, Heidegger claims that in making such a statement we are not primarily directed toward the content of the statement or toward some inner representation of the picture, but toward the picture itself as being so and so. What then happens as we face the picture is that we see that the picture shows up precisely in the way that our assertion presented it—as hanging askew. In this, the assertion demonstrates itself as true, that is, as "being-uncovering" (*entdeckend-sein*): "To say that a statement *is true* means that it uncovers the being in itself. It asserts, it shows, it 'lets' the being 'be seen' (*apophansis*) in its uncoveredness. The *being-true (truth)* of the statement must be understood as *being-uncovering*" (SZ: 218).

So far, Heidegger has basically recapitulated in his own words Husserl's account of truth in terms of the interplay between signifying and intuitively fulfilling intentional acts: first, it belongs to our intentional experiences that we are directed at the matters themselves; second, an intention is proved true when the matter intended is intuitively self-given in the way we intended it. However, he goes on to argue that the possibility of our statements corresponding with—uncovering— beings presupposes that Dasein is a being that is always already open to its historical world: "the uncoveredness of innerworldly beings is *grounded* in the disclosedness of the world" (SZ: 220). It is only on the basis of its prior disclosure of its world that Dasein can intend and apprehend beings as this or that, and, hence, make true or false statements about them. As a result, Heidegger names the "*disclosedness* of Dasein" the "*most primordial* phenomenon of truth" (SZ: 220–1). Does this mean that Dasein's primary world-disclosure, conceived as the condition of truth of all ontic statements about beings, cannot itself be true or false?

In his classic critique of Heidegger's concept of truth, Ernst Tugendhat ([1969] 1992, 1970) argues that Heidegger indeed holds that Dasein's primary understanding of its historical world, since it grounds all possible truth, is itself immune to and stands above the question of truth:

> If, namely, every propositional truth about intraworldly beings is relative to the historical horizons of our understanding, then the entire truth problem is now concentrated upon these horizons, and the decisive question would have to be: In what way can one also ask about the truth of these horizons, or is it rather the case that the question of truth can no longer be applied to the horizons themselves? For Heidegger, this question becomes invalid through the fact that he already gives the name of truth to the respective understanding as a disclosedness in and for itself. Thus, on the one hand, this makes it possible for us to still talk of truth in connection with understanding and its horizons. On the other hand, it is realized that we do not need to ask about the truth of these horizons, since that would only mean asking about the truth of a truth. ([1969] 1992: 295, translation altered)

According to Tugendhat, Heidegger, by calling Dasein's disclosedness "primordial truth," rules out the possibility of asking about the truth of our understanding of our world. The outcome of this is that Heidegger sanctions the dogmatic acceptance of our factical historical horizons in their arbitrariness and relativity, thereby renouncing the crucial task of critically interrogating these horizons.

Since its publication, Tugendhat's critique has been the object of fierce controversy and debate.[6] Although I do not find Tugendhat's way of arguing so convincing, I believe his central critical thesis—that Heidegger's makes Dasein's world-disclosure immune to the question of truth—is on target.[7]

Let me try to sum up Heidegger's view.

First off, I want to stress that Heidegger unequivocally accepts a phenomenologically clarified version of the traditional view that the truth of our statements about beings consists in correspondence with the beings in question.[8] Whereas true statements present the beings they intend as something that they themselves are, false statements present them as something that they are not. According to Heidegger, such correspondence is only possible and always takes place within the horizon of a historical world that determines our understanding of beings as phenomena. Given such a world, we can present true or false statements about the beings populating this world: tools, plants, animals, character traits, emotions, social institutions, and so on.

However, according to Heidegger's conception, Dasein's understanding of its historical world—including the instrumental networks of the world, the guiding life-possibilities and ideals, and the senses of being—cannot itself be true or false. Since our understanding of the world determines our possibilities of experiencing and understanding beings as phenomena—determines what beings are for us—this understanding cannot itself be true or false depending on how it corresponds with beings. Hence, our historical world—ultimately, all the meaning-possibilities bestowed by our history—takes on the status of the ungroundable and finite ground that determines our experience of meaningful beings and that is itself immune to the question of truth.

However, Heidegger's radical historicization of our understanding of the world is nothing that he can comfortably settle with. It immediately raises the question of how it is possible to distinguish between the historical prejudices in which we normally tend to live and the possibility of a genuine understanding of the matters at stake. Given Heidegger's historicism, this is the question of how historical being can be given and experienced as in some sense binding and primordial beyond the prejudices of the They. As we shall see, Heidegger fails to address this question in *Being and Time*, a failure which undermines and raises decisive obstacles both for his account of authenticity and for his conception of the hermeneutic-destructive method of thinking. In his later thinking Heidegger takes up and pursues the question of the bindingness of historical worlds in a bid to compensate for his denial that our understanding of such worlds can be true or false.

7

PROBLEMS OF AUTHENTICITY

The Challenge of Authenticity

Heidegger's analysis of authenticity is at the heart of his struggle with the problem of phenomena in *Being and Time*.

To begin with, Heidegger holds that realizing the possibility of authentic existence is methodologically decisive for the philosophical effort of explicating the historical structure of phenomena. The idea is that Dasein is essentially confronted with the challenge of acknowledging the groundlessness and finitude of the historical possibilities of its heritage and of choosing some of these possibilities as its identity. Whereas authenticity consists in opening up to and meeting this challenge, inauthenticity consists in repressing it, refraining from independent responsible understanding, and taking refuge in the interpretations offered by the collective They. Indeed, Heidegger maintains that the traditional understanding of being as presence-at-hand is rooted in the attitude of inauthentic existence. Denying the historical finitude of life, Dasein develops an interpretation of being that covers up and explains away what it does not want to know. By contrast, he claims that his existential analytic of Dasein must take its point of departure in Dasein's authentic existence. Since we can only hope to ontologically explicate what we are open to and acknowledge, authentic existence becomes a prerequisite for ontological understanding: it secures "the phenomenally adequate basis for a primordial interpretation of the sense of being of Dasein" (SZ: 234). The explication of the historical structure of Dasein must thus be based on Dasein's authentic experience of its historical groundlessness and finitude.

What is more, to grasp the philosophical stakes of the analysis of authenticity we need to see that it deals with Dasein's understanding of the ultimate phenomenal sources of ethical-existential normativity and significance. For Dasein, the challenge of authenticity is the challenge of understanding and choosing the life-possibilities that constitute its identity. It is these possibilities, Heidegger claims, that grant significance to our lives and to the phenomena we encounter: to actions, tools, animals, plants, and so on. Hence, they constitute the source and teleological horizon of all phenomenal significance. The question of how such possibilities are given and understandable is thus decisive for the philosophical and ethical-existential meaning of Heidegger's account of phenomena.

Let me begin by further specifying the stakes and meaning of the challenge of authenticity: How is Dasein faced with the challenge of authenticity? What does understanding and choosing one's life-possibilities involve?

The point of departure of Heidegger's analysis is that Dasein tends to live and understand itself in an inauthentic manner. This means that it represses and flees from the task of acknowledging the groundlessness and finitude of its life-possibilities and of independently choosing some such possibility as its own. Instead, inauthentic Dasein uncritically takes over whatever the collective group in which it happens to live—the anonymous "They" (*das Man*)—happens to endorse (SZ: 126). To live inauthentically means that we do not think and see for ourselves anymore; rather, we think what "They" think and do what "They" do just because our collective circle happens to value these things. According to Heidegger, inauthentic Dasein lets itself be uncritically guided by the They both in its understanding of the being of its possibilities and in its understanding and choice of its own possibility: first, it takes over the traditional understanding of being as presence-at-hand, which means that it covers up the historical finitude of its possibilities and instead explicates them as objective and universal entities; second, it does not take responsibility for but lets the They decide the choice of its possibilities: "The They has always already kept Dasein from taking hold of these possibilities of being. The They even conceals the way it has silently disburdened Dasein of the explicit *choice* of these possibilities" (SZ: 268).

There are, Heidegger contends, two basic experiences that disrupt the conformity of inauthentic existence and confront Dasein with the task of facing its predicament in a responsible manner: anxiety (*Angst*) and the call of conscience (*Ruf des Gewissens*).

According to Heidegger, *anxiety* differs from other forms of fear in that in anxiety we do not fear anything particular—for example, other human beings, animals, or diseases—that would threaten us. Rather, in anxiety we experience that our entire familiar world with all its beings is "of no consequence" and "collapses into itself": "The world has the character of complete insignificance" (SZ: 186). Dasein feels that it is "not-at-home" in the familiar world of the They, which shows up as "uncanny" (SZ: 189). Having taken over the possibilities of the They in an unquestioning fashion without independently choosing them, these possibilities now appear alien and meaningless.

Ultimately, that in the face of which Dasein experiences anxiety is itself in its essential mortality and finitude. Anxiety exposes Dasein to its death as its "ownmost, non-relational, insuperable (*unüberholbar*) possibility" (SZ: 250). That death is Dasein's *ownmost* possibility means that Dasein is referred to its *own* possibilities as that which it can be; that death is *non-relational* means that it is the individual Dasein *itself*, and no one else, that has to take over its own possibility of being; finally, that death is *insuperable* means that it constitutes the ultimate possibility that Dasein can never move beyond and that delimits all its finite life-possibilities. In anxiety, Dasein is thus faced with the task of independently disclosing and choosing its own finite possibilities from those historical possibilities available to it.

Like anxiety, the *call of conscience* is described by Heidegger as an experience that unsettles Dasein's tendency to be governed by the They. The call of conscience, he says, completely "passes over" the interpretedness of the They in terms of which Dasein normally understands itself, whereby it "pushes" the They into "insignificance" (SZ: 273). The call has nothing new or substantial to tell Dasein about how it ought to live its life in accordance with the available collective norms and paradigms of value. Instead, it speaks solely "in the mode of keeping silent" (SZ: 273). It addresses Dasein's inauthentic self as an alien voice that, neither planned nor anticipated, comes at once "from me" and "over me" (SZ: 275). The voice that calls, Heidegger says, is Dasein itself in its "primordial thrown being-in-the-world as not-at-home" (SZ: 276). As such, it awakens Dasein to its alienated existence in the They and to the task of authentically reclaiming itself.

But what does the call of conscience give to understand? According to Heidegger, the call of conscience says that Dasein is "guilty." What he has in mind here is not a moral guilt that Dasein could incur through its way of relating and acting toward others, but a guilt that belongs to Dasein prior to and regardless of all its ontic attitudes and actions. Dasein is said to be fundamentally guilty in two respects. Firstly, Dasein is characterized by the fact that it is always already thrown into its being. This means that Dasein is from the outset delivered over to a possibility to be that it has never been in a position to ground or instigate but which it is nevertheless referred to as its "thrown ground": "It [Dasein] is never existent *before* its ground, but only *from it* and *as this ground*. Thus being-a-ground means *never* to have power over one's ownmost being from the ground up" (SZ: 284). In short, it belongs to the being of Dasein that it is always already thrown into a field of factical historical possibilities which conditions all meaningful experience, and which constitutes the ungroundable ground that it can be. Secondly, in so far as Dasein chooses certain possibilities of being, it thereby chooses *not* to be all the possibilities that it passes over. Hence, in order for Dasein to be able to choose its own finite possibilities it must also be capable of enduring the negativity of letting go of all the alternative possibilities of life.

As we have seen, both anxiety and the call of conscience disrupt Dasein's irresponsible and uncritical living in accordance with the They and confront it with the task of disclosing and choosing its own possibilities. It is crucial to see that the task of authenticity strictly speaking involves two tasks.

First, there is the task of acknowledging and understanding the historically finite nature of the possibilities that Dasein is to choose. The call of conscience is said to disclose the groundlessness of the historical possibilities available to us: the fact that we are always already thrown into a historical heritage which bestows and limits our possibilities and which we have to accept as a groundless given that cannot be grounded in any transhistorical realities. Furthermore, both anxiety and conscience expose the finitude characterizing Dasein's choice of its possibilities: the fact that we have to choose some finite possibility as our own identity and leave all other possibilities unchosen.

It seems that most commentators would agree that acknowledging the groundlessness and finitude of our possibilities is an important dimension of authentic existence as depicted by Heidegger. Indeed, many would claim that it is the crucial and perhaps only dimension of authenticity.

However, achieving authenticity—as the problem is set up in *Being and Time*—also involves and calls for a second task: the task of disclosing and choosing one's own possibilities. We need to see what kind of challenge we are faced with here. Remember, the task is to independently grasp and choose the possibilities of life—the ideals and values—that are to constitute our personal identity—that are to make up the horizon of purposes for the sake of which we do what we do and that are to grant whatever significance we ascribe to the beings we encounter. Remember also that Heidegger underscores our tendency to inauthentically renounce responsibility for this task and let our understanding and choice of our possibilities be governed by whatever the They happens to recommend. Hence, Heidegger's analysis of authenticity calls for an account of how an independent critical choice of one's own possibilities transpires.

It is hard—indeed, impossible—to deny that it belongs to the kind of life-possibilities that we are to choose that they can be more or less meaningful or futile and more or less morally good or evil. The world we belong to can offer us many different possibilities and ideals: being successful and rich; being loving and open toward others; being sexy; being a devoted Nazi; being a Christian, being a heterosexual macho, being a campaigner for social justice; being a professional athlete, being a good mother or father. It is clear that any explication of what it means to disclose and choose such possibilities must—if it is not to repress what is at stake here—give some account of what understanding and critically judging the existential and moral substance of such possibilities amount to.

However, it is very common that this second task and challenge of authenticity is denied or played down in the secondary literature—above all by commentators who want to give an affirmative interpretation of Heidegger's historicist notion of authenticity.[1] The main reason for this is, I gather, that Heidegger himself does not clearly acknowledge the challenge that his concept of authenticity implies, which also means that his own account remains fundamentally lacking and problematic. In the end, I will argue that the question of the grounds and sources of ethical-existential understanding unsettles and cannot be answered within his historicist framework.

The Lacunae in Heidegger's Analysis

Heidegger's analysis of authenticity calls for an account of how authentic Dasein is to disclose and choose its guiding life-possibilities.

The point of departure is that Dasein first and foremost lives inauthentically such that it uncritically takes over the possibilities offered by the collective They. Clearly, the fact that our group endorses some ideals and values does not rule out or even make it implausible that these ideals are ethically-existentially corrupt or defective. As long as Dasein simply accepts the ideals without question, it lives in prejudice and without anything like an independent understanding of its possibilities. So the question is: How is independent and critical understanding of our life-possibilities possible?

According to Heidegger, the existential analysis cannot have anything to say about the specific criteria or content of Dasein's existentiell choice, since the determinants—the available possibilities and values—of the choice always depend on the historical situation of Dasein. Still, this "existentiell indefiniteness" has its "existential definiteness" (SZ: 298). Heidegger thus thinks it is fully possible to explicate the existential structures that characterize Dasein's choice of itself without entering upon the content of that choice.

Heidegger's conception of the radically historical character of Dasein's life-possibilities frames and sets limits to how he can account for the possibility of independent critical understanding. Since our historical possibilities are conceived of as our ultimate source of ethical-existential significance, there is no possibility of understanding and judging such possibilities on the basis of some supposedly more fundamental ethical-existential realities. Moreover, it is important to note that Heidegger's notion of authenticity is not a variant of the romantic–expressivist concept of authenticity.[2] Becoming authentic is not for Heidegger to express or realize something like one's true or inner self. On the contrary, he stresses that we are fundamentally referred to our historical heritage as our source of possibilities and significance. Prior to our appropriation of such possibilities, there is no true meaningful self to express. To become oneself is for Heidegger to commit oneself to some of the possibilities contained by the heritage and, by so doing, appropriate one's own identity as a person with such and such values, virtues, and life tasks.

Heidegger's historicism implies that he needs to account for the possibility of independent understanding and critique as a possibility within—and not transcending—our understanding of available historical possibilities. That is, the question Heidegger needs to answer is: How can historical possibilities address Dasein—and how can Dasein access and understand them—as in some sense binding and primordial in a way that is not reducible to the fact that they happen to be endorsed by the They?

However, Heidegger does not answer—or even clearly raise—this question in *Being and Time*.[3] According to Heidegger, authenticity involves taking over and committing oneself to possibilities bestowed by one's heritage. He calls the possibility of explicitly taking over one's possibilities "retrieval" or "repetition" (*Wiederholung*) (SZ: 385). However, he does not say a word about how Dasein is to achieve critical distance to and judge the possibilities of the They that it primarily lives in and how it is to access binding or primordial possibilities as a ground for judging the prejudices of the They. In the introduction to the book, Heidegger presented the argument that our immersion in the prejudiced traditional understanding of being as presence-at-hand makes it necessary to undertake a destruction of the tradition in order to access and retrieve a more primordial understanding of being. It seems that the analysis of authenticity would call for precisely this kind of account of what it means to retrieve primordial historical possibilities. However, Heidegger does not provide one. Indeed, as we shall see in the next chapter, Heidegger's programmatic assertions about the destruction as the central methodical way of his investigations remain unfulfilled precisely because he is unable to say what it would mean to access and retrieve primordial historical meanings and possibilities.

In what follows, I will argue that this basic lacuna leads Heidegger's analysis of authenticity into an ambivalent oscillation between collectivism and subjectivism. If I am right, it is no surprise that some of the most influential interpretations take opposing stands on this matter, stressing either one of the poles. Moreover, I want to suggest that it is impossible to answer the question of the ethical-existential meaning of life-possibilities within the strict historicist framework that Heidegger has set up for himself and that the meaning and weight of such possibilities is always rooted in our interpersonal motives and concerns. I will suggest that the basic existential attitude that Heidegger silently presupposes and draws upon is our concern with our social identity, a concern that is ultimately motivated by our simultaneously egoistic and collectivist desire for social affirmation.

Dasein's Self-Choice: Between Collectivism and Subjectivism

So what does Heidegger have to say about how authentic Dasein chooses its own possibilities? What does his analysis tell us about this choice?

As said above, I think Heidegger's analysis of authenticity exhibits an oscillation between collectivism and subjectivism. Let us begin by looking at the collectivist aspect and then examine the subjectivist element of the analysis.

Heidegger underscores that Dasein will never, even if it achieves authenticity, be able to completely emancipate itself from the dominion of the They: "*Authentic being-a-self* is not based on an exceptional state of the subject, a state detached from the They, but *is an existentiell modification of the They as an essential existentiale*" (SZ: 130). But what does it mean that authentic existence is a "modification of the They"? Heidegger's formulation admits, I think, both of a weak and of a strong interpretation. The weak interpretation would be that Dasein can never hope to free itself completely and definitely from the interpretedness of the They. Given Dasein's tendency toward inauthenticity and given the way our common understanding and language is dominated by the They, Dasein's struggle for authenticity will be a constant battle against collective uprootedness and prejudice, a struggle whose possible victories will always be provisional and incomplete. However, the formulation also allows for the strong interpretation that Dasein, in its choice of its own possibilities, is fundamentally referred to the world of the They as the ultimate source of its possibilities.

Many passages speak in favor of the strong interpretation. Heidegger stresses that Dasein's authentic choice of its possibilities does not imply any transformation of the world that Dasein has so far taken over from the They in an uncritical and prejudiced manner: "The 'world' at hand does not become another one 'in its content'; the circle of others is not exchanged for a new one; and yet, the being toward the ready-to-hand which understands and takes care of things, and the solicitous being-with others, are now determined in terms of their ownmost ability-to-be-a-self (*Selbstseinkönnen*)" (SZ: 297–8). However, if Dasein's authentic choice of itself does not bring with it any change of the content of the world dictated by the They—what can this mean, except that the prevailing norms and possibilities of the They are taken over and affirmed as ultimate and authoritative? A few pages later, this interpretation seems to be forcefully confirmed:

> Even resolutions remain dependent upon the They and its world. The understanding of this is one of the things that a resolution discloses, inasmuch as resoluteness is what first gives authentic transparency to Dasein. In resoluteness Dasein is concerned about its ownmost ability-to-be (*Seinkönnen*), which, as thrown, can project itself only upon definite factical possibilities. Resolution does not withdraw itself from "reality," but first uncovers what is factically possible in such a way that it catches hold of it as it is possible as its ownmost ability-to-be in the They. (SZ: 299)

Here, Heidegger not only writes that Dasein's choice of itself remains "dependent upon the They and its world." He even goes so far as to identify the possibilities of the They with Dasein's factical possibilities in general: that authentic Dasein uncovers "what is factically possible" means that it uncovers and embraces it as this is "possible … in the They." All of this seems to support an interpretation according to which Dasein would be fundamentally referred to the possibilities of the They, such that its authentic choice of itself would involve no need and no possibility to critically question the common interpretedness of the They in order to attain a more primordial understanding of the possibilities of a good and meaningful life.

Hubert Dreyfus and Jane Rubin have offered a well-known defense of this kind of interpretation.[4] Their point of departure is that "Heidegger never denies that *all* significance and intelligibility is the product of the one," and that "Dasein *is* a more or less coherent pattern of the comportment required by public 'roles' and activities—an embodiment of the one" (Dreyfus 1991: 156, 159). On this view, becoming authentic does not involve attaining a better or more primordial understanding than the one provided by the They. The authentic individual must "take over the average for-the-sake-of-which one has in one's culture just like everyone else" (157). The difference between inauthentic and authentic Dasein is that whereas the former conceives of the norms of the They as universal and timeless truths, the latter understands that they only amount to "what we in the West happen to do." Hence, the "only deep interpretation is that there is no deep interpretation" (157).

However, even though there is a tendency in Heidegger's argument to absolutize the collective norms of the They as our ultimate source of ethical-existential significance, the interpretation suggested above is problematic, both exegetically and—above all—philosophically. It is exegetically problematic because it misconstrues the sense and stakes of Heidegger's analysis of authenticity. As a result, it does not recognize the challenges and questions that it raises. It does not see that authenticity, for Heidegger, is all about disclosing and choosing our guiding life-possibilities and values—a task that calls for assessment of the ethical-existential substance of such possibilities. Moreover, it does not acknowledge the extent to which Heidegger's analysis of the They works against the notion that authenticity could simply consist in clear-sightedly accepting the opinions of the They as one's source of possibilities and reasons. According to Heidegger's analysis, following the They *means* taking over collectively sanctioned possibilities just because they are collectively sanctioned, without independently trying to understand and assess these possibilities. Philosophically, the interpretation ends up relinquishing the very distinction between collective prejudice and true understanding—however such a distinction is to be understood. However, such an elevation of the They into our ultimate source of ethical-existential normativity, if taken seriously, is tantamount to crude—cynical or naive—collectivism. To accept the interpretedness of the They as one's destiny—how could this be anything else than legitimizing one's thinking and acting by referring to what the prevailing collective concepts and norms happen to prescribe as good and true, even though one knows, in a basic yet more or less inarticulate way, that this is bad faith and self-deception?[5]

When we move from the question of the source of Dasein's possibilities to the question of its choice of its own possibilities, the collectivist tendency in Heidegger's account tends to give way to a tendency toward subjectivism.

Heidegger calls the authentic attitude in which Dasein responsibly discloses and chooses its finite possibilities "resoluteness" (*Entschlossenheit*) (SZ: 297). As soon as Heidegger has posed the question of which possibilities authentic Dasein will choose—"But upon what does Dasein resolve itself in resoluteness? To what should it resolve itself?" (SZ: 298)—he writes:

> *Only* the resolution itself can give the answer. It would be a complete misunderstanding of the phenomenon of resoluteness if one were to believe that it is simply a matter of incorporating and catching hold of possibilities that have been presented and recommended. *The resolution is precisely the disclosive projection and determination of the actual factical possibility.* (SZ: 298)

The same thought is repeated many times: in becoming authentic Dasein does not simply take up the possibilities that have been presented and proposed by the collective They. Instead, resoluteness essentially involves that Dasein independently discloses and determines its own possibilities.

But how?

As far as I can see, Heidegger's only concrete strategy for accounting for Dasein's disclosure and choice of its possibility consists in referring to Dasein's anticipation of its own death as that which grants light and certainty to the choice. Let me quote one of the main passages in which this notion is elaborated:

> The more authentically Dasein resolves itself, that is, understands itself unambiguously in terms of its ownmost eminent possibility in anticipating

death, the more unequivocally and unarbitrarily does it choose and find the possibility of its existence. Only the anticipation of death drives every accidental and "preliminary" (*vorläufige*) possibility out. Only being free *for* death gives Dasein its goal outright and pushes existence into its finitude. The finitude of existence thus seized upon tears one back out of the endless multiplicity of possibilities offering themselves as closest by—those of comfort, shirking and taking things lightly—and brings Dasein into the simplicity of its *fate* (*Schicksal*). (SZ: 384)

Heidegger's basic idea that it is "only the anticipation of death" that allows Dasein to free itself from the accidental and provisional possibilities provided by the They, and makes it possible for it to "choose and find" its own possibilities. Yet how does Dasein's anticipation of its death enable its choice of itself?

One the one hand, Heidegger could be seen as saying that Dasein's anticipation of its death merely opens it up to the *finitude* of its own factical possibilities. However, if anticipation of death only discloses the finitude of Dasein and confronts it with the task of choosing its own finite possibilities—then it does not give any clue at all as to which possibilities Dasein is to choose. On the other hand, Heidegger's formulations also support a stronger reading. He writes that anticipation of death "gives Dasein its goal" and "brings Dasein into the simplicity of its *fate*." In some sense, Heidegger seems to suggest, Dasein's anticipation of its death as its ultimate limiting possibility grants a measure that enables it to disclose and choose its own possibilities. However, Heidegger stops at this suggestion and does not give any hint about how Dasein is supposed to choose in the light of its mortality.

Heidegger's statement that "resoluteness is certain of itself only as a resolution" (SZ: 298) seems to confirm that prior to its resolute choice of its possibilities, Dasein has access to no ground or measure that would allow it to critically assess the historical possibilities available to it. Hence, it seems that Dasein is faced with a radically free and ungroundable choice of the possibilities that are henceforth to guide its life and understanding.

Heidegger's problems with accounting for the grounds of Dasein's authentic choice of its possibilities have led some commentators—for example, Karl Löwith and Ernst Tugendhat—to criticize his conception of authenticity as amounting to a sort of "decisionism."[6] The basic argument is that Heidegger's fundamental failure to describe how Dasein is to assess the truth and normativity of the factical possibilities provided by the They, implies that Dasein's resolute choice—which is in itself "immediate and without perspective" (Tugendhat 1970: 361)—determines the truth of the possibilities it happens to choose. As Tugendhat formulates it: "Resoluteness does not conform to the truth; instead, the 'truth' of the current possibility consists precisely therein, that Dasein resolves upon it from out of its authentic being-itself" (1970: 360). As I see it, the insight of this critical reading is that Heidegger is unable to account for any ground or measure that would allow Dasein to disclose and choose its own possibilities independently of the They. This means that in so far as Dasein's choice of itself is supposed to be independent of the They, the only thing left that could guide its choice is its own blind whims and impulses (if such are even thinkable apart from the They). However, the interpretation of Heidegger as a decisionist or subjectivist overlooks the extent to which Heidegger stresses Dasein's thrownness into its historical heritage as its absolute source of significance. At no point would Heidegger claim that the resolute choice of the individual Dasein could by itself determine the truth or significance of its available historical possibilities.

The oscillation between collectivism and subjectivism is not an oscillation between two viewpoints held by Heidegger. Rather, the tension in question is the unintended effect of the basic lacunae in Heidegger's analysis of authenticity mentioned above. When faced with the task of independently disclosing and choosing its possibilities, Dasein lacks any measure that would allow for anything like a critical and independent understanding of what is good and meaningful. Hence, Dasein's choice of its possibilities must either be totally conformist or totally subjective and arbitrary.[7]

The Basic Egoism of Dasein

So far, I have focused on Heidegger's inability to account for a ground or measure that would allow Dasein to understand and critically judge the ethical-existential substance of the possibilities of the They. However, the question about the ground of ethical-existential understanding and critique points to and implies the question of normative force and motivation: How do matters claim us and concern us as obligating in the first place? In virtue of what motives do we care about them at all? It is only by taking on these questions that we can hope to become clear about and assess the ethical-existential meaning and substance of different claims and motives.

In *Being and Time* Heidegger does not pose the question of how Dasein's life-possibilities and ideals can address it as binding or significant. Instead he is content with arguing that Dasein, due to the historical structure of phenomenal experience, is referred to the possibilities bestowed by its historical heritage as an absolute givenness that it has to accept. However, this kind of argument tells us nothing about the possible normative force exerted by such possibilities or about our motives for caring about them. A few years later, Heidegger will pose the question regarding the bindingness of historical being as a guiding question for his later thinking. However, even then, he will not venture into the kind of moral psychological investigations of our interpersonal relations and motives that would be needed in order to truly clarify this question.

Here, I will make an attempt to reconstruct, in a very sketchy and indicatory manner, the ethical-existential motives and attitude that silently inform and frame Heidegger's conception of the structure of our experience of meaningful phenomena and his account of authenticity. My suggestion is that Dasein, as depicted by Heidegger, is basically driven by motives that are at once egoistic and collectivist: by the urge to be affirmed by the group to which it belongs. In the epilogue I will offer a more detailed account of what our urge for social affirmation amounts to, of how it tends to get invested into our identity, and how it differs from the possibility of loving or caring for the other as such.

Let us begin by noting and underscoring that Heidegger's analysis of the basic historical structure of phenomenal experience rules out that any beings—for instance, human beings—may show up and address us as significant in themselves. The core claim of Heidegger's analysis is that we can only experience beings as significant phenomena on the basis of our understanding of the historical life-possibilities that we have chosen as essential to our identity. As is well-known, the critique suggested here—that Heidegger denies the primacy of our ethical relation to the other and makes the experience of the other dependent on our understanding of being—was originally developed by Emmanuel Levinas. I will return to this issue and to Levinas's criticism in the epilogue.

To get a sense of how Heidegger's denial of the possibility of caring for others as such is played out and of what motives actually drive Dasein, let us take a look at Heidegger's analysis of Dasein as "being-with" others.

Heidegger's treatment of Dasein's being-with others no doubt belongs to the weakest parts of the book. Apart from Heidegger's sharp reflections on Dasein's tendency to succumb to the collective pressure of the They, the analyses conducted here remain philosophically undeveloped, having the character of a halfhearted supplement to the main description of Dasein as engaged in coping with tools in the world. The aim of the chapter is to argue that Dasein is from the outset open toward and has an understanding of other human beings, beings who do not show up as present-at-hand or ready-to-hand entities, but, precisely, as other human beings who also have the character of Dasein. In this context, Heidegger states that Dasein as "being-with" is "essentially for the sake of others": "This ... disclosedness of the others thus also constitutes significance, that is, worldliness. As this worldliness, disclosedness is anchored in the existential for-the-sake-of-which" (SZ: 123). That is to say, the instrumental networks of significance making up the world are not only anchored in Dasein's own life-possibilities but also in others and their life-possibilities. However, does this formal definition of Dasein as being for the sake of others really imply that Heidegger would introduce the possibility of a care about the other human being for her own sake as a primary source of ethical-existential normativity and significance? As we shall see, this is hardly the case.

Heidegger begins his analysis by claiming that Dasein, in its everyday coping with the tools and tasks of its world, first and foremost encounters others "from out of the *world*" (SZ: 119): "In what we concern ourselves with in the surrounding world, the others are encountered as what they are; they *are* what they do" (SZ: 126). In coping with different tools, these tools by themselves refer to other Daseins as their users, owners, producers, and so on. Also, when we face or address others directly, they chiefly show up in terms of what they do and work with, that is, in terms of their social roles within the world: "we meet them 'at work,' that is, primarily in their being-in-the-world" (SZ: 120). However, in so far as we understand and relate to others primarily in terms of their social roles and tasks, we do not care about them as individual persons; rather, the others get whatever import we ascribe to them from their roles within our world and its horizon of life-possibilities.

However, according to Heidegger, the others do not merely concern us instrumentally, on account of their roles and functions in our coping with our world.

To begin with, Heidegger describes inauthentic Dasein as being motivated by the desire to comply with the collective pressure of the They. In living inauthentically, we are concerned about what our collective group values and praises, and we are driven by the urge to live up to and follow the collectively endorsed values and norms. Heidegger does not drill deeper into our motives for wanting to comply with the They. However, it seems that the kind of motive he has in mind—the motive that in fact generally underlies our sensitivity to social pressure—is our urge for social affirmation. By complying with the preferences of the They, we hope to gain acceptance and affirmation by our community. Conversely, by failing to do so, we fear drawing upon ourselves the contempt and hostility of our group. Here, we need to see that our urge for affirmation is essentially egoistic and self-concerned and does not amount to a care about others as such. What I care about when I care about what the others as a collective group think about me is myself—how I appear in the eyes of the others and how my prospects for achieving affirmation are enhanced or weakened or destroyed by how the others judge me.

In short, the inauthentic individual depicted by Heidegger chooses possibilities and ideals endorsed by the They for the sake of attaining collective affirmation– and it does this out of egoistic self-concern.

Although Heidegger mainly focuses on Dasein's inauthentic everyday being-with others, he also takes up the possibility of a positive "solicitude" (*Fürsorge*) toward others. There are, he claims, two "extreme possibilities" of solicitude (SZ: 122). On the one hand, we have the solicitude which "*leaps in*" for the other and "takes away" his "care" by performing the tasks that originally belong to her: "This kind of solicitude takes over for the other that which is to be taken care of. ... In such solicitude the other can become someone who is dependent and dominated, even if this domination is a tacit one and remains hidden from him" (SZ: 122). On the other hand, we have the possibility of a solicitude that does not "leap in" for the other, but which "*leaps ahead* of him ... not in order to take his 'care' away from him but rather to authentically give it back to him as such" (SZ: 122): "This kind of solicitude (*Fürsorge*) pertains essentially to authentic care—that is, to the existence of the other, not to a *What* with which he is concerned; it helps the other to become transparent to himself *in* his care and *free* for it" (SZ: 122).

As concerns the first kind of solicitude "which leaps in and dominates" (SZ: 122) the very fact that Heidegger describes the possibility of helping the other with her concrete tasks and burdens as inherently dominating, that is, as constituting a relation of power, shows that he has ruled out the possibility of a loving care about the other which is free of power motives and does not necessarily effect relations of domination and subordination. However, neither does Heidegger's depiction of the second kind of care "which leaps forth and liberates" (SZ: 122) introduce a care for the other for her own sake as a primary and irreducible source of motivation. To be sure, the aim of this care is not to dominate the other but to help her become authentic. However, the question is: Why—on account of what motives and concerns—would Dasein want to help the other become authentic?

The impossibility of answering this question within the framework of *Being and Time* indicates that we have reached a basic limit and lack of this framework. The whole point of authentic care is to help the other become authentic: to independently understand and choose her own finite historical possibilities as that which first opens up the possibility of experiencing beings as significant. Hence, the very nature and centrality of the challenge of authenticity presuppose that the other is not significant as such but gets whatever significance she has from the historical possibilities and ideals at our disposal. Since the challenge of authenticity is a universal challenge for Dasein that is not dependent on the particular life-possibilities we are committed to, it is out of the question to claim that our will to help the others become authentic is spurred by our particular historical possibilities. However, Heidegger has also ruled out the possibility of referring to something like our love for or care about the other as such. What is more, if he were to introduce care about the other as a motive for helping the other become authentic, this would undermine his entire conception of authenticity as the central existential challenge of existence.

Ultimately, Heidegger's repression of the possibility of love for the other as such shows itself in the lack of radical effects that the recognition of this possibility would necessarily have had on his philosophical project. Had he recognized this possibility for what it is, this would have unsettled both this basic thesis that Dasein's historical life-possibilities determine its experience of phenomenal significance and his idea that the basic challenge of authentic existence lies in choosing one's own possibilities.

Heidegger's denial of the possibility of loving and caring for others for their own sake suggests that Dasein is, at bottom, an egoistic or self-concerned creature. Yet how should this be understood?

Heidegger defines Dasein's being as "care" (*Sorge*). In so doing he states that the expression "care for oneself" (*Selbstsorge*) is strictly speaking a "tautology" (SZ: 193), given that Dasein's care for any being is grounded in its care for its life-possibilities. The definition is not an expression of straightforward egoism. Dasein may very well care about other persons and about tasks that do not directly serve its own interests. However, according to Heidegger, all such care about particular beings and projects is grounded in and motivated by Dasein's care about the life-possibilities and ideals of its identity.

So the decisive question is: How can Dasein's life-possibilities and ideals concern it as in some sense normative or important?

Later, in the epilogue, I will argue that our ultimate source of genuine moral normativity lies in our ethical relationship to other persons: in the ethical claim of the other on me and on the love and care that she calls for. There I will also argue that genuine moral understanding and critique of the ethical-existential substance of different ideals and values consists in seeing how they relate to our primary care for others: Do they express or serve what our care gives us to understand or do they distort and impede it?

Heidegger, however, rules out the possibility of loving and caring for others as such. What is it, then, that accounts for the possible normative force and appeal that different life-possibilities and ideals can exert on Dasein? My suggestion is that the central motive that drives Dasein—not just inauthentic Dasein but also authentic Dasein—is the self-concerned desire for social affirmation.

As regards the question of what binds Dasein to its life-possibilities, the only motive mentioned and acknowledged in *Being and Time* is inauthentic Dasein's desire to comply with the collective They. However, could there not be other motives in play? Well, what makes it plausible to suggest that the desire for social affirmation is indeed the basic motive of Dasein is that aside from our direct care about other beings—in particular, human beings—our urge for affirmation is in fact the central and most powerful motive that fuels our concern about our life-possibilities and our identity. Although I will not try to do this here, I think it would be possible to show in quite some detail that most—if not all—of Heidegger's theses that touch upon the question of what gives significance and weight to our lives bear witness to the critical presence of this motive. Above all: his insistence that we can only experience our lives as meaningful if we commit ourselves to and merge with our social roles and identities; moreover, his later vision that it is only by establishing, on the basis of an understanding of the groundless and finite *Ereignis* of being, a strong and cohesive collective world where everyone has a clear role to play—a world modelled on premodern honor-societies—that beings can start to engage us as important again.

As I will argue in the epilogue, our desire for social affirmation is a very basic and powerful motive: we want to be affirmed and accepted by our group and we dread the prospect of incurring its hostility and contempt. This motive goes deep in us and tends to fuel both our self-perception and our identity. We have a basic capacity to see and judge ourselves from the point of view of this desire: we have a sense or how we appear in the eyes of others and how it stands with our ability to achieve affirmation and liking. Hence, this kind of self-perception is essentially accompanied by strong emotions. Whereas seeing ourselves as likeable and affirmable incurs feelings of pride and self-confidence, seeing ourselves as unlikeable and despicable makes us feel embarrassment and shame. Moreover, our urge for affirmation is always a powerful motive in our formation of our identity. In so far as this urge drives our identity formation, this means that in developing our identity—and appropriating the ideals and values that constitute who we ideally are—what we develop is an image of ourselves as a person successfully enacting ideals and values that make us respectable and affirmable. Since our identity here functions as the bearer of our trust in our own capacity to achieve affirmation we feel very strongly that we have to live up it: if we manage to do this we feel confidence in our ability to achieve affirmation; if we fail to do so we feel that our capacity to gain social affirmation and respect has been damaged or destroyed.

What we need to see here is that to the extent that our concern about our life-possibilities and values is fueled by our urge for social affirmation we are driven by a motive that is at once egoistic and collectivist. When ideals and values address us as normative in virtue of our desire for affirmation they address as the standards that determine how our group judges us and how we, having internalized these standards, see and assess our own affirmability and respectability. In this, the ideals and values merely address us as means for realizing our egoistic-collectivist desire for affirmation. What we care about here is in the end our own capacity to achieve affirmation. In being concerned about what others think about us we do not care about them as persons; the others merely figure as the audience that judges us and what we care about is how *we* appear in their eyes.

To get a sense of the ethical-existential difference between love for others and concern about affirmation, consider the following example. A colleague of mine is being bullied by another colleague and I feel moved to intervene. Why do I feel this urge to help? Here are two possibilities: On the one hand, I may be motivated by desire for affirmation, which I have invested in my identity as a good and courageous person who intervenes in situations like this. On the other hand, I might want to act simply because I am open to the plight of my colleague and care about her. Although both motives might be present in me at the same time and interact in various ways they are essentially different from each other. In the first case, what I care about—given that no love is involved—is myself: about my ability to realize my identity and uphold my trust in my affirmability. In case I would fail to act, I would feel ashamed over the unaffirmable and unlikeable person I have become. In the second case, what I care about is the other person as such. Here, in case I would fail to act I would not feel shame but rather sorrow and remorse since I would be focused not on myself and my performance but on the other and on my relation to her.

In short, my suggestion is that Heidegger, in describing Dasein as fundamentally guided by the life-possibilities and ideals of its identity—possibilities that it has received from the collective They—and denying the possibility of care about others, presupposes the desire for social affirmation as the central motive that attaches us to our ideals and values. In so doing, he portrays Dasein as a fundamentally egoistic creature.

To sum up, then: Heidegger's analysis of authenticity in *Being and Time* is haunted by severe problems that concern both the criteria and the ethical-existential motives informing Dasein's understanding and choice of its possibilities. First, we diagnosed Heidegger's inability to describe any ground or measure that would allow Dasein to understand and critically assess the ethical-existential substance of the possibilities endorsed by the collective They. Second, we saw that Heidegger, by denying the possibility of direct care about the other as such, fails to account for any source of ethical-existential normativity and motivation beyond our urge for social affirmation. The first failure has its roots in the second failure. If what gives to Dasein's life-possibilities whatever normative force they have is our desire for collective affirmation, then the preferences of the They constitute our ultimate ground and source of ethical-existential understanding. In his later thinking, Heidegger will try to get out of this impasse by attempting to answer the question that *Being and Time* gave rise to and left hanging: How can our historical world—with its meanings and norms—address us as binding beyond the prejudices of the They? However, given that he will not rehabilitate our relation to the other person as such as our source of ethical-existential significance, it will be difficult, in fact impossible, for him to find a way out of the egoistic-collectivist loop.

8

HEIDEGGER'S METHOD IN *BEING AND TIME*

The Question of Method—the Question of Phenomenology

The question of Heidegger's method in *Being and Time* is at bottom the question of the fate of phenomenology during this central period of his thinking. It is a complex question involving many different aspects: How should we understand Heidegger's explicit appropriation of phenomenology as the method of *Being and Time*? What about his reinterpretation of phenomenology as historical interpretation and destruction? Does his program for a historical thinking imply a total break with Husserl's method of intuitive reflection and description? What is the relation between Heidegger's methodological self-understanding and the concrete manner in which he pursues his investigations?

Since the beginning of Heidegger research, the question of the method of *Being and Time* has constituted the central stage where the discussion about Heidegger's relation to phenomenology has been played out. Especially since the 1990s, the discussion has been characterized by the tension between the transcendental phenomenological reading and the hermeneutic-deconstructive reading. Let me briefly present two lucid and careful studies representing each of the opposing readings: Søren Overgaard's 2004 book *Husserl and Heidegger on Being in the World* and Charles Guignon's book *Heidegger and the Problem of Knowledge* from 1984.

Overgaard's basic thesis is that "Heidegger (at least the Heidegger of *SZ*) is a transcendental phenomenologist" (2004: 108). According to Overgaard, Heidegger's question of being involves two parts: first, the question concerning the being—the different modes of being as well as the unitary sense of being—of all beings; second, the question concerning the nature of our understanding of being. To investigate these questions, Overgaard claims, Heidegger employs Husserl's phenomenological method. As concerns the first question, Heidegger essentially makes use of Husserl's *epoché* to gain access to the modes of being. It is only by "bracketing" or "locking up" (43) our natural understanding of beings as present-at-hand objects that it becomes possible to thematize how beings manifest themselves in our experience. And, to intuitively explicate the modes of manifestation of different beings is for Heidegger precisely to explicate their "modes of being" (82). As concerns the second question, Heidegger employs the phenomenological *reduction* to investigate the conditions for understanding being.

According to Overgaard, the reduction—as used by Husserl and Heidegger—does not take the form of direct reflection on the experiences in which beings are given but rather proceeds through indirect regressive argumentation. Taking the bracketed object as our "transcendental guiding clue" we ask "*what ... subjectivity must, so to speak, 'look like' in order to be the experiencing subjectivity of such an object*" (52). Heidegger thus takes his point of departure in an intuitive explication of the modes of being of entities, and, taking these as transcendental guidelines, carries out a regressive investigation of the structures of Dasein that make understanding of being possible.

Against this background it is not surprising that Overgaard attributes only a secondary role to Heidegger's program of destruction. Although it is an important task to dismantle our traditional understanding of being and appropriate the insights of the tradition, Overgaard claims that the destruction "is *not* an *indispensable* methodological component in any investigation of being, at least the way the Heidegger of *Sein und Zeit* understood such an investigation." The reason for this, he claims, is that the destruction presupposes a "phenomenological basic experience" (98) of the being of beings, which is independent of the destruction, and which allows us to identify the tradition as a distortive understanding of being in the first place.

In contrast to Overgaard, Guignon advances a hermeneutic-deconstructive interpretation—more hermeneutic than deconstructive, in fact—of Heidegger's method in *Being and Time*. According to Guignon, Heidegger's analysis of Dasein as being-in-the-world implies a radical break with the traditional picture of the human being as an isolated contemplative subject faced with the task of representing reality. This break is also a break with what Guignon describes as Husserl's Cartesian effort to ground our knowledge of the world in the "apodictic evidence found in transcendental subjectivity" (1983: 43). In contrast to the tradition, Heidegger describes Dasein as always already acting with practical competence in "a world of cultural and historical meanings which make up the horizon in which anything is intelligible, but which cannot itself be grounded by something beyond that horizon" (60). Given that all understanding is determined by the historical contexts we occupy, Heidegger gives up the Husserlian idea of a direct "intuition of meanings and essences presented to consciousness" (67): "Our understanding is always discursive, never intuitive" (221).

Heidegger's method in *Being and Time* is said to involve four stages: (1) a *descriptive* stage in which Dasein's everyday factical understanding of being is exhibited; (2) a *hermeneutic* stage in which this factical understanding, which is primarily characterized by traditional prejudices, is interpreted through a transcendental analysis that uncovers the normally hidden background of practical competence and historical understanding that conditions our experience of beings; (3) a *dialectical* stage in which we are led back to retrieve the ultimate historical origins and sources of our understanding of being which constitute the bedrock of all interpretation; (4) a critical *diagnosis* of our seemingly self-evident traditional understanding, which exposes its historical roots and thereby helps to dissolve the pseudo-problems that arise from it (68).

According to Guignon, the task of destructing the history of ontology takes on a primary role in executing the project of fundamental ontology. Since Heidegger's investigation is "embedded in the history of ontology and dependent on it for its findings, it must be seen as an unfolding of possibilities already implicit in the tradition" (225). The destruction has both a diagnostic and a dialectical function: on the one hand, it diagnoses the prejudices of the tradition by tracing their roots in Greek ontology; on the other hand, it retrieves the most primordial possibilities harbored by our heritage, which the tradition has forgotten and covered up (225). Whereas the transcendental analysis of the temporal structure of Dasein undertaken in part one of *Being and Time* provides the "guideline" for destructing the history of ontology, the aim of the destruction—to be undertaken in part two—is to "authenticate the finding of the transcendental stage by showing their historical origins." Hence, Guignon concludes: "far from being a historical appendix ... the destruction contains the concrete ontological research that makes up fundamental ontology" (223).[1]

What is the truth of these divergent interpretations? In what follows, I will argue that the hermeneutic-deconstructive reading on the whole accords with Heidegger's methodological self-understanding in *Being and Time*. However, due to Heidegger's problems with accounting for the possibility of historical retrieval, he is actually unable to execute his program for a radically historical thinking proceeding by way of hermeneutic explication and destruction. Instead, I suggest that the concrete investigations of *Being and Time* basically take the form of intuition-based phenomenological reflections along Husserlian lines.

Heidegger's Methodological Self-Understanding

In the introduction to *Being and Time* Heidegger states that the method of the book is phenomenological. He traces the meaning of the expression "phenomenology" back to its Greek roots. Whereas *phainomenon* means "that which shows itself, the self-showing, the manifest" (SZ: 28), *logos* signifies a discourse the function of which is to *apophainesthai*, to "let be seen" or "make manifest" (SZ: 32) what the discourse it about. Hence, he presents the following formal definition of phenomenology: "Thus phenomenology means *apophainesthai ta phainomena*— to let that which shows itself be seen from itself in the very way in which it shows itself from itself" (SZ: 34).

The definition expresses the basic phenomenological principle that in order to understand the meanings of things we need to take as our absolute starting point our first-person experience of things as meaningful phenomena. There is no other access to meaning than our experience of beings as significant and mattering to us in different ways: as useful, demanding, frightening, and so on. To do phenomenology means to do nothing else than describe and explicate our experiences of different phenomena.

However, how should we more precisely understand Heidegger's proclamation that he is a phenomenologist? What is the matter of phenomenology and how does it get access to its matter? Heidegger begins to deformalize his formal concept of phenomenology by specifying what constitutes the specific phenomena of phenomenology:

> What is it that by its very essence is *necessarily* the theme when we exhibit something *explicitly*? Obviously, it is something that initially and for the most part does *not* show itself, something that is *concealed* in contrast to what initially and for the most part does show itself. But, at the same time, it is something that essentially belongs to what initially and for the most part shows itself, indeed in such a way that it constitutes its sense and ground. Yet that which remains *concealed* in an exceptional sense, or which falls back and gets *covered up* again, or which shows itself only *"in disguise,"* is not this or that being, but rather … the *being* of beings. (SZ: 35)

In short, the task of Heidegger's phenomenology is to exhibit being—the different modes of being as well as the sense of being as such—as the hidden ground of beings. Since our experience of beings is always already guided by our understanding of being, and since this understanding is first and foremost unthematic and prejudiced, the task of explicating being becomes an essential prerequisite for attaining a transparent understanding of ourselves and other beings. This implies an intimate relationship between phenomenology and ontology: whereas "phenomenology" is "the science of the being of beings—ontology" (SZ: 37), "*ontology is possible only as phenomenology*" (SZ: 35).

So how do we get access to the sense of being, that is, to the basic structures of Dasein? We already know that Heidegger's appropriation of the term "phenomenology" in the early 1920s goes hand in hand with a critical dismissal of Husserl's belief in direct intuitive givenness, and with the development of a hermeneutic phenomenology which understands itself as historical in a radical sense. Indeed, when Heidegger formally defines his method as phenomenological this does not imply any recourse to the idea of direct seeing as he is careful to point out: "*The* only peculiarity of seeing which we claim for the existential significance of sight is the fact that it lets beings accessible to it be encountered unconcealedly in themselves" (SZ: 147).

In the introduction to *Being and Time* Heidegger makes it clear that the phenomenology he has in mind is a "hermeneutics," which is to say that it transpires by way of "interpretation": "the methodological sense of phenomenological description is *interpretation*" (SZ: 37). As we have seen, "interpretation" for Heidegger signifies the thematic explication of what we already "understand." In elaborating this notion, he strongly emphasizes that all intuitive seeing is grounded in understanding: "By showing how all sight is primarily based on understanding … we have deprived pure intuition of its priority … 'Intuition' and 'thinking' are both already remote derivatives of understanding. Even the phenomenological 'intuition of essences' is based on existential understanding" (SZ: 147). The argument for the priority of understanding over direct intuition is based on Heidegger's conception of the hierarchical structure of phenomena, the core of which is this: to be able to intuitively experience a being as a meaningful phenomenon we already need to have an understanding of the life-possibilities and networks of significance in terms of which it can show up as this or that; moreover, our understanding of beings is always already guided by our understanding of being. Given that our understanding of being guides our experience of beings and cannot itself be intuitively grounded, Heidegger concludes that we can only explicate being through an interpretation of the factical historical preunderstanding of being in which we live. Fundamentally, then, the phenomenological ontology of *Being and Time* has the character of "'historical' interpretation" (SZ: 39).

However, according to Heidegger, our factical understanding of being is not only unthematic and hidden; it is also pervaded by the prejudices and concealments of the tradition which we primarily tend to take over in a blind and unquestioning manner. The tradition, he writes, "takes what has come down to us and delivers it over to self-evidence; it blocks our access to those primordial 'sources' from which the traditional categories and concepts were in part genuinely drawn" (SZ: 21). The upshot of this tendency to take over the tradition as self-evident without questioning its sources is that the entire tradition of philosophy has been dominated by the original Aristotelian understanding of being as presence-at-hand. Hence, Heidegger argues that to liberate ourselves from the tradition and access a more primordial understanding of being, we need—since we cannot rely on any direct seeing of the matters—to carry out a destruction of the history of ontology:

> If the question of being is to have its own history made transparent, then this hardened tradition must be loosened up, and the concealments which it has brought about must be removed. We understand this task as one in which by taking *the question of being as our guiding clue*, we are to *destruct* the traditional content of ancient ontology until we arrive at those primordial experiences in which the first, and subsequently guiding, determinations of being were gained. (SZ: 22)

In short, the aim of the destruction is to trace our factical traditional understanding of being back through the history of ontology to its historical sources or origins at the Greek beginning of Western philosophy. The destruction has a twofold task. First, the task is to dismantle our traditional conception of being as presence-at-hand until we arrive at its origin in Aristotle's thinking. In so doing, we become able to grasp the primordial experiences at the basis of this conception and, hence, achieve a concrete understanding of it in its limited validity. Second, by delimiting the traditional understanding of being it becomes possible to "bring ourselves into full possession of our ownmost possibilities of inquiry" (SZ: 21). That is to say, the ultimate task of the destruction consists in an "appropriation" (*Aneignung*) (SZ: 21) or "retrieval" (*Wiederholung*) (SZ: 26) of the most primordial possibilities of understanding harbored by the Greek beginning of our heritage.

We can now see that Guignon's reading, emphasizing the hermeneutic and destructive character of Heidegger's method, captures the gist of Heidegger's methodological self-understanding in *Being and Time*. Still, even though Guignon stresses the importance of the destruction it seems to me that he does not go far enough. Guignon argues that whereas the interpretation of our factual understanding of being uncovers—through a kind of transcendental argumentation—the primordial understanding of being as readiness-to-hand underlying the traditional conception of being as presence-at-hand, the destruction "authenticates the findings of the transcendental stage" by showing that they indeed constitute the most primordial understanding of being contained by the tradition (1983: 231). However, it seems that Guignon's idea that we could achieve a primordial understanding of being by interpreting and transcendentally analyzing our contemporary factual understanding of being does not find support in the text. Given that our factual understanding is laden with prejudice and at most contains traces of the historical sources that give it its sense, I think it is clear that Heidegger believes the function of the destruction is not only to authenticate the interpretation but to open up our basic access to the primordial historical sources of understanding.

According to Heidegger's original plan, the destruction of the history of ontology was to be undertaken in the second division of *Being and Time*. It was to take its "guideline" from the preliminary analysis of the temporal structure of Dasein and the temporality of being in division one and proceed backwards through the main stages of the history of ontology: Kant, Descartes, and Aristotle. Since the destruction constitutes our basic way of access to a primordial understanding of the sense of being, Heidegger insists that "the question of being achieves its true concreteness only when we carry out the destruction of the ontological tradition" (SZ: 26). This also means that in so far as the existential analytic of Dasein carried out in division one is able to articulate the primordial structure of Dasein and being it is because it already draws on and anticipates the results of the destruction as that which makes it possible.

Phenomenology in Practice

Despite Heidegger's presentation of his method as a radically hermeneutic-destructive mode of thinking, this methodological program does not really describe the concrete method of *Being and Time*. The reason for this is that Heidegger's program for a hermeneutic-destructive thinking is still beset with principal problems that hinder him from implementing it. As a result, he is led to have recourse to the method of intuition-based phenomenological description in his concrete positive investigations.

As we have seen, Heidegger thinks that since our factual understanding of being guides our comprehension of beings, it cannot be true or false depending on how it corresponds to beings; nor can its truth be measured through direct intuition of beings. Nevertheless, Heidegger's description of our traditional understanding of being as prejudiced and distortive, and his conception of the task of philosophy as that of attaining a more primordial understanding of being, presupposes that he is able to distinguish between prejudiced and primordial historical understanding. The crucial question is: How can historical being give itself as in some sense primordial and basic—not just amounting to a new set of prejudices—and how do we access and understand it as such? How does the primordiality of a primordial understanding show itself? Does—as the word "primordial," holding both a historical and a logical aspect suggests, suggests—the primordial understanding show itself as the historical origin that in some sense constitutes the transcendental-dialectical ground or horizon which determines the rest of the tradition?

However, Heidegger does not address or answer this question in *Being and Time*. Considering his methodological program, answering the question would be tantamount to accounting for the final stage of the destruction, that is, for what it means to "appropriate" or "repeat" the primordial being-senses harbored by our historical heritage. However, having outlined his hermeneutic-destructive program in the introduction, Heidegger never returns to the issue of what it could mean to achieve a primordial interpretation of the sense of being through appropriating or repeating primordial being-senses.

Heidegger's inability to account for the givenness of primordial historical being gives rise to a deep ambivalence between his methodological program and his concrete method in *Being and Time*. The lacuna depicted above implies that Heidegger lacks a clear vision of what it would mean to implement his hermeneutic-destructive program as an appropriation of the primordial being-senses harbored by our heritage. This, in turn, means that in order to be able to lay claim to a primordial explication of the being of Dasein and the sense of being, which transcends and delimits the traditional prejudiced conception of being as presence-at-hand, Heidegger in his concrete investigations has recourse to a method of intuitive phenomenological reflection of the sort that his analysis of the historical structure of phenomena has supposedly ruled out.

When we take a closer look at Heidegger's actual approach in *Being and Time* we see that the relationship between his hermeneutic-destructive program and his concrete analyses is much looser than he wants to believe. It is true, to be sure, that his investigations are characterized by a sharpened critical attentiveness to the traditional preunderstandings and concepts which tend to guide our questioning in a prejudiced way, and by an ambition to dismantle these preconceptions in order to access the primordial experiences from which they issue. However, it belongs to Heidegger's continuous hermeneutic-destructive reflection that it constantly converts into the effort to achieve a positive understanding of the phenomena through intuitive phenomenological reflection on the structures of our experience. Heidegger's analysis of how we primarily encounter beings as ready-to-hand tools is typical. It begins by disclosing our traditional conception of beings as present-at-hand objects. Then follows a phenomenological description of how we primarily encounter beings as ready-to-hand tools against the backdrop of the significance-relations of the world. This also allows Heidegger to dismantle and delimit the traditional conception by showing that the understanding of being as presence-at-hand is expressive of a theoretical attitude in which we observe beings as context-independent objectivities. The same methodological scheme manifests itself in all of his central analyses, for example, of worldliness, understanding, anxiety, conscience, temporality, and historicity.

It is clear, I think, that the concrete positive analyses doing the central philosophical work in *Being and Time* essentially transpire as intuition-based phenomenological descriptions of the basic sense structures of Dasein's factical experiences. These analyses do not have the form of interpretations that would merely explicate our implicit historical preunderstanding. Instead, what Heidegger continuously tries to do is to describe—through direct intuitive reflection and independently of our more or less prejudiced historical preunderstanding—the basic structural elements that constitute the meaning of central human experiences such as practical coping, anxiety, and conscience. The validity and clarificatory force of such phenomenological descriptions do not rest on their relation—for instance, historical-logical primordiality—to the other historical understandings of our tradition but lie solely in their ability to exhibit and illuminate what is there and intuitively discernible for us as the basic structures of our experiences.[2]

Heidegger's method of direct phenomenological description also implies that the structures described in *Being and Time* essentially have the status of universal necessary structures characterizing the human being as such. As Heidegger himself writes: "being-in-the-world is an *a priori* necessary constitution (*Verfassung*) of Dasein" (SZ: 53). Since the positive analyses of the existential analytic do not have the character of explications of our historical preunderstanding, their validity and scope are not relative to any historically and culturally specific preunderstanding. Roughly speaking, the analyses focus on two kinds of experience: first, experiences—such as anxiety, fear, and conscience—that are common to all human beings although their cultural role and interpretedness may vary; second, experiences—such as hammering, opening a door, hearing a car—that belong to a specific historical-cultural context. However, in both cases the aim of Heidegger's phenomenological descriptions is to explicate necessary universal structures that are constitutive of general kinds of experience shared by all human beings. Although the contents of our experiences and the cultural worlds we live in vary historically, Heidegger's approach presupposes that it is possible to describe basic structures that are constitutive of all such historically situated experiences: readiness-to-hand, being-in-the-world, care, mortality, temporality, and historicity.

We can now see that on the whole the transcendental phenomenological reading defended by Overgaard is a convincing interpretation of the concrete methodological approach employed by Heidegger in *Being and Time*. In actual practice, Heidegger's positive investigations unfold as intuitive-reflective descriptions of the basic structures of Dasein's experience of phenomena. However, although Heidegger in this sense remains a Husserlian phenomenologist, he also critically develops Husserl's method in at least three respects. I already explicated these developments in my treatment of Heidegger's early Freiburg lectures. However, since all three of them are to some extent articulated anew in *Being and Time* a brief repetition is in order.

First off, Heidegger stresses that the phenomenological explication is dependent on our personal ability to openly encounter and acknowledge what we experience: "The ontological 'truth' of the existential analysis is developed on the basis of the primordial existentiell truth" (SZ: 316). Indeed, it is this idea that motivates the decisive methodological role of the analysis of authenticity in *Being and Time*. According to Heidegger, Dasein is essentially confronted with the challenge of responsibly acknowledging the groundlessness and finitude of its historical possibilities. To be able to answer authentically to this challenge is a prerequisite for being able to explicate phenomenologically the structure and sense of what is revealed in the experiences of anxiety and conscience, namely the temporality and historicity of existence. By contrast, failing to acknowledge our predicament means to block our phenomenological access to it. Indeed, it means that we will be in urgent need of concepts that cover up and explain away what we do not want to see. Although I think Heidegger's depiction of the problem of authenticity as our greatest ethical-existential challenge is deeply problematic, his insistence that philosophical problems are always also ethical-existential problems is vital. Formally, the lesson is this: In so far as we are concerned with understanding matters that are important to us, that engage our desire and will and that we might be tempted to interpret in distortive and self-confirming ways, our philosophical ability to explicate them will be dependent on our ethical-existential ability to face and acknowledge them.

Second, Heidegger's notion of the need for a destruction of the philosophical tradition is an expression of his sharpened sensitivity to how our traditional concepts tend to determine our thinking and seeing in a prejudiced manner. In so far as we let some received concepts guide us merely on account of their normality and collective acceptedness, they function as prejudices that steer the way we think without our independently having inquired about their truth. According to Heidegger, paying critical attention to the preconceptions that press themselves on us from the outset of every inquiry is a condition for any independent and primordial explication of the matters themselves. Moreover, he claims that to free ourselves from the prejudices of the tradition we have to undertake a dismantling return to their historical origins in Greek philosophy. However, as argued above, the destructive program does not describe Heidegger's concrete method in *Being and Time*. In these years, the destruction mainly figures as a dependent aspect of Heidegger's method of intuitive phenomenological reflection. Indeed, what Heidegger's concrete destructive interpretations demonstrate is the potential of phenomenology to open up the concrete experiential ground and meaning of historical concepts and texts. What gives to Heidegger's interpretations their force and vitality is his prime effort to exhibit phenomenologically the concrete human experiences and situations that the historical concepts articulate in a more or less generalizing and unclear manner. Here, getting a concrete phenomenological understanding of what the concepts are about and determining their limited validity is one and the same thing. In addition to stressing the need for critically attending to our received prejudices, Heidegger thus also points to how phenomenology can be used to open up history and to how the history of philosophy can function as an important resource for widening our phenomenological imagination.

Finally, Heidegger stresses that the phenomenological reflection should not be understood as a reflective turn from the experienced object to the acts of the experiencing subject. Instead, the different structural aspects of Dasein's experience uncovered through reflection— "world," "being-in," and the "who"— should be seen as "equiprimordial" (*Gleichursprünglich*) (SZ: 131) elements that form a dynamic unity. To clarify the critical sense of this move, let me explain why I find Overgaard's conception of the phenomenological reduction as a form of regressive argumentation—*not* as a direct reflection on our experiences— problematic. If, as Overgaard claims, the experienced world—the *noema*—really is the sole phenomenal content of our experience, then it is hard to explain how we can explicate the noetic structures of subjectivity at all. If intuitive reflection on these structures is impossible, must not our regressive construction of the subject remain speculative to a high degree?[3] It seems that Overgaard's regressive account is motivated by his fear that conceiving of the reduction in terms of intuitive reflection would imply reducing the noematic meanings to the noetic acts of the subject. And yet, this is only a problem if we—as Husserl has a tendency to do—think of the reduction as a turn from the intended objects to the acts of the transcendental subject, conceived as the constitutive source of noematic meaning. However, as Heidegger's notion of equiprimordiality indicates, the idea of phenomenological reflection does not necessarily involve such a subjectivizing move. The basic sense of such reflection is that we take our absolute starting point in our concrete first-person experiences in order to reflect on the basic structural features that make them what they are. Here, nothing is presupposed about the role played by subject and object. Instead, in reflecting we attend to the whole of our experience, whereby it is an open question how the different features— the object, the acts and desires of the subject, other people, language, collective values—interact as more or less basic aspects of the experience in question.

Part Three

THE OPENNESS OF BEING

Introduction

Heidegger's later thinking is focused on the question of the event—*Ereignis*—that opens up and gives historical being. My claim is that Heidegger's turn to this question is centrally a turn in his way of interrogating the problem of phenomena.

Since the period under consideration is long and complex—stretching from 1928 to Heidegger's last writings from the early 1970s—let me begin by offering a rough overview of how I see his thinking as developing during these years.

In the first years after the publication of *Being and Time* in February 1927, Heidegger continues his effort to advance and complete his project of fundamental ontology. In the introduction to the lecture course "The Basic Problems of Phenomenology," delivered in the summer term 1927, Heidegger promises to take on the decisive task reserved for the suspended third division of the first part of *Being and Time*, namely, to explicate the sense of being as temporality. In his concrete lectures, however, he never gets beyond a very rudimentary sketch of this theme.

1928 is the beginning of a series of intensively probing lecture courses and other texts—for example, "The Metaphysical Foundations of Logic" (1928), "Introduction to Philosophy" (1928-9), "What Is Metaphysics?" (1929), "On the Essence of Ground" (1929), and "The Fundamental Concepts of Metaphysics" (1929-30)—in which Heidegger moves away from the project of fundamental ontology toward a new understanding of the guiding question and task of thinking. The primary aim of *Being and Time* was to explicate the historical as-structure of Dasein's phenomenal experience. However, while claiming that our experience of phenomena is determined by the historical contexts of meaning in which we always already live, Heidegger never raised the question of how such historical meanings can be given as binding or primordial to us—as somehow transcending and distinct from the factical collective prejudices of the They. His failure to deal with this question, I argued, undercut two of the book's central concerns. First, it pushed his account of Dasein's authentic self-choice into an inadvertent vacillation between subjectivism and collectivism. Second, it made it impossible for him to implement his programmatic vision of phenomenology as a historical, hermeneutic-destructive mode of thinking. What happens in 1928 is that Heidegger raises precisely the question concerning the binding character of historical being: How can our historical world of being-relations address us as binding and obligating? At this time, he tries to tackle this question by arguing that being opens up as binding to us as the result of a free projection of a historical world. The change of the question implies that his view of the task of philosophy also changes. The fundamental ontological task of explicating the structures of Dasein is, he claims, ultimately motivated by the "metontological" task of freely projecting a binding historical world. Furthermore, his strengthened emphasis on how our understanding of historical being determines all our ontic understanding of beings brings with it a need to depart from the method of phenomenological reflection used in *Being and Time*. By the beginning of the 1930s Heidegger insists that philosophy has to take the form of a radically historical thinking, a thinking that can only hope to overcome the metaphysical tradition by tracing and retrieving the latent resources harbored by the Greek beginning of the tradition (cf. GA 94: 52–3/39–40).

These transformations in Heidegger's thinking gradually lead him to give up the project of fundamental ontology. After the spring of 1929, we do not hear him talking about a continuation of *Being and Time* anymore (cf. Sheehan 1984: 186). However, although the years 1928–33 certainly initiate Heidegger's turn to his later thinking, his formulation of his guiding question still remains groping and unclear. Moreover, he is still unable to offer more than very crude indications of the dynamics that open up historical worlds and of the methodological character of his historical thinking.

In the beginning of the 1930s Heidegger becomes captivated by the growing National Socialist movement, which he sees as a counterforce against the nihilism of the modern age and as a possible beginning of the philosophical world-projection that he is envisioning. In 1933 he decides to engage himself politically. For one year—April 21, 1933 to April 12, 1934—he serves as rector of the University of Freiburg with the task of implementing the Nazi program for university reform. However, although Heidegger soon becomes disenchanted with the politics of the party and starts to view National Socialism as yet another version of nihilism, the story of his relationship with Nazism does not end here. Not only does Heidegger continue to believe in the metaphysical potential of National Socialism and to entertain anti-Semitic thoughts at least until the late 1940s. Indeed, it seems that he is never able to face and acknowledge the moral calamity of Nazism and the Holocaust, to say nothing of taking responsibility for his own actions. I will deal with the story of Heidegger's relationship with Nazism in greater detail in Chapter 10. There I will also raise the question about the connections between Heidegger's Nazism and his philosophy.

After his debacle as Nazi rector, Heidegger puts his effort into clarifying and articulating the question and task that is to guide his later thinking. This happens in a progression of lecture courses and papers from the mid to the later 1930s—for example, "Hölderlin's Hymns 'Germanien' and 'Der Rhein'" (1934–5), "Introduction to Metaphysics" (1935), "The Origin of the Work of Art" (1936), and "Basic Questions of Philosophy" (1937–8)—as well as in the massive self-reflective manuscripts *Contributions to Philosophy (of the Event)* written in 1936–8 and *Mindfulness* written in 1938–9. Apart from Hölderlin, who plays a pivotal role, Heidegger's main philosophical influences during these years are the early pre-Socratic thinkers and Nietzsche. As I will argue, Heidegger's turn basically consists in a redirection of his interrogation of the problem of phenomena. Whereas Heidegger in *Being and Time* concentrated on phenomenologically describing the historical structure of Dasein's experience of phenomena, he now insists that the basic philosophical question must concern precisely the openness or givenness of historical being itself: how does being open up and address us as a binding historical context of meaning? Heidegger's transformation of his central question opens up and determines all his subsequent later thinking. As concerns his conception of phenomena and phenomenology, this has two main consequences. First, the question of the openness of historical being leads Heidegger to provide a new account of the dynamic happening which allows a historical world to arise and shine. Second, it brings with it a change in the methodological character of his thought, so that the phenomenology of *Being and Time* gives way to a more radically historical reflection tracing the possibilities of understanding contained by our history.

From the mid-1930s until the end of the war in 1945 Heidegger is primarily occupied with articulating his new guiding question of the openness of being—which he primarily names "the event" (*Ereignis*) or the "clearing" (*Lichtung*) of being—and sketching the historical program of his later thinking. This essentially involves elaborating—chiefly through a set of extensive courses on Nietzsche—a new explication of the nature of metaphysics as well as a diagnosis of how the subjectivist and technical understanding of being characteristic of the metaphysical tradition gets radicalized into the modern technical understanding of being as a material reserve for human desire and manipulation. This destiny, Heidegger claims, can only be overcome through a return to the Greek beginning of the history of metaphysics, such that we attempt to reflect on the hidden and bypassed origin of this "first beginning" in order, thereby, to open up the basic philosophical possibilities required to prepare the way for an "other beginning." During these years—especially in the essay "The Origin of the Work of Art"—he also works out an analysis of the dynamics that allow a historical world to arise and shine, and which centrally take the form of a "strife" between the historical "world" and the material-sensuous "earth."

After the war, in 1946, Heidegger publishes his "Letter on Humanism," which is his first public written presentation of his late philosophy. His 1949 lectures at the private *Club zu Bremen*, titled "Insight into That Which Is," mark the beginning of a new phase in his philosophical development. Here Heidegger introduces a new lapidary and meditative style which from now on will characterize his thinking. In contrast to his texts from the 1930s and 1940s, which were often marked by terminological excess and grand historic-apocalyptic visions, he now attempts to open up the questions by pursuing finite paths of thinking which take their point of departure in specific contexts of questioning: philosophical texts, poems, or some aspect of the contemporary situation. Hence, the bulk of Heidegger's key texts from the 1950s onwards consist in shorter essays gathered in anthologies such as *Lectures and Essays, Identity and Difference, On the Way to Language,* and *On the Matter of Thinking.* Among Heidegger's main philosophical endeavors in the 1950s we may name his deepened reflections on language, poetry and technology as well as his rearticulation of the dynamics that open up a world in terms of the "fourfold." In the 1960s, Heidegger once more returns to the question of phenomenology. In *On the Matter of Thinking*—especially in the essay "The End of Philosophy and the Task of Thinking" from 1964—he offers his most thorough attempt to articulate the methodological nature of his late thinking.

The discussion of the later Heidegger's conception of phenomena and phenomenology has largely been dominated by the hermeneutic-deconstructive line of interpretation. This is no surprise, given the later Heidegger's focus us on how being is given as a historical destiny and given his express intention to abandon intuition-based phenomenology in favor of a deeply historical mode of reflection. For the transcendental phenomenological reading, Heidegger's early production culminating in *Being and Time* has naturally been the prime point of focus. Despite Heidegger's proclaimed intention to transform phenomenology into a historical mode of thinking, the method of intuition-based phenomenological reflection is at the core of his early lecture courses and *Being and Time.* From the point of view of this reading, Heidegger's turn in the 1930s is prone to appear as a more or less drastic parting with his earlier phenomenology in favor of a radical historical thinking that is essentially in jeopardy of collapsing into historicism and speculative construction. However, although the attitude toward the later Heidegger has generally been skeptical, there have been attempts to argue that even his later thinking contains elements of intuitive transhistorical grounding. As regards the question of phenomena, David Espinet has recently suggested that Heidegger's notion of the "earth" can be read as an attempt to salvage a dimension of sensuousness that transcends our historical contexts of meaning. As regards the question of phenomenology, it has been argued—for example by Steven Crowell—that Heidegger despite his strong insistence on the historicity of thought never completely abandons the method of phenomenological seeing.

I hope to shed some new light on the sense of and motives behind Heidegger's turn after *Being and Time* by interpreting it as a turn in his interrogation of the problem of phenomena. It seems to me that previous interpretations have not been able to articulate with sufficient clarity how and why Heidegger turns from interrogating the historical structure of phenomenal experience to interrogating the openness and phenomenality of historical being itself. There has also been a general failure to recognize his guiding ambition to account for how a historical world can open up and prevail as binding and obligating. In what follows, I offer explications of Heidegger's view of the dynamics that open up historical being and of the historical character of his later thinking. My interpretation can basically be seen as confirming and elaborating on the dominant hermeneutic-deconstructive reading. I will argue that although Heidegger, by introducing the notion of the "earth," points to an irreducible dimension of sensuousness and material nature, this does not unsettle his basic conception of the ontological difference, namely that our historical heritage constitutes our primary and determining source of meaning. Furthermore, I will argue that although Heidegger is unable to dispense completely with intuition-based phenomenology, his use of phenomenological descriptions in his later work is ambivalent and quite weak.

As concerns the philosophical questions at stake, I ultimately believe that Heidegger's effort to demonstrate the radical historicity of being and thinking is bound to fail and that it builds on a momentous denial of what I suggest is our intuitive transhistorical access to beings as an independent source of truth and ethical-existential normativity. In the epilogue of the book, I will make an attempt to critically examine the problems and limited insights of Heidegger's radical historicism.

This part comprises four chapters: In Chapter 9, I trace and explicate the sense of Heidegger's turn to the question of the openness of being. In Chapter 10, I discuss the philosophical roots and import of Heidegger's engagement in National Socialism. In Chapter 11, I explicate Heidegger's view of the dynamics that open up historical being as a binding destiny. Here, the primary focus is on Heidegger's analysis of the struggle between the "world" and the "earth" as it is developed in "The Origin of the Work of Art." In Chapter 12, I discuss the methodological character of Heidegger's late historical thinking and its relationship to phenomenology.

9

THE QUESTION OF THE OPENNESS OF BEING

The Question of the Turn

It is clear that Heidegger's philosophical approach undergoes a change, or a set of changes, in the decade following the publication of *Being and Time*. The change concerns both the guiding question and matter of his thought as well as the task and method of his thinking. In the secondary literature, this change has commonly been labeled the "turn"—following Heidegger's word "die Kehre"—and has generally been seen as the rough dividing line separating the early from the late Heidegger. However, it is far from obvious how the philosophical sense of Heidegger's alleged turn should be understood, the last fifty years having witnessed a massive scholarly debate regarding this issue.

In his pioneering work *Heidegger: Through Phenomenology to Thought* from 1963 William J. Richardson established the standard interpretation that has dominated the literature to this very day. According to Richardson, Heidegger's thinking undergoes a turn in the years 1930–5, a turn which consists in a "shift from There-being [Richardson's translation of "Dasein"] to Being" (1963: 624). Whereas the early Heidegger primarily focuses on Dasein and basically conceives of being as "the project of There-being" (238), the later Heidegger turns his principal focus to being itself as something which precedes and, of its own accord, gives itself to Dasein. This shift of focus, Richardson claims, is also linked to an alteration of Heidegger's methodological approach, such that the phenomenological explication of the structures of Dasein carried out in *Being and Time* gives way to a historical thinking which articulates being such as it gives itself historically (525).

Against this, Thomas Sheehan has emphatically argued that there never occurred a turn in Heidegger's central question. According to Sheehan, the standard interpretation of the turn has failed to distinguish between two quite different matters. On the one hand, Heidegger uses the word "turn" (*Kehre*) to designate the central issue of his thinking, namely the movement—characterized by the reciprocal co-belonging of being and Dasein—through which being is opened up. On the other hand, he uses it to name "the shift in the way [he] formulated and presented his philosophy beginning in the 1930s" (Sheehan 2001b: 3). Indeed, in his 1962 letter to Richardson, Heidegger makes a clear terminological distinction between the two turns. Here he contrasts the "turn" (*Kehre*) as a designation of the issue itself with the "change" (*Wendung*) in his thinking of that issue (Richardson 1963: XVI–XIX; GA 11: 149–50; cf. Sheehan 2010: 93). Sheehan argues that the common failure to see that the "turn" for Heidegger primarily names his central topic and not some reversal of his philosophical standpoint is a consequence of the failure to grasp what that topic actually is. Heidegger's central topic, Sheehan claims, is not being but "*that which 'gives' being*" (2001a: 192): "What produces (*poiei*, *läßt* sein) givenness? What enables being as *parousia* or Anwesen to be given at all?" (2001b: 7) Once we recognize that Heidegger's central issue was the event that opens up being, more specifically the reciprocity between being and Dasein operative in that event, it becomes impossible to interpret the changes in Heidegger's thinking in the 1930s as a radical turn of his guiding question from Dasein to being—as if these could be viewed as discrete entities. Instead, Sheehan maintains that Heidegger's central question "remains unchanged" (2010: 92), and that the shift in his thinking is only one of focus and emphasis. Whereas the early Heidegger focused on Dasein's projective understanding of being, the later Heidegger—realizing that "thrownness … always has priority over projection" (2001b: 15)—puts the emphasis "less on man projectively *holding* open the world and more on man's *being required* to hold open the world" (Sheehan 2010: 91).

It is clearly important to distinguish, as Sheehan does, between the turn as a name for the internal logic of the matter of Heidegger's thinking and the turn as a change in his strategies for thinking and expressing this matter. Nevertheless, I think that Sheehan's heavy emphasis on the continuity of Heidegger's central issue makes him oblivious to the transformations that Heidegger's questioning of this issue undergoes along the way. The aim of this chapter is to show that the turn of Heidegger's guiding question in the 1930s can essentially be seen as a turn in his questioning of the problem of phenomena. On this basis, it also becomes possible to specify in what sense, if any, his thinking exhibits a shift of focus from Dasein to being.

The Beginning of the Turn

Only a year after the publication of *Being and Time,* Heidegger begins to rethink his view of the guiding question and task of philosophy. This primarily happens in the lecture courses "The Metaphysical Foundations of Logic" (1928) and "Introduction to Philosophy" (1928–9) as well as in the essay "On the Essence of Ground" (1929).

The project of fundamental ontology launched in *Being and Time* was guided by the question of the sense of being, that is, the question of the basic structural framework characterizing Dasein's experience of phenomena. To answer this question, Heidegger provided an analysis of the historical as-structure of experience, according to which our experience of beings as phenomena is fundamentally determined by the historical context of meaning in which we live. However, he failed to raise the question of how the historical meanings of our heritage—the life-guiding possibilities and the understandings of being—can address us as in some sense binding and primordial. This lacuna made it impossible for him to account either for how authentic Dasein is to disclose its guiding life-possibilities or for how the hermeneutic-destructive thinking envisioned by Heidegger is to appropriate primordial historical understandings of being.

One year later, Heidegger directs his philosophical attention precisely to the question of the "origin of bindingness," the "making possible of bindingness and obligation in general" (GA 26: 25/20; GA 9: 164/126). The question is this: How can our historical world open up and address as binding and obligating?

Heidegger's redirection of his guiding question goes hand in hand with a change in his view of the task and existential import of philosophy. In these years, he divides the task of philosophy into "fundamental ontology" and "metontology." The idea is that when the fundamental ontological task of philosophy is radically elaborated, it effects an "overturning" (*Umschlag*)—*metabolē*—into "metontology" (GA 26: 199/157). And the task of metontology is no other than that of establishing a binding historical world.

How should this be understood?

When Heidegger raises the question of the bindingness of the world, his also modifies his analysis of Dasein in some important respects. To begin with, he expands his concept of world to include the manifold of being-senses in terms of which we understand different beings: "The world is the totality of the constitution of being, not only of nature and of the historical togetherness, but the specific totality of the manifold of being" (GA 27: 309). In the introduction to *Being and Time* Heidegger had declared that our understanding of beings is guided by our understanding of the manifold of different being-senses and by our understanding of the sense of being as such. However, in his concrete analyses the supposed priority of our understanding of being was passed over. Heidegger explicated the world as consisting of instrumental networks that were ultimately anchored in Dasein's life-possibilities. Moreover, he described Dasein's challenge of authentically choosing its possibilities as preceding and conditioning the philosophical task of explicating the sense of being. Now, however, Heidegger insists that our historical world comprises not only instrumental references and guiding life-possibilities but also the totality of being-senses that determine our understanding of beings as human beings, animals, tools and so on. To bring out the primary and determining role of our understanding of being, he articulates it in terms of Dasein's "transcendence." The central idea is that the "ontic transcendence" of Dasein toward beings—including ourselves—presupposes its "primordial transcendence" toward the being-world: "Dasein surpasses beings, in such a way that it is only in this surpassing that it can relate to beings" (GA 27: 306–7).

Furthermore, Heidegger now asserts that Dasein's primordial understanding of being has the form of a free "projection of world" (*Weltentwurf*) (GA 9: 166/128). Taking up the Kantian notion that the human being can only be obligated by laws that she has freely given herself, he claims that "freedom alone can be the origin of bindingness" (GA 26: 25/20). However, in contrast to Kant, who locates the origin of the law in universal reason, Heidegger suggests that the bindingness of the world is grounded in Dasein's free projection of the world. Such a projection is essentially groundless and productive. It cannot ground itself on any ontic understanding of beings and it cannot transpire as a discovery of some kind of pregiven being-senses since there are no such things to discover prior to the projection. Hence, Heidegger describes the projection as originating in "freedom," conceived as the "abyss of ground (*Ab-grund*) in Dasein" (GA 9: 174/134). Moreover, he underscores the productive character of the projection: "Dasein ... is in the essence of its being *world-forming (weltbildend)*" (GA 9: 158/123). At the same time, Heidegger maintains that Dasein's projection of a world in some sense needs to be grounded in and attuned to beings: "*Transcendence means projection of world in such a way that those beings that are surpassed also already pervade and attune that which projects*. With this *absorption* by beings that belongs to transcendence, Dasein has taken up a basis within beings, gained 'ground.'" (GA 9: 166/128). By this, Heidegger does not mean to gainsay his fundamental thesis—the ontological difference—that the projection of being precedes and determines our experience of beings as phenomena. Rather, what he suggests is that the free projection of being takes place through a kind of receptive interaction with the totality of sensuous-material beings—here still prephenomenal and undetermined—such that this projection first opens up the world that allows these beings to appear as phenomena.[1]

According to Heidegger, the fundamental ontological analysis of Dasein's understanding of being in terms of transcendence and free world-projection opens up the metontological task of realizing such a projection. Ultimately, the task of philosophy—together with art and politics—is to take part in establishing a binding historical world. As Heidegger sees it, the historical world in which we live can lose or gain its power to bind and obligate us, and whichever happens depends on how philosophy succeeds in its task. In the background we have his belief that the history of Western philosophy—by covering up the question of being, and, hence, failing to transparently take on the task of establishing a binding world—has brought about a situation in which our world does not address us as binding and important anymore, but rather appears hollow and meaningless. The philosophical task of establishing a binding world thus becomes fundamental and acute. It is only to the extent that our world claims us as binding that there are any meaningful possibilities for us to choose; indeed, it is only to this extent that beings can show up as significant phenomena at all.

To mark the primary existential importance of the metontological task of philosophy, Heidegger repeatedly stresses that Dasein is a fundamentally philosophical being: "To exist as a human being means to philosophize. Philosophizing belongs to the human Dasein as such" (GA 27: 3; cf. GA 26: 274/212). The point is that—contrary to what Heidegger thought in *Being and Time*—there is no prephilosophical challenge of authentic existence that is not already conditioned by the primary philosophical challenge of establishing a binding world. After all, only the successful philosophical projection of a binding world can set up meaningful possibilities for Dasein to choose as its own.

Heidegger's conception of the metontological task of philosophy and his account of the free projection of world remain rudimentary and undeveloped.

Still, his development in these years opens up the path toward his later thinking, the basic setup of which he will be able to articulate more clearly in the mid-1930s. The perceived need to account for how a historical world can open up as binding to us will remain guiding for all his later thinking. However, his view of the task and method of philosophy and of the dynamics that open up a world will change. To begin with, he will leave fundamental ontology behind and rethink the task of philosophy in terms of a radically historical reflection on the event that opens up historical being. Furthermore, he will replace his almost Nietzschean conception of the world-projection with a more complex account of how poetry and art open up a world by enacting what he will call the "strife" between the "world" and the "earth."

The Turn of Heidegger's Question

It is in the mid-1930s that Heidegger works out and achieves a clear articulation of the question that is to guide the rest of his thinking. By this time, Heidegger insists that philosophy has to take the form of "historical reflection." Since our possibilities of seeing and understanding are determined by the historical understandings of being bestowed by our history, we cannot rely on any supposedly direct transhistorical intuition. Moreover, he believes that the history of philosophy has been governed by the metaphysical understanding of being as presence that was established by Plato and Aristotle. Hence, to free itself from metaphysics, he claims, thinking has to return to the Greek beginning of metaphysics in order to see whether it harbors a more primordial understanding of being. Heidegger's guiding idea is that the pre-Socratic notion of being as *physis*, as well as the Greek word for truth, *alētheia*, in fact express an embryonic understanding of the event that opens up being, an understanding that was repressed and covered up by metaphysics.

Here, I will primarily focus on the lecture course "Basic Questions of Philosophy" from the winter term 1937–8, which in my view contains Heidegger's clearest and most detailed account of the turn in his guiding question. In this lecture course—as in many of the other texts establishing the stance of his later thinking—he takes his point of departure in the question of truth rather than the question of being.

Since the inception of Western philosophy in Plato and Aristotle, Heidegger claims, we have tended to understand truth as "correctness" (GA 45: 14/14). For us, truth basically materializes as the capacity of the human subject to represent beings correctly in explicit or implicit utterances. Yet for such representation of beings to be possible, these beings must somehow be open and accessible to us. There must prevail an "openness" (GA 45: 19/18) that allows the human being free access to the totality of beings. Since Heidegger holds that our contemporary conception of truth as correctness is determined by the onset of this conception in Plato and Aristotle, he insists that the only way to reopen the question of truth is through a historical reflection on this origin (cf. GA 45: 35/34).

As Heidegger returns to the Greek origin of our concept of truth, he says that the question of truth undergoes a decisive "turn" (*Kehre*):

> The question of the *essence of truth* (*Wesen der Wahrheit*) is *at the same time and in itself* the question of the *truth of the essence* (*Wahrheit des Wesens*). The question of truth—asked as a basic question—turns itself in itself against itself. This *turn*, which we have now run up against, is an intimation of the fact that we are entering the compass of a genuine philosophical question. (GA 45: 47/44)

How should this be understood?

According to Heidegger, Plato and Aristotle thought that the possibility of truth as correctness is grounded in our preceding understanding of essences. In order to experience beings as meaningful phenomena—and, hence, as that which makes our statements about them true or false—we already need to understand the essences that determine what beings can show up as for us. Hence, the Greeks determined the essences as *ideai*: "What is sighted is as what beings give themselves in advance and constantly. The *what-it-is*, the whatness, is the *idea*" (GA 45: 62/56). Even though Heidegger will critically revise the Greek understanding of essence as a constantly present and independently definable whatness, he unflinchingly endorses the hierarchical difference between our understanding of essences and our knowledge or particular entities:

> If, in our immediate comportment toward individual beings, we did not have the essence already in sight, or, Platonically expressed, if we did not have the "ideas" of individual things in view in advance, then we would be blind, and would remain blind, to everything these things are as individuals, i.e., as such and such, here and now, in these or those relations. And still more: according to the way and to the extent that we regard the essence, we are also capable of experiencing and determining what is particular in the things. What is viewed in advance and how it is in view are decisive for what we actually see in the individual thing. (GA 45: 65/59)

We can now see how the question of the essence of truth motivates a turn to the question of the truth of the essence. Given that the essence of truth as correctness is grounded in our understanding of essences, we are led to the question of the truth of the essences, that is, of how the essences themselves are opened up and given to us.

According to Heidegger, Plato and Aristotle conceived of the knowledge of essences in terms of a "bringing forth" of the essences from anonymousness and obscurity "into the light" so that we may sight them (GA 45: 85/76). This conception of knowledge of essences, he claims, in the end refers back to and claims as its own ground the basic experience of *alētheia* or "unconcealedness" (*Unverborgenheit*) (GA 45: 97/86). It is only in so far as the essences are open and unconcealed that it is possible for us to access and articulate them. And yet, even though Plato and

Aristotle experienced the unconcealedness of essences as the ground of truth they never asked the question about the nature of unconcealedness as such:

> And assuming that they [the Greeks] would have established the unconcealedness of beings as the ground of the correctness of the assertion, is this ground itself—*alētheia* in *its* essence—thereby sufficiently determined and questioned? Did the Greeks ever ask about *alētheia* as such; did the Greeks make the unconcealedness of beings as such into that which is worthy of questioning? Does this, that the Greeks experienced the essence of truth as unconcealedness, mean without further ado that the unconcealedness of beings was what was question-worthy for them? By no means. (GA 45: 111–12/98)

Heidegger claims that the first Greek beginning of philosophy in Plato and Aristotle was founded on the basic experience of *alētheia* as the ground that made possible all understanding of being and beings but which itself remained unquestioned. Plato and Aristotle never radically asked the question of how essences are opened up and given to us. The Greek beginning was thus essentially ambiguous and fragile. On the one hand, the experience of *alētheia* harbored an intimation—more originally manifested in the pre-Socratic notion of *physis*—of the epiphanic happening that lets essences open up and prevail as uncovered. On the other hand, the fundamental inability to question *alētheia* as such led the Greeks to interpret the unconcealedness of essences in terms of the stable presence—*ousia*—of the essences for the gaze of our understanding (cf. GA 45: 68/61).

For Heidegger, then, the decisive task of thinking is clear: "to *bring* the *openness* itself, in what it is and how it is, *upon its ground*" (GA 45: 189/162–3). The basic question, which is to guide Heidegger's later thinking—and which he names, for example, the question of the "truth of being" or the question of "being itself"—is none other than the question concerning the openness and givenness of historical being: How is a historical world of being opened up and given to us as a binding destiny?

According to Heidegger, the pre-Socratic thinkers had an incipient understanding of the event that opens up being. His thesis is that before Plato and Aristotle began to conceive of being as presence—*ousia*—thinkers and poets such as Parmenides, Heraclitus, Pindar, and Sophocles understood being in terms of *physis*: "*Physis* is being itself, by virtue of which beings first become and remain observable" (GA 40:17/16). Heidegger maintains that *physis* does not refer either to the structure of our phenomenal experience or to the historical being-world that determines this experience. Rather, in the context of pre-Socratic thought *physis*—the Greek word for "nature" and natural "growth"—is said to refer to what Heidegger calls the "epiphany of a world" (GA 40:67/69). *Physis*, he states, names "what emerges from itself (e.g. the emergence, the blossoming, of a rose), the unfolding that opens itself up, the coming-into-appearance in such unfolding, and holding itself and persisting in appearance—in short, the emerging-abiding sway" (GA 40: 16/15–16). In short, what Heidegger asserts is that *physis* refers precisely to the epiphanic event that lets a historical world emerge, unfold, open up and persist in appearance. To reflect on and articulate this event is the central task of his later thinking.

Heidegger's Turn Reconsidered

Heidegger paradigmatically articulates the turn of his thinking in the 1930s as a turn from the question of the essence of truth to the question of the truth of the essence (cf. GA 45: 47/44; GA 9: 201/153). This suggests that the project of fundamental ontology would still have transpired within the horizon of the question of the essence of truth. Elucidating this suggestion allows us to clarify the way in which Heidegger conceives of the turn as a self-critical advance beyond the horizon of *Being and Time*.

In fact, there is a clear sense in which *Being and Time* is concerned with the question of the essence of truth. To ask for the essence of truth, Heidegger writes, is to ask for what in general "distinguishes every 'truth' as truth" (GA 9: 177/136). In phenomenological terms, this amounts to asking about the basic structures that condition our experience of truth. This, however, is precisely what is done in *Being and Time*. Guided by the question of the sense of being, Heidegger here attempts to phenomenologically explicate the basic structures of Dasein that condition and constitute our experience of beings as meaningful phenomena and allow us to express true or false judgments about them.

However, the analysis carried out in *Being and Time* engenders results that in Heidegger's view necessitate a turn of the question of fundamental ontology. According to Heidegger, the as-structure characterizing Dasein's phenomenal understanding is essentially historical: our experience of beings as phenomena is determined by our preunderstanding of our historical world and this understanding is in turn guided by our preunderstanding of being. However, as we have seen, Heidegger never asks the question of how historical significances and being can be given to us as in some sense binding or primordial beyond the factical historical prejudices of the tradition. In this way, he remains stuck in the same predicament as Plato and Aristotle. While both these philosophers grounded the essence of truth as correctness in our preceding understanding of essences, they failed to radically interrogate the truth—the openness and givenness—of these essences. In contrast to Plato and Aristotle, who conceived of the essences as universal and eternal, Heidegger insists that our experience of phenomena is determined by our preunderstanding of our historically finite world of significances and being-senses. Yet like Plato and Aristotle, he leaves the question of the openness of this historical world unasked.[2] As we have seen, the result of this is that the existential analysis of *Being and Time* runs into insurmountable ambivalences. One could thus say that the fundamental ontological investigation of the sense of being—the essence of truth—gives rise to the question of the openness of being—the question of the truth of the essence—without, however, itself being able to carry out this turn of the question.

We should now be in a position to assess and delimit the truth of the standard interpretations of Heidegger's *Kehre*.

As mentioned above, Thomas Sheehan has insisted that Heidegger's central question concerns not being but that which gives being, and that this question remains the same from beginning to end. However, although it is true to say on a formal level that Heidegger always asks about the source and conditions of being—and not about its substantial determinations—it seems to me that Sheehan is unable to account for what is at stake in the turn of Heidegger's question and thus also underestimates the changes that his thinking undergoes. As I have tried to show, Heidegger's turn consists in a shift from a questioning of the basic structures of phenomenal understanding—a questioning that uncovered the ground of this understanding in historical being—to a historical interrogation of the openness and givenness of historical being itself. This, however, means that the same formal question concerning that which gives being essentially gets transformed both as concerns the focus of the question—from the structure of phenomena to the phenomenality of being—and as concerns the manner of questioning: from phenomenology to historical reflection.

But what about the influential notion that Heidegger's turn consists in a shift of focus from Dasein to being? According to Richardson, the earlier Heidegger understands being as the projection of Dasein whereas the later Heidegger gives priority to being as something that gives itself to Dasein. Sheehan for his part argues that the event that gives being has the character of a reciprocal dynamic between being and Dasein, and that the only thing that happens in the 1930s is that Heidegger shifts his emphasis from Dasein to being as the primary pole of this dynamic.

What is true is that whereas Heidegger in *Being and Time* focuses on the structures of Dasein, his later thinking is concerned with the event that gives being. However, this does not in any way imply that the earlier Heidegger would have given priority to Dasein as the one who through its projections produces or determines being, and that the later Heidegger would have reversed the order of priority. The fact of the matter is that the question of how being opens up—and, hence, how the dynamics between being and the human being characterizing this event should be understood—was not broached in *Being and Time*. In his analyses of how the individual Dasein chooses and projects itself toward its life-possibilities, Heidegger quite unambiguously stresses that Dasein can only choose possibilities that are given as part of the historical heritage into which it is thrown. In no way can Dasein's projections produce historical possibilities or being. In this, the question about how the heritage opens up as a binding world remains unasked. When Heidegger in the 1930s turns to the question of the openness of being he will analyze the event that opens up being in terms of a dynamic strife between the address of the history of being, the sensuous-material milieu at hand, and the simultaneously receptive and formative function of the work of art. Although he will tend to emphasize the priority of being itself as something that gives and sends itself to us, the human being will still play a decisive role in the preparation and formation of historical worlds.

10

THE PROMISE OF NATIONAL SOCIALISM

Heidegger's engagement in National Socialism has always haunted his thinking as a painful question and the ongoing publication of his *Black Notebooks* has again made this question acute. How could one of the arguably greatest and most influential philosophers of the twentieth century, a philosopher claiming to uncover the deepest structures of human existence, fall for one of the most evil and murderous regimes known throughout history? What does this show about the ethical and existential substance of his philosophy?

Obviously, it is impossible for me to offer anything like a comprehensive treatment of Heidegger's relationship to National Socialism here. To begin with, it is unfeasible within the framework of this book to elaborate the philosophical horizons—constituted by the relations between philosophy, ethics, politics, and psychology—that this question opens up. Moreover, it is not possible to engage in any detail with the massive scholarly literature that has evolved around this issue. In what follows, I will focus on the relationship between Heidegger's philosophy and his Nazism and try to pinpoint some of the central philosophical commitments that motivate or facilitate his pull toward this movement. My hope is that my analysis of Heidegger's struggle with the question of how a historical world can open up as binding and holy, and of the ethical-existential stakes and problems of this effort, might shed some new light on this difficult issue.

The Superior Task of Philosophy

Where does the road begin that eventually leads Heidegger to engage himself—and his philosophy—in National Socialism in the beginning of the 1930s?

I will not attempt to trace the development of the psychological motives and ideological-political ideas—for instance, his conservatism, his nationalism, and his anti-Semitism—that will inform his penchant for Nazism.[1] Instead, I will concentrate on those traits of his philosophy that prepare the way for and are linked to his politics.[2]

Heidegger's early thinking that culminates in *Being and Time* was basically apolitical. The project of fundamental ontology was aimed at explicating the sense of being through an analysis of the basic structures of Dasein. The central focus of the analysis was on the individual Dasein's struggle for authenticity. Here, there is still no trace of the idea that will be vital to Heidegger's Nazi-engagement, namely the idea that it is the task of philosophy to take part in projecting a binding historical world—a task that essentially involves politics. Nevertheless, as we have seen above, there are aspects of Heidegger's analysis of authentic existence that are ethically-existentially problematic and that will later play into his philosophical politics.

To start with, Heidegger's conception of authenticity builds on a principal denial of the possibility that the other human being as such can be the source of an absolute ethical claim, and that we can care about her for her own sake. In fact, it involves a superordination of the challenge of authenticity over the ethical challenge of opening up and responding to the claim of the other. According to Heidegger, the primary existential challenge of Dasein consists in transparently appropriating its own finite historical life-possibilities, the heroes that constitute its identity. Since these possibilities are supposed to determine the significances and roles with reference to which we can experience particular beings—including human beings—as meaningful, the outcome is that our struggle for authenticity conditions our ethical relationship to human beings. The world we live in and the identity we choose determine what we will be able to experience as significant and normative in the first place. Furthermore, Heidegger's account of the motives driving Dasein's authentic self-choice gives expression to an attitude that is simultaneously egoistic and collectivist. To be primarily concerned—as Dasein is—about the social roles that constitute one's identity is essentially to be concerned about oneself, about how one appears in the light of one's collectively formed identity and in the eyes of the collective group that endorses and gives weight to the social roles in question. Dasein, Heidegger maintains, has to choose its own possibilities from the historical heritage into which it has always already been thrown and which it shares as a "destiny" (*Geschick*) with the "community" (*Gemeinschaft*) or "people" (*Volk*) (SZ: 384) to which it belongs. In this, the possibilities bestowed by the collective heritage are said to constitute "the sole authority that a free existing can have" (SZ: 391).

Heidegger thus describes Dasein as a fundamentally egoistic creature guided by the factical norms and values of its collective historical world. Although such an egoistic-collectivist attitude certainly exposes the person who holds it to the possible evils of the collective context that she identifies with, it does not imply an internal connection to any particular values or political programs, for example, National Socialism. In fact, such an attitude can take many different forms, and although it is ethically-existentially defective it may even motivate political actions that we recognize as good. Driven by our egoistic-collectivist urge for affirmation, we may become businesspersons, philosophers, political heroes defending justice and equality, or fascists.[3]

Not long after the publication of *Being and Time*, Heidegger's view of the task of philosophy undergoes a change. In 1928, he introduces the idea that philosophy is not exhausted by the fundamental ontological task of explicating the structures of Dasein but is essentially motivated by the task of establishing—through a free projection—a binding and meaning-laden historical world. What according to Heidegger makes this task acute is that the Western world has lost its power to bind and overwhelm us, with the result that our lives have suffered a devastating loss of meaning. This nihilistic condition, he claims, is the final outcome of the metaphysical understanding of being as steady presence for the human subject. Hence, the philosophical task of rethinking the origin of being in our free world-projection, and of executing such a projection, becomes urgent.

Heidegger's rearticulation of the task of philosophy implies that the central existential challenge of life is not the authentic self-choice of the individual Dasein anymore. If there is no binding world to live in, becoming authentic is not enough for attaining a meaningful life. Hence, for Heidegger the primary existential challenge becomes to establish a binding world for a historical people. This is primarily the task of the philosophers and the poets, but it is also, as we shall see, the task of the political leaders.

In Heidegger's account, the philosophical-political task of opening up a binding world emerges as superordinate to every possible ethical concern with particular beings. The establishment of the world cannot be grounded on or measured against any direct experience of beings as significant since it first opens up the world on the basis of which such beings—including human beings—can show up as significant and normative. It is the world that first gives to all beings whatever importance and moral appeal they can have for us—that first makes them possible objects of love, concern, and responsibility. Heidegger's conviction that the contemporary world has lost its bindingness sharpens the conflict between philosophy and ethics. Whereas the philosophical-political task of opening a world appears as absolutely primary and pressing, the human beings we encounter are unable to address us as binding anymore. Should there be a conflict between the two tasks, the philosophical-political task would override every possible ethical claim or concern.

It is important to note that Heidegger's superordination of philosophy over ethics is not to be understood as a temporary suspension of the ethical that would be annulled if we would be able to overcome nihilism by establishing a binding world. It is, I think, quite possible to imagine the possibility of a general political-ideological situation—for example, a murderous totalitarian regime—that would be so cruel and oppressive that we would be forced to weigh the task of forcibly and even violently transforming this political situation in order to make possible a better life for the people living there against our ethical concern for some particular human beings. Still, what makes this a moral problem in the first place is that the motivation and guideline for our action lie in our love and concern precisely for particular human beings. For Heidegger, however, this way of thinking is excluded from the outset. Since it is the binding historical world that first confers significance on human beings, the need to establish such a world cannot itself be motivated by a concern for such beings. Furthermore, even if the establishment of a binding world were to succeed, and this world were to contain the idea of the absolute value of human beings, this would not in itself open us to the ethical appeal of the other as such. The idea of the absolute value of human beings would appear binding to us not because we would care about the others as such but because it would be prescribed as a norm by our collective historical world.

What we need to see here is that it is precisely the above vision of the task of thinking in the face of the impending apocalypse of the Western world that centrally pervades Heidegger's understanding of National Socialism as a possible beginning of a philosophical projection of being. Of course, Heidegger's superordination of philosophy over ethics does not by itself imply that there would be a need to violate or do violence to anybody in order to establish a new world. However, what it does do is offer a basic justification for transgressing or ignoring the ethical claim of the other in case the philosophical-political revolution would involve such violence—as it is bound to do when it takes the shape of National Socialism.

The Basic Facts

Here is, to begin with, a brief overview of the main facts of the story of Heidegger's engagement with National Socialism.

Heidegger begins to express his sympathy and philosophical hopes regarding Adolf Hitler's National Socialist movement in 1932 (cf. GA 94: 61-3/46-8). On April 21, 1933, he is elected as rector of the University of Freiburg and two weeks later he becomes a member of the NSDAP. As rector, he supervises the enactment of the Nazi university reform, including the implementation of the *Führer* principle and the application of the Nazi laws of racial cleansing to the student body of the university. He secretly denounces colleagues and students that he finds troublesome. However, having taken over the position as rector with a mixture of high hopes and serious misgivings, Heidegger quite soon starts to grow increasingly frustrated with the university politics of the party. Toward the end of 1933, he also begins to lose faith in the philosophical potential of National Socialism. On April 12, 1934, he hands in his application to resign—not least for the reason that he had made too many academic enemies in his dictatorial role as *Führer*-rector (cf. GA 94: 109-99/80-146).

However, the story of Heidegger's relationship to Nazism does not end with the rectorate. In the mid-1930s, Heidegger develops a critical interpretation of National Socialism as a drastic manifestation of the nihilist technical-subjectivist metaphysics that he first hoped it would overcome. However, Heidegger's critique—which, as we shall see, is fraught with problems—does not imply a clean break with Nazism. For Heidegger, the fact that Nazism is a fierce form of nihilist metaphysics is no reason to resist it. On the contrary, he believes that Nazism should be affirmed as the "barbaric principle" that it is (GA 94: 194/142). The idea is that by letting Nazism run its course—and not oppose it on the basis of outdated nihilistic alternatives such as liberalism and democracy—the nihilism of the modern age will enter its extreme end phase. As a result, nihilism will self-destruct and the possibility of a new beginning of history will grow stronger. This is the main philosophical reason why Heidegger continues to express support for Hitler and remains a member of the NSDAP until the end of the war. Furthermore,

Heidegger's critique of nihilist Nazism is targeted at the "vulgar National Socialism" (GA 94: 142/104) that manifests itself in the existent policies enacted by the party. By contrast, he continues to view his own thinking as a pursuit of what he calls "spiritual National Socialism" (GA 94: 135/99) or the "inner truth and greatness" of National Socialism (GA 40: 208/222). By these terms, he designates the philosophical-political possibility that he thinks was there to be grasped in 1933 but which the Nazis failed to realize. In 1946, Heidegger can still write that Hitler's rise to power in 1933 offered the "opportunity for a total self-reflection of the Occident" (GA 97: 174), and it is as yet not clear when—if ever—he gives up this belief.

Finally, anti-Semitism. Although Heidegger criticizes the biological racism of the Nazi regime, from the late 1930s onwards his *Black Notebooks* contain several passages in which he gives voice to blatantly anti-Jewish sentiments and makes use of common anti-Semitic stereotypes—the calculating, rootless Jew—in his philosophical diagnosis of the history of being. Heidegger's basic move in these passages is to characterize the nihilist technological metaphysics that he sees dominating the modern era as "Jewish": "The question of the role of *world-Judaism* (*Weltjudentum*) is not a racial question, but a metaphysical one, a question that concerns the kind of humanity which in an *utterly unattached* way can undertake as a world-historical 'task' the uprooting of all beings from being" (GA 96: 243/191). That is, what Heidegger claims is that the word "Judaism" as he uses it does not refer to race but names the technological, calculating thinking of metaphysics that results in our being uprooted from our finite, local contexts of meaning. In this sense, "Judaism" would encompass everything from American capitalism and Soviet communism to German Nazism. However, Heidegger's application of the word "Judaism" to nihilist metaphysics is nothing but a philosophically inflated version of the kind of cultural racism that vilifies a certain culture or religion on the basis of crude and falsifying stereotypes. After all, the only reason for calling nihilism "Jewish" lies in the contention that Judaism or the Jews are essentially characterized by calculative reasoning and rootlessness. Moreover, by talking about metaphysical "Judaism" alongside references to the Jews themselves Heidegger frequently blurs—as cultural racists tend to do—the distinction between Judaism as a metaphysical-cultural category and Judaism as a racial type. For instance, he suggests that it was Husserl's Judaism that hindered him from reaching "into the domains of essential decisions" (GA 96: 46/37). For this claim to rise above a mere tautology—Husserl's metaphysics makes him metaphysical—it has to refer to the biological race of Husserl, the Protestant, as the cause of his supposed philosophical inability.

The perhaps most outrageous manifestation of Heidegger's anti-Semitism is found in the already infamous claim that he makes about Jewish "self-annihilation" (*Selbstvernichtung*) during the war:

> Only when what is essentially "Jewish" in the metaphysical sense battles against the Jewish is the pinnacle of self-annihilation in history attained; assuming that what is "Jewish" has everywhere monopolized dominance entirely for itself, such

that even the battle against "the Jewish," and this above all, becomes subjection to it. (GA 97: 20)

Again, what Heidegger primarily claims to be saying in this passage is that the current situation of industrialized war and killing signals or forebodes the self-annihilation of technical metaphysics, that is, of "Judaism." However, by using this vocabulary he cannot fail to insinuate in the most outlandish manner that the Jews themselves were somehow the cause—were somehow themselves to blame—for the fanatic Nationalist Socialist effort to annihilate them in the death camps.

The sad fact is that Heidegger was never able to respond morally and philosophically to National Socialism and the Holocaust. In fact, the comments we have from Heidegger on the death camps are terribly belittling and self-serving. In his *Black Notebooks* he writes that the "terror of ultimate nihilism is still more uncanny than the massiveness of the hangman's assistants and the concentration camps" (GA 97: 59). Moreover, he suggests that the "guilt" of the victorious powers for impeding the metaphysical "destiny" of the Germans would be greater than the guilt stemming from all the "publicly 'denounced' 'crimes,'" such that it "could not even be measured against the horrors of the 'gas chambers' [note the quotation marks]" (GA 97: 99–100). As far as we know, Heidegger never showed any remorse, never apologized for his actions, and never seriously acknowledged the moral disaster of Nazism and his own entanglement in it.

The Philosophical Roots of Heidegger's Politics

Heidegger's engagement in National Socialism in the beginning of the 1930s was deeply rooted in his philosophical program. In a letter to Elisabeth Blochmann from the end of March 1933, he sums up his view of the Nazi seizure of power in the following manner:

> For me, the present events—precisely because much remains opaque and unmastered—have an unusual gathering power. They enhance the will and the certainty of acting in the service of a great assignment, and of assisting in the construction of a world grounded in the people (*volklich gegründete Welt*). For some time, the pallidness and shadowiness of a mere "culture," and the unreality of so called "values" have sunk down into nothingness for me, allowing me to search for the new ground in Dasein. We will find this ground, and also the vocation of what is German in the history of the occident, only if we expose ourselves to being as such in a new manner and appropriation. Hence, I experience the present entirely from the future. Only thus can a genuine participation grow, and the *standing-within* (*Inständigkeit*) our history, which is indeed a precondition for true acting. By contrast, we need to calmly put up with the overly hurried playing along with the new things that is mushrooming all over, that is to say, with the clinging to the superficial, which takes anything and everything as "political" without taking into consideration that this can

only remain *one* way of the first revolution. However, for many people this can become and has already become a way of the first awakening—supposing, that is, that we are ready to prepare for a second and deeper awakening. (GA 16: 71-2)

In short, to Heidegger the Nazi accession to power appears as a "first revolution" which has the potential of being a "way of awakening" toward a "second and deeper" philosophical revolution. The ultimate deeper revolution that is at stake is that of establishing a new binding world for the German people. This, Heidegger claims, can only be achieved through a thorough philosophical critique of the Western tradition of philosophy that has given rise to nihilism. For a new beginning to be possible, what is needed is a critical retrieval of the Greek origin of the tradition. This task—which is the task of the philosophers—is the prerequisite for the task—to be performed by the other creators, the poets and the political leaders—of concretely establishing a new world.

Heidegger understands the contemporary politics of National Socialism "entirely from the future," as the possible beginning of a future projection of being. Although he invests great hopes in the potential of the movement he is from the outset clear that it is quite uncertain whether this potential will be realized or not. What he sees in Nazism is basically an intensified mood of departure and resolve: a "first awakening" (GA 16: 72), a "departure" (*Aufbruch*) (GA 16: 95) from the old world, and a "resolve ... to stand firm in the face of the German fate in its extreme distress" (GA 16: 112/34). That is, even though Nazism does not yet involve a clear understanding of its ontological task—and though it is uncertain if it ever will—Heidegger believes that it expresses an awakening to the need to depart from the contemporary world and a resolute determination to take part in the establishment of a new destiny for Germany. In the end, everything depends on whether Nazism will find and follow its philosophical calling. The aim of Heidegger's own rectorship is precisely to take hold of the mood of departure and resolve pervading the Nazi revolution and place it under the direction and leadership of his own philosophical vision. This comes to clear expression in his inaugural address as rector of the University of Freiburg, "The Self-Assertion of the German University," which can be read as his philosophic-political manifesto. On the one hand, he here welcomes the rise of Nazism and makes it the main task of the university to work for this "departure" toward a new beginning in its "glory" and "greatness" (GA 16: 117/38). On the other hand, he elevates the university, headed by the philosophical questioning of being, as the "paramount school, which from science and through science educates and disciplines the leaders and guardians (*Führer und Hüter*) of the fate of the German people" (GA 16: 108/30). What then happens is that he quickly loses his belief in the possibility of directing the Nazi movement by becoming its philosophical leader.

We can thus see how Heidegger's apocalyptic diagnosis of the Western world and his notion of the superior and urgent task of projecting a new world pave the way for his philosophical affirmation of the Nazi revolution as the possible dawn of an ontological revolution to come. There are at least three aspects of Heidegger's philosophical program that explain the lure that Nazism exerted on him.[4]

First, Heidegger's diagnosis of the nihilistic end phase of the Western world and his dream of founding a new binding historical world is mirrored in the Nazi contempt for the futile and dirty modern bourgeois world and the desire for a strong collective community. Although Heidegger's ontological conception of the task of opening up a world has little to do with official Nazi ideology, they shared a more or less unclear dream of founding a powerful collective world modelled on premodern honor-societies: a meaning-laden world in which all people would identify so strongly with their social roles and callings that they would be prepared to die for their sake. Here, it is also good to note that Heidegger's interest in National Socialism was never about politics in the usual sense but about what he called "metapolitics" (GA 94: 116/85, 124/91). That is to say, he sees the potential of Nazism solely in its possible ability to play a role in the ontological establishment of a world, namely by developing the institutional structures needed for this task. In this, Heidegger understands his philosophical metapolitics as prior to all political questions concerning, for example, how to form a just and economically flourishing society. This way of understanding politics also makes him apt to ignore and disdain democracy. If the primary task is to open up a strong and binding world, and if this task must be led by an elite of philosophers, poets, and political leaders, then a state headed by a strong leadership is by definition preferable to democratic institutions.

Second, there are aspects in Heidegger's philosophy that predispose him to be attracted by the furious nationalism of the Nazis. For Heidegger, to establish a historical world is essentially to establish a world for a particular historical people, in this case the German people. It is true that Heidegger is highly critical of the Nazis' genetic definition of the essence of the people, and that he insists that the identity of the people is first determined by the world that is opened up as its destiny (cf. GA 94: 223/163). However, although the projection of a world is to some extent free and creative it is also predetermined both by the history and by the natural milieu of the people. According to Heidegger, the people always already stands in a specific history that contains the possibilities out of which a new world can be formed. Moreover, the projection of the world must be attuned to the natural sensuous-organic setting of the people. In fact, in a remark from 1934, Heidegger claims that "race" constitutes "*one* necessary ... condition of historical Dasein (thrownness)" (GA 94: 189/139). Although the remark is intended as a criticism of the National Socialist tendency to highlight race as the defining trait of a people, it nevertheless suggests that he considers race to be one of the natural factors that determine the shape of the coming world and identity of the people. In addition to this, Heidegger will always underscore that in order for the world to arise as binding and luminous it must exhibit a strong unity, something that implies that all alternative understandings of being and life that do not fit into the projected world must be negated and left out. Apart from the general tendency to promote national unity and reject pluralism, Heidegger—succumbing to naive mythologizing—ascribes a unique and primary role to the Germans within the history of the West. Because of the special historical kinship supposedly obtaining between the Greeks and the Germans, he tells us, it is the unique task of the Germans to realize a new beginning for the entire Western world (cf. GA 94: 27/21; GA 36/37: 6/5–6).

Third, Heidegger's conception of the urgency of the task to open up the world, and his superordination of this task over all ethical concerns, make him liable to be attracted by the revolutionary zeal of the Nazis, and to explain away their crimes and transgressions as regrettable misfortunes counterbalanced by the import of the coming philosophical revolution.

Of course, this exposition of the philosophical reasons behind Heidegger's Nazi-engagement is no complete account of the motives—psychological, political, philosophical—that determine his attraction to Nazism. As concerns the loose aggregate of ideas making up National Socialist ideology—for example, the biologistic racism and the eugenics program, the national revanchism and militarism, the cult of power and health—most of these do not have any direct counterparts in Heidegger's philosophical thinking, although his deeply conservative and nationalist worldview, his anti-Semitism, and his emotional dynamics possibly made him feel attracted to some of them.

The Failed Critique

Heidegger's hopes concerning National Socialism were from the outset tempered by doubts whether the present political revolution would lead over into the ontological revolution that he envisioned. Toward the end of 1933, a little over half a year into the rectorate, he starts to lose his faith in the potential of the politics of the party. As he sees it, the Nazi university politics amounts to little more than empty programs and ideological conformism, and he criticizes Nazi ideology as a manifestation of "ethical materialism" (GA 94: 142/104) and "murky biologism" (GA 94: 143/105). As a result, he starts to conceive of his own task as that of continuing his lonesome struggle for a "spiritual National Socialism" outside the realm of official party politics (GA 94: 132/96–7; 155/113–14). This also means that he gives up his hopes of an imminent turning in the history of being. Instead, he will from now on think of the task of the thinker as that of preparing the way for a new beginning that will perhaps only come to pass after hundreds of years and that he himself—doomed to loneliness and to being misunderstood by his contemporaries—will never be able to witness (cf. GA 94: 280–1/205–6).

From the mid-1930s Heidegger develops what will be his basic critique of National Socialism, namely that it constitutes a radical manifestation of the metaphysical techno-subjectivist understanding of being, the overcoming of which he first hoped it would initiate (cf., e.g., GA 96: 195/153; GA 66: 168–9/146–7). The nihilistic essence of this metaphysics, he claims, is that it robs being—and, hence, all beings—of its significance and worth by reducing it to a material reserve for the human subject to exploit and manipulate.

Considered as a general diagnosis of the technical and subjectivist tendency of Western metaphysics, Heidegger's analysis is not without merit. Although it is wildly simplifying—singling out one aspect among many as *the* basic dimension of the historical development—it offers an original perspective on the way in which the Western understanding of being and knowledge is internally linked to a will to control and manipulate the world and ourselves. However, Heidegger's critical diagnosis of National Socialism as a species of techno-subjectivist metaphysics is unable to shed much light on the socioeconomic, psychosocial, and ideological developments that open up the possibility and appeal of a movement like Nazism. Above all, it totally fails to acknowledge and illuminate the ethical and political meaning of this murderous regime.

It is clear, I think, that Heidegger's interpretation of Nazism as a form of nihilist metaphysics represses and serves to cover up the moral disaster of Nazism in general and the Holocaust in particular. In understanding Nazism as a species of metaphysics, what Heidegger worries about is only and exclusively its status as a representative of modern nihilism that his own thinking is aimed at overcoming. In this, he is not concerned about and pays no attention to the abysmal moral corruption of the collectivism and racism that Nazism promotes or the murder and suffering that it results in. This is why he can conceive of Nazism as on a par with all the other ideologies of the nihilistic age, for example, communism, liberalism, and democracy. This is why he can consider the extreme nihilism of Nazism as a reason for affirming it and for continuing to support Hitler's murderous policies. Furthermore, this is also why he contemptuously rejects the moral outrage of the Allies over the atrocities committed by the Nazis, stubbornly maintaining that the Allies failed to recognize the metaphysical status of the events and the philosophical calling of the Germans.

In the end, Heidegger's repression of the moral reality of National Socialism makes it impossible for him to give meaning and urgency to his critique of Nazism as nihilism. His basic charge is that Nazism qua nihilism robs being of its power to bind and concern us, with the result that all beings—including human beings—are deprived of their normativity and weight. Hence, the basic problem with Nazism is not that it is morally evil but that it hinders us from experiencing anything as ethically-existentially normative. Consider the infamous yet quite paradigmatic passage from the lecture-cycle "Insight into That Which Is" from 1949 where Heidegger interprets the gas chambers of the concentration camps as one among many consequences of nihilism: "Agriculture is now a mechanized food industry, in essence the same as the production of corpses in the gas chambers and extermination camps, the same as the blockading and starving of countries, the same as the production of hydrogen bombs" (GA 79: 27/27). The point of the remark is to highlight the way in which nihilism transforms all beings into meaningless objects that can be manipulated at will, such that even killing people appears as normal technical procedure. We are thus in bad need of a world in which things would matter again. However, Heidegger's remark is an exercise in double play. On the one hand, he conceives of nihilism as a condition that actually prevents us from experiencing other human beings as ethically obligating and significant. This is what makes nihilism worse than murder and gives absolute priority to the task of overcoming nihilism by establishing a binding world. On the other hand, his description of nihilism gets its entire moral significance and urgency from the fact—denied by Heidegger—that human beings *do* claim us as absolutely normative and significant whatever metaphysical worldview happens to dominate our society. If this were not the case, nihilism would not be a moral problem in the first place. If we, like Heidegger, deny the absolute ethical claim of the other, it becomes impossible to articulate without inconsistency the moral challenge that nihilism supposedly poses to us and the moral urgency of overcoming it.

The Black Hole in Heidegger's Thinking

The recent publication of the first four volumes of Heidegger's *Black Notebooks* has caused a major shock effect, reverberating far beyond the world of Heidegger scholarship. Ultimately, it seems that the ongoing publication might even threaten Heidegger's status as one of the greatest philosophers of the twentieth century.[5]

So what is so shocking about the *Black Notebooks*?

So far, the shock effect has mainly been seen as the result of the incontrovertible and detailed testimony that the *Black Notebooks* give of the depth and the duration of Heidegger's entanglement in Nazism, and especially of the gravity of his anti-Semitism and the use he makes of it in his narrative of the history of being. However, given that most of these things have been known before—excepting the depth of Heidegger's anti-Semitism—it seems implausible that the shock is just the result of the *Black Notebooks'* disclosing new aggravating facts about Heidegger.

To start with, it is hard to avoid the thought that the astonishment and outrage caused by the publication is at least to some extent conditioned by previous bad faith, such that it is part of the shock that the *Black Notebooks* force us to confront questions that we have so far allowed ourselves to deny or mitigate in different ways. The notebooks make it impossible to deny the gravity of Heidegger's Nazi engagement, whereby the question of the relationship between his philosophy and his Nazism is opened up in all sharpness as a primal question for all future research. However, I also believe that the shock effect has another source. What I want to suggest is that the *Black Notebooks* unsettle our understanding of the *spirit* of Heidegger's thinking and that it is this perhaps more than anything else that seriously threatens our assessment of his philosophical status.

What do I mean by the "spirit" of a philosopher's thinking?

My suggestion is that when we read philosophical texts—in particular, texts that touch on vital ethical and existential matters—it belongs to the reading itself that we project a certain understanding of the spirit of the text, that is, of the emotional atmosphere and ethical-existential attitude of the voice that speaks to us. To understand the spirit of thinking is basically to understand what kind of person it is that does the thinking, from what kind of ethical-existential universe the thinking springs. Our more or less indeterminate grasp of the spirit of a text centrally guides how we read it and understand its philosophy: What kinds of motives and concerns drive the philosophical explication? What are the emotional charge and existential weight of its central theses? What other kinds of things would we expect this voice to think and say? What kinds of things would feel far-fetched or unthinkable? If our sense of the spirit of the text changes, our way of understanding the logic and meaning of what it says may also change drastically.

As I see it, listening and relating to the spirit of the text is an internal feature of reading philosophical texts. However, even though we always co-read the authorial voice that speaks to us, this does not allow us to directly deduce the spirit of the text from whatever we think we know about the psychology of the author. It is always possible in principle that the emotional and existential character of the text transcends—widens or contradicts—our preunderstanding of the psychological type of the author. Then again, it is precisely because we are always already projecting the spirit of the text that our understanding of the life and psyche of the author cannot fail to matter to us in our philosophical interpretation of the text. Even though our beliefs about the author do not permit us to predetermine the spirit of the text, they nevertheless raise questions and suggest tentative answers that we cannot ignore and that are bound to color our reading. This is the reason why philosophers—even though they habitually write off the philosophical relevance of biography—tend to be extremely sensitive about biographical data that affect their understanding of the ethical-existential substance of their philosopher-heroes.[6]

When it comes to our understanding of Heidegger, the situation we stand in could be described as follows. Since the beginning of his philosophical fame, Heidegger's thinking has not only been seen as one of the most profound critical confrontations with the traditional ontological and epistemological paradigms determining the character of Western philosophy. It has also been seen as one of the foremost modern attempts to articulate the being of the human being—the basic existential challenges and the fundamental structures that constitute our experience of significant phenomena. Indeed, it is precisely Heidegger's way of anchoring the ontological-epistemological problems of philosophy in the existential problems of life that gives to his philosophy its peculiar radiance and sense of depth.

Nevertheless, I think it is pertinent to say that Heidegger's thinking has generally taken the form of quite abstract explications of the general structures of our experience and of the dynamics of being. Although Heidegger has insisted on the need to ground these explications in phenomenological descriptions of concrete experiences, he has tended to avoid digging deeper into the ethical-existential experiences and motives that the explications ultimately refer to. This will certainly be disputed by many Heidegger scholars but I think it is true. As concerns Heidegger's earlier thinking, the phenomenological analyses are primarily aimed at exhibiting the structures of our everyday coping with the tasks and tools of our environment. However, when it comes to the central ethical-existential experiences and attitudes that give sense to our everyday coping, the phenomenological effort has been much poorer: the analysis of authenticity does little to illuminate the ethical-existential motives characterizing authentic resoluteness; the analysis of Dasein's relations to others, without which the analysis of authenticity must remain fundamentally unclear, is inadequate to say the least;

although the account of the They points to important mechanisms of collective pressure and conformism, it fails to elucidate the motives and attitudes that sustain the They; finally, although Heidegger has a lot to say about the experiences of anxiety and conscience it seems to me that his guiding effort to construe them as experiences disclosing the ontological structures and predicament of Dasein allows him to avoid further questions concerning their ethical-existential motives and meaning. As concerns Heidegger's later thinking, it is more obvious that his meditations on the openness of being, the strife between the world and the earth, and so forth mainly unfold without much concrete analysis of the experiences and attitudes that inform these matters.

This distance between Heidegger's philosophical theses and their ethical-existential meaning has allowed for a certain indeterminacy or leeway as regards our understanding of the spirit that his thinking is rooted in. There has, so to speak, been a hole in the Heideggerian textuality into which his readers have been able to project their more or less unclear phantasies about the spirit of his thinking. It is this hole that has conditioned the common way of reading Heidegger, especially his later texts, very reverently as giving expression to deep insights, insights whose ethical-existential meaning, however, has been left quite indeterminate. It is also this hole that has made it possible for many readers to conceive of Heidegger's philosophy as concerned with so fundamental ontological questions that it is prior and/or neutral to all ethical-existential questions, and thus in principle compatible with, for example, the kind of ethics represented by Martin Buber and Levinas.

The effect of the *Black Notebooks* is that they narrow our opportunities for wishful speculation about the spirit of Heidegger's thinking and instead cast a dark shadow over it. Reading the notebooks is to listen to a man who shuts his ears and eyes—and above all his heart—to the wave of persecution, violence and war that rises around him from the beginning of the 1930s to the end of the war, and who after that continues to deny what has happened and his own role in the events. Instead of opening himself to the ethical challenge that he is faced with, Heidegger is obsessed with interpreting—that is, explaining away—the meaning of the political events in terms of the roles they play in the dynamics of the history of being. Everything—from political ideologies to mass murder—is leveled down and conceived of as moments in the history of being: either as manifestations of nihilism or as the first stirrings of a new beginning.

The glaring discrepancy between Heidegger's philosophical meanderings and all that he shuts out and denies makes it difficult not to read his notebooks as an expression of repression and self-deception, as a desperate effort to explain away the ethical problems that he is unable to face and transform them into impersonal episodes in the history of being. The emotional landscape of the notebooks is largely dominated by bitterness, contempt, and self-aggrandizement. The bitterness and contempt is primarily directed at the urban bourgeois world, the intellectuals and philosophers at home in this world, the vulgar Nazis, and the victorious powers that first wage war on Nazi Germany, after which they hinder Heidegger from realizing his philosophical calling by banning him from teaching. Finding himself surrounded by all these small-minded agents of nihilism, Heidegger stages himself as the lonesome thinker who—misunderstood and unappreciated by his contemporaries—sacrifices himself for the sake of the new beginning, a beginning that he in his role as philosophical forerunner is doomed never to experience.

The spiritual atmosphere of the *Black Notebooks* is not only a window to Heidegger's psychology, but also concerns our understanding of his thinking. The fact that Heidegger's later thinking is elaborated and articulated in this atmosphere suggests that it is compatible with and at least to some extent motivated by an attitude that represses the central ethical challenges of life and that is characterized by a blend of bitterness and self-aggrandizement typical of ressentiment. This, of course, does not allow us to reduce Heidegger's philosophy to a pure expression of repression and ressentiment. Explicating and assessing the meaning, truth, and ethical substance of Heidegger's later thinking is an autonomous task that can only be done by reflecting on the thoughts themselves and phenomenologically relating them to the experiences they refer to—either expressly and willfully or implicitly and inadvertently. What the *Black Notebooks* do is that they forcefully suggest that Heidegger's thinking is steeped in a spirit that is problematic in many respects. In so doing, they are bound to color our reading of his texts and sharpen the critical question of the ethical-existential substance of his thought—both early and late.

One issue that may appear in a different light when considered against the backdrop of the emotional landscape of the *Black Notebooks* is the curiously nebulous and evasive character of the later Heidegger's vision of an "other beginning," of the possible dawning of a binding world. In a fresh review of the English translation of the first volume of the *Black Notebooks* Richard Polt deplores the fact that the "long-term goal" of Heidegger's philosophical-political program remains "frustratingly vague." Hence, he writes that unless we find more "specific analyses and rationales," for example, in Heidegger's still largely unpublished correspondence, we are "forced to speculate" (Polt 2016). However, what if it is no coincidence but rather a kind of emotional necessity that Heidegger's vision remains vague? If it is true that Heidegger's later thinking of the openness of being is energized by a spirit of repression and ressentiment—by his bitterness in the face of the contemporary world and his dream about a collective community that shall free him from his alienation and his conscience, and hail him as the philosopher-hero that has made this community possible—then it should come as no surprise that his dream of an other beginning will always remain unclear and ambivalent. Indeed, it would have to be such in order not to dissipate. Why would not the binding world that Heidegger envisions be strongly characterized by the tyranny of the They that he criticizes in *Being and Time*, perhaps even more so than the modern urban society that he despises? Why would the holy gods of this world not just amount to more variants of the collective mass spectacles that Heidegger was offered by the Nazi regime and that he seems to have tired of pretty swiftly? Why would not the individual person living in the binding world still be faced with the difficulties of the ethical challenge to open up to the others and with the impossibility of merging with her social role? Perhaps these questions—and many others—must remain unanswered for the simple reason that Heidegger's dream of a new beginning is essentially a dream of a historical situation in which the problems that face every person in every epoch have been magically dissolved.

I do not intend this as a definite claim about the existential meaning and function of Heidegger's vision of an other beginning. The point is rather to show what kinds of questions are at stake here. Perhaps the philosophical vision guiding Heidegger's affirmation of Nazism had the character of a ressentiment-driven utopian dream? Indeed, seeing Nazism as an answer to an unclear phantasy—a phantasy that also involves covering up the evils of Nazism—would not have been a peculiarity of Heidegger. Rather, it is the typical way in which we are drawn to this kind of movement and to evil more generally.

The publication of the *Black Notebooks* has caused widespread moral outrage and condemnations. It is no doubt important that we unflinchingly acknowledge and critique all the facts and dimensions of Heidegger's Nazi-engagement and his anti-Semitism. Still, it seems to me that this issue ultimately confronts us with questions that go far beyond any restricted attempt to determine to what extent Heidegger and his philosophy were Nazi. In fact, by concentrating exclusively on the question of Heidegger's Nazism—whether we condemn his entire thinking as Nazi-philosophy[7] or whether we try to distinguish between those parts of his philosophy that are infected by Nazism and those that are not—we risk dodging the further challenges that this issue points to, challenges that concern our understanding of Heidegger's philosophy, of philosophy more generally, and of ourselves as human beings.[8]

Heidegger's Nazism raises the question of the ethical-existential problems characterizing his entire thinking: the denial of the ethical claim of the other, the egoistic-collectivist attitude informing both his view of authenticity and his later account of the bindingness and holiness of the world, and so on. To critically investigate these matters is not the same as disclosing the hidden Nazism of his philosophy. Rather, it is to interrogate the ethical-existential attitude that his thinking is rooted in and articulates, and of which his Nazism is just an especially poisonous and dangerous manifestation. In the end, our ability to understand and learn something from Heidegger's relationship to Nazism depends on our seeing that it is a symptom of ethical-existential problems that will always, no doubt, constitute challenges for ourselves and for philosophy in general: the problem of acknowledging and opening up to the ethical claim of other persons; the temptation to deny and repress this claim and succumb to an attitude that is fundamentally egoistic and collectivist; the temptation to cover up and explain away the ethical challenges that face us by appropriating philosophical theories and worldviews that do this job for us; the lure of the logic of ressentiment, according to which our difficulties with attaining collective affirmation make us despise the people we secretly envy, and generate phantasies of revenge and of a glorious return to our collective circle. And so on.

11

THE EVENT THAT OPENS THE WORLD

Heidegger's later thinking is guided by the question of the event—the *Ereignis*—that opens up and gives a historical world as a binding destiny. The purpose of this chapter is to explicate Heidegger's conception of the dynamics of this event.

I will begin by outlining Heidegger's view of the purpose and stakes of the event that opens the world: to establish a world that is, in some sense, binding and holy. I then present his view of the tasks of thinking and poetry, of their complementary roles in making possible the establishment of a binding world. After that, I offer an extended analysis of Heidegger's main attempt to account for the dynamics of the event that opens the world, which is found in "The Origin of the Work of Art," where he explicates the opening of the world in terms of a "strife" between the "world" and the "earth." Finally, I take a brief look at Heidegger's later rearticulation of this dynamic in terms of what he calls the "fourfold."

The Question of the Binding Power of the World

For Heidegger, what is at stake in the event that opens up a historical world is not only the determination of the meanings and purposes constituting the world, but also the power of the world to bind and obligate us.

The later Heidegger's concern with the bindingness of the world has, however, largely been neglected or downplayed in the secondary literature, which has primarily focused on the epistemological-ontological aspects of the event of being: on the self-withdrawing character of the *Ereignis*, on concealment as a condition for unconcealment, on the historicity, finitude, groundlessness, and linguisticality of being, and so on.[1] One plausible reason for this neglect is that Heidegger mainly articulates the problem of the binding power of the world by introducing a heavy religious vocabulary into the center of his thought—a vocabulary that is exegetically challenging and prone to alienate some of his readers. From the mid-1930s onwards, he persistently talks about the holy, the gods, the divinities, and so forth. As late as in the 1966 interview for *Der Spiegel* he famously states, as a comment on the contemporary metaphysical situation, "Only a god can still save us" (GA 16: 671/107).

However, I think the main philosophical reason for the neglect is that Heidegger's pursuit of the question of the bindingness of the world brings us face to face with questions that are difficult and unsettling for all those who believe in the radical historicity of meaning and value—among them most Heideggerians. This question is rarely asked by philosophers who subscribe to some version of the idea that our experience of ethical-existential normativity and significance is based on the values and norms of our historical context. Instead, one tends to be content with appealing to general epistemological-ontological arguments to the effect that our historical values are all that we have and that we simply have to accept them as our groundless predicament. Heidegger's pursuit of the question of the bindingness of historical values is rare, and this for a reason. The problem is— as I shall argue in the epilogue—that by pursuing this question Heidegger is bound to bear witness to how difficult—and, in the end, impossible—it is to corroborate the idea that our historical meanings and values constitute our ultimate source of ethical-existential normativity.

Let us take a look at how Heidegger articulates the issue of the binding power of the world in terms of his religious rhetoric.

According to Heidegger, the history of Western metaphysics with its basic forgetfulness of the openness of being reaches its peak in the modern techno-subjectivist understanding of being as a mere object reserve for human manipulation. With Hölderlin and Nietzsche, Heidegger describes the modern age as an age characterized by the "flight of the gods" (GA 40: 48/49)—an age where "God is dead" (GA 5: 124/214). Heidegger also names the predicament of the present age "nihilism" (GA 45: 185/160). Due to its fundamental obliviousness to the openness of being, the modern age suffers from a lack of holiness and gods, the result of which is that we experience a deep "purpose- and meaninglessness of all beings" (GA 45: 196/168).

In this situation, Heidegger sees it as our primary task—the task of thinking and poetry—to work toward establishing a world that is holy and binding and where the gods are present again. However, what does he mean by "the holy" and "the gods"?

Heidegger characterizes "the holy" as the "essential sphere of divinity" that "affords the dimension for the gods and the god" (GA 9: 338/258). In some sense, the holy is the dimension or realm where gods can be present. To understand what Heidegger has in mind it is crucial to see that by talking about holiness and gods he is far from introducing any kind of transcendent super-entities that would exist beyond our finite historical world.

In "The Origin of the Work of Art" Heidegger writes: "In the tragedy ... the battle of the new gods against the old is being fought." This means that tragedy puts up for decision "what is holy and what unholy, what is great and what small, what is brave and what cowardly, what is noble and what fugitive, what is master and what slave" (GA 5: 29/22). Here is his description of how the artwork lets the gods be present in their holiness:

> Such setting up [of the work of art] is an erecting in the sense of dedication and praise. To dedicate means to consecrate (*heiligen*), in the sense that, in the

workly construction, the holy (*das Heilige*) is opened up as holy and the god is called forth into the openness of its presence. Praise belongs to dedication as doing honor to the dignity and splendor of the god. Dignity and splendor are not properties beside and behind which there stands, additionally, the god. Rather, it is in the dignity, in the splendor, that the god comes to presence. In the reflected glory of this splendor there glows, i.e., there clarifies, what we called the world. (GA 5: 30/22)

The above quotations allow us to specify what Heidegger means by "holiness" and "gods." Heidegger makes it perfectly clear that "behind" the holiness and splendor of the artwork there exist no transcendent gods that the artwork would represent and give voice to. On the contrary, it is precisely the holiness and splendor opened up by the artwork that allow the gods to be present as gods in the first place. Hence, for Heidegger, the gods signify nothing but the highest values and ideals of our historical world in so far as they are able to be present to us as holy gods that bind and have authority over us.[2] Only by conceiving of our guiding historical values and ideals as holy and binding, can we experience the beings of our world as meaningful and important phenomena.[3]

However, is it not wrongheaded and distortive to characterize—as I have done—Heidegger's gods in terms of "values," given his well-known and severe criticism of this concept? Let me briefly explain why think this objection is misguided and threatens to cover up and mystify what Heidegger has in mind.

Heidegger denounces the concept of "value" as a monstrosity originating in modern techno-subjectivist metaphysics. In the nihilistic situation of the present where the gods have fled, we are left with the concept of value—"the last and at the same time the weakest offspring of *agathon*" (GA 9: 227/174)—as our way of conceiving of the ideals and purposes of our world. However, when we conceive of our ideals and purposes in this way they cannot address as binding and important anymore. "Values," Heidegger states, are the "powerless and threadbare mask of the objectification of beings, an objectification that has become flat and devoid of background. No one dies for mere values" (GA 5: 102/77). So what is the problem with values? Heidegger explains:

> It is important finally to realize that precisely through the characterization of something as "a value" what is so valued is robbed of its worth. That is to say, by the assessment of something as a value what is valued is admitted only as an object for human estimation. Every valuing, even where it values positively, is a subjectivizing. It does not let beings: be. (GA 9: 349/265)

In attacking the concept of value, the central thrust of Heidegger's critique is always that in conceiving of our purposes and ideals as values, we subjectivize them and see them as products of the human capacity to evaluate things and create values. To avoid this connotation and emphasize that our ideals and purposes are given to us out of our history as something ultimate that we have to receive and accept, Heidegger prefers to use other words, such as the "gods" (GA 5: 30/22), the "directives" (*Weisungen*) (GA 9: 361/274), the "measure" (*Maß*) (GA 5: 30/22), or the "law and rule" (*Gesetz und Regel*) (GA 9: 361/274). However, it seems to me that Heidegger's view of values as issuing from the evaluating activity of the human subject does not capture an internal trait of the concept of value as it is normally used. Both in our everyday talk and in contemporary philosophy it is common to use the notion of historical values to denote the historically given conceptions of what is good and valuable that always already guide or condition our experience of ethical-existential significance and that cannot be created at will. If we understand values in this kind of non-subjectivist manner, there is nothing that prevents us from using the word to articulate and elucidate what Heidegger prefers to call the gods or the measure of our historical world. Moreover, there is nothing that prevents us from reformulating Heidegger's question of the bindingness of being as the question of what is needed in order for our values to open up and address us as holy gods that we are prepared to die for.[4]

The Task of Thinking and the Task of Poetry

According to Heidegger, it is only be reflecting on and taking part in the event that opens up historical worlds that it is possible for the event to unfold and open up a world that is holy and binding to us.

Although Heidegger stresses that being gives itself to the human being of its own accord—and is no human creation—the human being is nevertheless needed in order to accomplish the self-giving of being. This is the task of the thinkers and the poets who play different yet complementary parts in the dynamics that open up the world. Heidegger describes the difference between thinking and poetry like this: "The thinker says being. The poet names the holy" (GA 9: 312/237). That is, whereas thinking reflects on and articulates the fundamental ontological status and dynamics of the basic happening which opens up the world, art in general and poetry in particular establish the gods and the world and make them shine forth as a holy domain of purposes and meaning.

Let us spell out the complementary roles of thinking and poetry in a little more detail. Heidegger describes the task of thinking as the primary task that conditions and prepares the way for the task of poetry: "But the holy, which alone is the essential sphere of divinity, which in turn alone affords a dimension for the gods and for the god, comes to radiate only when being itself beforehand and after extensive preparation has been cleared and is experienced in its truth" (GA 9: 338-9/258). That is, it is only when "being has been … experienced in its truth"—which is the task of thinking—that the holy can open up and the gods can come to presence in the work of poetry. By reflecting on the openness of being, thinking dismantles our metaphysical attempts to ground historical being and lets us conceive of being in its givenness as a groundless and finite destiny. By so doing, it opens up our understanding of poetry as the "holy" domain harboring our "gods." Within the horizon of this understanding of the event of being, the task of poetry is then to establish—and give splendor and dignity to—the ideals and gods that are to guide our experience of phenomena.

Since the later Heidegger conceives of the world as fundamentally linguistic, he sees poetry as the primary form of art.

In *Being and Time*, Heidegger basically conceived of language in terms a medium of communication that does not constitute but refers to and expresses our primarily prelinguistic understanding of our historical world. During the 1930s this conception undergoes a change. As early as 1931, in the lecture course "Aristotle's Metaphysics Θ 1–3: On the Essence and Actuality of Force," Heidegger intimates a critical reversal of his view. Explicating Aristotle's concept of *logos*, he claims that language should be understood "not merely as a means of asserting and communicating, which indeed it also is, but ... as that wherein the manifestness and message of the world first of all bursts forth and is" (GA 33: 128/109). In the 1936 lecture "Hölderlin and the Essence of Poetry" Heidegger makes one of his first attempts to spell out his new conception of language. Here he states the constitutive role of language bluntly: "Only where there is language, is there world" (GA 4: 38/56). But how so? In order to be able to speak with each other about different matters at all, Heidegger argues, we first need to able to hear and comprehend the common words that carry our speech and understanding:

> We are a conversation (*Gespräch*)—and that means: we are able to hear from one another. We are a conversation, that always also means: we are *one* conversation. The unity of a conversation, however, consists in one and the same thing being manifest in the essential word, something we agree upon, and on the basis of which we are united and thus properly ourselves. The conversation and its unity support our existence. (GA 4: 39/57)

That is to say, it is only on the basis of the primary unity of our language, the capacity of our words and expressions to say and present the same meanings, that the possibility is opened up to experience and communicate the world as a common historical context of significance. For the later Heidegger, language is thus the fundamental element that constitutes the world; it is the "clearing-concealing arrival of being itself" (GA 9: 326/249). Hence, it is only by receptively appropriating our given historical language that we are able to understand the world and experience beings as phenomena.[5]

The task of poetry is none other than to found the language that constitutes the world:

> The poet names the gods and names all things with respect to what they are. This naming does not merely consist in something already known being furnished with a name; rather, by speaking the essential word, the poet's naming first appoints the beings as that, which they are. Thus they become known *as* beings. Poetry is the founding (*Stiftung*) of being in words. (GA 4: 41/59)

Since there are no meaningful phenomena available prior to the emergence of language, poetry cannot transpire as an activity of naming or description accommodating itself to such phenomena. Rather, by establishing the words capable of assembling the significances of the world into their unity, the poet appoints the entities to what they are. In this way, the poet founds the language that opens up our historical world, determining all our subsequent speech and understanding. This is why poetry is the primary art that guides all the other arts—painting, architecture, music, and so on—in their conjoined effort to open up the world.

The Superiority of the Task of Opening a World

About a year after the publication of *Being and Time*, Heidegger began to think of the task of opening up a binding world as the primary ethical-existential task of the human being. Provided that we live in a nihilistic era where all beings have lost their bindingness and significance for us, the task of establishing a binding world takes on absolute primacy over and against all ethical concerns with different beings. This superordination of ontology over ethics, I claimed, played a central role in Heidegger's engagement in National Socialism by allowing him to cover up the moral corruption and terrible deeds of Nazism, and think of these events as a purely ontological matter.

Although Heidegger from the mid-1930s starts to interpret Nazism as a species of nihilist metaphysics, he will always hold on to the idea of the absolute superiority of the task of thinking and poetry. Here is how he formulates the import and motivation of his thinking on the opening page of the "Letter on Humanism":

> Thinking accomplishes the relation of being to the essence of the human being. Thinking does not become action only because some effect issues from it or because it is applied. Thinking acts insofar as it thinks. Such action is presumably the simplest and at the same time the highest because it concerns the relation of being to humans. But all working or effecting lies in being and is directed toward beings. Thinking, in contrast, lets itself be claimed by being so that it can say the truth of being. Thinking accomplishes this letting. (GA 9: 313/239)

That is to say, since the possible significance of all particular beings and all our actions in relation to such beings is determined by historical being, and since thinking plays an essential part in the realization of the happening that decides over the occurrence or failure to occur of a binding being-world, thinking acquires the absolute dignity of "highest action." Later in the same text, Heidegger explicitly raises the question of how his thinking relates to a possible ethics. To answer this question, he returns to Heraclitus's use of the word *ēthos*, which he interprets as signifying the "abode, dwelling place ... the open region in which the human being dwells" (GA 9: 354/269). Since it is precisely the task of his own thinking to reflect on and articulate this openness of being, he argues that his own thinking is already in itself "primordial ethics" (*ursprüngliche Ethik*) (GA 9: 356/271). However, by calling his own thinking a primordial ethics, Heidegger in no way questions but rather reaffirms the radical priority of his thinking of being over ethics.

The superior import that Heidegger ascribes to his thinking of being is a direct consequence of his basic idea that the historical happening of being possesses the power of granting to the world—and, hence, to the beings of the world— any significance they might have, and that thinking plays a decisive role in the realization of this happening. What is ultimately at stake in the task of thinking is thus not only to clarify the ontological horizons of our existential understanding, but also to co-realize—assist or hamper—the happening which decides whether a binding holy world arises at all. Consequently, the task of thinking emerges as the highest thinkable task, a task that conditions and thus in principle overshadows every other possible existential-ethical concern, even our concern for other human beings.

Although Heidegger's conception of the task of thinking—its import and motivation—basically remains the same, it also undergoes some changes. In 1933, there were some aspects of his thinking that supported his seeing the Nazi regime as the possible beginning of a deeper ontological revolution. First, in viewing the Nazi takeover as a "first awakening" or "departure," Heidegger presupposed that the prephilosophical mood of departure and resolve that he felt around him could later be developed into a truly philosophical understanding of the task that lay ahead. Second, by conceiving of the establishment of the world in terms of a free projection, he ascribed great power to the human creators—the philosophers, artists, and political leaders—in changing the course of the history of being and in projecting a new world. In his later thinking, both these things change. To begin with, Heidegger will insist on the absolute priority of the task of understanding— via a return to the Greek origin—the openness of being as the decisive prerequisite for a new beginning. Prior to this, whatever looks like a prephilosophical emotional preparedness to project new worlds inevitably still remains stuck in the old nihilistic metaphysics of the first beginning. Furthermore, he will give up his notion of a free world-projection and emphasize that the opening of a world is nothing that the human subject can bring about at will. Although the establishment of a world still involves the creative and formative work of the poets and artists, Heidegger will describe it as essentially receptive in relation to the history in which it stands as the ultimate source of all gods and meanings. Both these modifications make it harder for Heidegger to yield to the temptation of seeing a political movement like Nazism as the possible onset of a new beginning in the history of being. Nevertheless—as I shall argue in the epilogue—the later Heidegger's conception of the superior task of founding a binding world will always remain philosophically and morally-politically deeply problematic.

The Strife between the World and the Earth

Heidegger's long essay "The Origin of the Work of Art" constitutes his most elaborate attempt to depict the dynamics that, in and through the work of art, allow a historical world to open up and shine forth. Although written in the early phase of his later thinking, I think the essay establishes the basic schema that his later reflections, particularly on the "fourfold," will to some extent elaborate but never radically alter.

The central aim of Heidegger's essay is to describe how the work of art "opens up a world" (GA 5: 28/21) by carrying out the "strife" between the "world" and the "earth." It is important to note from the start that Heidegger rejects the traditional conception of art as an object of the subject's aesthetic experience, and instead focuses on the question of the truth of art. However, by this he does not mean the ability of the artwork to correctly represent any pregiven meanings of the world or express the inner life of the artist. Rather, the truth-task of the artwork is "the opening up of beings in their being, the happening of truth" (GA 5: 24/18). His model example of an artwork is a Greek temple:

> It is the temple work that first fits together and simultaneously gathers around itself the unity of those paths and relations in which birth and death, disaster and blessing, victory and disgrace, endurance and decline acquire for the human being the shape of its destiny. The all-governing expanse of these open relations is the world of this historical people. (GA 5: 27–8/20–1)

And:

> Standing there, the temple first gives to things their look (*Gesicht*), and to men their outlook (*Aussicht*) on themselves. (GA 5: 29/21)

As Heidegger's choice of example indicates, he understands the world-establishing function of the artwork in analogy with how a religious world of beliefs, norms, and practices is set up and upheld by a compound of writings, artworks, music, buildings, and other public installations and practices. The task of the work of art is thus none other than to enact the epiphanic happening which opens up the world as the unified and binding historical context of ideals and purposes determining our possibilities of experiencing and grasping ourselves and the entities of the world as meaningful. Prior to the work of art we do not have access to a world or to meaningful entities; it is only through the work that a world of being and meaning opens up and shines forth: "In the work of art the truth of beings has set itself to work (*sich ins Werk gesetzt*). 'To set' means here: to bring to stand. The being of beings comes into the constancy of its shining" (GA 5: 21/16).

The essay takes its starting point in the question concerning the character of the artwork as a material thing. Since the "thing" has always functioned as the "paradigmatic being" (GA 5: 6/5), it may seem natural to begin by explicating the thingness of the thing in order, then, to go on and specify the features that make the thing into an artwork. However, Heidegger argues, the traditional conceptions of the thingness of the thing are insufficient. He first rejects two concepts of the thing that are grounded in the theoretical experience of present-at-hand objects: the thing as an underlying substance and the thing as a unity in the stream of sensations. He then turns to the notion of the thing as a "synthesis of matter and form" (GA 5: 11/8) which, he claims, has its origin in our experience of tools. It is a basic characteristic of the tool that its material is subordinated to its form, so that both the material and the form are ultimately determined by their usefulness for human purposes. Yet according to Heidegger, the notion of the tool as formed material is unable to account either for the peculiar quality of the material thing as something "having-grown-by-itself" (*Eigenwüchsig*) (GA 5: 13/10) or for the "standing-in-itself" (*Insichstehen*) (GA 5: 25/19) or "self-sufficiency" (*Selbstgenügsamkeit*) (GA 5: 14/10) characteristic of the work of art.

If we bear in mind that Heidegger's own analysis of the structure of phenomenal understanding in *Being and Time* was rooted precisely in the experience of tools, we can see that his critique of the model of the tool in fact opens up a reassessment of his own conception of phenomena. Not only did his earlier analysis obliterate the material aspect of the phenomena by reducing them to instantiations of pre-understood significances and purposes. As a result of taking its starting point in the experience of the tool and proceeding by explicating the structural ground of this experience in Dasein's understanding of the world, it also failed to radically ask the question concerning the openness and givenness of the historical world itself. Heidegger's initial reflections on the thingness of the thing thus indicate the philosophical agenda of the essay. To begin with, Heidegger's entire investigation of the nature of art is motivated by the hitherto unasked question of how being itself is opened up. Granted that the work of art constitutes the site that keeps the world open, the question of the openness of being here takes the form of a question concerning the "standing-in-itself" of the artwork. Moreover, this intensified pursuit of the question of the openness of being gives rise to a felt need to account for the material-sensuous aspect of the world. What is it, apart from the facticity of history, that grants to the world its concretion and specificity?

Heidegger's account of the dynamics—namely, the strife between the world and the earth—that open up a historical world constitutes the heart of his later conception of phenomena. Hence, it is not surprising that it has become the object of opposed readings, readings mirroring the conflict between the transcendental phenomenological and hermeneutic-deconstructivist interpretations of Heidegger.

Recently, David Espinet has argued that Heidegger's notion of the "earth" can be read as a phenomenological corrective to his radical conception of the historicity of understanding. According to Espinet, the "earth" signifies both our material-natural surroundings and the manifold of sensuous qualities: colors, sounds, scents, and so on (2011: 53–4, 58). In our everyday life, we have a strong tendency to cover over the sensuous aspect of our experience, and grasp things solely in terms of the significances they have in our historical world. The upshot of this is that our understanding rigidifies into a closed repetition of received patterns of meaning: "What is silenced through the intentional yet distortive transparency of the world, is the sensuously experienceable as such, the earth. Thus intelligibility often thrusts itself between our listening and seeing and that which shows itself, so that we often superimpose fixed patterns of interpretation on the latter—on this unexpected, literally unheard-of and, as such, unrepresentable sense" (58, my translation). It is, Espinet argues, precisely because the work of art merges "our experience of sense and our experience of sensuousness" (60) in an intensified manner that it is able to shatter our common understanding of the world and open us up to "a new and unexpected sense" (57). According to Espinet, Heidegger's "earth" thus constitutes nothing but the material-sensuous ground which at the same time transcends and co-constitutes our world: a "*constantly* historical and, as such, *trans*historical ground" (54). Hence, our experience of the earth—as it is made possible by the work of art—has the potential of critically unsettling our factical understanding of the world and give us access to new meanings. Notwithstanding the fact that Heidegger in the end tends to downgrade the role of the material-sensuous earth in the artwork by overemphasizing its linguisticality and historicity, Espinet maintains that Heidegger's account of the earth "systematically" implies "the equal rank of earth and world" (64).

In Julian Young's hermeneutic-deconstructive interpretation of Heidegger's later thinking, we find a different account of the "earth." According to Young's Heidegger, we always live in a "historically and culturally relative" world, which regulates what we can understand as meaningful (2002: 9). This means that "in addition to what is intelligible to us, reality possesses an indefinitely large number of aspects, a 'plenitude' of 'sides' or 'facets' which would be disclosed to us were we to inhabit transcendental horizons other than the one we do, horizons which, however, we can neither inhabit nor even conceive. Truth, then is concealment, ultimate truth concealment of the, to us, *ineluctably* mysterious" (9). Heidegger, Young claims, introduces the notion of "earth" precisely to name the self-secluding manifold of meaning-possibilities encircling our world: "'Earth' … is … the dark penumbra of unintelligibility that surrounds … and grounds … our human existence" (2002: 9; cf. also Young 2001: 38–40). The function of the artwork is to make manifest the earth as the mysterious source of the world that we normally tend to cover over and forget. In the end, Young argues, the materialization of the earth in the work of art makes the world shine forth as "holy": "Experienced as the self-disclosure of an unfathomable 'mystery' it acquires radiance, becomes as one might also say, numinous, a 'holy' place" (2002: 45). For Young, then, the earth does not signify a sensuousness that would in any way disturb the priority that Heidegger ascribes to the historical world as that which determines the significance of all material-sensuous beings, but rather names the origin of our world in a manifold of alternative worlds and histories.

So how does Heidegger conceive of the strife between the world and the earth?

As Heidegger began the turn toward his later thinking after the publication of *Being and Time*, he put forward the idea that the world is established through a free world-projection. Even though he suggested that our projections of being in some sense need to be grounded in the totality of beings, this idea was never developed, and it remained fundamentally unclear how such projections could ever establish a unitary binding world. Now, by contrast, Heidegger stresses that the world-establishing work of art is not the result of a free and creative projection on the part of the poet or the artist. In "Hölderlin and the Essence of Poetry" he spells out the twin bonds to which poetry is subject: "As the founding of being, poetry is bound in a *twofold* sense" (GA 4: 45/63): on the one hand, poetry is bound by the "hints of the gods" (GA 4: 46/63), by which Heidegger means the determinations granted by our history; on the other hand, it is bound by "the voice of the people" (*die Stimme des Volkes*) (GA 4: 46/63), that is, "the tales (*die Sagen*) in which a people is mindful of its belongingness to beings as a whole" (GA 4: 46/63), by which he indicates what he in the art-essay will call the "earth": the factical material milieu in which we live. To understand the dynamics that open up a world is to understand how the work of art founds and gathers a world on the basis of these twin bonds. Let us examine them in turn.

Firstly, Heidegger claims that the world-founding activity of art is not free but bound by the "hints of the gods": "But the gods can come to expression only if they themselves address us and place us under their claim. The word that names the gods is always a response to such a claim. This response always stems from the responsibility of a destiny" (GA 4: 40/58; cf. GA 5: 64/48). Hence, as Heidegger repeatedly emphasizes, the articulations of poetry must be seen as responses, which receive and comply with the relations of being and meaning that are already given through our history. But how does the receptive founding of a world take place? Here is Heidegger's attempt to specify:

> The poet's saying is the catching of these hints [of the gods], in order to pass them on to his people. This catching of the hints is a reception, and yet at the same time a new giving; for in the "first signs" the poet already catches sight of the completed whole, and boldly puts what he has seen into his word, in order to predict what is not yet fulfilled. (GA 4: 46/63)

That is, the poet does not only receive and represent the hints of the gods as a ready and obvious set of pregiven concepts just lying there in our history waiting to be expressed. Rather, in what is first only given as "first signs" the poet "catches sight of the completed whole, and boldly puts what he has seen into his word." Hence, at the same time as the poet opens herself up to the address of history as our as yet undetermined manifold of being-possibilities she also through her founding words determines—decides and gathers—this manifold into a unified and limited historical world: in "fitting together" and "gathering" the "paths and relations" (GA 5: 27–8/20–1) of the world the work of art puts up for decision "what is holy and what unholy, what is great and what small, what is brave and what cowardly, what is noble and what fugitive, what is master and what slave" (GA 5: 29/22).

The fact that the world has its origin in the gathering performed by artwork for Heidegger means that it is centrally characterized by the logic of what he calls the "clearing" (*Lichtung*) (GA 5: 40/30). By gathering the world into a finite unity of meaning-relations, the artwork simultaneously refuses and covers up all the alternative meanings and values that could have entered the world but which did not. Hence, the "clearing in which beings stand is in itself at the same time concealment" (GA 5: 40/30). The world that is opened up in the work of art is thus essentially a finite historical world surrounded by a potentially endless dark field of neglected alternative meanings. In fact, it is precisely this dark multitude of dissimulated meanings that Young calls the "earth." However, although Young certainly describes a central aspect of Heidegger's conception of the dynamics of the event of being, I will argue that the "earth" names another aspect of these dynamics.

Secondly, Heidegger maintains that in order to establish a world the artwork has to ground it on the "earth." But what is the "earth"? Let me begin by quoting Heidegger's description of the Greek temple in its groundedness on the earth at length:

> Standing there, the building rests on the rocky ground. This resting of the work draws out of the rock the darkness of its unstructured yet unforced support. Standing there, the building holds its place against the storm raging above it and so first makes the storm visible in its violence. The gleam and luster of the stone, though apparently there only by the grace of the sun, in fact first brings to radiance the light of day, the breadth of the sky, the darkness of the night. The temple's firm towering makes visible the invisible space of the air. The steadfastness of the work stands out against the surge of the tide and, in its own repose, brings out the raging of the surf. Tree and grass, eagle and bull, snake and cricket first enter their distinctive shapes and thus come to appearance as what they are. Early on, the Greeks called this coming forth and rising up in itself and in all things *physis*. At the same time *physis* lights up that on which and in which man bases his dwelling. We call this the *earth*. What this word means here is far removed from the idea of a mass of matter and from the merely astronomical idea of a planet. Earth is that in which the arising of everything that arises is brought back—as, indeed, the very thing that it is—and sheltered. In the things that arise the earth occurs as the sheltering one. (GA 5: 28/21)

This description already shows that the earth cannot, as Young claims, be interpreted as a designation of the hidden plurality of historical significance constituting the mysterious source of our finite world. Indeed, what Heidegger means by "earth" is "nature," understood not as the theoretical object of natural science, but as the material and sensuous setting we inhabit and experience. As such, the "earth" comprises both the manifold of sensuous qualities—the "massiveness and heaviness of the stone," the "firmness and pliancy of the wood," the "brightening and darkening of color," the "clang of tone," the "naming power of the word" (GA 5: 32/24)—as well as the material-organic milieu in which we establish and live our lives: the sun, the air, the waters, the climate and the weather, the rhythms of the days and the years, the terrain and the soil, the plants and the animals, the metals and the minerals.

To open up a world, Heidegger argues, the work of art needs to base the world on the earth as its material-sensuous ground. Conceived as this ground, the earth exhibits two basic traits. First, it is "that which, unforced, is effortless and untiring" (GA 5: 32/24), that is, it rests in itself irrespective of all human purposes and is thus able to function as the concrete ground on which the world is set up. Second, it is "the essentially self-secluding (*Sich-verschließende*)" (GA 5: 33/25), that is, it withdraws from the open meaning-context of the world and from all attempts to penetrate into it, operating as the hidden and self-secluding ground of the world. Eventually, Heidegger describes the interplay between the world and the earth as a "strife" (*Streit*) that the work of art enacts: "The earth cannot do without the open region of the world if it is to appear as earth in the liberating surge of its self-seclusion. The world in turn cannot float away from the earth if, as the prevailing breadth and path of all essential destiny, it is to ground itself on something decisive. In setting up a world and setting forth the earth, the work is an instigation of this strife" (GA 5: 35-6/27). Hence, in enacting the strife between the world and the earth, the artwork does not only open the world by grounding it on the earth but also sets forth and presents the earth as the hidden material-sensuous ground that it is: "The rock comes to bear and to rest and so first becomes rock; the metals come to glitter and shimmer, the colors to shine, the tones to sing, the word to speak. ... *The work lets the earth be an earth*" (GA 5: 32/24).

But what is the systematic sense of Heidegger's idea that the artwork needs to ground the world on the earth? If Espinet would be right in claiming that the earth signifies an independent transhistorical source of meaning that co-constitutes the world, this would imply a radical breach with Heidegger's central notion of the ontological difference. Is Espinet right? Does Heidegger's concept of the earth unsettle his fundamental idea that our possibilities of experiencing beings as meaningful phenomena are determined and delimited by the historical world into which we have always already been thrown?

In fact, we can find statements by Heidegger that seem to encourage this kind of interpretation. In some of his later writings he asserts that the ontological difference already presupposes a more fundamental belonging together of being and beings (cf. GA 65: 250-3/197-8; GA 11: 71/65) In a very late text on Cézanne—originally, the text was published in a supplement of the French quarterly *L'Herne* in 1971, yet Heidegger had occasion to rework it as late as 1974—he even goes as far as to suggest that Cézanne's paintings imply the "overcoming of the ontological difference between being and beings" (CZ: 342/311). His claim is that in Cézanne's art the "duality" between being and beings "is bound up in the simplicity of the pure shining of his images" (CZ: 341-2/311). However, Heidegger says nothing more to substantiate or clarify his claim about overcoming the ontological difference. Hence, the only way to give sense to the claim—and not leave it as purely formal and empty phrase—is to refer it back to his efforts to account for the dynamics that open a world first in terms of the strife between the world and the earth and then in terms of the fourfold. Since I believe that Heidegger's analysis of the strife between the world and the earth in "The Origin of the Work of Art" constitutes his most ambitious account of the way in which being and beings interact in the opening of a world—and since his account of the fourfold does not alter it in any relevant way—we need to look at this analysis to see whether there is any ground for his statement about overcoming the ontological difference.

So does Heidegger's description of the strife between the world and the earth unsettle the ontological difference? I think not, at least not in any radical manner.

To begin with, it is crucial to see that Heidegger never questions the thesis that constitutes the heart of the ontological difference, namely that it is our historical world that determines our possibilities of experiencing beings as significant phenomena. Hence, he holds that when we experience beings as phenomena they show themselves as instantiations of the meanings and values that make up our world and that are our ultimate source of truth and significance. Prior to the establishment of a world in and through the work of art, we do not have access to any meaningful phenomena.

This means that the strife between the world and the earth depicted by Heidegger takes place prior to and as a condition for the experience of beings as phenomena. What does it mean that, within these dynamics, the world has to be grounded on the earth? How does the earth function as the ground of the world?

It is clear, I think, that Heidegger wants to anchor the world in the materiality of the earth in order to ensure that the world does not remain a set of abstract and floating conceptual schemata. The work of art, he claims, grounds the world on the earth as "something decisive" (GA 5: 36/27): "In the earth, however, as the essentially self-secluding, the openness of the open region finds the highest form of resistance; it thereby finds the site of its steady stand in which the figure must be fixed in place" (GA 5: 57/42). That is, in order to gather and decide the meanings granted by history and make them stand forth in a concrete and specific form, the artwork needs to ground them in the material-sensuous milieu at hand. Although Heidegger does not spell out how this happens, it is possible to discern two aspects of this grounding, answering to the two aspects covered by the notion of earth. On the one hand, the world must be grounded in—that is, specified and fleshed out according to—the natural surroundings in which we live and in which the guiding purposes or our world can be concretely enacted and instituted. On the other hand, the world must be grounded in—that is, expressed and shaped by—the materiality and sensuousness of the medium in and through which the artwork projects the world. By anchoring the meanings of history in the earth, the work of art lets the guiding purposes and meanings making up the world arise and shine forth in a concrete paradigmatic form.

What is the status of the earth in the strife with the world? The fact is that in Heidegger's descriptions, the earth constantly figures as the subordinate pole in a hierarchical relationship: the artwork "sets" the world "back" on the earth whereby the earth functions as "the sheltering one" (*das Bergende*) (GA 5: 28/21). Even though the earth constitutes a necessary and irreducible element in the constitution of the world, it essentially functions as the receiving dimension which gives concrete and specific form to meanings ultimately stemming from our historical heritage. There is nothing in Heidegger's account that indicates how our experience of the materiality and sensuousness of the earth could ever constitute the source of those central existential purposes and meanings which in the end organize our world and give all things any possible significance they might have. The inability of the earth to function as an autonomous source of meaning also becomes manifest in Heidegger's claim that it is only the opening of the world through the work of art that lets the earth emerge as the earth: "The temple work, standing there, opens up a world and at the same time sets this world back on the earth, which itself only thus emerges as native ground (*heimatliche Grund*)" (GA 5: 28/21). Taken as such—before and irrespective of the world—the earth is nothing but a meaningless manifold of material-sensuous data; then again, to the extent that the world is established in the artwork, the earth shows up as the concrete sensuous-material setting of this historical world.[6] Indeed, if the earth would comprise beings that would be significant and normative in themselves, this would undercut the very idea that we need to open up a binding world in order to encounter meaningful phenomena.

Hence, we must conclude—against Espinet's suggestion—that Heidegger's earth does not constitute a transhistorical ground capable of harboring new meanings. Although Heidegger accords an irreducible role to nature as the sensuous-material ground and setting of every world, he does not breach the ontological difference, which remains the corner stone of his conception of phenomena to the end. This also means that although Young's reading of the earth as the hidden manifold of alternative historical meaning-possibilities goes astray and bypasses the constitutive role played by the materiality and sensuousness of the earth, his guiding intuition that Heidegger's notion of earth does not shake the primacy of history is basically correct. In the epilogue, I will raise the critical question of whether Heidegger's description of the strife between the world and the earth can account for how a historical world can bind and obligate us as our ultimate source of ethical-existential normativity and weight.

The Thing and the Fourfold

Later, beginning with the lecture cycle "Insight into That Which Is" that he gave in Bremen in 1949, Heidegger goes on to elaborate the dynamics that open up a world in terms of what he calls the "fourfold" (*Geviert*). In my view, the notion of the fourfold is essentially a rearticulation of his earlier analysis of the strife between the world and the earth and does not alter that analysis in any radical way. Hence, I will only briefly indicate the basic role and characteristics of this notion.[7]

Heidegger's conception of the fourfold grows out of his renewed effort to reflect on the "thing." He calls the dynamics that allow a thing to be a thing and have the significance that it has in our lives, the "fourfold": the "mirror-play of the simple onefold of sky and earth, divinities and mortals" (GA 7: 181/179). To be a thing is thus to be a gathering point in the fourfold and be constituted by the interplay of its different aspects: the sky, the earth, the divinities, and the mortals. What do these words signify? The "earth" ("the building bearer, nourishing with its fruits, tending water and rock, plant and animal" (GA 7: 179/178)) and the "sky" ("the year's seasons, the light and dusk of the day, the gloom and glow of the night, the clemency and inclemency of the weather" (GA 7: 180/178)) basically name two aspects of our material-sensuous surroundings that Heidegger in "The Origin of the Work of Art" summed up as the "earth." The "divinities" ("the beckoning messengers of the godhead" (GA 7: 180/178)) in turn correspond to what he earlier called the "gods," that is, the holy values and ideals that form the horizon of purposes of the world. Finally, the "mortals" ("they [the human beings] are called mortals because they can die" (GA 7: 180/178)) is simply a new name for humans beings in their finitude. Although the "fourfold" does not—as some commentators would have it—just amount to a dim mytho-poetical vision but has a relatively clear sense, it is nevertheless the case that Heidegger never offers a substantial enough analysis of the interplay between its different aspects that would make it a genuinely autonomous and clarifying figure of thought.[8]

There is, however, one respect in which Heidegger's thinking of the thing and the fourfold entails a critical expansion of his earlier view. In "The Origin of the Work of Art" Heidegger held that the task of opening up the world was the exclusive responsibility of the thinkers, the poets, and the political leaders. In this, the only role that was left for ordinary people—the receivers of the world—was to take over and commit themselves to the world that was opened up by the poetical artwork. By contrast, in reflecting on the thing and the fourfold, Heidegger ascribes to our dealings with concrete everyday things an irreducible role in the realization of the openness of being.

To be sure, Heidegger never gives up his view of language as the fundamental constituent of the world. In the 1958 essay "The Word" he affirmatively quotes Stefan George's line "Where the word breaks off, no thing may be" (*Kein ding sei wo das wort gebricht*), which he explicates as follows: "The word's rule springs to light as that which makes the thing be a thing. The word begins to shine as the gathering which first brings what is present to its presence" (GA 12: 224/155). From this, it follows that the poet has a primary role in establishing the language that harbors the meaning-relations of the world: "Poetizing is the basic capacity of human dwelling" (GA 7: 207/228). However, even though Heidegger conceives of our living among things as always already guided by our poetical language, he does not reduce the thing to an instantiation of prior meaning-relations anymore. The "thing" is for Heidegger not just a name for the significant phenomena we encounter in the world but plays a key role in opening up and maintaining the world. The thing is seen as itself gathering and co-constituting the play of the "fourfold": "The thing things (*das Ding dingt*). The thinging gathers. Appropriating the fourfold, it gathers the fourfold's stay, its while, into something that stays for a while: into this thing, into that thing" (GA 7: 175/174). The things are thus the concrete places in which the play of the fourfold gets gathered and specified. Just as in the case of the work of art, Heidegger describes the gathering of the thing as simultaneously receptive and formative. On the one hand, in building things, Heidegger says, we receive the "directive" (GA 7: 161/360) from the different aspects of the fourfold— the gods of our history and the material-sensuous milieu of the earth and the sky. On the other hand, the thing itself "*admits* … and *installs* the fourfold" (GA 7: 160/360), which means that it gives to the fourfold the concrete paradigmatic form that it has for us.

The upshot of this is that what Heidegger calls our "dwelling" among "things" assumes the character of a task that we can succeed or fail in. To truly dwell among things means to build and relate to things as a kind of micro-temples that gather and maintain the fourfold. Heidegger presents the following formula to articulate what such dwelling amounts to:

> The mortals dwell in so far as they save the earth ... in so far as they receive the sky as sky ... in so far as they await the divinities as divinities ... in so far as they guide their own essential being—their being capable of death—into the use and practice of this capacity, so that there may be a good death. (GA 7: 152/352)

To spell out what he means by this, he provides the following concrete description of a thing—a bridge:[9]

> The bridge swings over the stream "with ease and power." It does not just connect banks that are already there. The banks emerge as banks only as the bridge crosses the stream. ... The bridge *gathers* the earth as landscape around the stream. ... Resting upright in the stream's bed ... the bridge is ready for the sky's weather and its fickle nature. ... Always and ever differently the bridge initiates the lingering and hastening ways of men to and fro, so that they may get to other banks and in the end, as mortals, to the other side. The bridge *gathers*, as a passage that crosses, before the divinities—whether we explicitly think of, and visibly *give thanks for*, their presence, as in the figure of the saint of the bridge, or whether that divine presence is obstructed or even pushed wholly aside. (GA 7: 154–5/354–5)

Heidegger's description is meant to picture how the bridge preserves the fourfold by gathering and commemorating its different aspects. The bridge can be built so that it "saves" the earth and "receives" the sky, that is to say, in such a way that it complies with our natural surroundings and lets them shine forth as our material-sensuous setting, not just exploiting them as raw material for our needs and desires. Moreover, the bridge can be built so that it "awaits" the divinities, that is, in such a way that it institutes and reminds us of the need to receive the holy ideals and values that our history harbors, and not "make" our "gods" for ourselves (GA 7: 152/352). Finally, the bridge can be constructed so that it "guides" us in our mortal being, namely, in such a way that it serves our highest purposes in the best possible while bearing witness to the finitude of our life.

Heidegger never offers a more thoroughgoing phenomenological elucidation of what it means to dwell in and preserve the fourfold, and I will not attempt a more detailed explication of this theme here. For us, the important thing to see is that for Heidegger the task of dwelling among things is all about taking part in opening up and keeping open the historical world we live in as our finite and binding destiny. Hence, when Heidegger talks about preserving the fourfold he is not saying that we need to care for particular things and beings—for example, for human beings—as significant in themselves, prior to and irrespective of our historical world. Rather, what Heidegger's call to preserve the fourfold is meant to express is that in all our dealings with things we co-realize—foster or hamper—the happening which allows these things to be present and engage us as things in the first place, as meaningful phenomena.

12

HEIDEGGER'S LATE HISTORICAL THINKING

The task of Heidegger's later thinking is to reflect on the event that opens up and gives historical being. How is such a thinking to proceed?

There cannot be much doubt that the turn that Heidegger's thinking undergoes in the 1930s in some sense involves a break with the phenomenological approach employed in the existential analytic of *Being and Time*. At this time, Heidegger gives up the word "phenomenology" as a label of his thinking. Instead, he speaks of it as "historical reflection" (*geschichtliche Besinnung*) (GA 45: 35/34), "reflection" (*Besinnung*) (GA 7: 63/180), "being-historical thinking" (*seynsgeschichtliches Denken*) (GA 65: 3/5), and, finally, just "thinking" (*Denken*) (GA 14: 74/59).

Given Heidegger's programmatic intent to turn from phenomenology to historical reflection, it is not surprising that the hermeneutic-deconstructivist reading has established itself as the main interpretation of the methodological character of his later thought. Still, there have been some attempts by representatives of the transcendental phenomenological reading to argue that even the later Heidegger remains a Husserlian phenomenologist in important respects. For instance, Steven Crowell maintains that although Heidegger's later thought contains "strong elements of postphenomenological and postmodern suspicion" (2001: 204), Heidegger never abandons the phenomenological impulse. Crowell, it seems to me, alternates between a stronger and a weaker claim. The stronger claim is that Heidegger himself conceives of his late thinking as containing an essential element of phenomenology. Quoting a passage from "Letter on Humanism," Crowell writes that "Heidegger's post-metaphysical thinking ... draws upon the 'essential help of phenomenological seeing,'" and that "even the late Heidegger ... remains committed to the possibility of phenomenology" (2001: 218, 221; GA 9: 357/271). By contrast, the weaker claim put forward by Crowell is that the later Heidegger de facto continued practicing phenomenology regardless of what he thought he was doing: "Heidegger never abandoned [phenomenological seeing and description] in practice even if he abandoned it as a designation for his project" (2001: 220).

Our questions are, then: What is the methodological character of Heidegger's later thinking? Is it still—despite Heidegger's claims about its historicist character—to some extent phenomenological in our sense of the word? That is, does it appeal to or draw on intuitive transhistorical reflection on our first-person experience?

In what follows, I will begin by examining Heidegger's critique of Husserl in "The End of Philosophy and the Task of Thinking" and his presentation of his own thinking as a more rigorous way to execute the phenomenological demand to go to the matters themselves. After that, I go on to investigate in more detail the matter and method of Heidegger's late thinking and its relation to phenomenology. Later, in the epilogue, I will offer a critical assessment of the later Heidegger's effort to develop a radically historical mode of thinking.

The Question of Phenomenology

It is only late in his life—in the beginning of the 1960s—that Heidegger takes up and thematizes the question concerning the specific mode and rigor of his late thinking. This happens in the texts gathered in the anthology *On the Matter of Thinking*, above all in the essay "The End of Philosophy and the Task of Thinking" from 1964.[1] Heidegger's late attempt to account for the methodological character of his thinking also involves a last confrontation with Husserl's phenomenology.

"The End of Philosophy and the Task of Thinking" may be read as one extended attempt to critically reappropriate Husserl's phenomenological motto "To the matters themselves!" Indeed, the title of the book of which it is part—*Zur Sache des Denkens,* which literally means: to the matter of thinking—can be read as a paraphrase of this motto. By confronting Husserl's basic phenomenological demand for rigor and claiming to realize this demand in a more primordial manner, Heidegger gives himself the opportunity of raising the question of the specific rigor of his own late thinking.

The question Heidegger wants to pose is whether there is still a task left for thinking at the end of philosophy. As he sees it, philosophy is essentially metaphysics. It understands being as presence and it is driven by the urge to establish the ground for beings: it starts out from "what is present, represents it in its presence and thus presents it as grounded out of its ground" (GA 14: 70/56). That is, metaphysical thinking attempts to ground our understanding of beings by seeking out the present being-ground—for example, God, the eternal ideas or the transcendental subject—that allows beings to be present as what they are. The metaphysical impulse to ground beings in their presence reaches its fulfillment in the modern diffusion of philosophy into a manifold of technified sciences, whose one and only aim is to plan and manipulate beings. Heidegger calls this ultimate end-stage of metaphysics, in which we currently live, the "end of philosophy" (GA 14: 70/57).

Heidegger's question is this: Does the history of philosophy, apart from the "*last* possibility" just mentioned, harbor within itself a "*first* possibility" from which philosophy had to "start out" but which it was never able to "expressly experience and adopt" (GA 14: 73/59)? To ask for the task of thinking is, Heidegger claims, first and foremost to ask for its "matter" or "issue" (*Sache*) (GA 14: 75/61). It is only by attending to the matter at stake that we can say more about the task and method of thinking. Heidegger begins by discussing two thinkers who have both urged us to go to the matters themselves: Hegel and Husserl. Here I will concentrate on his treatment of Husserl.

For Husserl, the motto "To the matters themselves!" constituted something of a gathering battle cry for the whole phenomenological movement. According to Heidegger, the function of Husserl's motto is in the first place negative: to ward off prejudiced theorizing either—as in the case of naturalism—barring the way to the phenomena of consciousness by applying a dogmatic method or—as in case of historicism—deteriorating into empty speculation on the basis of received philosophical concepts and standpoints. So how should we reach the matters themselves? Heidegger's thesis is that Husserl's call to go to the matters primarily concerns the "securing and elaboration of the method" (GA 14: 77/63). This, he claims, comes to clear expression in the way that Husserl in *Ideas I* articulates the basic attitude of phenomenology in terms of the "principle of all principles," which states that "*every originarily giving intuition is a legitimizing source of knowledge*" and that we as phenomenologists must do nothing but receive and describe what is "*offered to us in 'intuition'*" (Hua 3: 51/44). Heidegger argues that the principle of all principles entails a thesis about the priority of the method. Prior to any reflection on what constitutes the matter of philosophy, the principle already tells us *how* phenomenology is to proceed, namely in the manner of a strict registration and description of that which gives itself in our originary conscious intuition. This, however, implies that the principle has already unwittingly decided over "what matter alone can suffice for the method" (GA 14: 78/63):

> The method is not only directed toward the matter of philosophy. It does not just belong to the matter as a key belongs to a lock. Rather, it belongs to the matter because it is "the matter itself." If one wished to ask: Where does "the principle of all principles" get its unshakable right, the answer would have to be: from transcendental subjectivity, which is already presupposed as the matter of philosophy. (GA 14: 78–9/63)

According to Heidegger, the basic problem with Husserl's understanding of his guiding motto is thus that it does not grant radical primacy to our attention to the matters themselves but rather determines the phenomenological method before and irrespective of an open look at the matters in question. Due to this failure to attend to the matter of philosophy, Husserl naively succumbs to the traditional metaphysical conception of the task of philosophy, so that his entire phenomenology develops as a qualified attempt to realize this task: to ground beings in transcendental subjectivity. It is, Heidegger claims, only because Husserl has determined being as presence for the transcendental subject that he can fashion the phenomenological method as a demand for intuitive givenness and outline the phenomenological reduction as the central methodological maneuver that gives us access to transcendental consciousness as the ground of the "objectivity of all objects" (GA 14: 78/63).

Heidegger's late critique of Husserl bears witness to how much the distance to his teacher has grown since the 1920s. In his earlier critiques, Husserl appeared as a radically ambivalent figure. On the one hand, he was the philosopher par excellence who through his phenomenology had opened the path to Heidegger's own thinking. On the other hand, he had hampered and disfigured the principal possibilities of his phenomenology by remaining stuck in the theoretical attitude of traditional philosophy. Hence, Heidegger conceived of his own thinking as a critical appropriation of Husserl, stressing the primacy of our pretheoretical experience and explicating the historicity and understanding of being at work in all phenomenal givenness. Now, by contrast, Husserl comes into sight alongside Hegel as an emblematic representative of the metaphysical effort to ground the presence of beings in subjectivity. In this, Husserl's phenomenology is not given any precedence as the possibility Heidegger himself develops but simply appears as a qualified method for realizing the misguided aim of metaphysics.

In Part Two, I already dealt with Heidegger's criticism of Husserl's reliance on direct intuition and his supposed failure to acknowledge and heed the radical historicity of being and thinking. Here, I only want to comment on Heidegger's charge that Husserl's idea of direct intuitive givenness is an expression of the metaphysical urge to ground and secure our knowledge of beings.

As I see it, the limited truth of this charge is that in developing his transcendental phenomenology Husserl is undoubtedly influenced by the traditional scientistic desire of philosophy to achieve certain and fundamental knowledge. It is true that Husserl's appeal to intuitive givenness is to some extent motivated by his desire to present phenomenology as a rigorous evidence-based science. As I have argued above, Husserl captivation by such ideals manifests itself in the focus and method of his phenomenology: in the tendency to pass by our pretheoretical experience of ethical-existential significances—and the challenges involved in intuitively understanding such significances—and instead focus on the supposedly basic layer of sensory object-perceptions with the aim of reflecting on the acts that allow different objects to be perceptually-cognitively given.

However, there is no warrant at all for Heidegger's claim that Husserl's very idea of phenomenology as intuition-based reflection would be reducible to the metaphysical urge for grounding. Although Husserl's elaboration of this idea is to some extent influenced by prejudiced ideals, the idea also works as an open formal indication that is not completely determined—either for Husserl of for us—by these ideals. In its essence, the idea of direct intuitive givenness is the idea that we have open intuitive access to meaningful experiences and beings as something that transcends our factical historical understandings and concepts. As such, the idea of intuitive givenness is not inherently motivated by an ambition to ground our knowledge but can also be motivated by a will to openly encounter and account for what we actually experience—regardless of any concern for certain, absolute, or universal knowledge—instead of falling back on preconceived concepts, theories, or other grounds that detract us from and distort these phenomena.

Heidegger's harsh critique of Husserl must in the end be understood against the background of his driving ambition to demonstrate that his own late thinking in fact realizes the phenomenological demand for rigor in a more primordial manner than Husserl's phenomenology. In the closing paragraph of the last text of *On the*

Matter of Thinking, the brief autobiographical sketch "My Way to Phenomenology," Heidegger sums up his relationship to phenomenology as follows:

> And today? The age of phenomenological philosophy seems to be over. It is already taken as something past which is only recorded historically along which other schools of philosophy. But in what is most its own phenomenology is not a school. It is the possibility of thinking, at times changing and only thus persisting, of corresponding to the claim of what is to be thought. If phenomenology is thus experienced and retained, it can disappear as a designation in favor of the matter of thinking whose manifestness remains a mystery. (GA 14: 101/82)

What happens here? To begin with, Heidegger separates his own thinking from the dwindling movement of "phenomenological philosophy," by which he means Husserl's development of phenomenology into a transcendental philosophy reflectively investigating the structures of intentional consciousness. Second, he puts forward the claim that his own thinking realizes phenomenology as "the possibility of thinking ... of corresponding to the claim of what is to be thought." Now, granted that Husserl's phenomenology fails precisely in the task of attending to its matter and granted that his own thinking succeeds in this, then Heidegger can claim that his thinking indeed constitutes "true phenomenology" (*die eigentliche Phänomenologie*) (GA 14: 54/45). However, Heidegger adds, as soon as phenomenology is thus conceived as the pure possibility of thinking to attend and answer to its matter we might as well give up the term phenomenology as a potentially misleading name—due to its association with Husserl's intuitive method—for this possibility of thinking.

Historical Reflection and the Need to Return to the Greek Beginning

Heidegger's later thinking is very much an attempt to deliver on the idea of the radical historicity of thought elaborated in *Being and Time* but not realized in its full consequence: the idea that our experience and understanding of beings as meaningful phenomena is determined by the meaning-possibilities inherent in the historical understanding of being in which we always already live.

From the mid-1930s onwards, Heidegger insists that thinking must renounce intuition-based phenomenology and instead take the form of a historical reflection. As he puts it in "Introduction to Metaphysics": "The question, 'How does it stand with being?' must maintain itself within the history of being" (GA 40: 99/101). There seems to be no support for Crowell's stronger claim that the later Heidegger still conceives of his thinking as essentially making use of phenomenological seeing.[2] Heidegger is adamant that thinking cannot hope to examine or ground our factical understanding of being through some kind of direct phenomenological intuition of the structures of our experiences; rather, it needs to transpire by way of a historical reflection that traces and articulates the most primordial possibilities of understanding harbored by our own history.

Heidegger elaborates the basic movement of his historical thinking as a transition from the "first beginning" (*der erste Anfang*) to the "other beginning" (*der andere Anfang*) (GA 45: 199/171). According to Heidegger, the "first beginning" of Western metaphysics takes place as Plato and Aristotle interpret being as presence—*ousia*—for the human subject. The early pre-Socratic conception of being as *physis* still harbored a vague and embryonic understanding of the event that conditions and opens up being as presence—an understanding which is also discernible in the Greek word for truth, *alētheia*, whose literal meaning is unconcealment. However, in the thinking of Plato and Aristotle the roots of *ousia* in *physis/alētheia* are cut off and being is interpreted as pure presence for the human being. This understanding of being—which is also, at the same time, a forgetfulness of the origin and nature of being—then determines the entire history of metaphysics, which essentially takes the form of an ever-increasing subjectification of being. When this tendency reaches its peak in the modern techno-subjectivist understanding of being as a standing reserve for the human being to exploit and manipulate, this gives rise to nihilism, which means that being fails to address us as binding and significant anymore.

As Heidegger's radical historicism is supplemented by the idea that the entire history of philosophy is dominated by the metaphysical understanding of being as presence, he comes to believe that the only way to overcome this understanding is by returning to the first beginning of Greek philosophy where it took shape. There are two aspects to this. To begin with, it is only by returning to the first beginning that it becomes possible to understand our modern techno-subjectivist understanding of being as a variant of the Greek understanding of being as presence. Only in this way can we grasp the fundamental meaning of our own conception of being. Furthermore, Heidegger thinks that the Greek beginning—especially the texts of the pre-Socratics—contains within itself a nascent understanding of the openness of being, an understanding that was never developed and that Plato and Aristotle simultaneously presupposed and covered up as they established what was to become the dominant understanding of being as presence. Hence, it is only by critically retrieving the implicit and unthought possibilities of the "first beginning" that an "other beginning" is possible: a thinking that articulates the openness of being as the primordial source of historical being, and which by so doing opens up the possibility of establishing a historical world that addresses us as a binding destiny.

This idea—that the only way for thinking to free itself from metaphysics and to open up a more primordial understanding of being, is through a confrontation with the first beginning, and a critical appropriation of its unthought possibilities—will henceforth determine Heidegger's conception of the task of thinking.[3]

The Matter of Thinking

So far, we have seen that the task that Heidegger sets for his thinking is to articulate the event that opens up being and to do this by reflecting on the primordial possibilities of thinking harbored by the Greek beginning of philosophy. However, how does such a thinking transpire concretely? How does the event of being announce itself, how is it accessible to thought? What is it that gives to Heidegger's historical reflection its concrete measure and rigor and hinders it from deteriorating into dogmatic historical-dialectical constructions?

According to Heidegger, the heart of the phenomenological rigor expressed in Husserl's maxim "To the matter themselves!" does not consist in intuitive givenness but in the ability of thinking to attend to its matter prior to and as a condition for determining its method. It is only by attending to its matter that thinking can materialize as a qualified way of answering to this matter. Conversely, every attempt to determine the method prior to the matter will necessarily entail a dogmatic postulation of the matter.

What is the matter of thinking?

In "The End of Philosophy and the Task of Thinking," Heidegger states that the matter of thinking is the "clearing" (*Lichtung*). The tradition of metaphysics has always understood being as presence without ever asking how presence as such is possible. However, he argues, in order for something to be present for us as an intelligible phenomenon it has to be illuminated by a light, that is, by a preceding understanding of being. This light, in turn, has to transpire in an openness, a free space, in which it can shine forth and illuminate beings. Heidegger calls this openness the "clearing": "We call this openness, which grants a possible letting-shine and show, the clearing. ... Light can stream into the clearing, into its openness, and let brightness play with darkness in it. But light never first creates the clearing. Rather, light presupposes it. ... The clearing is the open region for everything that is present and absent" (GA 14: 80-1/65). What for Heidegger makes the clearing the matter of thinking is that it constitutes the ultimate condition for all phenomenal presence and intelligibility. This also means that metaphysics, which attempts to think and ground being as presence, has always already unwittingly presupposed the clearing as its own constitutive element: "All philosophical thinking that explicitly or inexplicitly follows the call 'to the matter itself' is in its movement and with its method already admitted to the free space of the clearing. But philosophy knows nothing of the clearing" (GA 14: 82/66).

How does the clearing work?

To get a grasp of this notion, it is important to see that the clearing is not just another name for the particular historical context of meaning that happens to prevail. Rather, the clearing is the open space that conditions and characterizes such worlds. Heidegger's notion of the clearing is rooted in his account of how poetry and art open up historical worlds by enacting the strife between the world and the earth. According to this account, the artwork gathers and determines the world in a manner that is simultaneously receptive and creative. On the one hand, the artwork is referred and hearkens to the manifold of still undetermined possibilities contained by the historical heritage and to the sensuous-natural milieu of the earth. On the other hand, it creatively decides which possibilities that will prevail as gods and values in this particular world and gives to these possibilities their concrete shape by grounding them in the earth. The dynamics that open up the world essentially involve the kind of logic that Heidegger calls the "clearing." By this, he means that in order for a historical world to emerge as a finite and unified context of meaning, some values and meanings have to be singled out and established as constitutive of this world whereas all alternative potential values and meanings have to be discarded and covered up. As Mark Wrathall puts it: "The clearing is that some truth of being prevails because other truths of being do not" (2011: 15). The world thus necessarily emerges as the clearing of an open free space surrounded by a darkened field of other possible gods and ways of life.

Heidegger maintains that the concealment characterizing the clearing is twofold. Not only are the alternative possibilities excluded from the world covered up. What is more, the very logic of the clearing itself—the fact that all other alternative possibilities are covered up—is also covered up:

> This [the clearing] remains concealed. Does it happen by chance? Does it happen only as a consequence of the carelessness of human thinking? Or does it happen because self-concealing, concealment, *lēthē*, belongs to *a-lētheia*, not as mere addition, not as shadow to light, but rather as the heart of *alētheia*? Moreover, does not a sheltering and preserving rule in this self-concealing of the clearing of presence, from which alone unconcealment can be granted, so that what is present can appear in its presence? (GA 14: 88/71)

For Heidegger, then, it is a central feature of the clearing that it conceals its own logic. In living in a particular world, this world is present to us as the historical space of meaning that determines and delimits our possibilities of understanding and experiencing phenomena. In this, the logic of the clearing, which allows the world to be present, is not itself a presence in the world but withdraws from all presence. Still, it is important to note that even though the clearing unavoidably conceals itself, it is not completely inaccessible. As we shall see, Heidegger thinks that the clearing always already announced itself and that it is an essential task to reflect on and articulate it.[4]

At this point, a brief comment on the relationship between the two central terms that Heidegger uses to name the matter of his later thinking—the event (*Ereignis*) and the clearing (*Lichtung*)—is in order. Basically, these terms name the same matter from different angles. The event signifies the dynamic happening that opens up a world whereas the clearing signifies the play between concealment and unconcealment that is an essential aspect of the event and that characterizes every historical world. In fact, the double meaning of the word *Ereignis*—event and appropriation—points to the logic of the clearing. Since the event that opens up the world has the form of an appropriation—a making one's own—of certain historical possibilities, this implies that all other possibilities need to be excluded and concealed.

The Way of Thinking

For Heidegger, the decisive question when it comes to determining the rigor and methodological way of his thinking is this: How does the clearing announce itself to thinking? How do we concretely get access to it?

Addressing this question, Heidegger writes that the clearing constitutes what Goethe called a "primal phenomenon" (*Urphänomen*), whereafter he immediately adds: "We would have to say: a primal matter" (*Ur-Sache*) (GA 14: 81/65). That is, as the primal phenomenon which constitutes the origin of phenomenal givenness the clearing cannot be understood as a self-showing phenomenon anymore, but rather has the character of a "matter," a "primal matter." But what is a "matter"? Heidegger explicates the word "matter" by invoking its old juridical meaning as "case" or "controversy." The "matter" of thinking thus denotes "that which concerns thinking, is still controversial (*strittig*) for thinking, and is the controversy (*der Streitfall*)" (GA 14: 75/61; cf. GA 14: 46/38; GA 11: 53).

The central phenomenal characteristic of the clearing is that it addresses us as something controversial and polemical. What does this mean?

By using the word *Streit*—strife, controversy, *polemos*—to describe the phenomenality of the clearing, Heidegger anchors it in his account of the strife between the world and the earth that opens up our world. This strife, to repeat, transpires as a receptive-creative gathering of a world, such that some of the more or less indeterminate being-senses and values contained by our history are appropriated and shaped as the horizon of this world, whereas all other potential meanings are discarded and concealed. Hence, the world of meaning and being that we inhabit is constituted by an ungrounded seizure of some possibilities at the expense of others. Furthermore, the specific shape it takes also depends on the way it is grounded in the alogical sensuous-natural milieu of the local earth. This, however, implies that the controversial logic of the clearing will inevitably announce itself in the world that it establishes. Our world will always be an ungroundable, arbitrary, and finite historical world, a world whose guiding values and understandings will always be underdetermined and full of tensions. This is something that we will continuously run up against, for example, in our efforts to justify and adjudicate between the guiding values of our society and in our encounters with alien cultures. In short, the historically arbitrary and ungrounded nature of our world and its lack of necessity and systematic closure will always press itself upon us whether we want to know about it or not. According to Heidegger, metaphysics reacts to the finite and controversial character of the world—in which its origin in the clearing announces itself—by repressing and concealing it. Instead, it conceives of being as presence and of its own task as that of grounding beings in some absolute paradigm of presence.

Although the controversiality of the clearing still makes itself felt in our contemporary world, Heidegger's radical historicism makes him believe that we can only get a positive understanding of the clearing in so far as our history already harbors some preunderstanding of this matter: "every attempt to gain insight into the supposed task of thinking finds itself moved to review the whole history of philosophy" (GA 14: 74/60). What is more, he thinks that in order to access the clearing we have to return to the Greek beginning of metaphysics, in particular to the pre-Socratic thinkers whose notion of *physis* harbors an implicit embryonic understanding of the clearing. This understanding was covered up and forgotten when Plato and Aristotle established what was to become the dominant understanding of being as presence. The matter of thinking, that is, the clearing, "was already said a long time ago, precisely at the beginning of philosophy and for that beginning but has not been explicitly thought" (GA 14: 75/60–1).

The considerations above determine the concrete way in which Heidegger's later thinking unfolds. I think it is fair to say that from 1949—when Heidegger finds the paradigmatic style of his later thought—onwards his texts in different ways tend to enact the following three main steps. First, depending on the guiding question, Heidegger sets out from a given textual or conceptual constellation which in an exemplary way manifests our metaphysical understanding of being, for example, a text by a philosopher or a poet (Nietzsche, Hegel, Hölderlin, Trakl, Kant, Husserl, Aristotle, Heraclitus), some word or concept (being, time, truth, identity, science, metaphysics, *logos*), or some other aspect of the contemporary situation (the modern technical world, our relationship to things, the specialization of the sciences, the flight of the gods). Second, he carries out a destructive explication of the text or concept in question. This centrally involves laying bare the basic ontological commitments of the text and showing that these commitments are variations and elaborations of the metaphysical understanding of being as presence that was established in the first Greek beginning. The task of the third step—the decisive step—is to demonstrate that our traditional understanding of being as presence cannot account for itself but refers back to the clearing as its unthought origin.

How is this done?

As far as I can see, there are two kinds of argumentative strategy at work in the texts. To begin with—the first strategy—Heidegger's critical explication of metaphysical texts involves demonstrating that they are fundamentally unable to account for the basic understanding of being as presence to which they have always already committed themselves. When we ask about the origin and legitimacy of this understanding of being as presence, metaphysics will have no answer to give. As a result, we are faced with the question of the origin of presence. However, what this kind of critical investigation is able to establish is, at most, the negative failure of metaphysics to account for itself. What is still needed is some kind of positive demonstration that the clearing indeed constitutes the origin of presence. The problem for Heidegger is that he has ruled out the very possibility of a phenomenological—or some other kind of positive—investigation of the clearing as the transhistorical dynamics that open up and sustain historical being. Hence, the only way to demonstrate the clearing is by making use of historical texts that in his view refer to the clearing. There are two primary kinds of text to which he ascribes this potential: first, the writings of the pre-Socratic thinkers and poets; second, poems by a hand-picked group of poets including, for example, Hölderlin, Georg Trakl, and Stefan George.

Concretely, what Heidegger does—the second strategy—is that he attempts to show that there are passages or words in the text under consideration that point to the clearing (or the event, or the fourfold) as the origin of presence. He then goes on to explicate the central passages in question, which are often very vague and indeterminate, in terms of his own conception of the logic of the event/

clearing of being. Another way that Heidegger uses to get historical starting points for his descriptions is to make use of etymology. Again and again he tries to demonstrate that the etymological roots of our words give expression to an implicit understanding of the clearing that has been covered up by the triumph of metaphysics. For example, he claims to demonstrate the roots of the word "Lichtung" in the old German verb "lichten," which is said to mean "to make something light, free and open" (GA 14: 80); the roots of the word "Ereignis" in the verb "eräugen," which is said to mean "to catch sight of, to call something to oneself through looking, to appropriate" (GA 11: 45/291–2); the roots of the word "Sache" in an older usage in which it still meant "legal case" or "controversy" (GA 14: 46/38; 75/61); the roots of the word *logos* in the verb *legein*, which is said to mean "gather" (GA 40: 131/135). Such an employment of etymologies in philosophical reasoning quite naturally gives rise to the critical question: how can references to etymology ever give any grounds for our systematic understanding of the matter in question? Heidegger, being well aware of this objection, already common in his lifetime, responds as follows:

> It might look as though the essence of the thing as we are now thinking of it had been, so to speak, thoughtlessly poked out of the accidentally encountered meaning of the Old High German *thing*. The suspicion arises that the understanding of the essence of the thing that we are here trying to reach may be based on the accidents of an etymological game. The notion becomes established and is already current that, instead of giving thought to essential matters, we are here merely using the dictionary. The opposite is true. ... The truth ... is not that our thinking feeds on etymology, but rather that etymology has the standing mandate first to give thought to the essential content involved in what the words, as words, denote in an undeveloped way. (GA 7: 176–7/174–5)

Hence, what Heidegger here claims is that his tracing of etymologies in no way implies that he would try to ground his articulation of the matters themselves on some information about the earlier meanings of our words available in dictionaries and etymological studies. On the contrary, etymology itself already presupposes an understanding of the matters that the words signify. Only thus can the old words and usages appear and be explicated as embryonic expressions of these matters.

However, even though Heidegger insists on the priority of thinking in relation to etymology his abundant use of etymologies is not a superficial or accidental feature of his thinking but is deeply motivated and prompted by his notion of the historicity of thought. Given the idea that we are essentially referred to the meaning-possibilities harbored by our history, his reflections on the clearing strictly speaking have no positive guidance except the de facto indications of the clearing that he claims to find in certain texts and in the etymological roots of certain words. As a result, Heidegger's late thinking transpires in a zigzag movement: on the one hand, an exposition of the basic groundlessness and unaccountability of metaphysics which negatively opens up the question of the origin of presence; on the other hand, a historical explication of a text or a word, which allows him to articulate and offer a positive answer to this question.

Heidegger maintains that the task of thinking the clearing is a finite and interminable one. The only way to access the clearing is by making use of finite historical texts that either negatively presuppose and call for the question of the clearing, or that positively indicate the clearing. As a result, we are never in a position once and for all to determine something like the necessary and universal structure of the clearing as such. Instead, thinking must take the form of a historical interrogation whose paths will always remain determined by the finite historical-textual situation in which we find ourselves and that will never arrive at final answers. At the end of the day, the point of reflecting on the clearing is not to come up with some sort of answer, but to "correspond to" (*entsprechen*) the clearing, that is, to let the clearing be and do its work as the origin that opens up a binding world (GA 14: 25/20). This is why Heidegger thinks that ultimately thinking must have recourse to silence (GA 12: 255/135) and tautologies (GA 15: 400/81) as modes of expression that, as it were, make us halt and bow before the ungroundable happening that lets our world be.

The Fate of Phenomenology

Above we noted that the later Heidegger's conception of the historicity of thought rules out the possibility of making use of intuition-based phenomenological descriptions as the ground and vehicle of thought. But what about the weaker claim put forward by Crowell, that although the later Heidegger may have rejected phenomenology in principle he still continues to make use of it in his concrete investigations?

Heidegger's later production exhibits a gradually increasing effort to answer to the historicity of thought by developing the kind of historicist strategies for thinking described above. After 1930, when the project of fundamental ontology has definitely been abandoned, we look in vain in Heidegger's later texts for the kind of ambition to ground and clarify every central concept of his thinking through phenomenological analyses that still characterized *Being and Time*. Nevertheless, in many of the texts from the 1930s, when his thinking is still in search of its new form, we still find greater or smaller pieces of traditional phenomenological description. This happens in several lecture courses and texts, for example, in the lecture courses "On the Essence of Truth: On Plato's Parable of the Cave and the Theaetetus" (1931–2) and "Basic Questions of Philosophy," and especially in the essay "The Origin of the Work of Art." Although Heidegger mainly proceeds by way of historical explications and quasi-dialectical arguments, he also every so often has recourse to phenomenological descriptions that aim to bring out the structures of our concrete experiences of truth, art, nothingness, and so on. In the 1940s and 1950s, the phenomenological element of his thinking diminishes as his effort to develop a thinking that is true to its historicity intensifies.

Now, it is certainly possible to point to the fact that many of Heidegger's later texts contain concrete descriptions that can easily be taken as examples of phenomenology. However, I think the role of phenomenology in these texts, and the character of the phenomenology practiced here, are problematic. Since Heidegger has ruled out the possibility of intuitive phenomenology, he naturally tends to minimize his use of phenomenological description. What is more, when the later Heidegger offers what seems to be phenomenological descriptions it generally is the case that they do not actually offer the kind of intuitive phenomenological explication of the concrete experiences in question that would be needed to shed light on the matters under investigation.

Previously I quoted Heidegger's description of how a bridge may function as the gathering point of the fourfold. Here is his description of a jug performing the same function:

> The jug's jug-character consists in the gift of the pouring out (*Geschenk des Gusses*) ... The gift of the outpouring can be a drink. The outpouring gives water, it gives wine to drink. The spring stays on in the water of the gift. In the spring the rock dwells, and in the rock dwells the dark slumber of the earth, which receives the rain and dew of the sky. In the water of the spring dwells the marriage of sky and earth. It stays in the wine given by the fruit of the vine, the fruit in which the earth's nourishment and the sky's sun are betrothed to one another. In the gift of water, in the gift of wine, sky and earth dwell. ... The gift of the pouring out is drink for mortals. It quenches their thirst. It refreshes their leisure. It enlivens their conviviality. But the jug's gift is at times also given for consecration. If the pouring is for consecration, then it does not still a thirst. It stills and elevates the celebration of the feast. The gift of the pouring now is neither given in an inn nor is the poured gift a drink for mortals. The outpouring is the libation poured out for the immortal gods. ... The consecrated libation is what our word for a strong outpouring flow, "gush," really designates: gift and sacrifice. ... In the gift of the outpouring, mortals and divinities each dwell in their different ways. (GA 7: 174–5/172–3)

According to Heidegger, the essence of the jug consists in its ability to give, to pour out water and wine to the mortal human beings. In the quoted passage he describes how this giving at once refers to and celebrates the four dimensions of the fourfold. In a sense, the description is concrete. In emotionally elevated language, it paints a picture of how the earth, the sky, the mortals, and the divinities are present and constitute the pouring out of water and wine that is the essence of the jug. Nevertheless, from a phenomenological point of view, the description remains fundamentally lacking. When Heidegger describes how the fourfold is present in the pouring of the jug, his basic point of reference is a situation in which human beings have gathered to drink, celebrate, bring out toasts, and commemorate the gods. The problem is that this paradigmatic situation, in which the entire description is anchored, remains almost totally implicit and unreflected. Heidegger does not offer anything close to a trenchant reflection on how the situation is experienced by the people present: What mood and what way of relating to each other characterizes the gathering (a sense of open and wholehearted interpersonal relations, a sense collective community and unity, or something else)? How are we to understand the ethical-existential motives constituting the mood in question (love, an egoistic urge for collective affirmation, or something else)? In refraining from pursuing these kinds of questions and inquiries, Heidegger flouts the decisive phenomenological insight that we can only clarify the significances that matters have for us by reflecting on the first-person experiences—the motives, the emotions, the ways of relating to others and to oneself—in which they appear and concern us. As a result, his descriptions of the different dimensions of the fourfold and the way they interact with each other are doomed to remain vague and unclear.

The outcome of this is that the later Heidegger's quasi-phenomenological descriptions threaten to remain unphenomenological constructions of the same kind as all other conceptual and theoretical projections that dogmatically postulate meanings that they cannot account for. This does not mean that such constructions are empty and without meaning. It means that the philosopher in question is unable to shed light on and clearly understand the experiences and meanings that she draws upon in an unclear and unacknowledged way.

EPILOGUE: BEING OPEN TOWARD BEINGS

Introduction

In this book, I have tried to trace and explicate Heidegger's lifelong struggle to come to terms with the problem of phenomena.

This struggle can be described as an ever more radical effort to work out and account for the historicity of phenomena and phenomenology. In the 1920s, Heidegger first elaborates what he thinks is the basic structure of our experience of phenomena. The core of this structure consists in the ontological difference, that is, in the idea that our prior understanding of historical being—the life-possibilities and values and the being-senses bestowed by our heritage—determines our possibilities to experience and understand beings as phenomena. In *Being and Time* Heidegger did not yet raise the question of how historical being can be given as binding and primordial beyond our common collective prejudices. By contrast, his entire later thinking is guided by the task to account for the event/clearing that allows historical being to open up and prevail as a binding destiny. In this, he also to a large extent renounces intuition-based phenomenology in favor of a radically historical reflection on the unthought possibilities of meaning harbored by our history.

So far, I have mainly engaged in a kind of internal critique of Heidegger's effort to work out his historicist conception of phenomena. While largely leaving his historicist framework unquestioned, I have focused on the internal problems and ambivalence that haunt his thinking, and on his attempts to overcome them. In this way, it has been possible to diagnose the philosophical motives that drive the development of his thinking. In this epilogue, I will make an attempt to critically interrogate Heidegger's basic conception of the historical character and structure of phenomena and phenomenology. The aim is to take some steps toward delimiting the truth—and the untruth—of some of the central aspects of this influential conception.

It is only possible to critically delimit Heidegger's thought on the basis of an independent account of the philosophical matters of stake. Hence, I will offer a provisional outline of my own view of these matters. My ambition is not to provide anything like a full-fledged alternative conception since this would require engaging with the relevant literature and working out my arguments in a much more thorough and comprehensive manner. Indeed, it would require another book—at least. Rather, the point is to open up, in a provisional and sketchy manner, a perspective that allows us to get into view the distortions and also the limited truths of Heidegger's historicism.

In what follows, I will concentrate on three main themes. First, I discuss Heidegger's thesis that our historical norms and values constitute our ultimate source of ethical-existential normativity and significance, as well as his attempt to account for the bindingness of such values. Against Heidegger, I argue that we are essentially open to the other human being as someone who concerns us and claims us as such; moreover, that our historical values can only have genuine ethical significance in so far as they express our concern for the other as such. Second, I discuss Heidegger's claim that since our understanding of historical meaning determines what we can experience as meaningful phenomena it constitutes our ultimate source of truth. Against Heidegger, I suggest that when it comes to understanding the ethical significance and structures of our experience, understanding essentially consists in openly seeing and grasping human realities that transcend all our factical concepts. Third, I provide a critical delimitation of Heidegger's historicist strategies of thinking. Here, I argue that such strategies can never replace direct phenomenological intuition as our basic concrete access to our experience of meaning.

My critique of Heidegger's radical historicism has its background in and further develops the kind of critique previously put forward by Levinas, Ernst Tugendhat, and Cristina Lafont.

As concerns the question of ethical-existential significance, the primary background for my thought is found in the ethics of Levinas and in the tradition of dialogical thinking initiated by Martin Buber and Franz Rosenzweig. Recently, this tradition has received a new and original articulation in the work of my friends and colleagues Joel Backström and Hannes Nykänen, to whom my own account is indebted (cf. Backström 2007; Nykänen 2002; Backström and Nykänen 2007). As concerns the question of truth and phenomenology, I take myself to be showing how the idea of direct realism—which Hilary Putnam originally developed with reference to empirical knowledge—also applies to our intuitive phenomenological understanding of meaningful phenomena.

Even though—as I will argue—Heidegger's radical historicism cannot be upheld, it nevertheless points to the many ways in which our experience and understanding is guided by and indebted to the history in which we stand. Indeed, the critical task of exposing the problems and unclarities of Heidegger's highest philosophical ambitions is also geared to clarifying and appropriating the genuine insights of his thinking within their proper limits.

13

THE SOURCES OF ETHICAL-EXISTENTIAL NORMATIVITY

Heidegger's analysis of the historical structure of our experience of phenomena implies that the values and norms of our historical world constitute our ultimate and ungroundable source of ethical-existential normativity and significance. In this, Heidegger denies that any beings—for example, human beings—could claim us as normative and important in themselves regardless of historical context. It is our historically received values and norms that determine what we can experience as ethical-existential claims and reasons in the first place and what actions and character traits that can strike us *as* good or bad, honorable or despicable, meaningful or futile, and so on.

The idea that historical values constitute the source of ethical-existential normativity has for a long time been highly influential not only in academic philosophy but also in the humanities more generally and in the wider public debate. Heidegger not only plays a central role in establishing and articulating this paradigm of thought. He is also unusual in that he pursues the question concerning the normative force of historical values. Mostly, the representatives of historicist value-philosophy have avoided raising this potentially awkward and unsettling question. By contrast, Heidegger's later thinking is guided by the question of the bindingness or normativity of historical values and norms. In what way can the values and ideals of our historical world address us as binding and obliging? How do we experience and feel the claim and normative force of such values?

As I shall argue, what makes the question of the normative force of historical values unsettling is that it is difficult—and in the end impossible—to pursue it in an open and radical manner without undermining the very idea of historical values as the source of ethical-existential normativity. This is why the champions of historicist value-philosophy—among them the representatives of the hermeneutic-deconstructivist reading of Heidegger—have normally been content with presenting epistemological-ontological arguments to the effect that our historical values constitute the ultimate ground of our ethical-existential experience and understanding and that we have to accept them as this ungroundable and finite ground. These kinds of argument, however, tell us nothing about why historical values can address us as normative and obliging and why we care about them at all. In the wake of *Being and Time* Heidegger recognizes the need to pursue this question and he is also bold—or arrogant—enough to do it. However, since he holds on to his radically historicist framework, he is bound to fail. Nevertheless, his attempt is very instructive. Indeed, as I hope to show, by pursuing the question of the sources of ethical-existential normativity and motivation more drastically than Heidegger did, and by critically assessing his attempt to answer it, we are able to attain a clearer understanding of the role and function of historical values and norms in our ethical-existential experience and life with each other.[1]

I begin this chapter by briefly outlining Levinas's classic critique of Heidegger as the starting point of my own analyses. After that, I offer an account of what I suggest are the two basic motives—our urge for collective affirmation and our love for the other as such—that underlie our experience of ethical-existential normativity and that account for whatever normative force historical values may exert on us. My central claim is that whereas the desire for affirmation is egoistic-collectivist in nature, our love for and care about others constitutes our genuine source of moral claims. I end the chapter by critically assessing the later Heidegger effort to account for the binding force of historical values.

Levinas's Critique

As is well known, it is Emmanuel Levinas who first and paradigmatically presents the critique that Heidegger's ontological thinking sidesteps and reduces the primacy of our ethical relationship to the other human being.

According to Levinas, Heidegger's ontology exceeds the "classical intellectualism" of the philosophical tradition in stressing that our comprehension of being is not a merely theoretical attitude but fundamentally involves the whole of our pretheoretical—temporal, practical, social—existence in the world (1996: 4). Nevertheless, Heidegger retains the central idea that our relation to particular beings basically has the form of comprehension, such that our ability to grasp a being as a meaningful phenomenon is conditioned by our prior understanding of its being: "For Heidegger, an openness upon Being, which is not *a being*, which is not a 'something,' is necessary in order that, in general, a 'something' manifest itself" (1969: 189). Although Levinas believes that Heidegger's ontological difference captures the structure of our knowledge of impersonal beings, he insists that it implies a radical reduction of the other human being to an entity which can only address us as significant on the basis of our prior understanding of being: "To affirm the priority of *Being* over *existents* is to already decide the essence of philosophy; it is to subordinate the relation with *someone*, who is an existent, (the ethical relation) to a relation with the *Being of existents*, which, impersonal, permits the apprehension, the domination of existents (a relationship of knowing)" (45).

Against Heidegger, Levinas argues that the other human being does not primarily meet me as an object of comprehension at all. Rather, the other in her presence as a face addresses me as someone who "counts as such" (1996: 6), as someone who claims me and whom I am called to address and welcome regardless of the historical context or situation I happen to live in: "the face speaks to me and thereby invites me to a relation incommensurate with a power exercised, be it enjoyment or knowledge" (1969: 198). In this, the other puts my egoistic urge to dominate all beings into question and reveals my "infinite responsibility" for the other person (240).

As will become clear, I think Levinas's central critique of Heidegger is basically correct and of decisive importance. Even though Levinas's explication of Heidegger is in some respects insufficient and does not always do justice to the complexity of Heidegger's thinking, he is certainly right in claiming that Heidegger's thinking of being reduces and covers up the primacy of our direct ethical relationship to the other person. Although there are aspects of Levinas's ethics that I find problematic, my own analysis in the following pages is much in line with the ethical perspective he opens up.[2]

Desire for Social Affirmation versus Love for Others

It is of course perfectly clear—as Heidegger and others have stressed—that we always already live in some historical contexts of values and norms. Moreover, it is true that these values, or some of them, tend to exert powerful normative force on us.

However, how can historical values address us as normative at all? And with what kinds of normative force?

The first thing to note is that this question cannot be answered by simply referring to the fact that values and norms are part of our culture and community and that we, in some unspecified sense, are familiar with them. Taken by themselves, values and norms are merely conceptions of what is valuable, important, and required and of what is worthless, meaningless, and forbidden. That different values and norms somehow exist and are present to us does not explain why they might concern us as normative or important. The only way to shed light on the possible normative force of values is to acknowledge and attend to the interpersonal concerns and motives in virtue of which matters may engage us as normative and significant in the first place. Here, I will outline two such basic human motives that account for two different kinds of normative force: first, our desire for social affirmation; second, our love for and care about the other person as such.

I think there can be little doubt that the motive which primarily and for the most part underlies our experience of the values and norms of our community as normatively pressing is our desire for social affirmation. It is one of our most basic and strongest desires. We long for being accepted and affirmed by our community; conversely, we dread the possibility of being met with hostility, contempt, hatred, and violence by our group. The urge for affirmation goes deep in us and accounts for much of the emotional charge that normally accompanies our self-perception and self-evaluation. As humans, we have a basic ability to see and evaluate ourselves in terms of how we think we are seen and judged by other people. This means that in so far as our urge for social affirmation is at play, we can always sense how we fare in the light of this urge. And what we see here engenders powerful emotions. When we see ourselves as affirmable and admirable we feel pride and self-esteem. However, when we perceive ourselves as non-affirmable and despicable we are overcome by painful feelings of embarrassment, shame, and self-loathing.[3]

The desire for affirmation is the main motive that accounts for why the values and norms of our historical community tend to wield such strong normative force on us. These values are there for us as the conceptions of what is good and bad, meaning and futile, obligatory and forbidden, which are endorsed by our community. As such, the values regulate how the community evaluates different actions and character traits. This implies not only that the values address us as the standards that we need to follow if we are to gain acceptance and affirmation by our community. It also implies that we are prone to appropriate them as the horizon of our self-perception and self-evaluation. In seeing and judging how we appear in the light of our desire for affirmation, we tend to evaluate ourselves in terms of the values of the community whose affirmation we desire. Here, our historical values function as the measures that determine our emotionally charged judgment of ourselves as honorable and affirmable or as shameful and despicable.

Our urge for affirmation is also a key motivating force in our formation of our identity: our conception of who we, ideally, are. To the extent that this urge drives our identity-formation, we develop our identity by appropriating values and ideals, which, if realized in real life, promise to make us socially affirmable and respectable. Our identity, understood in this sense, functions as the bearer of our trust in our ability to gain collective affirmation. Hence, we strongly feel that we need to live up to the values of our identity in our actual attitudes and actions. When we manage to do this, we feel pride and confidence in our capacity for achieving affirmation. By contrast, when we fail to do—or do the opposite of—what our values demand, our trust in our capacity for achieving affirmation is undermined and we see ourselves as shameful losers.

We can now see that our urge for social affirmation is indeed a powerful motive that makes us responsive to the normative force of the values of our community and our identity. However, is this motive a source of genuine moral claims?

It is not.

What makes our desire for social affirmation fundamentally deficient from a moral point of view is that in so far as we are moved by this motive our attitude is fundamentally egoistic or self-concerned. What we care about in caring about social affirmation is *ourselves*: about our own prospects for achieving social affirmation and about the affirmability of our appearance. At the same time, the attitude is collectivist in the sense that we are concerned about how others think about and judge us, and we are prone to succumb to the judgments and values of our group in order to achieve affirmation. However, in caring about what the others think about us we do not love and care about them as persons. We only care about them as the audience that judges us and that we feel we must win over.

The egoism of the desire for social affirmation is not necessarily straightforward in the sense that we would here only pursue our own particular interests at the expense of the interests of others and other non-self-serving purposes. In fact, the urge for affirmation may very well lead us, for example, to help other people and engage ourselves in environmental issues—indeed, we may be ready to sacrifice ourselves for the sake of such greater goods—if this is demanded by our values and ideals. However, if our concern about such values is motivated by our desire for affirmation, it is essentially egoistic-collectivist in character. What accounts for the normative force that the values wield on us is the fact that they address us as the standards that determine our sense of who we need to be and what we need to do to emerge as respectable and affirmable. As such, they merely function as vehicles for realizing our self-concerned urge for collective affirmation.

The moral blindness of our urge for social affirmation is the reason why it— and all the emotions that it fuels: pride, self-esteem, embarrassment, shame, and so on—can attach us to values and ideals irrespective of their ethical-existential substance. From the point of view of this attitude, it is not possible to distinguish between good and evil values. If no love whatsoever is involved, there is no ethical-existential difference between, for example, the attitude of the Christian priest who, on account of his values and ideals, helps political refugees and feels shame when he fails to do it, and the attitude of the neo-Nazi who, on account of his values and ideals, persecutes refuges and feels shame when he fails in his task. In both cases, the persons are merely concerned about their social affirmability. Of course, there is a huge ethical-existential difference pertaining to the effects of their actions. However, this difference can only be seen and felt from the perspective of love.

Next, I want to suggest that our ultimate source of genuine moral normativity and motivation lies not in our urge for social affirmation but in the fact that other persons essentially claim and concern us as such and that we are open to the possibility of responding to them with love and care.

Clearly, the thesis that love for the other constitutes the irreducible source and heart of morality raises many potential questions and objections. The only thing I want to do here is to insist that love and care—understood in a very fundamental sense—is always present as a possibility between people and that without this ever-present possibility there would be no such thing as morality. It seems to me that it is possible to point to this possibility—and to use it as a backdrop for critically discussing Heidegger—while leaving many questions about the nature of such love and its relation to other motives open.

It is, I want to claim, a basic phenomenal fact of life that others essentially claim and concern us as persons and that we have the possibility of opening up to and caring about. The other is always there for me as a person that concerns me and appeals to my love and care, and to love the other—in this very basic sense— means to open up to her, let oneself be touched by her and care about her. Whereas in being motivated by our urge for affirmation we are focused on ourselves and our social affirmability—and experience emotions like pride, self-esteem, shame, and self-disgust depending on how we evaluate ourselves—in love we are concerned about the other and our relationship to her. Hence, love comes to expression in a different emotional register. For example, if I sense, from the perspective of love, that I have let down or betrayed a friend, I do not experience shame; rather,

I experience bad conscience—the voice of the other in me—or remorse—in so far as I am able to relate to the other with love again and face what I have done to her.

My claim is that the personal address of the other and the possibility of loving her is there in every historical situation—that is, regardless of the values and norms that happen to govern my society and my identity. To take an extreme example: Even in a society where slavery has been institutionalized and normalized since time immemorial, it is perfectly possible to see and welcome the slave as a you who claims me as an equal human being. Hence, I think Levinas is quite right in writing: "When man truly approaches the Other he is uprooted from history" (1969: 52).

However, opening up to the other with love is difficult, so difficult that this possibility is habitually repressed and covered up. The prime reason for this is that our anxious egoistic-collectivist urge for affirmation constitutes an extremely powerful force that tends to dominate our ways of seeing and relating both to others and to ourselves. In so far as we are in the grip of this urge, the possibility of love appears dangerous—often overwhelmingly so—because it calls us to welcome and care about others regardless of how this effects our desire for affirmation. Not only does it demand that we renounce all values and norms—values that may be deeply rooted in our community and identity, and into which we may have invested our desire for affirmation—that in different ways condemn or deny or run counter to the claim of the other. In the end, the possibility of love calls us to open up to and care about the other without caring about how whatever we say or do affects our standing in the community and our own prospects of achieving affirmation.

The difficulty of love and our need to repress it explains why the fact that people do not always, or very often, relate to others with love does not imply that this possibility is not there for them. Indeed, it would be possible to show that the constant presence of love shows itself in the emotional dynamics of the ways in which we repress it. For example, it seems inconceivable to imagine a slave owner who would be totally oblivious to the humanity and ethical appeal of his slaves—because, supposedly, the values of his culture would not allow him to recognize this possibility—and who in a calm and open-minded manner would treat his slaves as the pure tools that they are. No, whatever his culture and values, the slave owner is doomed to live in the tension between his irreducible openness to the slaves and his desperately felt need to repress this openness and legitimize his own attitude by dehumanizing and demonizing the slaves.

Insisting on the centrality of love does not imply naturalizing ethics in the manner of moral sentimentalists like Shaftesbury and Hume who tend to make the claims of ethics dependent on our de facto feelings of sympathy and benevolence. What I am suggesting is that the claim with which the other addresses us is an absolute one, and that our open response to this claim *consists* in care and love. Furthermore, when I talk about love I am not talking about particular feelings of sympathy or liking. I am talking about relating to the other person in an open and caring manner, about reaching out to her as a personal you. My reaching out toward the other may manifest itself in feelings of sympathy and joy but also in feelings of sorrow and anger, say, when the other closes herself to and relates in immoral ways toward me or other people. Of course, there is no doubt that we often fail to open up to others with love. However, these are not neutral facts pertaining to human emotional life. The failure to care about the other person is nothing but an ethical failure to respond to her.

Furthermore, it is important to note that rooting morality in our love for others does not imply any kind of moral particularism. To be sure, to be open to and care about others is always essentially to care about particular persons and not about some abstract notion of humanity. Still, since the claim of the other addresses us regardless of any particular circumstances—historical context, personality traits, and so on—we are always already open to the understanding that *all* people, universally and without exception, claim our love and care. This understanding of the absolute ethical appeal of all human beings is to some extent independent of our de facto ability to respond to particular others with love. Hence, although more or less unclear and repressed, it can serve as the critical light with guides both our ethical-existential and political thinking and acting.

So, is there a way in which values and norms can address us as genuinely morally significant—apart from the immense pressure they exert on us in virtue of our egoistic-collectivist urge for social affirmation?

As argued above, values and norms cannot in themselves be a source of moral claims. However, the perspective of love—the true source of morality—in fact opens up the possibility of experiencing and assessing values in terms of their moral meaning, that is, in terms of how they relate to this perspective. A value can strike us as more or less good and true in so far as it serves or articulates what the perspective of love gives us to understand; conversely, a value may strike us as evil or untrue in so far as it counteracts or distorts this perspective. As a result, the question of which values are endorsed by historical communities and individuals is a morally significant one. It is significant because the values and norms regulating our desire for affirmation—and hence the collective dynamics of honor and shame—is one of the most powerful forces determining collective and individual thinking and acting. Hence, in so far as we care about other people we are called to engage in the paradoxical challenge of fighting for the best values of our community while at the same time recognizing and unmasking the moral deficit of all collective morality. In this, the very possibility of caring about and distinguishing between good and evil in the first place, lies in our personal love and care for others as such.

Heidegger and the Binding Power of the World

It is a central task of Heidegger's later thinking to show how historical worlds can arise and address us as binding and holy. Our question is: Is Heidegger able to account for a genuine source of ethical-existential normativity and motivation beyond collective pressure and egoistic yearning for affirmation?

Heidegger's argument for the bindingness of the world proceeds in two stages—stages corresponding with how he conceives of the task of thinking and the task of art and poetry in establishing a binding world.

To begin with, the task Heidegger sets for his later thinking is to reflect on and articulate the event—*Ereignis*—that opens up historical being. To understand the *Ereignis* is ultimately to understand that being is given as ungroundable and finite historical epochs out of the groundless and self-withdrawing event of the *Ereignis*. Hence, the insight into the *Ereignis* achieved by thinking confronts us with the task of taking over and affirming our historical world as the ungroundable and finite destiny that it is.

However, this argument is strictly speaking an epistemological-ontological argument about the primacy of historical being. The point is that since our historically given meanings and values are epistemologically-ontologically fundamental, conditioning all our experience and understanding of ethical-existential significance, we have to accept them as a groundless destiny and realize that every attempt to ground them or flee them is futile. However, this argument tells us nothing about the possible normative force of our historical world. It does not point to any dimension of ethical-existential normativity beyond the collective pressure that our values tend to exert on us; it only asks us to accept these values as an ultimate historical given. At the end of the day, I think Heidegger's picture of our ontological predicament is radically distortive. Firstly, it seems that we are never referred to certain limited contexts of meaning and value as our given lot; rather we are in principle open to the possibility of other values, whether we access them in other cultures or in our own culture or through our imagination. Secondly—and most importantly—Heidegger's argument is predicated on his suppression of the fact that we are basically open to the call of the other person as someone to love and to care about as such, and that this is a source of moral meaning irreducible to historical values and gods. Hence, we are never faced with the necessity of accepting some set of values as our destiny.

In addition to this epistemological-ontological argument, Heidegger also offers an account of how art—especially poetry—can establish a binding world by enacting the strife between the world and the earth. Previously, I described in some detail how this happens. The central idea is that the work of art gathers—in a simultaneously receptive and creative manner—the world into a unified and finite totality of meanings and values on the basis of the still undetermined manifold of meaning-possibilities harbored by the historical heritage. The artwork gives concrete shape to the world by grounding it in the earth, that is, in the local natural-sensuous milieu at hand. Heidegger contends that in so far as this establishment of the world succeeds, the values that constitute our world will be present to us as gods, as holy and binding ideals that we are prepared to die for.

The question I want to raise is what kind of normative force could in principle issue from the dynamics of the artwork as depicted by Heidegger? Apart from his description of the strife between the world and the earth, Heidegger does not offer any additional elucidation of how the different aspects of the strife are supposed to grant to the world its binding power. Hence, we must attempt to do this ourselves with the risk of over- or misinterpreting the text.

Here are some suggestions:

1. In so far as the work of art gathers the ultimate horizons of meaning harbored by our history, this could imply that these meanings are able to address us both as familiar and age-old and as cognitively-dialectically superior to all the other meanings available to us.
2. In so far as the work of art grounds the world on the earth, this could entail that the world is able to address us as rooted in our local natural-sensuous milieu, to which we are adapted and attuned.
3. In so far as the artwork gathers and presents the meanings of the world in the form of concrete paradigmatic figures, this could be taken to enhance the aesthetic-dramatic power of the world.
4. In so far as the artwork involves consecration and praising of our values as holy gods this could be taken to entail employing various mechanisms of collective pressure to strengthen the power of the world to impress and overawe us, for example, putting the gods on a pedestal in the public space, surrounding them with limits and taboos, singing their praise and condemning their denial.

It seems to me that in addition to the collective pressure exerted by our historical values Heidegger's description of the artwork is only able to add various sorts of *rhetorical-persuasive force:* cognitive-dialectical force in so far as the meanings address as cognitively-dialectically superior in relation to other meanings; aesthetic-dramatic force in so far as they address us as familiar, striking, and overpowering.

However, we need to see that the collective pressure exerted by our historical world and the rhetoric-persuasive amplifications of this force are far from constituting anything like a source of genuine moral claims. To experience certain historical values and ideals as holy in Heidegger's sense is basically just to be impressed by their status within our community and by their rhetoric-persuasive power. Correspondingly, our motives for wanting to comply with some values on account of the collective pressure and persuasive force they exhibit are not moral motives. What we care about here is only how we perform in the eyes of our community or about the cognitive-aesthetic impressiveness of the values in question—in so far as the latter is separable from the former at all.[4]

The normative force of the world that Heidegger depicts is a far cry from our openness to the moral claim of other persons. This is why it would be possible in principle for a historical world to appear binding and holy in Heidegger's sense, although the values and ideals of this world would be morally corrupt. Consider, for example, a historical community whose collectively endorsed values and norms would dictate that some group of people are humanly inferior and that it is honorable to treat them as such: subjugate them and persecute them. Such a world, it seems, could well appear as holy and binding according to Heidegger's criteria: it could address us as familiar and alluring on account of its ability to bring to expression ancient historical ideals as well as the local earth; its highest ideals—its gods—could appear as cognitively-dialectically superior to other ideals; the paradigmatic shaping of the gods in art and poetry could be aesthetically-dramatically striking and sublime; the gods could finally be invested with all the collective force issuing from their function as standards for what the community holds to be honorable and shameful.⁵

The moral problems of Heidegger's radical historicism become politically acute in his conception of the logic of fall-and-rebirth characterizing Western history. Given that we live in the nihilistic end-stage of the history of metaphysics, in which the world has grown dim and powerless and all beings—even human beings—have lost their significance for us, Heidegger argues that our primary task consists in reflecting on the openness of being in order to make possible the establishment of a binding world. Since it is only the realization of this task that can make beings binding and significant again, the task has superiority over every ethical concern for particular human beings.

Previously I claimed that it was precisely the above scheme of thought that constituted a basic motivation for Heidegger's engagement in National Socialism. However, even after he starts to view Nazism as an extreme version of nihilism, Heidegger retains his notion of the priority of ontology over ethics, as well as the idea of the loss of meaning characterizing the modern world and the need to project a new binding world. The moral deficit of this scheme manifests itself especially plainly in those passages where he highlights the import of his own thinking by contrasting it to merely ontic matters and catastrophes. For example, in "On the Question of Being" from 1955 Heidegger compares the *polemos* of the history of being with ordinary wars: "This is no war, but the polemic event that first lets gods and humans, freemen and slaves, appear in their respective essence and leads to a differentiating dispute of *Being*. Compared to this dispute, world wars remain superficial. They are less and less capable of deciding anything the more technological their armaments" (GA 9: 424–5/321). In "The Thing" Heidegger makes use of a similar contrast:

> Man stares at what the explosion of the atom bomb could bring with it. He does not see that the atom bomb and its explosion are the mere final emission of what has long since taken place, has already happened. Not to mention the single hydrogen bomb, whose triggering, thought through to its utmost potential, might be enough to snuff out all life on earth. What is this helpless anxiety still waiting for, if the terrible has already happened? (GA 7: 168)

What is it that makes these passages so worrying? The basic problem is not, of course, that they are too gloomy and pessimistic in their diagnosis of our time as characterized by a reductive and dehumanizing metaphysics. What makes them so sad and problematic is rather the contempt and closedness toward the lives and suffering of concrete human beings that they express, which in effect make Heidegger's apocalyptic projection of a greater metaphysical catastrophe appear as a petty flight from the moral heart of life: if the lives of others human beings are not more important than that—if they are not absolutely important in themselves, regardless of the historical framework of meaning within which we happen to encounter them—then it is unintelligible why Heidegger's metaphysical catastrophes would be anything to worry about.[6]

Heidegger's vision of a binding meaning-laden world to come remains extremely vague and schematic to the end. What we can say is that the world he has in mind is a strong and unified collective world modeled on premodern honor societies but rooted in a philosophical understanding of the groundless and finite character of every such historical world. It is a world gathered around a shared set of ideals and values revered as holy gods by the people; a world in which each individual is supposed to resolutely appropriate her collective role as an identity that determines the meaning and narrative of her life; a world headed by an elite of thinkers, poets, and political leaders. As I see it, the basic ethical problem with this vision is that it builds on a repression of our primary ethical relationship to others as persons that concern us and claim us as such. On closer scrutiny, the people Heidegger envisions and idealizes emerge as people thoroughly dominated by their egocentric desire to realize their collective identities, as people to whom others are only important as the collective audience whose affirmation they seek or as instruments for enacting their own identities. To be sure, Heidegger's envisioned world does not necessarily imply totalitarian control and/or persecution of alien elements. However, it would seem that due to its character as a strong collective community gathered around a unified set of ideals and values, such a world would very easily give way to collective control, repression, and, in the end, persecution. Heidegger himself never talks about such dangers, just as he never talks about the moral crimes of National Socialism. His lack of worry is yet another sign of the moral dearth of his vision of a binding world.

14

THE SOURCES OF TRUTH

Heidegger's analysis of the historical structure of phenomena has radical consequences for how we are to think about truth. According to Heidegger, the traditional conception of truth as correspondence is quite pertinent as regards statements and beliefs about beings and states of affairs. For example, the statements "the picture on the wall is hanging askew" and "Socrates is courageous" are true or false depending on whether they present the beings that they are about correctly. However, to be able to understand these phenomena in the first place, we already need to possess an understanding of the historical network of meaning in which such matters as human beings, pictures, and courage have the meaning they have for us. Since our understanding of being determines what we can experience and grasp as meaningful beings, it cannot itself be true or false in virtue of its ability to correspond to or depict such beings. Hence, Heidegger rules out the possibility of interrogating the truth of our primary understanding of historical being and meaning. Instead, he insists that, ultimately, we need to take over our historical context of being as a groundless and finite destiny that allows us to experience beings as meaningful at all.

My aim here is to take some steps toward delimiting the truth of Heidegger's historicized notion of truth: What aspects of our understanding does it capture? What aspects are covered up or distorted? I begin by taking a look at Cristina Lafont's severe critique of Heidegger's conception of truth. After that, I go on to review Heidegger's phenomenological arguments for his conception, suggesting that he refers to and draws on certain particular kinds of understanding—what I will call pragmatic understanding of practices and pragmatic understanding of values— that may be said to be radically historical in his sense. However, I argue that his general thesis about the historicity of our understanding of phenomena is unsupported and, in the end, untrue. Against Heidegger, I maintain that understanding the ethical-existential meaning and structure of our experience of meaningful phenomena is, in its most central and basic aspects, a matter of grasping existential realities that transcend our historical concepts and preunderstandings and that constitute the source of truth—and untruth—of our understanding.

Lafont's Critique

In my view, the most powerful critique so far of Heidegger's historicist conception of truth has been delivered by Cristina Lafont in her book *Heidegger, Language, and World-Disclosure* from 2000.[1] Lafont's critique is very much in line with and an elaboration of Tugendhat's classical and much-debated critique, which I briefly touched upon in Part Two. Both hold that Heidegger, in conceiving of our historical understanding of being as the ground that determines what we can experience as phenomena, makes this understanding immune to the question of truth. In her book, Lafont explicates and critically interrogates Heidegger's notion of the ontological difference by drawing on the theories of direct reference developed by Hilary Putnam and Keith Donnellan.[2]

Lafont's principal thesis is that Heidegger understands language as world-disclosure, which means that he believes that our experience of beings is determined by the meanings and categories of our language. Although this conception of language receives a clear and consistent articulation only in Heidegger's writings after the *Kehre*, Lafont claims that it is already—albeit in an ambivalent way—at the basis of his thinking in *Being and Time*. The idea of language as world-disclosure is, in turn, grounded in the ontological difference. According to Lafont, Heidegger's notion of the ontological difference implies the semantic thesis that meaning determines reference in the radical sense that our understanding of being determines not only what we can refer to with our words but also what we can experience as meaningful entities: "Given that our understanding of being is *constitutive* for what these entities are *for us*, it determines how we understand, perceive, and experience the world" (2000: XIII). Even though Heidegger insists that our understanding of being is factical, that is, historically contingent and changeable, he nevertheless conceives of it as strictly *a priori*: it precedes and determines in advance—as an absolute and uncircumventable historical destiny—our experience of beings and it is, consequently, unrevisable by such experience (2000: 110–12, 253–7). As a result, Lafont argues that Heidegger's thinking of the ontological difference in the end amounts to a kind of linguistic idealism and leads to a relativization of the truth—understood by Heidegger as unconcealment—to our different historical ways of linguistically constituting the world (2000: XV, 111).

According to Lafont, Heidegger's ontological difference cannot be upheld. Drawing on Putnam and Donnellan, she argues that our understanding of the factical concepts and meanings that always already guide our experience of beings is, in so far as it has empirical content, essentially hypothetical and fallible in character, and cannot determine in advance the possible content of our experience. Moreover, it is a central feature of our language that we can use words to refer directly to beings without possessing an *a priori* knowledge of meaning supposedly necessary to allow us to pick out the referent. In referring to beings directly, we use our factical understanding to refer to the beings themselves as independent of our understanding, that is, regardless of how they are ultimately to be described: "We can see that the referential use of terms presupposes the unproblematic availability of the distinction between *language* and *what language is about*. Only on the basis of grasping this difference can we adopt a *hypothetical* attitude toward the ascriptions we undertake vis-à-vis the objective world, a world presupposed by the activity of designation" (2000: 244). Heidegger, Lafont maintains, is certainly right in claiming that we always already live in a factical understanding of being which guides our referring to and experience of beings. However, this understanding does not *a priori* determine our experience but merely has the status of fallible hypotheses about independent beings.

It seems clear to me that Lafont's critique is on the right track and I see my own account as a radicalization of this critique. However, I want to draw attention to two problems with Lafont's critical argument, the second of which limits the force of her critique to a considerable degree.

To begin with, I do not agree with Lafont's exegetical claim that Heidegger would already in *Being and Time* put forward the thesis that our understanding of being is linguistically constituted. As I argued earlier, the early Heidegger basically conceives of Dasein's understanding of being and the world as an understanding of prelinguistic patterns of meaning, so that these meanings form the basis for our possibilities of linguistic expression and communication. However, regardless of whether Heidegger conceives of the understanding of being as linguistic or not, I think Lafont is right in maintaining that Heidegger's conception of the ontological difference implies that our historical understanding of being *a priori* determines our experience of beings, and that this conception suffers from deep problems of the kind she points to.[3]

A more serious problem with Lafont's critique, however, is that it fails to target what I think is the central philosophical concern underlying Heidegger's ontological difference. Lafont basically explicates the ontological difference as the general thesis that our factical preunderstanding of being determines what we can experience as beings. Her central critical argument is that Heidegger fails to see that our understanding of being, in so far as it has empirical content, must be conceived as fallible hypotheses about the world such as it is in itself independently of our understanding. Here, the theoretical concepts of the empirical sciences provide the paradigm that Heidegger in her view cannot account for and that the theory of direct reference can account for.

However, in framing her critique in this way, Lafont from the outset overlooks that the primary question guiding Heidegger's analysis of the ontological difference concerns the structure of our experience and understanding of *significant phenomena*. Central to this analysis is Heidegger's claim that our pretheoretical experience of ready-to-hand beings in terms of their functions and significances is irreducible to and determines the possible relevance of our theoretical knowledge of present-at-hand beings. As Heidegger writes: all the "properties" of the equipment are "bound up" the ways in which it is "appropriate or inappropriate" in relation to some task or purpose (SZ: 83). Ultimately, Heidegger contends that our experience of phenomena is determined by our understanding of the historical values and ideals that grant significance to the phenomena; this understanding is in turn guided by our historical understanding of being.

Heidegger's notion of the ontological difference implies the claim that our understanding of the values and being-senses that determine and guide our experience of beings as phenomena cannot be true or false depending on how it corresponds with such beings. This claim, however, does not commit Heidegger to the thesis ascribed to him by Lafont, namely that our access to and knowledge of empirical present-to-hand objects—of the kind studied by the natural sciences—would be determined by our factual empirical preconceptions of these objects. Heidegger's view of the truth of empirical concepts is not, to be sure, crystal clear.[4] Still, from a systematic point of view it is clear that he could retain his thesis that our primary understanding of significance is structured by the ontological difference, while admitting that the concepts of the empirical sciences function as fallible hypotheses about the beings under investigation.

I believe Heidegger is right in insisting that our understanding of the significance of beings is irreducible to, and not primarily constituted by, our empirical knowledge of the material-causal traits of these beings. This, however, implies that Lafont's critical thesis about the fallible nature of the concepts of the empirical sciences—although in my view true of them—strictly speaking does not unsettle Heidegger's central notion of the historicity of our understanding of phenomena. For us, then, the decisive question remains: Is our understanding of phenomenal significance radically determined by our historical understanding of values and being, or must this understanding rather be conceived in terms of our fallible provisional grasp of independent realities?

Heidegger's Arguments

What is the phenomenological basis of Heidegger's principal thesis about the historical structure of phenomena? By probing his phenomenological arguments for this thesis, we will get a better grip on its truth and limits.

To be clear what we are talking about, let us begin by once more reiterating Heidegger's thesis and noting that he conceives of the prior understanding of historical meaning constituting our experience of phenomena as structured in three layers: first, our experience of beings as phenomena—as tools—is determined by our understanding of the instrumental contexts of the tasks and practices we are engaged in; second our understanding of these contexts and practices is determined by our understanding of the values and ideals that are the source of ethical-existential significance of all phenomena; third, all the experience and understanding above is guided by our understanding of the different modes of being and of being as such. According to Heidegger, all these three layers of understanding disclose historically given meanings that determine our experience of beings as phenomena and that cannot be true or false by virtue of how they correspond with such beings.

I will start by discussing an argument that Heidegger continually employs to support the idea that all our understanding of general meanings and concepts is radically historical in his sense. The argument is this: In order to be able to experience and identify beings as distinguishable phenomena we always need to have an understanding of the general meanings or concepts that the beings instantiate. Only if I already have an understanding of what a dog is can I apprehend a being as a dog; only if I already have an understanding of what courage is can I judge somebody to be courageous. This description certainly captures a condition for identifying beings as this or that. However, it is no argument for the thesis that our preunderstanding of general meanings is radically historical and cannot be true or false about the matters that it is about. This is especially clear when it comes to our preunderstandings of empirical matters (although I will shortly be arguing that the same goes for our understanding of ethical-existential matters). Obviously, our conceptions of engines, viruses, genes, and planets can be more or less true or false. In this, their truth does not depend on how they correspond with particular beings or states of affairs. Rather, the truth or falsity of such general conceptions depends on how well or badly they conceive of such things as the being-character, structure, causality, and behavior of the kind of beings in question. In short, the fact that our experience is always already guided by general understandings that allow us to identify phenomena in no way rules out the possibility that these understandings may be true or untrue to the matters they refer to.

Let us now go on to review how Heidegger specifically argues—or fails to argue—for the historicity of each of the three layers of our prior understanding of historical meaning.

As concerns the first layer, Heidegger—in his various analyses of our coping with ready-to-hand tools—offers a strong phenomenological account of how our practical engagement in and understanding of the practices of our world conditions our ability to experience beings as relevant to the practice in question. What Heidegger seems to have in mind here are the basic practices and habits of acting established in a given historical community, such as hammering, riding bicycles, using clocks, living in houses, playing football, and using money. As Heidegger argues, we can only encounter beings as tools for this or that within the instrumental context of a certain practice. The practices of our world open up the possible functions and roles in terms of which beings may show up, for example, as a good hammer or as an insufficient amount of money. Moreover, the practices themselves prescribe what it means to skillfully handle or make true or false judgments about the tools and situations that they allow us to encounter.

Now, it seems to me that it is quite accurate to say that the pragmatic understanding involved in mastering and engaging in historical practices of the above kind constitutes our understanding of certain beings, namely, the beings that emerge as relevant beings within the contexts of the practices. Furthermore, it makes sense to say that such pragmatic understanding does not in itself involve any question about the truth or untruth of the practice in question. To understand here simply means to grasp the internal norms and workings of a certain historically given practice and be able to engage in it.⁵ Of course, we can ask questions, for example, about the values and ideas motivating the practice or about the role of the practice in our society—questions that introduce the issue of truth. However, this implies leaving the pragmatic understanding that consists in mastering the practice behind.

As regards the second layer, Heidegger provides little phenomenological support for his thesis that understanding the historical values and norms of our world—which he calls the "heroes" or "gods"—means appropriating them as the groundless and finite destiny determining our experience of ethical-existential significance and that it makes no sense to ask about their truth or untruth. Of course, in proposing this thesis Heidegger is drawing on the familiar fact that we always live in historical communities with varying collectively endorsed values that tend to exert powerful normative force on us. However, he offers no phenomenological explication of our experience and understanding of values to support his claim about the historicity of this understanding.

To be sure, it is possible to conceive of an entirely pragmatic understanding of values and norms that may be said to be radically historical and truth-immune in the same way as the pragmatic understanding of practices discussed above. What I have in mind here is a pragmatic understanding that merely consists in learning to know and skillfully cope with the historical values of given community without any interest in or questions about the ethical-existential meaning or truth of these values. However, Heidegger's conception of historical values and norms as our ultimate source of ethical-existential significance calls for an account of what it means not just to pragmatically handle but to understand and judge the moral and existential substance of such values. Yet he gives no phenomenological support for his thesis that this kind of understanding would be radically historical and immune to questions of truth. In fact, in the previous chapter I claimed that this thesis is false. I argued that other persons claim and concern us as a primary source of ethical significance regardless of historical context. Moreover, I argued that understanding and judging the existential and moral substance of values means understanding how they relate—in ways that are more or less true—to our primary ethical relationship to others.

Finally, as concerns the third layer, it must likewise be said that Heidegger does not really offer phenomenological arguments for his idea about the historicity of our understanding of being. Indeed, the thesis that our understanding of being is radically historical gets much of its persuasive force from the fact that Heidegger formally inserts it as the uppermost layer of our prior understanding of historical meaning. In this, the seeming credibility of the thesis is parasitic upon and rests on a flawed analogy to the other layers of historical understanding. There is the sense that just like the historical practices and the historical values of our world, the senses of being are also historical givens. What is more, there is the sense that since our understanding of being is an understanding of the basic ontological meanings guiding all our ontic experience and understanding, it cannot be true or false by corresponding to particular beings. However, although the latter is certainly true it in no way rules out all possibilities of conceiving of the truth of such understanding. Indeed, in what follows I will argue that the truth or untruth of our understanding of being consists in how truthfully it renders the structures of our phenomenal experience.

Our Openness to Transhistorical Realities as the Source of Truth

My suggestion is that when it comes to understanding the structures and ethical-existential significance of our experience of phenomena, we are essentially open to and directed toward realities that transcend our historical concepts and preconceptions and that constitute the source of truth of our understanding.

What I primarily have in mind here is, first, our understanding of the ethical claim of the other person and our existential relation to her; second, more generally, our phenomenological understanding of the structures of our experience of meaningful phenomena. In both cases, I want to suggest, understanding is essentially a matter of seeing and grasping transhistorical realities in ways that are more or less true or false. To openly acknowledge the claim of the other and my relation to her is to truthfully understand the ethical-existential reality of our encounter—a reality that is not determined by any historical values or understandings; by contrast, not to open up to the other is to untruthfully deny what goes on between us. Furthermore, to phenomenologically understand and explicate the structures of our phenomenal experience is fundamentally a matter of grasping—in more or less truthful ways—the structural elements that make our experiences what they are and that are, at their most fundamental, transhistorical in nature: our ethical relation to others, our basic desires and fears, our perceptual and cognitive structures.

Whereas I already discussed our ethical relationship to others in the previous chapter I will present my view of phenomenology in the last chapter. What I want to do here is to articulate and give some phenomenological substance to my claim that it belongs to the very sense of these kinds of understanding to be open to and grasp independent existential realities as the source of truth of understanding.

Let us begin by considering the case of a soldier fighting for some country, say, in the Second World War. The soldier in question has a deep-seated concept of courage according to which courage signifies the ability to face physical danger and stand up for one's group no matter what happens. Accordingly, he has always looked down on conscientious objectors and their likes as cowards. However, one day the army group that he belongs to takes a prisoner behind enemy lines. Because of the difficulties in keeping him detained, his comrades decide to kill him on the spot. Let us imagine that at this point our soldier is struck by the fact that the enemy soldier is in fact a human person that claims him ethically, and that he and his fellow soldiers are about to commit murder. He also senses the overwhelming difficulty and even danger of opposing the consensus of the group. As a result, his concept of courage changes as he comes to see that maintaining one's moral autonomy in the face of collective pressure might be at least as demanding as facing physical danger. We could also imagine that our soldier would begin to grasp the extent to which his allegiance to the group is motivated by fear and by the desire for collective affirmation.

The crucial thing to see here is that we can only account for the dynamics of truth operative in the example if we conceive of our understanding in terms of our grasp—be it better or worse—of independent realities. What makes the soldier's initial understanding of courage untrue is that it fails to account for and instead covers up and distorts what is actually there and given as significant in his experience. What, by contrast, makes his new understanding more true is that it allows him to see and account for the phenomena in question: the ethical appeal of the other soldier, the evil of killing him, the courage needed to stand firm in the face of collective pressure, the anxious desire for collective affirmation motivating his adherence to the group. These ethical and existential phenomena are there for us regardless of the factical concepts we and our culture happen to possess. Hence, the dynamics of truth constitutes an irreducible aspect of our understanding of such matters.

To be sure, Heidegger is right in claiming that our experience is always already guided by the factical conceptual preunderstanding we live in. This preunderstanding contains the typical general patterns of meaning which determine what we first and foremost tend to identify as unified phenomena and situations, what possibilities and scenarios we tend to anticipate, and which conceptual contexts we tend to draw on when we think about or discuss the matters in question. It also forms the point of departure for every modification of our concepts. If the culture we live in has only a poor or distortive conceptuality for accounting for a certain matter, this might make it difficult to grasp and articulate—both for ourselves and for others—what we experience. Modifying the above example, we could think of our soldier as belonging to a historical community where, for ages, the idea that courage consists in standing up for one's group in the face of danger has been the only game in town. In such a situation, he might have severe difficulties with articulating and accounting for his genuine moral seeing of the enemy soldier. He would lack the conceptual resources for grasping the moral meaning of his reaction. In addition, the collective values that he would have inherited would prompt him to reject it as something bad and shameful. Hence, it is likely that the voice of his conscience would appear unintelligible and immoral to him.

Mark Twain's story of Huckleberry Finn's friendship to the runaway slave Jim offers an illuminating example of the kind of moral confusion and conflict that might occur when one lives in a community governed by corrupt collective values. Huck's having helped Jim escape from his owner, Miss Watson, the two are on the run. In this situation, Huck finds himself torn between conflicting claims. On the one hand, the collective values that he has internalized tell him that the only good and decent thing to do is to hand Jim over to the authorities. On the other hand, his heart—that is, his love for and care about Jim—tells him that this would be utterly wrong. As we know, Huck follows his heart. However, given the collective morality he has internalized, he has a hard time making sense of his own moral reactions, and conceives of them as fundamentally immoral. Having decided not to write to Miss Watson and denounce Jim, Huck—acknowledging his own "wickedness"—exclaims: "All right, then, I'll *go* to hell" (Twain [1884] 1994: 162).[6]

Even though our factical conceptual preunderstanding always guides our experience and understanding of phenomena, it does not determine what we can experience as meaningful. Although the prejudicing force of our pre-understanding might be strong, it is no more than our factical provisional grasp of the ethical-existential realities we experience. Hence, it possesses no epistemic authority other than its potential ability to help us account for what our open intuition lets us experience.

It seems that any attempt to account—or compensate—for the truth of understanding by conceiving of it in terms of some kind of internal critical reflection on our historical concepts is doomed to lose sight of truth altogether. There have of course been many attempts to argue that radical historicism does not imply relativism or irrationalism. Philosophers such as Gadamer, Charles Taylor, and Alasdair MacIntyre have in different ways put forward the claim that even though our historical concepts cannot be true or false by corresponding to some independent reality, there nevertheless remains a possibility for engaging in critical, rational reflection on the basis of the concepts at our disposal:[7] concepts can be exposed as incoherent or unclear or they can be shown to contravene or have the character of ad hoc constructions in relation to more basic concepts; some concepts may appear rationally superior to other concepts since they are able to account for the latter but not the other way around; regarding the possibility of critically assessing different historical frameworks of meaning— epochs, traditions—it always seems possible to find some common conceptual ground on the basis of which a discussion can be enacted. Still, whatever forms such a critical intraconceptual reflection could take, it seems that it cannot account for the truth of understanding. However strong or justified a constellation of meaning may appear in relation to our most basic concepts, or however basic a concept or meaning may be within our historical context—this does not make it true. The cognitive force or weakness of a concept issuing from its role within some conceptual context simply does not coincide with its being true of false in the irreducible sense of illuminating or distorting what is experientially given to us as independent of our concepts. Even if a certain concept would be the only one available in a culture—or, for that matter, in all the world's cultures—this would still not make it true.

Ultimately, the idea that our understanding is radically determined by our historical concepts makes it impossible to account for what it *means* to understand ethical and existential phenomena. It is precisely the openness of our conceptual understanding toward the matters we conceive that makes it possible for it to be illuminating and clarifying or misleading and distortive. Not only does this openness form an integral trait of our understanding and appropriation of concepts within our own culture; it also lets us see how the encounter between different worlds and cultures always revolves around an irreducible dimension of shared experience. As soon as we recognize this, the very idea that we are referred to finite historical contexts of meaning and that there can be radical conceptual gaps between different worlds loses its grip on us and emerges as a dogmatic construction. If our concepts would not offer themselves to us as possibilities to grasp or misinterpret matters that we experience irrespective of these concepts, would not our understanding of concepts be reduced to something like a skill in playing a self-contained game with more or less determinate rules? A game which, strictly speaking has nothing to do with truth, falsity, illusion, self-deception and insight? A *Glasperlenspiel*.

15

PHENOMENOLOGY AND HISTORICAL REFLECTION

Heidegger's analysis of the historical structure of our understanding of phenomena induces him to develop a radically historical mode of thinking. While this ambition largely remained at the level of program in *Being and Time*, his later texts constitute a series of attempts to elaborate and enact such a thinking concretely. But how does this attempt succeed? What kind of truth or cognitive force can Heidegger's historical thinking lay claim to? What are the principal possibilities and limits of such thinking?

In what follows, I am going to argue that Heidegger's ambition to replace intuition-based phenomenology with historical reflection is bound to fail. My contention is that in so far as we want to understand our experience of significant phenomena, the only way to do this concretely and not speculate is to reflectively look at and explicate our de facto first-person experiences of such phenomena. Hence, if one denies the possibility of phenomenology—as Heidegger does—one in effect loses the possibility of saying anything substantial about our experience of significance without either resorting to prejudiced speculation or secretly appealing to phenomenological seeing. However, although historical reflection cannot replace phenomenology as the primary method of philosophy, it can still serve important supplementary and critical functions.

I will begin by critically examining Heidegger's central idea that thinking needs to return to the Greek origin of our understanding of being in order to retrieve the most primordial possibilities of understanding at our disposal. I will then go on to discuss the method of deconstruction as another possible means to demonstrate the logic of the event/clearing. Although Heidegger's thinking about the clearing points to the possibility of such a method, he does not develop it concretely in the way Derrida later does. Still, since Heidegger is often thought of as the progenitor of deconstruction, and since it is often assumed that this method offers a qualified means for revealing the work of the *Ereignis* or *différance*, it may be a good idea briefly to attend to it. I end the epilogue by outlining my view of the possibility of phenomenology and of the central challenges that face the phenomenological approach.

The Method of Returning to the Historical Origin

Heidegger's conviction that phenomenology must be transformed into a historical mode of thinking is based on his analysis of the structure of phenomena. Since, as he argues, our experience of phenomena is determined by our prior understanding of the historical contexts of meaning that we live in, the possibility of thinking must consist in interpreting and retrieving the most qualified meanings that our history harbors.

In *Being and Time*, Heidegger thought that thinking must take the form of a destruction that dismantles our uprooted ontological concepts by tracing them back to their historical origin. This origin he found in Aristotle, whose texts, he believed, not only established the understanding of being as presence-at-hand dominating the history of philosophy but also harbored a more primordial understanding of the temporal sense of being. By returning to Aristotle, he believed it would be possible to clarify the meaning of our received understanding of being, to free ourselves from this understanding, and to retrieve the more primordial understanding of the temporality of being which Aristotle's texts had in store. However, since Heidegger did not yet pursue the question of how a primordial historical understanding of being is achievable, his investigations in *Being and Time* did not in fact transpire through a retrieval of Aristotle but through direct phenomenological descriptions of the structures of Dasein.

In his later work Heidegger conceives of his thinking as a radically historical mode of reflection inquiring into the event/clearing of being.

According to the later Heidegger, all our historical meanings and values have their origin in the event that opens up historical worlds. Such an event, he believes, is precisely what took place in ancient Greece. On the backdrop of the early pre-Socratic—still vague and groping—conception of the event/clearing of being as *physis*, Plato and Aristotle developed an understanding of being as *ousia*: presence. The fateful thing about this metaphysical understanding of being was that it left unthought, covered up and forgot the historical happening that made it possible. Since the guiding metaphysical understanding of philosophy thus lacked a grasp of the historicity of being, philosophy henceforth became the prisoner of this understanding, following and transmitting it in a prejudiced fashion without questioning its origin or legitimacy. Heidegger thus pictures the history of Western thinking as a closed monolithic series of ever more uprooted understandings of being that remain determined by the Greek beginning.

This picture of the logic of the history of metaphysics forms the background for Heidegger's idea that thinking, to achieve a primordial understanding of the event/clearing of being, needs to return to the Greek beginning. To begin with, we can only hope to get clear about our contemporary techno-subjectivist understanding of being as material reserve for our subjective desires by returning to the Greek beginning in Plato and Aristotle where the original understanding of being as presence—of which our own understanding is but a modification—was forged. Furthermore, Heidegger contends that in understanding being as presence metaphysics leaves unthought and covers up the event/clearing that opens up and gives being in the first place. The only way to get access to the matter of thinking is to trace and retrieve the primordial yet vague and embryonic understanding of the event/clearing of being that he thinks the Greek beginning—in particular the pre-Socratic thinking preceding the era of metaphysics—harbors within itself. Heidegger's strategy for doing this involves two steps. Negatively, he tries to demonstrate that metaphysics is fundamentally unable to account for its understanding of being as presence. Positively, he tries to show that there are historical sources that in fact point to the event/clearing. Not only does metaphysics itself contain references to the event/clearing as its own presupposition. Heidegger also thinks that the texts of the pre-Socratics and the etymological roots of central words bear witness to the event/clearing as the origin of being.

So what about the truth of Heidegger's idea that it is both possible and necessary to return to the historical beginning in order to achieve a primordial understanding of the event/clearing of being?

Crucially, I think Heidegger's basic idea that our understanding of being is determined by our historically inherited meanings is false. In so far as our understanding of being is all about understanding the structures of our experience of meaningful phenomena, there is no ground for the idea that this understanding is determined by our history. Rather, such understanding essentially consists in openly seeing and grasping the structures of our experiences as something that transcends whatever historical preconception we might have of them. Although it is true that we always already live in historical conceptualities which primarily tend to guide our understanding, and which may be false and distortive, we are nevertheless free in principle to openly see and examine the structures of our experience as the source of truth of our concepts.

From this, it follows that even though the factical concepts primarily guiding our sight would have the character of distortive prejudices, there would be no need to return to their historical origin in order to emancipate ourselves from their grip and access the matters themselves. Indeed, it also follows that Heidegger's depiction of the history of Western philosophy as a closed and unified series of events completely determined by the metaphysical understanding of being issued by the first Greek beginning cannot but emerge as a dogmatic construction. Since we are essentially free to look at and try to understand what we experience regardless of our historical preunderstandings, no historical beginning or paradigm could ever determine and delimit our possibilities of understanding with any necessity. To be sure, Heidegger's diagnosis of the metaphysical nature of philosophy in my view captures a basic tendency in the history of philosophy and I also agree that the context of Greek philosophy provides an exemplary zone for reflecting on the driving problems and motives of philosophy. Still, I think there is no doubt that Heidegger's mythologizing narrative about the history of philosophy as a monolithic unity determined by a singular Greek origin belongs to the weakest parts of his thinking (cf. Derrida 1989). As concerns the matter of philosophy, he dogmatically shuts out all alternative questions and problems that do not confirm his view that philosophy is all about understanding being as presence. As concerns the historical sources of philosophy, he systematically disregards other traditions and contexts that do not fit into the Euro-Greco-Germano-centric line of development he so badly wants to draw up from the Greeks to his own thinking.

So far, I have claimed that we are not determined by our history and that it is not necessary for thinking to return to its historical origin. However, more than this I want to argue that the method of returning to and retrieving the historical origins of our tradition cannot in itself yield understanding of the matters at stake—in Heidegger's case, the event/clearing of being—at all.

Heidegger's radical historicism makes him believe that the only way to demonstrate the event/clearing as the origin of being is by showing that our history actually harbors such a notion within itself. By explicating central Greek texts and tracing the etymologies of key concepts, he tries to show that the metaphysical understanding of being as presence de facto refers back to a more primordial understanding of the event/clearing that opens up being. In this, the notion of the event/clearing it thought to emerge as both historically and ontologically primordial: it precedes the onset of metaphysics as the ultimate condition of the metaphysical understanding of being as presence. As such, it constitutes the conditioning horizon for Western thinking in its entirety.

However, it seems unfeasible to use this kind of historical method to demonstrate that the event/clearing is the source of historical being. As argued above, the fact that a notion presents itself as ontologically primordial—or otherwise cognitively basic—within a certain tradition does not make it true or illuminating. Although Heidegger would succeed in showing that the event/clearing constitutes the most primordial notion of the Western tradition—something that he in my view is not able to do—this would in no way prove that the event/clearing is the source that opens up being. It would only show that the notion of the event/clearing would have functioned as the philosophical horizon of the Western tradition. In this, the question of the truth and meaning of this notion would remain completely open.

In short, the method of tracing and retrieving the historical origins of our concepts is not necessary nor fundamental for attaining philosophical understanding. This, however, does not mean that reflection on historical origins would have no role to play. For example, by tracing the historical roots of some concept we may come across a field of related historical concepts and contexts that potentially widen our view of the different questions and aspects related to the matter in question. Perhaps we find that tracing the origin of our concept opens up a contrast between the present concept and some previous concept that is instructive. Perhaps we are confronted with concepts and meanings that transcend and destabilize our normal understanding and suggest new and perhaps even insightful ways of looking at things. This said, it is important to remember that the potential gain in philosophical understanding here depends entirely on our independent seeing and understanding of the matters. It is only our ability to independently understand the matters that allows us to give concrete sense to historical concepts, to see how such concepts relate to one another, and to recognize what is insightful and what is not in historical conceptions. Whatever historical concepts we might find and however great their potential insight or interrogatory force, they are bound to remain nothing more than abstract ideas or prejudices as long as they have not been engaged in an open effort to see and understand the matters they are all about.

It is important to note that my thesis is *not* that due to his method of historical reflection, Heidegger's later thinking would amount to groundless and speculative constructions. My thesis is rather that Heidegger's metaunderstanding of the radically historicist character of his method does not allow him to account for what it is that gives to his thinking whatever truth or clarificatory force it possesses. In his texts from the mid-1930s onwards, Heidegger employs many different strategies for demonstrating and articulating the event/clearing of being, strategies that are often fused and hard to distinguish clearly: historical and etymological explications, quasi-dialectical and quasi-transcendental arguments, as well as phenomenological descriptions. My claim is that—whatever Heidegger thinks he is doing—these strategies get their potential clarificatory force from their ability to describe and make sense of the phenomenal experiences that they ultimately refer to. Although Heidegger may articulate a line of thought in terms of a historical explication or dialectical argument, this thought may nevertheless rest on and give expression to astute phenomenological observations. For us who read Heidegger philosophically, the decisive task is no other than to see what sense we can make of Heidegger's thinking, and to critically delimit its truth and untruth, by phenomenologically relating it back to the relevant concrete experiences.

The Method of Deconstruction

Heidegger's conception of the event/clearing contains within itself the train of thought that Derrida will later develop into the method of deconstruction. According to Heidegger, our historical world essentially arises as the result of a strife, a polemic gathering, in which certain historical meanings and values are singled out as the teleological horizon of the world, whereas other alternative meanings are denied and covered up. Hence, the world arises as a clearing surrounded by a dark field of suppressed possibilities. The origin of the world in the strife will always announce itself in the controversial character of the world. By this, Heidegger means that it belongs to the world that its constitutive relations of meaning do not form a coherent self-contained system but will always be strained and underdetermined, bordering on other possibilities that have been stifled.

Heidegger's notion that the logic of the strife expresses itself as the controversiality of the world points to the possibility of a deconstructive method. Nevertheless, Heidegger himself does not implement such a method. When Derrida later develops his deconstructive strategy of thinking his prime sources of inspiration are Husserl, Heidegger, Saussure, and Hegel. His key notion of *différance* gives expression to the idea that all our historical meanings are determined by the way they differ from and contrast with other historical meanings. Hence, the ambition of Western metaphysics to ground stable and self-contained systems of meaning can only be achieved by repressing and omitting meanings that do not fit into the system but nevertheless constitute it. Deconstruction is the practice of exposing the logic of *différance* at work in the central texts of the tradition. This is done by showing how the texts are unable to circumscribe the meaning they purport to communicate, and by tracing the repressed and marginalized meanings that the text simultaneously denies and refers to as its constitutive other.

The only question I want to pose here is the following: Can, in principle, this kind of deconstructive method be used to demonstrate the reality of what Heidegger calls the *Ereignis* and what Derrida calls *différance*?

The answer must, again, be no.

There are of course a lot of things that a deconstructive analysis can do. It can demonstrate that a philosophical or some other kind of text is unable to determine and control its own meaning in a systematic fashion; it can expose meanings that the text marginalizes or stifles despite—or because of—their essential relevance to the issues that it claims to investigate. However, even if this kind of deconstructive analysis would be successful in a manifold of cases, this would in no way prove that our understanding of meaningful phenomena would essentially be constituted by the differential logic of *différance* or by the polemical logic of the *Ereignis*. There would be no ground for such a conclusion. To establish and give sense to the positive thesis about the fundamental role played by *différance* or the event/clearing, one would need to pursue some kind of positive transhistorical phenomenological investigation of the nature of understanding, a kind of investigation that both Heidegger and Derrida have ruled out in advance.

My suggestion is that such an investigation in fact shows the opposite, namely that our philosophical understanding is essentially directed and open toward our experience as a source of truth that transcends our factical concepts. Although we have to make use of our factical concepts—and of contrasts between these concepts—to clarify and articulate the matters we try to understand, there is no reason to conclude from this that our understanding as such would be determined through negative contrasts between our factical concepts. Rather, if we engage in understanding a matter—for example, the emotion of shame—this means that we look at and try to grasp the structures of the relevant experiences. In this, the factical concepts we employ—our common concepts regarding shame and other related phenomena—essentially gain their meaning and truth from our de facto ability to grasp and describe the relevant experiences. It is quite possible for us to use concepts in a more or less clear and meaningful way that is not dependent on our ability to systematically define and circumscribe their meaning. When it comes to reading and interpreting texts, this also means that no purely historical—for instance, deconstructive—explication of the factical concepts employed could by itself attain the meaning of the text. To get at the meaning of the text in question, and the meaning of the factical words as used in the text, one would have to leave historical thinking behind and engage in independent phenomenological reflection on the concrete experiences, for example, of shame, that the text attempts to explicate.

Clearly, the ambition to establish self-contained, quasi-deductive, or quasi-dialectical systems of thought has for all too long been a guiding ideal in the tradition of philosophy. Moreover, the temptation to marginalize or cover up—or otherwise subdue—what does not fit easily with the philosophical theory or worldview one wants to put forward will always be present in thinking. As a result, the deconstructive effort to attend to and expose the unacknowledged cracks, limitations, omissions, and marginalizations that generally haunt philosophy—as well as other forms of thinking and writing—will continue to be an important element of our critical thinking. However, deconstruction can never replace but rather presupposes phenomenology as the positive intuitive thinking that puts us into contact with the matters themselves.

What goes for all other forms of radically historical reflection also goes for deconstruction. In so far as our analysis of factical historical texts and conceptualities is to contribute to genuine philosophical understanding, it must be led by an effort to openly see and understand the experiential matters themselves. At the end of the day, it is only such an effort that allows us to grasp and access the concrete meanings of the particular conceptual tensions and repressions exposed by deconstruction. In and by itself, the strategy of internal historical deconstruction can never achieve a positive understanding of the philosophical matters—nor, thus, of its own sense and limits—but is bound to remain a critical supplement to the primary task of phenomenologically describing and conceptualizing what we experience.

The Challenge of Phenomenology

My suggestion is that in so far as philosophy takes as its task to understand our experience of ethical-existential significance it must primarily take the form of phenomenology. If we want to understand the significances that matters have for us, and the structures and dynamics of our experience, the only way to do this without resorting to speculation is to reflect on our concrete first-person experiences of phenomena.

At its most elementary, phenomenology means just this: to engage in intuitive reflection on our first-person experiences with a view to understanding their essential structures of sense. As such, phenomenology is simply the possibility of understanding ourselves and the meaningful world concretely. To remain phenomenologically open it is crucial not to identify, in a premature and dogmatic manner, the possibility of phenomenology with some specific historical interpretation of the phenomenological method, for example, with Husserl's theoretical-epistemological interpretation or with Heidegger's historicist interpretation. Ultimately, our understanding of phenomenology can only grow out of our concrete phenomenological investigations of the matters at stake. It is only by grasping our central problems and questions and by reflecting on the relevant experiences that we can understand the challenges and the nature of the phenomenological method.

But what about the two common criticisms of phenomenology: (1) that its claim to uncover universal structures flouts the radical historicity of understanding; and (2) that its claim to detect general essences is prejudiced and dogmatic?

(1) As Heidegger has shown, we always already live in historically transmitted and collectively sanctioned concepts and preunderstandings that tend to guide our philosophical understanding. However, as I have argued above, this does not mean that our possibilities of seeing and understanding would be determined by our preunderstandings. Far from it. We are essentially free to openly look at and reflect on our experiences themselves as the independent source of truth of our understanding. Nonetheless, there is good reason to stress that freeing ourselves from our own prior understandings and attending to what is given in our experiences in an open and unprejudiced manner is a demanding task, so demanding that phenomenologists fail in it more often than not.

In addition to this, our experiences themselves are to a greater or lesser extent formed by the historical contexts in which they occur: by the norms, practices, concepts and discourses of the historical community. Still, history does not determine our experiences from the ground up. After all, it is the *same* human beings with the *same* kinds of basic desires, fears, and sensual makeup that manifest themselves in different ways in different historical-cultural settings. For this reason, it is quite possible to explicate experiential structures that are common and universal to all human beings. Take shame, for example. Obviously, the norms for what is considered honorable and shameful vary greatly from one culture to the other. This also goes for our ways of expressing shame and for our conceptions of the status and role of shame. Nevertheless, it is possible to describe basic structural elements that are constitutive of shame whatever historical form it may take. For instance, it seems essential to shame that I see myself as believe I appear to others, in this case: as shameful and despicable. This structure, if correctly described, is constitutive of our experience of shame such that without it we could not have this kind of emotional experience. Beyond this, we could go on and try to describe basic human motives and desires that make us susceptible to shame in the first place, above all our elementary yearning for collective affirmation. These structures and motives are not historically specific but human universals. They are precisely what allow us to identify and understand different historical manifestations of shame as different variations of the same kinds of experience and motivation. Without these common structures, human beings from different cultures would be quite incomprehensible, which in reality they are not. In fact, the deeper our understanding of the human, the greater our ability to understand different individuals and cultures as sharing the same humanity.

There is thus nothing wrong with the phenomenological ambition to explicate the basic universal structures of our experiences. In so far as we try to understand the human, we are always grappling toward the universal. That said, there is clearly a great and constant risk of error here, of taking and presenting some culturally specific features or norms as the necessary universal structure of human experience. The history of philosophy is full of such errors. However, what we are dealing with here is not a fundamental obstacle to phenomenology; it is one of its central challenges.[1]

(2) Another criticism—common especially among Wittgensteinians—is that the ambition of phenomenology to describe necessary essential structures comes

down to an unjustified and dogmatic sort of essentialism. The charge I have in mind here is that the ambition to pin down the essential structure of some concept is fundamentally unjustified since there is no ground for assuming that the structure in question pertains to all the possible experiences and situations that fall under this concept. For all we know, these experiences and situations may just be related to each other by loose family resemblances. This criticism does not target the universalism of the phenomenological research into essences, but the very idea that it is possible to determine the necessary essential structure of some phenomenon. In fact, it is quite possible to insist—as in the case of Heidegger—on the radical historicity of meaning and still maintain that the phenomena exhibit essential, yet historically finite, structures that we can understand and explicate.

What makes the criticism of essentialism misguided as a criticism of phenomenology is that it is forged in the context of philosophy of language, which means that it primarily focuses on linguistic concepts. As a phenomenologist, I see no reason not to agree with Wittgenstein that our words tend to refer to different kinds of phenomena that do not have an essential structure in common but are linked together through family resemblances. However, phenomenology is not about detecting the structures that supposedly regulate our use of words but about describing the structures of our experiences. For example, it may very well be that we normally use the word "shame" to refer to many different experiences—some of which we also use other words, for example, "embarrassment" or "guilt," to refer to—that do not share the same basic structure. However, this does not in any way rule out the possibility of explicating the essential structures pertaining to the different kinds of experience that the word "shame" is used to pick out.

It belongs to the very sense of phenomenological understanding and description that we attempt to grasp essential and necessary structures. That is, we attempt to elucidate and describe the central structural features that constitute the experience under investigation: the structures that account for the meaning and character of the experience and without which it could not be the kind of experience that it is. Nevertheless, it must be remembered that phenomenological descriptions are not only fallible, such that they can be false, distortive, confused, or non-illuminating in different ways. Furthermore, it is always an open question exactly what experience—or level or aspect of experience—we are describing and how it resembles or differs from other related experiences. Hence, there is always the risk that we dogmatically generalize the structure of one kind of experience and postulate it as the essential structure of a more general group of experiences, whereby we falsely claim that it holds for experiences that it does not hold for. This often happens in phenomenology. To return to the case of shame: It is quite legitimate to try to describe the necessary structures of a certain emotional experience that is normally called "shame." However, dogmatic essentialism arises as soon as we claim that our description pertains to a wider set of experiences, including experiences that significantly differ from our paradigm. To avoid ambivalence and essentialism and get a sense of the possibilities and limits of phenomenological descriptions we need to take seriously the fact that the clarificatory scope of such descriptions is always an open issue.[2]

* * *

As I see it, the primary task of philosophy is to reflect on the central ethical-existential challenges and the psychological dynamics characterizing our lives with each other. This task is primary because it is the task that every human being is faced with and that is decisive for our understanding of good and evil, of authenticity and bad faith, of our motives and desires, of the possibility of happiness, and so on. It also has primacy in relation to other philosophical tasks since it deals with the question of how things concern us as significant and emotionally charged in the first place. In so far as the other possible tasks of philosophy—general ontology, epistemology, philosophy of language, political philosophy—are concerned with the significance and meaning that things have for us, they must be rooted in philosophical ethics and psychology.

As indicated above, phenomenology is a demanding endeavor even when it comes to investigating experiences that can be studied as ethically-existentially neutral, such as sense perceptions of different objects and tools. However, when the task is to clarify ethically and emotionally charged experiences—such as love and shame—we are faced with at least two additional challenges.

First, as Heidegger himself was aware, we have a very strong tendency to repress and cover up phenomena that we find difficult to face and acknowledge. We are prone to repress the ethical claims of others, our own ethical failures, as well as all sorts of things that threaten our sense of self-esteem. Instead, we develop understandings and emotional patterns that effectively cover up what we do not want to see, and instead show the world in a light that confirms our desires and interests. This means that the task of clarifying our central ethical-existential experiences and motives is not just an intellectual challenge. It is a task that essentially requires that we are willing and able to openly face and acknowledge ethical and existential realities that are demanding and painful, and the acknowledgment of which may transform our basic self-understanding. Without such a personal willingness to open up to the challenges and difficulties that our lives revolve around, no amount of intellectual sharpness will give as access to ourselves.[3]

Second, our ethically and emotionally charged experiences are not readily available for reflection in the way everyday sense perceptions are. It is a common feature of our emotive experiences that our emotions or moods overcome us and pervade our experience much like an emotional ether that determines how things now touch us and matter to us. Without our having taken any conscious decision to feel or be affected this way, or at least without our being aware of such a decision, we find ourselves moved by an emotional reaction. This is one of the reasons—but certainly not the only one—why philosophy has tended to treat our feelings and emotions as an external arational force that intrudes upon our rational consciousness.[4] However, contrary to what it may seem, our emotional experiences are in fact far from arational and amorphous but exhibit more or less determinate intentional structures. They are constituted by particular motives and desires and by particular ways of understanding and relating to oneself and to others. To access these structures and explicate our emotional experiences, what is needed is a form of phenomenological reflection that is akin to therapeutic self-reflection: an ability to sound and attend to one's emotionally charged experience with a view to their focus of pain or pleasure, the motives and desires at stake, the understandings and ways of relating that are at their basis.

Often, the difficulties that have to do with our resistance to understanding ourselves and the difficulties that have to do with reflective access interact to make the task of phenomenology so demanding. After all, since it is hard to understand our emotions anyway, it makes it all the easier to repress and dissimulate them in case we do not even try to or want to understand them.

The challenges mentioned above make phenomenology demanding and problematic as a science. To the extent that phenomenology is concerned with our first-person experience of ethical-existential significance, it not only has to rely on a personal form of reflection led by a will to understand. In communicating its findings, it also has to ask its interlocutors to engage in the same kind of reflection in order to probe whether its descriptions are able to shed light on the experiences in question. It is impossible for phenomenology to prove its results as objectively verifiable for all persons, regardless of their willingness and ability to reflect for themselves. Hence, it is always in principle possible to dismiss phenomenology as subjective, speculative or unscientific. As a result of this, it will always be a temptation for phenomenologists to boost their scientific credibility by falling back on non-phenomenological forms of argumentation—theorizing, exegesis, and so on—that in fact squander the true potential and rigor of phenomenology.

In a word, it will always be hard for phenomenology to become what it is: a concretely intuitive—and, ultimately, personal—reflection on the ethical-existential logic of the soul.

NOTES

Introduction

1 For some of the main works defending this interpretation, see Crowell 2001, 2013; Dahlstrom 2001; Overgaard 2004; Moran 2007; Zahavi 2003b; Hopkins 1993. See also Stapleton 1983; Gethmann 1974.
2 The central works defending this interpretation include Gadamer [1960] 2004, 1986, 1987; Guignon 1983; Bernasconi 1984; Sallis 1978, 1990; Figal 1992, 2009; van Buren 1990, 1994a; Krell 1986, 1992; Theodore Kisiel 1993; Ruin 1994; Dastur 1999; von Herrmann 2000; Young 2002; Carman 2003; Wrathall 2011; Backman 2016. In addition to the works listed so far, which basically affirm Heidegger's hermeneutic-deconstructivist thinking, there are also works that explicate Heidegger as a representative of a hermeneutic-deconstructivist approach but are more or less critical of this approach. Cf., e.g., Tugendhat 1970, [1969] 1992; Apel 1973, 1989; Lafont 2000.
3 In a similar way Friedrich-Wilhelm von Herrmann has argued that Heidegger's later "being-historical thinking" is "phenomenological through and through, that is, it is guided solely by the letting-itself-be-shown of the matter itself" (1990: 11, my translation).
4 Heidegger's comments on the title are found in a letter that he sent to Richardson in April 1962, and which was published as the "Preface" of Richardson's book. Cf. Richardson 1963: VIII–XXIX; GA 11: 145–52.

Part 1 A Phenomenology of Factical Life

Introduction

1 Henceforth referred to as "The Idea of Philosophy" in the main text.
2 For an account of the pioneering role of this lecture course, see Kisiel 1992, 1993: 15–20.
3 Already in his student years 1909–15 Heidegger became electrified by Husserl's phenomenology without yet being able to achieve an independent philosophical opening. For a brief account of Heidegger's first steps as regards phenomenology and the problem of phenomena, see Westerlund 2014a: 20–4. For more detailed treatments of Heidegger's pre-war philosophical writings, see Crowell 2001: 76–111; van Buren 1994a: 51–129; Sheehan 1981, 1988a; Denker 2004; Kisiel 1993: 25–38.
4 As a result of my suggested periodization, some of the texts that have been central to previous interpretations of Heidegger's early Freiburg lecture courses—e.g., the lecture course "Phenomenological Interpretations of Aristotle: Initiation into Phenomenological Research" from the winter semester 1921–2, the important text "Phenomenological Interpretations of Aristotle (Indication of the Hermeneutic Situation)" from 1922, and the lecture course "Ontology—The Hermeneutics of Facticity" from the summer semester of 1923—fall outside the scope of my interpretation of the *earliest* lecture courses. Furthermore, from the perspective

of my explication many of the interpretations of Heidegger's early Freiburg lecture emerge as more or less anachronistic. To begin with, the earliest lecture courses from 1919 to 1921 are almost without exception lumped together with the later ones from 1921 to 1923, in such a way that the Freiburg lecture courses emerge as a uniform period of thinking. Moreover, the Freiburg courses are regularly interpreted as the beginning of—and, hence, as belonging to—Heidegger's early thinking, which is thought to continue through the Marburg years and reach its climax in *Being and Time*. The presupposition of such interpretations is that the periods thus posited—"Heidegger's early Freiburg lectures," "the early Heidegger"—would display a more or less uniform philosophical approach. Hence, it is not uncommon that texts written after 1921 are used to substantiate claims about the radically historical character of Heidegger's thinking in 1919–21 or that texts from these earliest years are used to substantiate his commitment to phenomenology in *Being and Time*. My own suggestion, however, is that Heidegger's earliest Freiburg lecture courses in 1919–21 display a relatively distinct philosophical approach, which is very much a critical continuation of Husserl's intuition-based phenomenology. This approach, I will argue, undergoes a shift in 1921–2 when Heidegger, through his reading of Aristotle, develops a new account of the historical structure of phenomenality. This also leads him to stress the need for phenomenology to proceed historically through a destruction of the philosophical tradition.

5   Dilthey's influence on the early Heidegger has been stressed by many interpreters starting with Gadamer. See, e.g., Gadamer 1987: 417–30; Guignon 1983; Kisiel 1993; Bambach 1995; Scharff 1997; Maakreel 2004. For studies of the impact of contemporary life-philosophy on Heidegger's thought, see Krell 1992; Fehér 1994. For studies of the influence of Christian thinkers, see van Buren 1994a, 1994b; Kisiel 1993; Crowe 2006. The Neo-Kantian context of Heidegger's early philosophy has been examined in Kisiel 1995; Friedman 2000; Crowell 2001; Steinmann 2004.

1 Phenomenology as Primordial Science of Life

1   Henceforth referred to as *Ideas I* in the main text.
2   Husserl articulates the possibility of explicating essences in terms of what he calls "eidetic variation"—the methodological procedure that he sees as the key to grasping essential structures. However, I believe Husserl's analysis of eidetic variation fails to capture the nature of intuitive phenomenological description and understanding, thus also amounting to a misdescription of his own phenomenological work. I deal with this matter in some detail in Chapter 4.
3   Heidegger picks up the notion of "worldview" from Husserl who in his article "Philosophy as Rigorous Science" famously distinguishes between "worldview philosophy," which is content with producing practice-guiding overviews of the preeminent opinions of a particular historical time, and "scientific philosophy," which aims at achieving evident and universal knowledge (Hua 25: 8/253). However, Heidegger transforms the sense of Husserl's concept of "worldview" when he claims that the aim of all previous philosophy has been to establish a basic theoretical worldview. Indeed, since he believes that Husserl's phenomenology still belongs to the tradition of theoretical philosophy, he characterizes it as "scientific worldview philosophy" (GA 59: 11/7).

4 In his early Freiburg lectures Heidegger uses the word "givenness" as his general designation of the problem of givenness or phenomenality.
5 This first attempt of Heidegger's to articulate a critique of Husserl's phenomenology has received almost no attention in the secondary literature. In fact, none of the major studies of Heidegger's relationship to Husserl's phenomenology—e.g., Crowell 2001; Dahlstrom 2001; von Herrmann 2000; Overgaard 2004—contain any explication of this early Freiburg critique. I have dealt with Heidegger's critique in previous texts (see Westerlund 2010, 2014a: 60–74). However, since I found my earlier attempts to pinpoint the philosophical substance of Heidegger's criticisms too vague, I decided to use the opportunity of writing this book to reformulate and specify my view on the matter.
6 For a lucid exposition of the existential stakes of Husserl's phenomenology, see Cerbone 2003. As Cerbone points out, Husserl believes not only that phenomenology is ultimately geared to and necessary for bringing about the "ideal human life" (3), guided by an all-inclusive praxis of reason. Husserl also maintains that phenomenological seeing is always the self-responsibility and personal affair of the phenomenologist. However, my thesis is that Husserl is never able or willing to give primacy to and take on—and acknowledge the personal challenges involved in taking on—the ethical-existential issues that are decisive for any vision of the ideal human life. As a result, his phenomenology exhibits a tendency to resort to dubious grounding in relation to the aims that it sets for itself.
7 Heidegger criticizes Husserl's layer-ontology in the lecture courses "Ontology—The Hermeneutics of Facticity," "Introduction to Phenomenological Research," and "History of the Concept of Time: Prolegomena" (see GA 63: 88–92/67–70; GA 17: 271–2/209; GA 20: 171–4/123–6). For an incisive treatment of this critique, see Overgaard 2004: 173–83.

2 Heidegger's Phenomenology of Factical Life

1 For a recent interpretation of Heidegger's early Freiburg lectures along the same lines as Buren and Kisiel, see Campbell 2012.
2 In "The Idea of Philosophy" Heidegger considers two criticisms voiced by Natorp against Husserl's idea of phenomenology as reflective description (cf. GA 56/57: 99–109/83–92). Natorp objects, first, that in reflectively observing our experience we "still and interrupt the continuous stream of becoming," so that we "detach [the finding] from the experienced, from the subjective" and "make it into an object" (1912: 102–3, my translation); second, that in describing our experience we necessarily make use of generalizing and subsuming concepts, which transform whatever we describe into examples of universal concepts and categories (91–2, 190). Heidegger seems to take Natorp's criticisms seriously and remarks that Husserl has not responded to them. However, Heidegger makes it clear that he does not see the criticisms as undercutting the idea of reflective phenomenology; rather, they only point to the need for articulating the proper character of phenomenological reflection and description. In fact, it seems to me that Natorp's objections are quite weak. His critique of reflection involves two arguments. The first is that in reflecting on our pretheoretical experience we detach ourselves from it in order to observe it. The second is that in observing it

we reify it and make it into an object. However, whereas the detachment involved in reflection does not seem to be a problem at all—the reflective detachment does not hinder us but rather allows us to go along with and thematically attend to the dynamics and structure of our prereflective experience—the claim that reflection is inherently reifying is plainly false. Both for Husserl and Heidegger, the point of phenomenology is precisely to reflect on the transcendental structures of experience that constitute different objects. As concerns Natorp's second criticism, it must be objected that the concepts used by phenomenology essentially refer to and express the phenomenally given. They are not applied as external general concepts and categories under which the given is subsumed. Both Husserl and Heidegger know this, although it is true that Heidegger is more aware of the challenge of keeping open to what is actually given and not allowing ourselves to be led by our factical concepts or by any prejudiced ideals of conceptual order. Cf. Westerlund 2014a: 69–73; Zahavi 2003b.

3 My treatment of Heidegger's notion of "formal indication" will be limited to the texts from the period under consideration here, i.e., the period starting at the beginning of 1919 and ending in the summer term of 1921. In fact, Heidegger provides his most detailed account of this notion in the lecture course "Phenomenological Interpretations of Aristotle: Initiation into Phenomenological Research" from the winter semester of 1921–2. However, since I believe this course is already part of Heidegger's attempt to reorient his thinking through an interpretation of Aristotle—a reorientation that centrally involves a new analysis of the historical as-structure of understanding as well as of the question of being, and which, accordingly, modifies the sense of "formal indication"—I will refrain from using it as a source here. Heidegger continues to make use of the term "formal indication" in the Marburg years and he also uses it in *Being and Time* without explicitly reflecting on its sense.

4 Heidegger's notion of "formal indication" has been discussed in, e.g., Dahlstrom 1994, 2001; Inkpin 2010; Kisiel 1993; van Buren 1994a, 1995; Oudemans 1990; Pöggeler 1989; van Dijk 1991.

5 It could perhaps be taken as evidence against my view that Heidegger in "Basic Problems of Phenomenology" argues that formal indications receive their indicative force through negative contrasts with other concepts. Since, Heidegger writes, "negation" constitutes the "creative force" (GA 58: 240/181) of phenomenological concepts, the fact that the phenomenologist continuously says "no" to different alternative concepts should not be understood as a purely negative gesture. Heidegger calls the negatively dialectical logic of formal indications "diahermeneutics": "philosophical dialectic is '*diahermeneutics.*' Through the overturnings (*Umkippungen*) of the understanding and the intuition (use of negation?), the phenomena come to expression" (GA 58: 263/198). However, Heidegger is not here defending the quasi-Derridaean view that that the meaning of formal indications would be determined by the way they negatively contrast with other concepts. To the contrary, his point is that it is precisely on account of such negative contrasts that formal indications are able to point to our concrete experiences as an autonomous source of meaning that is intuitively accessible. Indeed, having just stressed the central role of negation in phenomenological expressions, Heidegger adds: "All understanding is enacted in the *intuition*. From this stems the *descriptive* character of phenomenological work" (GA 58: 240/181).

6   For a concise and illuminating account of how the dichotomy of history and systematics surfaces and is played out in Dilthey, Rickert, and Husserl, thus setting the stage for Heidegger's early thinking, see Ruin 1994: 37–42.
7   It is quite common among representatives of the hermeneutic-deconstructive reading of Heidegger—and among historicists more generally—to make use of problematic generalizations of this kind: to point to some kind or level of understanding that is historically determined—e.g., our understanding of historically changing values or practices—and conclude from this that, at bottom, all our experiences and understandings are historically determined in this way. It is this kind of invalid generalization that is at the basis of the familiar but confused criticism that there is a contradiction in the early Heidegger's effort to carry out a transhistorical phenomenological investigation of the essential historicity of life or Dasein. Here is how Günter Figal articulates this kind of criticism in relation to *Being and Time*: "[Philosophy] frees itself ... from the tradition in order to exhibit a structure, which, in spite of its temporality, is not temporal and historical anymore. The structure of Dasein persists as long as there is Dasein" (1992: 94, my translation). However, there is no necessary contradiction in the phenomenological claim that it is a universal and ahistorical feature of our experience of significance that it is radically historical in nature. As I will argue in the epilogue, Heidegger's own thesis—elaborated in the 1920s—about the radical historicity of our understanding of being also largely relies on this kind of untenable generalization.
8   Hans Ruin has argued that Heidegger already in his early Freiburg lectures gives up Husserl's trust in "original intuition" (1994: 48) and advances the thesis that "history, as that which is past, and thus non-present, is incorporated into a supposedly present givenness" (48). However, is seems to me that Ruin is here downplaying Heidegger's problems with accounting for the historicity of thinking beyond his programmatic declarations. In fact, if one takes a closer look at Ruin's argument, it appears that he is vacillating between a weaker and a bolder claim. On the one hand, he claims that Heidegger conceives of the phenomenological explication as a thematizing enactment of previous experiences: "there is a circular temporality inscribed in the method itself, in that the phenomenological reflection establishes an origin through a recapitulating enactment of previous intentional accomplishments" (51). This seems correct to me, yet it does not imply a radical historicization of thought. The fact that our experiences are always already there as the factical ground of every explication does not mean that they are historical in the strong sense of amounting to a changeable historical constellation of meaning. Rather, it only implies that they are contingent experiences that we humans happen to have, such as love, memory, pain, and anxiety. This does not shut out the possibility of intuitively reflecting on their necessary and universal structures. On the other hand, Ruin advances the bolder claim that "[the subject] understands its history by being that history, and it is that history in understanding it" (64). However, this claim does not follow from the first, and Heidegger does not yet open up the notion of thinking as a retrieval of historically transmitted meanings. Rather, whereas the significances encountered in our experiences are considered historical, the phenomenological explication essentially unfolds as an intuitive reflection on the universal features of the pretheoretical experiences as such. For an illuminating discussion of the distinction between the factical as a designation of the contingent character of our experiences and the factical as a designation of their historically situated and changeable nature, see Crowell 2003.

3 Life and the Task of Philosophy

1 There is an interesting kinship between Heidegger's early view of the negative task of philosophy and Wittgenstein's conception of the therapeutic function of philosophy, which would deserve closer examination. Cf. § 6.54 of Wittgenstein's *Tractatus Logico-Philosophicus*: "My propositions are elucidatory in this way: he who understands me finally recognizes them as senseless, when he has climbed out through them, on them, over them. (He must so to speak throw away the ladder, after he has climbed up on it.) He must surmount these propositions; then he sees the world rightly." Cf. also Wittgenstein's remarks on the task of philosophy in his *Philosophical Investigations*, §§ 109–133. Heidegger and Wittgenstein share the notion that our everyday pretheoretical experience and language-use constitute the primary and ungroundable domain where things mean what they mean for us. Moreover, both think that the traditional philosophical quest for a more fundamental and certain knowledge of life builds on an alienation from life and is bound to generate prejudiced constructions. However, whereas Wittgenstein consistently sees it as the task of philosophy to therapeutically dismantle the theoretical cloud-castles of philosophy, in Heidegger this impulse from the outset coexists with the opposed tendency to think of philosophy as called to achieve a positive explication of the basic sense of life or being that is essential for how we understand and relate to the central phenomena of life. The latter tendency dominates Heidegger's thought from the early 1920s onwards, when Heidegger first develops the idea that we always already live in a more or less vague preunderstanding of being that determines how we can experience beings and that it is the task of philosophy to elucidate.

Part 2 The Historical Structure of Phenomena

Introduction

1 There are some notable exceptions to this general tendency. See, e.g., Gethmann 1974 and Stapleton 1983.
2 According to Heidegger's plan, the analysis of temporality in division two of *Being and Time* is intended to be the highpoint of the existential analytic. However—contrary to what Heidegger and many commentators want to believe—I think that it fails to live up to that role. In fact, the decisive philosophical work of the book is done in Heidegger's analyses of being-in-the-world and authenticity. These analyses provide the systematic basis for his analysis of temporality, which then basically takes the form of a schematic articulation of the different temporal aspects of Dasein's being-in-the-world. Heidegger, of course, denies this, stating that the analysis of temporality "does not lead us to run through our analyses again superficially and schematically" (SZ: 332).

4 Toward a New Conception of Phenomena

1 Heidegger's relationship to Aristotle has been the subject of several studies. Cf., e.g., Sheehan 1978, 1988b; Sadler 1996; McNeill 1999; Weigelt 2002; Brogan 2005; Backman 2005; Denker et al. 2007.
2 Heidegger introduces the term "ontological difference" in his 1927 lecture course "The Basic Problems of Phenomenology." However, as many commentators have pointed

out, this notion is already at the center of Heidegger's thinking in *Being and Time*. Cf., e.g., Rosales 1970; Marion 1998: 108–40; Overgaard, 2004: 69–103. My suggestion is that it is in the context of his reading of Aristotle around 1922 that Heidegger first articulates the hierarchical structure of phenomenality that he will later name the "ontological difference."

3 As regards the ambiguity of Heidegger's explication of Husserl in "Prolegomena," cf. Bernet 1990: 136–7; Dahlstrom 2001: 52; von Herrmann 1981.

4 For studies emphasizing the paramount importance of Husserl's notion of categorial intuition for Heidegger's philosophical development, cf. Taminiaux 1977, 1991: 1–54; Wanatabe 1993; van Buren 1994a: 203–19; Critchley 2008. By contrast, Steven Crowell and Søren Overgaard—cf. Crowell 2001 and Overgaard 2004—defend the view that Husserl's main influence on Heidegger's thinking is to be found in his basic phenomenological method of reflection on the structures of our intentional experience. In so doing, they largely downplay or ignore the role of Husserl's notion of categorial intuition. Dismissing the importance often attributed to this notion, Overgaard writes: "Husserl's doctrine of categorial intuition might be a source of inspiration to Heidegger, but I find it hard to see how Heidegger could feel truly indebted to Husserl on this point" (2004: 80).

5 This criticism—that Husserl's method of free variation is circular in the sense that it can only explicate our prior factical understanding of the types or ideas under investigation—has been voiced before. See, e.g., Levin 1968; Zaner 1973a, 1973b; Mohanty 1989: 25–38. For a recent defense of Husserl's notion of free variation, see Kasmier 2010.

6 As Daniel Dahlstrom and others have pointed out—cf. Dahlstrom 2001: 84–8; Dastur 1991: 45–50; Mulligan 1995: 183–91—even in *Logical Investigations,* Husserl's conception of the founding relationship between sensuous and categorial intuition is not without ambivalence. For example, in the first edition of the book, Husserl writes: "It is part of perception that something appears in it; however, *interpretation constitutes what we call appearance*, be it right or not …. The *house* appears to me—in no other manner than that I interpret actually perceived sense-contents in a certain fashion. I hear a *barrel-organ*—the tones that I hear are interpreted by me precisely as *tones of a barrel-organ*" (Hua 19/2: 762/341). In the second edition, the terms "interpretation" and "interpret" have been replaced with "apperception" (*Apperzeption*) and "apperceive" (*apperzipieren*).

7 In Dahlstrom 2001: 48–174, Daniel Dahlstrom offers an extended and detailed treatment of Heidegger's explications of Husserl in the Marburg years, in which he also assesses the force of Heidegger's criticisms, tracing the points where Heidegger simplifies or distorts Husserl's conception. However, although I mostly agree with Dahlstrom's comments it seems that his effort to emphasize the continuity between Husserl and Heidegger, makes him lose sight of the fact that Heidegger appropriation of the "categorial intuition" opens a basic rift between the two philosophers as concerns the question about the nature of intuitive givenness.

5 *The Project of Fundamental Ontology*

1 Heidegger's identification of being with phenomenality has been noted before. Cf. Figal 2009: 85–7; Marion 1998: 63–4.

6 Being-in-the-World

1. However, even though Heidegger here tends to conceive of nature as a sort of ready-to-hand equipment, there are also passages in *Being and Time* which suggest a concept of nature that does not fit into the dichotomy of presence-at-hand or readiness-to-hand. For instance, Heidegger writes: "'Nature,' which 'surrounds' us, is indeed an innerworldly being; but the kind of being which it shows belongs neither to the ready-to-hand nor to what is present-at-hand as 'things of nature' (*Naturdinglichkeit*)" (SZ: 211). This passage points forward toward Heidegger's later attempts to reflect on the self-withdrawing material-sensuous aspect of the world, which in "The Origin of the Work of Art" he will call the "earth." Cf. Overgaard 2004: 123–6; Dahlstrom 2001: 261–7.
2. Cf., e.g., Overgaard 2004: 121–3; Gorner 2007: 45–6; Mulhall 1996: 48–50.
3. Here, we may note that Heidegger's claim about the *pragmatic meaning* of our understanding of tools is different from his claim that such understanding primarily has the character of *unthematic coping*. Indeed, the argument about the pragmatic meaning of the phenomena we encounter is compatible with a broader view of how different kinds of understanding and knowledge can serve a pragmatic function. Heidegger sometimes talks about the matter as if unthematic coping would simply be our primordial and true way of encountering tools whereas all thematic or theoretical forms of thinking would be secondary or alienated. However, it seems misleading to discard theoretical thinking as an alienated way of relating to the tools and tasks of the world. All depends on the nature of the task at hand. In turning the doorknob or riding a bicycle, what is needed is precisely the kind of unthematic coping that Heidegger has in mind. However, in order for a doctor or an architect to be able to excel at her task, the unthematic skillfulness, which is also essential here, must be accompanied by—interact with and to some extent build on—various forms of theoretical knowledge about anatomy, chemistry, physics, and mathematics. In order to build a space rocket destined for Mars, the knowledge needed is to a very high degree theoretical in nature. Instead of saying that our ability at unthematic skillful coping constitutes our ontologically-existentially primary way of comporting ourselves toward tools, it would be more to the point to say that such coping has a certain functional primacy: it allows us to handle tools in a smooth and efficient way and its unthematic know-how-character allows it to serve as the necessary background and horizon for all our thematic attention and thinking.
4. For some criticisms of Dreyfus's interpretation, see Olafson 1994a and Overgaard 2004: 178–9. Cf. also the debate between Frederick Olafson and Taylor Carman (Olafson 1994b; Carman 1994). For a more detailed critique of the pragmatist reading of Heidegger, see Dahlstrom 2001: 199–200, 305–6, 423–33.
5. For a helpful account that treats Heidegger's response to skepticism in more detail, see McManus 2013.
6. Among Heidegger scholars, the dominant tendency has been to dismiss Tugendhat's critique. See, e.g., Gethmann 1989; Pöggeler 1989; Richter 1989; Wrathall 1999; Dahlstrom 2001; Carman 2003. By contrast, some critics have hailed his critique as pointing to an essential problem in Heidegger's thought. Cf., e.g., Habermas 1987 and Apel 1973. Recently, Cristina Lafont has taken up and offered a substantial elaboration of Tugendhat's critique in her book *Heidegger, Language, and World-Disclosure* from

2000, a book that I will deal with in detail in the epilogue. For a helpful overview of the latest developments in this debate, see Smith 2007.

7   As I have argued elsewhere (Westerlund 2014a: 228–36), I believe that while Tugendhat's main critical thesis is accurate the arguments that lead him to it are problematic. Basically, Tugendhat argues that Heidegger, in defining the truth of statements in terms of their being "being-uncovering," he from the outset uses the term "uncover" in an ambiguous way. On the one hand, Heidegger is said to use "uncover" in a narrow sense, according to which only true statements are "uncovering" while false statements merely "cover up." On the other hand, he is said to use it in a broad sense to signify "showing up" or "exhibiting" in general. Tugendhat claims that Heidegger's definition of truth as "being-uncovering" in the broad sense is unjustified and implies that he loses the capacity to distinguish between the truth and falsity of assertions: "In this sense, every assertion uncovers, the false just as well as the true" ([1969] 1992: 84). Once Heidegger has defined truth in this way, "everything else follows almost deductively" ([1969] 1992: 81; cf. 1970: 350). That is, by exploiting the broad sense of "being-uncovering," Heidegger is able to apply the concept of truth to Dasein's primary world-disclosure. However, by characterizing Dasein's understanding of its world as "primordial truth," Heidegger in fact makes this understanding immune to the question of truth. In contrast to Tugendhat, I maintain that Heidegger when it comes to assertions about beings unequivocally accepts a phenomenological version of the correspondence-theory of truth: an assertion is true if it presents the beings that it intends as they really are, and false if it does not. Moreover, I believe that Heidegger's rejection of the question of the truth of Dasein's understanding of the world is not, as Tugendhat claims, the result of Heidegger's supposedly ambiguous definition of propositional truth as "being-uncovering." Rather, it springs directly from his basic analysis of the historical structure of phenomena according to which Dasein's understanding of its historical world determines what it can experience as phenomena that it can be right or wrong about.

8   On this point I agree with Wrathall 1999 and Carman 2003, who both argue—criticizing Tugendhat—that Heidegger does not replace the traditional concept of propositional truth as correspondence, but rather offers an account of the ontological conditions of such correspondence. However, it seems to me that neither of them is able to offer a persuasive response to Tugendhat's central charge that Heidegger unjustifiably forfeits the question of the truth of Dasein's primary world-disclosure. Whereas Wrathall does not recognize the challenge but is satisfied with pointing to Dasein's disclosedness as the condition of propositional truth, Carman attempts to articulate the normativity of Dasein's world-disclosure in terms of what he calls "hermeneutic salience," by which he means "the way in which what we say and think is always organized and articulated according to some dominant interpretation of things that holds sway in our local discursive community" (2003: 261). However, it seems to me that in so writing Carman is simply restating Heidegger's idea that we have to accept the authority of our historical world, of its meanings and values, because it constitutes the ultimate finite ground of our experience the truth or untruth of which cannot be interrogated. It is precisely this idea that Tugendhat—quite rightly—objects to.

7 Problems of Authenticity

1. As I will argue in the following, the common interpretation that authenticity consists in transparently accepting the groundless historical possibilities of the They as our ultimate authority generally builds on a denial of the challenge involved in becoming authentic. As a result, it tends toward a kind of crude collectivism. Let me mention two other interpretations that in my view misconstrue the philosophical stakes of Heidegger's analysis of authenticity. First, there is the interpretation that conceives of authenticity as an existentialized version of Aristotle's notion of *phronesis*. This interpretation starts from the idea that authentic Dasein transparently takes over the possibilities bestowed by the They and adds to this the idea that the authentic individual develops a capacity to see and relate wisely to the particular projects and situations she encounters. In this fashion—although drawing on Kierkegaard rather than Aristotle—Dreyfus and Rubin portray the authentic individual as someone who accepts that "no specific project can fulfil me" and who, on the basis of this insight, is able to appreciate the details of the project she engages in and be ready to let go of it when it "ceases to show up as being what needs to be done" (Dreyfus 1991: 322–3, 326; cf. also Carman 2005: 292). Second, Charles Guignon has offered a narrativist interpretation of Heidegger's concept of authenticity. According to Guignon, inauthenticity consists in becoming dispersed in the latest trends of the public world. By contrast, authenticity means that Dasein, facing up to its own mortality and finitude, is led to view its life as a "coherent story," and focus itself—with "decisive dedication"—into a finite range of possibilities: "Authentic self-focusing, understood as resolute reaching forward into a finite range of possibilities, gives coherence, cohesiveness, and integrity to a life course" (1993: 229). However, in my view both these interpretations fail to recognize that for Heidegger the challenge of authenticity—i.e., the challenge of understanding and choosing the life-possibilities that are to constitute one's identity and give significance to one's life—is prior to and conditions both the challenge of relating wisely and attentively to specific projects and situations and the challenge of achieving a coherent life-story. As a result, neither interpretation is able to account for what it would mean to emancipate oneself from the They and achieve an independent critical understanding of the ethical-existential meaning of different life-possibilities. In the end, both the phronetic wisdom and the ability to give narrative unity to one's life depicted by these interpretations are fully compatible with an attitude of collectivist submission to the They.
2. For a critique of the idea that Heidegger would have such an expressivist notion of authenticity in mind, see Guignon 2004.
3. Charles Guignon has also pointed out this lack in Heidegger's analysis of authenticity: "Heidegger says that authenticity will lead us into a 'sober understanding' of the 'basic possibilities for Dasein'. … But there is no clue as to what these 'basic possibilities' are. Although resoluteness might bring us face to face with our unique responsibility for making something of our lives, it does not seem to provide us with any indication as to which of the concrete possibilities circulating in the Anyone are the ultimate or basic sources for our understanding of being" (1983: 218).
4. For other works that argue that the norms of the They constitute Dasein's source of intelligibility and normativity, see, e.g., Guignon 2004; Carman 2005; Crowell 2013.

5   As argued above—in Chapter 6—it seems that what allows Dreyfus and Rubin to develop—and not recognize the immense problems of—this kind of interpretation is that they misconstrue the level and stakes of Heidegger's analysis of authenticity. At the basis of their account is the idea that the basic level of intelligibility is found in the background practices of our community, in the ways we do such things as walk, use money, and play chess. These practices, and the intelligibility and norms they incorporate, are identified with the They. However, Heidegger himself emphasizes that these kinds of practices receive whatever significance they have from the guiding life-possibilities and ideals of Dasein's identity. As concerns such possibilities, it is obvious that they can be more or less good or evil or meaningful or futile. To insist in earnest that there can be no deeper understanding of such possibilities and ideals than the de facto interpretation of the They would be equal to succumbing to collective pressure while repressing the possibility of critically judging and taking responsibility for the question of the goodness or evil and the meaningfulness or futility of one's ideals and way of life.

6   Cf. Löwith 1960: 93–4; Tugendhat 1970: 360–1. Cf. also Wolin 1990.

7   Recently, Steven Crowell, although maintaining that all Dasein's norms and reasons derive "from das Man" (2013: 300) has argued that Heidegger's account of authenticity is meant to articulate our "capacity to enter the space of reasons," (198) which is a prerequisite for critical deliberation. Crowell argues that whereas the inauthentic self acts according to the norms of the They in a "mindless" (202) and "quasi-mechanical manner" (204), the call of conscience opens up Dasein to a "responsiveness to norms as norms" (205). That is, the call of conscience opens up Dasein to the demand of taking responsibility for the norms to which it commits itself, and of accounting for itself and giving reasons for its choices. However, Crowell—like Heidegger—offers no account of an alternative source of ethical-existential normativity and significance beyond the factical norms endorsed by the They. As long as he does not do this, it seems to me that it is impossible to tell in what sense the authentic individual's sense of accountability as depicted by Crowell differs from and transcends the inauthentic individual's sense that she needs to account for herself and give reasons for her choices to the They. If the accountability and critical deliberation of the authentic person remain guided by what the They happens to endorse, it is unclear how this attitude differs from inauthentic collectivism. Toward the end of Crowell 2008, Crowell—commenting on Heidegger's essay "… Poetically Man Dwells …" from 1951—makes the suggestion that Heidegger, when reflecting on the character of the normative force that binds us, recognizes the claim of the other human being in a manner that resembles Levinas's ethics: "This does not mean that Heidegger and Levinas are saying 'the same.' But it does indicate that Heidegger too, when reflecting upon the normative force of the originary meaning-event, the orientation toward measure that makes all meaning possible, finds his way to relations between human beings" (2008: 276). Philosophically, I have no doubt that this is the right—in fact, the only—way to go if we want to understand the sources of genuine ethical normativity and obligation. However, as I will argue in what follows, Heidegger never recognizes the absolute claim of the other person as something which addresses me beyond every historical norm and value, and it is hard to see that the passage quoted by Crowell—in which Heidegger comments on some lines by Hölderlin—would support such a radical notion. Indeed, if Heidegger would really recognize the claim ascribed to him by Crowell, this would upset the basic philosophical framework which motivates and organizes both his thinking of authenticity in *Being and Time* as well as his later conception of the task of thinking.

8 Heidegger's Method in Being and Time

1. For another interpretation stressing the methodological primacy of the destruction, see Ruin 1994: 84.
2. It is quite common to characterize Heidegger's method in *Being and Time* by saying that it explicates what is normally implicit and hidden in our understanding. However, it is important to see that this kind of formulation can have—and often vacillates between—two quite different meanings. On the one hand, it can mean that the analysis spells out and explicates the historical preunderstanding that we always already live in, so that its validity and scope remains relative to that finite preunderstanding. On the other hand, it can mean that the analysis describes and explicates what is there and discernable—although normally unnoticed—in our experiences, in which case the description does not necessarily rest on our factical historical preunderstandings.
3. For an account of how the phenomenological idea of intuitive reflection helps us overcome the problems inherent in Kant's idea of regressive transcendental arguments, see Westerlund 2014b: 259–61.

Part 3 *The Openness of Being*

9 *The Question of the Openness of Being*

1. It has been common among commentators to suppose that the metontological task of philosophy envisioned by Heidegger in these years is to investigate the ontic ground of ontology. See, e.g., Bernasconi 1993; Grondin 1995; Crowell 2001: 222–43. However, it seems to me that such an interpretation misses the fact that the aim of metontology is to carry out an ontological projection of a world of being-senses. What is true—and what the commentators seize upon—is that Heidegger conceives of the world-projection as somehow grounded in and attuned to the totality of beings. However, this does not change the fact that the world projected by metontology conditions the possibility of ontically experiencing and understanding beings as phenomena. For a more detailed exegetical argument for my interpretation of the metontological task of philosophy, see Westerlund 2014a: 321–9. For another perceptive account of Heidegger's conception of philosophy as world-projection, see Figal 1992: 94–110.
2. Indeed, at one point Heidegger explicitly claims that his earlier way of interrogating being remained "stuck within the Platonic approach," that is, within the Platonic conception of being in terms of present ideas or essences (GA 9: 131c/104a). Accordingly, he understands his own advance toward the question of the openness of being as a retrieval of the earlier Greek concept of *physis*, which Plato and Aristotle presupposed but left uninterrogated. For more on this, see Westerlund 2014a: 353–9.

10 *The Promise of National Socialism*

1. The most comprehensive and reliable biographical accounts of Heidegger's political life are still Ott 1993 and Safranski 1998. For good studies of the broader political and ideological context of Heidegger's Nazi engagement, see Zimmermann 1990 and Sluga 1993.

2   For a long time, many prominent commentators—see, e.g., Schürmann 1990; Rorty 1999; Olafson 2000—have tried to argue that Heidegger's politics had nothing do with and should be sharply separated from his philosophy. It seems that with the publication of the *Black Notebooks* this strategy for containing Heidegger's Nazism has become incredible and obsolete.

3   Heidegger himself told Karl Löwith that the conception of "historicity" presented in *Being and Time* was the philosophical "basis" of his political "engagement" (Löwith 1994: 60). Later, the question of whether the analysis of authentic historicity in *Being and Time* motivated Heidegger's plunge into Nazism has divided the commentators. Some (e.g., Wolin 1990; Löwith 1994) have argued that it did; others (e.g., Guignon 1983; Olafson 2000) have claimed that it did not. My thesis is that in *Being and Time* Heidegger had not yet opened up the philosophical framework—the question of how a historical world can be established as binding, and the perceived need to project such a world in the face of the nihilism of modernity—that made it possible for him to see Nazism as playing a potential role in his own philosophical-political program. Nevertheless, Heidegger's analysis of authenticity gives expression to an ethically problematic egoistic-collectivist attitude. Moreover, the ultimate existential task of Dasein is seen as that of resolutely and transparently appropriating one's collective role and mission in the community.

4   Some commentators have argued that the philosophical roots of Heidegger's Nazi involvement are found in his radical program of university reform, which he started to develop as early as 1911. See, e.g., Crowell 2001: 152–66; Milchman and Rosenberg 1997; Thomson 2001, 2003. I will not pursue this lead here. Although it is certainly true that Heidegger's university reform program—according to which philosophy, as the investigation of the sense/truth of being, should play a leading role in the university and in society at large—was an important factor behind his decision to engage himself as rector of the University of Freiburg in 1933, it does not seem to be the central philosophical motive that explains Heidegger's pull toward National Socialism.

5   The literature on the *Black Notebooks* is growing rapidly. So far, it includes Trawny 2015; Trawny and Mitchell 2015; Farin and Malpas 2016; Heinz and Kellerer 2016; Gander and Striet 2016; Denker and Zaborowski 2017; Mitchell and Trawny 2017; Espinet et al. (2018).

6   Here I cannot do much more than indicate what I have in mind when talking about the spirit of the text. To simplify matters, I have assumed that the philosophical texts under discussion are of the kind where the implicit voice of the text can be more or less easily identified with the voice of the actual author. However, when it comes to literary texts the situation is obviously more complex. It is a central feature of literature—especially of fiction—that the main character, the narrator or the implicit author need not represent the real author. The text may give voice to and pursue viewpoints and ethical-existential attitudes that are not shared by the author at all. This may also happen in philosophy, the typical examples being Kierkegaard's pseudonymous authorship and the genre of philosophical dialogue. Nevertheless, it seems to me that it also belongs to our reading of literature that we inevitably project ourselves toward the ultimate source and spiritual context out of which the text is written: the author. How we read and relate to the text is always connected to how we imagine—in more or less implicit and indeterminate ways—the ethical-existential setting and perspective from which whatever gets expressed or happens in the text is seen and written. It seems to me that even in reading fiction this is always an issue for us.

7 It seems to me that the inclination to discard Heidegger's entire thinking as Nazi philosophy—the most flamboyant recent example of this being Faye 2009—is both philosophically and morally confused. To begin with, our knowledge of Heidegger's political biography and of the rhetorical connections between his philosophy and National Socialist ideology does not in itself allow us to critically understand and judge the truth and untruth of his central philosophical analyses. By dismissing Heidegger's philosophy in this way, we actually forfeit every chance of understanding the possibly deep connections between his philosophy and his Nazism. Moreover, by morally condemning Heidegger and his thinking as Nazi we easily demonize him and refuse to acknowledge that the philosophical and ethical-existential difficulties that motivated his Nazism may still constitute serious temptations for ourselves—perhaps in ways that we do not readily recognize.

8 The imperative not to demonize Heidegger—or his philosophy—when judging him, but rather to be open to what lessons his philosophico-political problems might teach us about *ourselves* is expressed well by Jeff Malpas: "true judgment never sets the one judged apart from the one who judges, but rather proceeds from recognition of the human character of evil as well as good—which is why all judgement ought properly to contain an element of sorrow or compassion, even if it may be hard to recognize or feel. The language of contamination, infection, and taint, and with it the tendency toward exclusionary forms of judgment, becomes especially problematic inasmuch as it readily serves to conceal our own areas of blindness, our own failings, and even our own complicity in some of the phenomena that we rightly condemn" (Malpas 2016: 11). Cf. also Sheehan 1993: 92.

11 *The Event That Opens the World*

1 For some exceptions to this general tendency, see Young 2002 and Wrathall 2011.

2 Julian Young has noted that "'the gods' of the late Heidegger" are "the reincarnations of early Heidegger's heroes" (2002: 96). I agree. However, it seems to me that Young's definition of the gods as "exemplary, charismatic and therefore authoritative, figures memorialized in the collective memory of the culture" (33) is unduly narrow. As far as I can see, what Heidegger has in mind is not necessarily real historical persons but rather values and ideals that can be manifest in many forms: they may be present to us in the form of—as exemplified by—real historical persons or more or less mythological figures (like Jesus, Mother Theresa, and Odysseus); or they may be present as ideals and virtues that figure in narratives, proverbs and other discourses without being tied to any specific persons.

3 Against the kind of interpretation suggested here, Günter Figal has argued that Heidegger does not anticipate anything like a return of the gods: the modern "experience of the flight of the gods" explicated by Heidegger "must not turn into an expectation of a return of the gods" (Figal 2000: 184, my translation). According to Figal, the experience of the flight of the gods is an "experience of being, inasmuch as being itself—or, rather, beyung—in this experience comes to fruition in its basic character of self-refusal" (183). Since the experience of the gods as departed and absent is essential for accessing the openness of being as that which makes all relations of the human being to the world possible, Figal argues, the return of the gods would "immediately cover up the experience of being-possible" (184). However, it seems to me that Figal too strongly identifies the experience of the flight of the gods with

the experience of the openness of being. To be sure, Heidegger believes that the nihilistic experience of the departure of the gods is a symptom and an indication of the forgetfulness of the openness of being characterizing the tradition of metaphysics. Still, as far as I can see, Heidegger's later thinking is guided by the notion that it is possible to think the event of being in its very withdrawal and, by thus attending to the source of all historical being, to open up the possibility of instituting a holy and binding world, a world where our highest values address us as gods.

4   Here, I have interpreted Heidegger's "gods" as referring to the substantial values and ideals of an historical world in so far as they address us as holy and binding. It seems that when Heidegger talks about "gods" and "divinities" in the plural, this is what he primarily has in mind. However, when Heidegger speaks about "the god" or "the last god" in the singular, he tends to refer not to the substantial values of the world but to the hidden source of the world. As we shall see, Heidegger thinks that the artist can only open up a binding world by receiving and gathering the divine hints—the most primordial conceptions—bestowed by the history in which she stands and by grounding the world in the material-sensuous milieu of the earth. Hence, the world that is opened up emerges as ultimately springing from a source beyond the artist and the artwork, a source that essentially remains hidden and mysterious. This hidden source of the unity of the world, which the artwork lets appear precisely as hidden, Heidegger tends to call "the god." As he writes in the essay "… Poetically Man Dwells …": "the unknown god appears as the unknown through the manifestness of the sky" (GA 7: 201/223). Young (2002: 94–5) makes a similar distinction between "the gods" and "the God."

5   For studies of Heidegger's conception of language see, e.g., Kockelmans 1972; Bernasconi 1984; Taylor 1995b; Lafont 2000; Powell 2013.

6   Hence, I think Espinet is mistaken in his suggestion that Heidegger's thinking of the earth would imply a critical dismissal of the analysis of *Being and Time* according to which we primarily experience things not as sensual data but in terms of their significance in our world (cf. Espinet 2011: 57–8). This analysis essentially remains in place. What Heidegger's thinking of the earth *does* do is develop the material-sensual dimension of the world itself as a dimension specifying and giving the world its paradigmatic shape. Espinet's attempt to argue that the material-sensual "earth" has the capacity of harboring new meanings is mirrored in his notion that the experienceable manifold of sensual qualities—which Espinet names *physis*—is played out on the "surface" of the earth, the "inner" of which remains concealed: "What becomes manifest in the appearing of the earth is an inaccessible interior that is concealed by an outer surface, an interior which can only come to fruition as outer surface" (56, my translation). The idea, however, that the experienceable dimension of sensuality is a manifestation of a hidden inner dimension, seems misleading. As I have tried to show Heidegger's "earth" is nothing but the material-sensual setting of the world, and beyond this it is just a meaningless abstraction. This also means that the self-secludedness of the earth does not signify the hidden interiority of sensuality but sensuality itself in its contradistinction to the openness of the world: sensuality as something that does not itself radiate phenomenal meaning but which constitutes the specifying and formative yet phenomenally inaccessible and closed dimension of the historical world.

7   For some studies of the fourfold, see Mitchell 2015 and Young 2006.

8   Andrew J. Mitchell has called the fourfold Heidegger's "most phenomenological thought": "The simple things around us—indeed, the things themselves—become

the focus of his attention and lead him to a phenomenologically more robust sense of the world than heretofore found in his work" (2010: 208–9). However, as I see it, Heidegger's conception of the fourfold is neither very phenomenological nor very robust. First, I will argue that the notion of the fourfold in no way unsettles Heidegger's conviction that our experience of things is determined by our history and that we have no access to meaningful beings that transcend our historical contexts of meaning. Second, I will argue that the later Heidegger's insufficient and ambivalent use of phenomenological descriptions makes him unable to give a very robust and concrete sense to the notion of the fourfold.

9   Cf. also GA 7: 174–5/172–3 for Heidegger's description of how a jug gathers the elements of the fourfold.

12 Heidegger's Late Historical Thinking

1   Other texts touching on this question are: Heidegger's letter to William J. Richardson from 1962, "On the Question Concerning the Determination of the Matter for Thinking" from 1965 (GA 16: 620–33), and some sections from the four seminars that Heidegger conducted in Le Thor and Zähringen 1966–73 (GA 15).

2   Crowell's claim leans heavily on what may appear to be Heidegger's affirmation of "phenomenological seeing" in "Letter on Humanism." Looking back at *Being and Time* as a first effort to advance toward the question of the truth of being Heidegger writes: "In the poverty of its first breakthrough, the thinking that tries to advance thought into the truth of being brings only a small part of that wholly other dimension to language. This language even falsifies itself, for it does not yet succeed in retaining the essential help of phenomenological seeing while dispensing with the inappropriate concern with 'science' and 'research.' But in order to make the attempt at thinking recognizable and at the same time understandable for existing philosophy, it could at first be expressed only within the horizon of that existing philosophy and the use of its current terms" (GA 9: 357/271). This Crowell interprets as meaning that from the viewpoint of the later Heidegger it is the "concern with 'science' and 'research'" and not with "phenomenological seeing" that "spoils the project of *Being and Time*" (2001: 227). However, even though the text can be taken to support Crowell's reading, it is also open for a divergent reading. Bearing in mind that Heidegger is always apt to use the word "seeing" as a formal indication of whatever mode of thinking that answers to the matter in question, his dismissal of the "concern with 'science' and 'research'" could also be read to include the Husserlian ideal of intuitive givenness as the paradigm of phenomenological seeing.

3   Beginning in 1949, Heidegger develops the style that will henceforth characterize his thinking. In lieu of the mighty, almost Hegelian, historical projections of the late 1930s he now develops his thinking in the form of shorter texts which, in a lapidary style avoiding the metaphysical conceptuality of the tradition and drawing on the resources of everyday language and its etymologies, stake out finite paths of thought through limited historical-textual contexts. This also means that the idea about the necessity for thinking to proceed through a transition from the first to the other historical moves into the background. However, it is never completely absent or discarded. As late as in 1973, in a seminar in Zähringen, Heidegger states: "According to me, the entry (*Einkehr*) into the essential domain of Da-sein, discussed at the end of yesterday's session—that entry which would render possible the experience of the

instancy (*Inständigkeit*) in the clearing of being—is only possible through the detour of a return to the beginning (*Rückkehr zum Anfang*). But this return is not a 'return to Parmenides.' It is not a question of returning (*zurückzukehren*) *to* Parmenides. Nothing more is required than to *turn toward* (*zukehren*) Parmenides. The return occurs in the *echo* of Parmenides. It occurs as that hearing which opens itself to the word of Parmenides from out of our present age, the epoch of the sending (*Schickung*) of being as enframing (*Ge-stell*)" (GA 15: 394/77).

4   Mark Wrathall has tried to make sense of the self-withdrawing character of the clearing by arguing that the clearing works most effectively when it is invisible: "For the available possibilities to have authority as possibilities ... we cannot be aware that other possibilities are being ruled out or concealed from us" (2011: 34). The downside of this is that "having lost sight of the concealment that makes it all possible, we become convinced of the necessity and unique correctness of our way of inhabiting the world" (35). However, it seems that by arguing in this way Wrathall cannot account for the fact that Heidegger's entire effort to reflect on the clearing is motivated by the thought that only through such reflection can the world again become binding for us. Indeed, it seems that Heidegger's thinking on this point is almost the opposite to what Wrathall suggests. According to Heidegger, it is precisely our suppression of the clearing—of the finitude of historical being—and our metaphysical will to ground beings that is at the root of nihilism. Our metaphysical effort to ground and conceive of our historical world as universal and necessary is a symptom of our inability to accept the true source of its authority—namely, the fact that it constitutes our finite destiny. By contrast, Heidegger believes that acknowledging and articulating the clearing implies letting our historical world regain its authority over us as our finite ultimate given while recognizing that it is finite and surrounded by other potential worlds. Still, although Wrathall's analysis is exegetically dubious it seems to me that it is philosophically on target. That is to say, it seems quite true that the almost unshakeable authority pertaining to the dominant values and norms and gods of many historical societies has in large part been due to the conception of these values as necessary and natural. Moreover, it seems that the growing consciousness of the historical finitude of all collective values and ideals has gone hand in hand with a diminishing of the previously unquestioned authority enjoyed by such values. Heidegger reacts to this situation by insisting that only by radically accepting the finitude of historical being can we experience such being as binding again. However, as I shall argue in the epilogue, his account of the bindingness of historical being is bound to fail.

Epilogue Being Open Toward Beings

13 The Sources of Ethical-Existential Normativity

1   As is well known, there is a long tradition of criticism directed against the alleged relativism, irrationalism, and anti-realism of historicist value-philosophy. The classic criticisms of Heidegger by Tugendhat ([1969] 1992, 1970) and Habermas (1987) fall squarely within this tradition. However, whereas the traditional critique has primarily been concerned with epistemological-ontological questions—focusing on the criteria for judging the validity of values and on the ontological status of such values—my critical question concerns the sources of normative force and motivation.

Although I cannot argue this here, I want to note that pursuing this question is not only unsettling to historicist value-philosophy; rather, it is unsettling to the very idea that such impersonal things as values, norms, and principles could in themselves be the source of moral normativity and motivation. The insistence of the moral realist or universalist that there are values that are real and/or universally valid does nothing to explain the possible normative and motivating force of such values. As long as we attempt to make sense of morality in terms of a relationship between the human being and impersonal values and principles, we are barred from understanding what it means to experience genuine moral claims and from differentiating between the different kinds of normative force—moral, amoral, immoral—that values and principles may exert on us on account of different motives.

2   Since this is not the place for a detailed critical engagement with Levinas, suffice it to mention what I see as two of the main problems in his thinking on ethics. First, even though Levinas stresses the other's claim on me and my responsibility for the other, he does not acknowledge the possibility of a direct loving care and desire for the other person as such. The claim of the other is described in terms of an obligation or demand imposed on my basic egoism, and my possibility of goodness is characterized as a "sacrifice without reserve" (Levinas 1981: 15). Ultimately, Levinas conceives of our direct relation to the other human being—who, in himself, is characterized as "the nondesirable, the undesirable *par excellence*" (1998: 68–9)—as an indirect means to realize our primary desire for God as the totally other. Second, Levinas's inability to account for the possibility of a positive love for the other goes hand in hand with an inability to distinguish clearly between such love and its opposite, namely our egoistic desire for collective affirmation. It is precisely Levinas's blindness on this point that makes him unable to recognize the extent to which his desire for God can be seen as yet another strategy for covering up the possibility of loving and caring for the other, a strategy characterized by a narcissistic logic of resentment according to which my sacrifice and self-denial evidence the superior dignity and godliness of my soul. For an excellent critique of Levinas, which pursues the same kinds of critical claims indicated here, see Backström 2007: 183–92.

3   In Westerlund (2019a) I provide a phenomenological analysis of shame as rooted in the desire for social affirmation and conditioned by our capacity for social self-consciousness.

4   I will not discuss Heidegger's notion of the fourfold separately here since I do not believe that it changes his way of accounting for the binding force of the world in any decisive manner. Seeing the issue differently, Mark Wrathall has argued that Heidegger's analysis of the fourfold shows a way out of the nihilism of the modern age. Wrathall's central argument is that the modern technological world rids all beings of their existential importance by taking them as purely instrumental resources that are removed from their local settings and appear universally available and interchangeable to us. In such a world, he writes, we can be completely "indifferent to particular places, people, and things" (2011: 201). Wrathall goes on to argue that dwelling in the fourfold is tantamount to allowing the different aspects of the fourfold—our particular earth, the temporal cycles of our heaven, the particular mortals of our community, and the particular matters that we revere as holy—to condition our way of life. In this way, the particular local things and people around us are not treated as interchangeable but are taken as constitutive of the lives we live: "When our practices incorporate the fourfold, such things will have importance beyond their instrumental use in our current activities because they and only they are geared to our way of inhabiting the

world. As a result, they, and only they, can be used to be who we are" (2011: 209). It seems to me that Wrathall is able to articulate a central aspect of how, according to Heidegger, dwelling in the fourfold may increase the bindningness and weight of our finite world and the things within it. However, this kind of account cannot compensate for Heidegger's basic denial of the other person as an absolute source of ethical-existential normativity and significance. Ultimately, the givenness of the things around us as unique and constitutive parts of our lives only amounts to an increase in the bindingness of our collective practices and norms. Such bindingness has nothing to do with genuine ethical claims, without which we remain trapped in our egoistic-collectivist motives. In fact, Wrathall from the outset defines the intrinsic "existential importance" that dwelling in the fourfold is supposed to grant to entities as "importance for our self-realization" (200). However, what this implies is that the intrinsic importance that things and persons are thought to manifest in the post-technological Heideggerian world is reducible to the instrumental value they have for our egocentric urge to realize our collective identity.

5 Heidegger's analysis of the They in *Being and Time* exhibited a keen awareness of our tendency to succumb to collective pressure: renounce our personal responsibility and do what They do and think what They think. However, in his magnum opus Heidegger offered no account of how our historical meanings and values can address us as binding beyond the de facto norms of the They. When in his later thinking he tries to provide just such an account, he lets his earlier analysis of the They drop out—for good. This is not a coincidence. If I am right in claiming that Heidegger's later account of the bindingness of our highest ideals or values remains anchored in our egoistic-collectivist motives, then his earlier notion of the They would necessarily have challenged and potentially upset this account. It would have forced him to specify the difference between the collective pressure of the They and the bindingness of a collective historical world; moreover, it would have insinuated the possibly corrupt nature of the motives underlying the grand rhetoric of holiness and gods. Hence, Heidegger has to repress his earlier concept of the They with its more or less latent insights into the workings of collective pressure. In fact, Heidegger's ability to drop this concept could perhaps also be taken as a token that his analysis of the They did not delve so deep into the existential motives behind our tendency to yield to collective pressure. If it had, it would have been difficult for him to persuade himself that his thinking of the *Ereignis*—or, for that matter, his analysis of authenticity in *Being and Time*—would have been free of these motives.

6 In fact, these statements are quite analogous to Heidegger's terrible assertion in his *Black Notebooks* that the "nihilism" of the final stage of metaphysics is "more uncanny" than the "concentration camps" (GA 97: 59). Only the victims have been changed. Instead of the Jews—and the other victims of the Holocaust—in particular, we now have whoever would be killed by the wars and bombs that Heidegger fantasizes about.

14 *The Sources of Truth*

1 Lafont's book is an extensively revised translation of the original German book *Sprache und Welterschließung. Zur linguistischen Wende der Hermeneutik Heideggers* from 1994.
2 Jacques Derrida is also known for having proposed a critical deconstruction and delimitation of Heidegger's notion of the ontological difference. However, I will

not be considering Derrida's critique since I believe it does not really question the ontological difference in the sense attempted here but rather amounts to a kind of critical elaboration of the ontological difference, an elaboration that rests on a basic affirmation of that very difference. Derrida writes: "entity and being, ontic and ontological, 'ontico-ontological,' are, in an original style, *derivative* with regard to difference; and with respect to what I shall later call *différance*, an economic concept designating the production of differing/deferring. The ontico-ontological difference and its ground (*Grund*) in the 'transcendence of Dasein' are not absolutely originary. Différance by itself would be more 'originary,' but one would no longer be able to call it 'origin' or 'ground,' those notions belonging essentially to the history of onto-theology, to the system functioning as the effacing of difference. It can, however, be thought of in the closest proximity to itself only on one condition: that one begins by determining it as the ontico-ontological difference before erasing that determination. The necessity of passing through that erased determination, the necessity of that *trick of writing* is irreducible" (1997: 23–4). However, even though Derrida suggests that the ontological difference is "derivate" with respect to *différance*—that "*différance* ... (is) 'older' than the ontological difference" (1982: 22)—his own idea of *différance* presupposes the ontological difference: the notion that our direct intuitive experience of beings as meaningful is determined by the historical contexts of meaning into which we are thrown. It is the ontological difference which forms the basis of Derrida's attempt to articulate *différance* as the logic of differing/deferring which, he claims, characterizes our historical contexts of meaning, and which supposedly produces what appears as the identifiable meanings of our direct experience. Hence, the ontological difference cannot be conceived as another historical effect of *différance*. Instead, it must be presupposed as the basic hierarchical structure that grounds the possibility of postulating différance as the "non-full, non-simple, structured and differentiating origin of differences" and deconstruction as the primary task of thinking (1982: 11). If it turned out that Heidegger's notion of the ontological difference is flawed and misleading; if it turned out that our factical historical contexts of meaning do not determine what we can experience but merely constitute our fallible preconceptions and concepts which receive their truth/untruth from our direct experience of beings—then Derrida's conception of *différance* as the basic logic regulating the production of meaning and truth would also collapse.

3 Taylor Carman and Mark Wrathall have both contested Lafont's claim that Heidegger is already a linguistic idealist in *Being and Time,* and I basically agree with their critique on this point (see Carman 2002: 206–13; Wrathall 2002: 222–4). However, both of them wrongly take this as evidence for the untenability of Lafont's central thesis that, according to Heidegger, our understanding of being radically determines what we can experience as beings. In this, it seems to me that they do not see or acknowledge the challenge that Lafont's critique actually poses to Heidegger's basic notion of the ontological difference, and the additional arguments they offer against Lafont are quite meager and unconvincing. Although Lafont, in replying to Carman and Wrathall, retains her thesis about the linguisticality of Dasein's understanding of being, she also—quite rightly—notes that this thesis is not relevant for the force of her basic critique: "Here, I must confess that I do not understand how the issue of whether meaning is prelinguistic or not could have any impact whatsoever on the question of whether (and in which way) our experience is essentially prejudiced by a prior understanding, linguistic or otherwise. My concern here is the allegedly a priori *status* of such an understanding and not its specific structure or *content*. If it turned out that

our cognitive capacities are essentially determined by our prelinguistic interpretative access to the world, I would not feel any better about it" (Lafont 2002: 244).

4 To clarify Heidegger's view on the truth of empirical concepts, we would have to take a closer look at his discussions of the empirical sciences. Here, there are at least two aspects that may seem to confirm Lafont's interpretation of Heidegger as a relativist far removed from Putnam's fallibilist realism (cf. Lafont 2000: 259–75). To begin with, Heidegger repeatedly insists that the positive sciences are grounded in a basic ontological understanding of the being of their object domain. This ontological understanding is not achieved—and cannot be questioned—by the sciences themselves since it always already guides their positive investigations (cf. SZ: 10–11). Furthermore, he claims that the scientific revolution of the sixteenth and seventeenth centuries should not be seen as a simple advance in our knowledge of nature. Rather, the primary happening of the scientific revolution is that a new ontological understanding of nature as a "closed system of spatio-temporally related units of mass" (GA 5: 78) is established. Since this understanding, which guides the natural science of Galileo and Newton, is radically different from the old Aristotelean understanding of nature, there is no point in saying that the new natural science would be better at discovering nature: "A historical reflection will recognize that it makes utterly no sense to measure the Aristotelian theory of motion straightforwardly against the results of the research of *Galileo* and to judge the former as antiquated, the latter as progressive; for in each case, nature means something completely different" (GA 45: 52–3/48). According to Lafont, the above claims imply that, according to Heidegger, the understanding of being guiding the natural sciences determines in advance what the sciences can identify and discover as facts of nature. Hence, the Aristotelian and the modern natural science share no "identical reference" (Lafont 2000: 273)—no common beings—that they could be said to investigate more or less successfully. However, although I cannot argue this in detail here, I want to suggest that the main thrust of Heidegger's argument is *not* that our preceding understanding of being would determine any of the specific results of the natural sciences. Rather, his point is that the natural sciences presuppose a certain understanding of nature that determines their basic methodology and prescribes what kinds of being they will be able to discover. As regards the scientific revolution, his decisive idea seems to be that since the new natural science rests on an understanding of nature that radically differs from that of Aristotle, the knowledge of the new science does not address or answer the questions and concerns of the old one. This, however, does not rule out the possibility that the concepts and theories of the empirical natural sciences can be true or false, depending on their ability to depict and explain facts that are what they are independently of these conceptions. What is more, in so far as premodern natural philosophy had any ambition at all to explain and control the causal workings of nature—as I am sure it did—there is no reason not to view the modern natural sciences as a superior realization of *that* ambition. Whether or not Heidegger would be willing to countersign this interpretation, I think it is in line with the main point of his argument.

5 It seems to me that it is this dimension of understanding that is the focal point of Denis McManus's recent major study (2012) of Heidegger's conception of truth. One aim of the study is to defend an interpretation of Heidegger that escapes the criticism—of Tugendhat and Lafont—that Heidegger unjustifiably makes our understanding of our historical world immune to the question of truth. McManus suggests that Heidegger's notion of Dasein's prior understanding of the "world" or of "being" refers to our basic understanding of and familiarity with the practices of our historical community, such

as hammering or—to take McManus's example of choice—measuring. According to McManus, such practices "'constitute' ... the objects that they allow us to describe" (136). That is, the understanding involved in mastering different practices makes it possible to encounter and pass true or false judgments about the kinds of entities opened up by the practice in question. Given that the historical practices constitute the beings that they allow to appear, McManus argues, they cannot be said to be true or false depending on whether they correspond with these beings: "it makes no sense to evaluate the 'truth' of the descriptive practices themselves, in the sense of assessing a correspondence of fit or a lack of correspondence or fit between them and the objects that they allow us to describe" (166). My sense is that McManus analysis captures and illuminates a particular dimension of Heidegger's analysis of being-in-the-world. However, this dimension of understanding is just one layer in Heidegger's conception of the historical understanding that supposedly determines what we can experience as phenomena. My claim is that when it comes to our understanding of the values and ideals that give ethical-existential significance to phenomena and our understanding of the sense of being, which links our experience in its entirety, Heidegger's historicist dismissal of the question of truth is indeed unjustified and untrue.

6   I owe the example of Huck and Jim to Joel Backström (2007: 240–2), who also uses it to bring out the difference between love and social morality.
7   Cf. Gadamer [1960] 2004, 1990; Taylor 1989, 1995a; MacIntyre 1977, 1985.

15 *Phenomenology and Historical Reflection*

1   Here, it might also be good to point out that phenomenological descriptions of necessary and universal structures in the end rest on human experiences that are not in themselves necessary but contingent (which is not the same as saying that they are culturally and historically specific and changeable). As Steven Crowell has put it: "For Husserl, essences are grasped *in re* through imaginative variation of what is given. Hence their necessity is always conditional: given such and such a thing, it must have these and those features. Whereas Kant attempts to establish that a certain *type* of experience is necessary by arguing that without it no unified self-consciousness is possible, Husserl can only reflect on the essential features of experiences that the subject *happens* to have. ... For the same reason, phenomenological necessity differs from traditional metaphysical or absolute necessity. It cannot explain why there *must be* certain things. For instance, phenomenological reflection can establish a necessary connection between memory and perception: the act of remembering something refers necessarily to a previous act of perceiving it. But phenomenology can give no reason why there must be anything like memory, as a Leibnizian might argue that memory is necessary to the best of all possible worlds" (Crowell 2003: 108). That is to say, whereas phenomenology cannot say anything about the necessity of the experiences that it investigates—for all we know, our human ways of experiencing could have been different—it can nevertheless explicate the essential and necessary structures characterizing these experiences.
2   In a previous article (Westerlund 2014b) I put forward the view that the claim of phenomenology to disclose essential and necessary structures of experience is problematic. I argued that phenomenological descriptions are always—necessarily, eh?—descriptions of particular experiences and that there is no phenomenological

basis for claiming that they necessarily hold for all experiences of the same kind. Instead, I suggested that all phenomenology can do is "to project, on the basis of descriptions of particular experiences, general paradigms of meaning whose range and explanatory force is principally open and shows itself in the *de facto* ability of the paradigms to illuminate the particular experiences and situations we encounter" (272). I now believe this argument was misguided. It now seems clear to me that to phenomenologically understand an experience *means* to understand not just one particular experience but the essential structures that constitute a certain kind or possibility of experience and make it what it is. To be sure, phenomenological descriptions are fallible and it is always an open question exactly what kind or level of experience that the description is able to describe. In my former article I mistakenly took this as a reason for rejecting the necessity claims of phenomenology as unjustified.

3 For more on this, see Westerlund (2019b).
4 Cf. Solomon 2007: 127–200.

BIBLIOGRAPHY

Apel, Karl-Otto (1973), *Transformationen der Philosophie. Band 1. Sprachanalytik, Semiotik, Hermeneutik*, Berlin: Suhrkamp Verlag.
Apel, Karl-Otto (1989), "Sinnkonstitution und Geltungsrechtfertigung. Heidegger und das Problem der Transzendentalphilosophie," in Siegried Blasche, Wolfgang R. Köhler, and Wolfgang Kuhlmann (eds.), *Martin Heidegger: Innen- und Außensichten*, 131–75, Frankfurt am Main: Surhkamp.
Backman, Jussi (2005), "Divine and Mortal Motivation: On the Movement of Life in Aristotle and Heidegger," *Continental Philosophy Review* 38 (3–4): 241–61.
Backman, Jussi (2016), *Complicated Presence: Heidegger and the Postmetaphysical Unity of Being*, Albany: State University of New York Press.
Backström, Joel (2007), *The Fear of Openness: An Essay on Friendship and the Roots of Morality*, Åbo: Åbo Akademi University Press.
Backström, Joel, and Hannes Nykänen (2007), "Collectivity, Evil and the Dynamics of Moral Value," *Journal of Evaluation in Clinical Practice* 22: 466–76.
Bambach, Charles R. (1995), *Heidegger, Dilthey, and the Crisis of Historicism*, Ithaca, NY: Cornell University Press.
Bernasconi, Robert (1984), *The Question of Language in Heidegger's History of Being*, Atlantic Highlands, NJ: Humanities Press.
Bernasconi, Robert (1993), "'The Double Concept of Philosophy' and the Place of Ethics in *Being and Time*," in Robert Bernasconi, *Heidegger in Question: The Art of Existing*, 25–39, Atlantic Highlands, NJ: Humanities Press.
Bernet, Rudolf (1990), "Husserl and Heidegger on Intentionality and Being," *Journal of the British Society for Phenomenology* 21 (2): 136–52.
Boedeker, Edgar C., Jr. (2005), "Phenomenology," in Hubert L. Dreyfus and Mark A. Wrathall (eds.), *A Companion to Heidegger*, 156–72, Malden, MA: Blackwell.
Brogan, Walter (2005), *Heidegger and Aristotle: The Twofoldness of Being*, Albany: State University of New York Press.
Campbell, Scott M. (2012), *The Early Heidegger's Philosophy of Life: Facticity, Being, and Language*, New York: Fordham University Press.
Carman, Taylor (1994), "On Being Social: A Reply to Olafson," *Inquiry: An Interdisciplinary Journal of Philosophy* 37 (2): 203–23.
Carman, Taylor (2002), "Was Heidegger a Linguistic Idealist?," *Inquiry: An Interdisciplinary Journal of Philosophy* 45 (2): 205–15.
Carman, Taylor (2003), *Heidegger's Analytic*, Cambridge: Cambridge University Press.
Carman, Taylor (2005), "Authenticity," in Hubert L. Dreyfus and Mark A. Wrathall (eds.), *A Companion to Heidegger*, 285–96, Malden, MA: Blackwell.
Cerbone, David R. (2003), "Distance and Proximity in Phenomenology: Husserl and Heideger," *The New Yearbook for Phenomenology and Phenomenological Philosophy* III: 1–26.
Critchley, Simon (2008), "Heidegger for Beginners," in Steven Levine (ed.), *On Heidegger's Being and Time*, 9–55, London: Routledge.

Crowe, Benjamin D. (2006), *Heidegger's Religious Origins: Destruction and Authenticity*, Bloomington: Indiana University Press.
Crowell, Steven (2001), *Husserl, Heidegger, and the Space of Meaning*, Evanston, IL: Northwestern University Press.
Crowell, Steven (2003), "Facticity and Transcendental Philosophy," in Jeff Malpas (ed.), *From Kant to Davidson: Philosophy and the Idea of the Transcendental*, 100–21, London: Routledge.
Crowell, Steven (2008), "Measure-Taking: Meaning and Normativity in Heidegger's Philosophy," *Continental Philosophy Review* 41 (3): 261–76.
Crowell, Steven (2013), *Normativity and Phenomenology in Husserl and Heidegger*, Cambridge: Cambridge University Press.
Dahlstrom, Daniel O. (1994), "Heidegger's Method: Philosophical Concepts as Formal Indications," *Review of Metaphysics* 47 (4): 775–95.
Dahlstrom, Daniel O. (2001), *Heidegger's Concept of Truth*, Cambridge: Cambridge University Press.
Dastur, Françoise (1991), "Heidegger und die 'Logische Untersuchungen,'" *Heidegger Studies* 7: 37–51.
Dastur, Françoise (1999), *Heidegger and the Question of Time*, trans. François Raffoul and David Pettigrew, New York: Humanity Books.
Dawkins, Richard (1989). *The Selfish Gene*, Oxford: Oxford University Press.
Denker, Alfred (2004), "Heidegger's Lebens- und Denkweg 1909–1919," in Alfred Denker, Hans-Helmuth Gander, and Holger Zaborowski, *Heidegger-Jahrbuch 1: Heidegger und die Anfänge seines Denkens*, 97–122, Freiburg: Karl Alber Verlag.
Denker, Alfred, and Holger Zaborowski, eds. (2017), *Heidegger-Jahrbuch 11: Zur Hermeneutik der "schwarzen Hefte,"* Freiburg: Karl Alber Verlag.
Denker, Alfred, Günter Figal, Franco Volpi, and Holger Zaborowski, eds. (2007), *Heidegger- Jahrbuch 3: Heidegger und Aristoteles*, Freiburg: Karl Alber Verlag.
Derrida, Jacques (1982), *Margins of Philosophy*, trans. Alan Bass, Chicago, IL: University of Chicago Press.
Derrida, Jacques (1989), *Of Spirit. Heidegger and the Question*, trans. Geoffrey Bennington and Rachel Bowlby, Chicago, IL: University of Chicago Press.
Derrida, Jacques (1997), *Of Grammatology*, trans. Gayatri Chakravorty Spivak, Baltimore, MD: John Hopkins University Press.
Dreyfus, Hubert L. (1991), *Being-in-the-World: A Commentary on Heidegger's Being and Time, Division I*, Cambridge, MA: MIT Press.
Espinet, David (2011), "Kunst und Natur. Der Streit von Welt und Erde," in David Espinet and Tobias Keiling (eds.), *Heideggers Ursprung des Kunstwerkes. Ein kooperativer Kommentar*, 46–65, Frankfurt am Main: Vittorio Klostermann.
Espinet, David, Günter Figal, Tobias Keiling, and Nikola Mirkovic (2018), *Heidegger's "Schwarze Hefte" im Kontext: Geschichte, Politik, Ideologie*, Tübingen: Mohr Siebeck.
Farin, Ingo, and Jeff Malpas, eds. (2016), *Reading Heidegger's Black Notebooks 1931–1941*, Cambridge, MA: MIT Press.
Faye, Emmanuel (2009), *Heidegger: The Introduction of Nazism into Philosophy in Light of the Unpublished Seminars of 1933–1935*, trans. Michael B. Smith, New Haven, CT: Yale University Press.
Fehér, István M. (1994), "Phenomenology, Hermeneutics, *Lebensphilosophie*: Heidegger's Confrontation with Husserl, Dilthey, and Jaspers," in Theodore Kisiel and John van Buren (eds.), *Reading Heidegger from the Start: Essays in His Earliest Thought*, 73–89, Albany: State University of New York Press.

Figal, Günter (1992), *Martin Heidegger zur Einführung*, Hamburg: Junius Verlag.
Figal, Günter (2000), "Gottesvergessenheit. Über das Zentrum von Heideggers *Beiträgen zur Philosophie*," *Internationale Zeitschrift für Philosophie* 2: 176–89.
Figal, Günter (2006), *Gegenständlichkeit: Das Hermeneutische und die Philosophie*, Tübingen: Mohr Siebeck.
Figal, Günter (2007), "Heidegger als Aristoteliker," in Alfred Denker, Günter Figal, Franco Volpi, and Holger Zaborowski (eds.), *Heidegger-Jahrbuch 3: Heidegger und Aristoteles*, 53–76, Freiburg: Karl Alber Verlag.
Figal, Günter (2009), *Zu Heidegger. Antworten und Fragen*, Frankfurt am Main: Vittorio Klostermann.
Figal, Günter, and Hans-Helmuth Gander, eds. (2013), *Heidegger und Husserl. Neue Perspektive*, 2nd edition, Frankfurt am Main: Vittorio Klostermann.
Friedman, Michael (2000), *A Parting of the Ways: Carnap, Cassirer, and Heidegger*, Chicago, IL: Open Court.
Gadamer, Hans-Georg ([1960] 2004), *Truth and Method*, 2nd revised edition, trans. Joel Weinsheimer and Donald G. Marshall, London: Continuum.
Gadamer, Hans-Georg (1986), "Destruktion und Dekonstruktion," in *Gesammelte Werke. Band 2. Hermeneutik II*, 361–72, Tübingen: J. C. B. Mohr.
Gadamer, Hans-Georg (1987), *Gesammelte Werke. Band 3. Neuere Philosophie I*, Tübingen: J. C. B. Mohr.
Gander, Hans-Helmuth, and Magnus Striet (2016), *Heideggers Weg in die Moderne. Eine Verortung der "schwarzen Hefte*," Frankfurt am Main: Vittorio Klostermann.
Gethmann, Carl Friedrich (1974), *Verstehen und Auslegung. Das Methodenproblem in der Philosophie Martin Heideggers*, Bonn: Bouvier Verlag Herbert Grundmann.
Gethmann, Carl Friedrich (1989), "Heideggers Wahrheitskonzeption in seiner Marburger Vorlesungen. Zur Vorgeschichte von 'Sein und Zeit' (§44)," in Siegried Blasche, Wolfgang R. Köhler, and Wolfgang Kuhlmann (eds.), *Martin Heidegger: Innen- und Außensichten*, 101–30, Frankfurt am Main: Surhkamp.
Gorner, Paul (2007), *Heidegger's Being and Time: An Introduction*, Cambridge: Cambridge University Press.
Grondin, Jean (1995), "Prolegomena to an Understanding of Heidegger's Turn," in Jean Grondin, *Sources of Hermeneutics*, 61–98, Albany: State University of New York Press.
Guignon, Charles (1983), *Heidegger and the Problem of Knowledge*, Indianapolis, IN: Hackett.
Guignon, Charles (1993), "Authenticity, Moral Values, and Psychotherapy," in Charles Guignon (ed.), *Cambridge Companion to Heidegger*, 215–39, Cambridge: Cambridge University Press.
Guignon, Charles (2004), "Becoming a Self: The Role of Authenticity in *Being and Time*," in Charles Guignon (ed.), *The Existentialists: Critical Essays on Kierkegaard, Nietzsche, Heidegger, and Sartre*, 119–32, Lanham, MD: Rowman & Littlefield.
Habermas, Jürgen (1987), *The Philosophical Discourse of Modernity: Twelve Lectures*, trans. Frederick Lawrence, Cambridge, MA: MIT Press.
Heinz, Marion, and Sidonie Kellerer (2016), *Martin Heideggers "Schwarze Hefte". Eine philosophisch-politische Debatte*, Berlin: Suhrkamp Verlag.
Hopkins, Burt C. (1993). *Intentionality in Husserl and Heidegger: The Problem of the Original Method and Phenomenon of Phenomenology*, Dordrecht: Kluwer Academic, 1993.

Inkpin, Andrew (2010), "Formale Anzeige und das Voraussetzungsproblem," in Friederike Rese (ed.), *Heidegger und Husserl im Vergleich*, 13–33, Frankfurt am Main: Vittorio Klostermann.

Kasmier, David (2010), "A Defense of Husserl's Method of Free Variation," in Pol Vandevelde and Sebastian Luft (eds.), *Epistemology, Archaeology, Ethics: Current Investigations of Husserl's Corpus*, 21–40, London: Continuum.

Kisiel, Theodore (1992), "Das Kriegsnotsemester 1919: Heideggers Durchbruch zur hermeneutischen Phänomenologie," *Philosophisches Jahrbuch* 99 (1): 105–20.

Kisiel, Theodore (1993), *The Genesis of Heidegger's Being and Time*, Berkeley: University of California Press.

Kisiel, Theodore (1995), "Why Students of Heidegger Will Have to Read Emil Lask," *Man and World* 28 (3): 197–240.

Kisiel, Theodore, and Thomas Sheehan, eds. (2007), *Becoming Heidegger: On the Trail of His Early Occasional Writings, 1910–1927*, Evanston, IL: Northwestern University Press.

Kockelmans, Joseph J. (1972), *On Heidegger and Language*, Evanston, IL: Northwestern University Press.

Krell, David Farrell (1986), "Fundamental Ontology, Meta-Ontology, Frontal Ontology," in David Farrell Krell, *Intimations of Mortality: Time, Truth, and Finitude in Heidegger's Thinking of Being*, 27–46, University Park: Pennsylvania State University Press.

Krell, David Farrell (1992), *Daimon Life: Heidegger and Life-Philosophy*, Bloomington: Indiana University Press.

Lafont, Cristina (2000), *Heidegger, Language, and World-Disclosure*, trans. Graham Harman, Cambridge: Cambridge University Press.

Lafont, Cristina (2002), "Replies," *Inquiry: An Interdisciplinary Journal of Philosophy* 45 (2): 229–48.

Levin, David Michael (1968), "Induction and Husserl's Theory of Eidetic Variation," *Philosophy and Phenomenological Research* 29 (1): 1–15.

Levinas, Emmanuel (1969), *Totality and Infinity: An Essay on Exteriority*, trans. Alphonso Lingis, Pittsburgh, PA: Duquesne University Press.

Levinas, Emmanuel (1981), *Otherwise Than Being or Beyond Essence*, trans. Alphonso Lingis, The Hague: Martinus Nijhoff.

Levinas, Emmanuel (1996), "Is Ontology Fundamental?," in Adriaan T. Peperzak, Simon Critchley, and Robert Bernasconi (eds.), *Basic Philosophical Writings*, 1–10, Bloomington: Indiana University Press.

Levinas, Emmanuel (1998), *Of God Who Comes to Mind*, trans. Bettina Bergo, Stanford, CA: Stanford University Press.

Löwith, Karl (1960), *Gesammelte Abhandlungen*, Stuttgart: Metzler.

Löwith, Karl (1994), *My Life in Germany before and after 1933*, trans. E. King, London: Athlone Press.

Maakreel, Rudolf (2004), "Dilthey, Heidegger und der Vollzugssinn der Geschichte," in Alfred Denker, Hans-Helmuth Gander, and Holger Zaborowski (eds.), *Heidegger-Jahrbuch 1: Heidegger und die Anfänge seines Denkens*, 307–21, Freiburg: Karl Alber Verlag.

MacIntyre, Alasdair (1977), "Epistemological Crises, Dramatic Narrative, and the Philosophy of Science," *The Monist* 60 (4): 453–72.

MacIntyre, Alasdair (1985), *After Virtue: A Study in Moral Theory*, 2nd edition, London: Duckworth.

Malpas, Jeff (2016), "On the Philosophical Reading of Heidegger: Situating the *Black Notebooks*," in Ingo Farin and Jeff Malpas (eds.), *Reading Heidegger's Black Notebooks 1931-1941*, 3-22, Cambridge, MA: MIT Press.
Marion, Jean-Luc (1998), *Reduction and Givenness: Investigations of Husserl, Heidegger, and Phenomenology*, trans. Thomas A. Carlson, Evanston, IL: Northwestern University Press.
McManus, Denis (2012), *Heidegger and the Measure of Truth: Themes from His Early Philosophy*, Oxford: Oxford University Press.
McManus, Denis (2013), "Heidegger on Scepticism, Truth and Falsehood," in Mark A. Wrathall (ed.), *The Cambridge Companion to Heidegger's "Being and Time,"* Cambridge: Cambridge University Press.
McNeill, William (1999), *The Glance of the Eye: Heidegger, Aristotle, and the Ends of Theory*, Albany: State University of New York Press.
Milchman, Alan, and Alan Rosenberg (1997), "Martin Heidegger and the University as a Site for the Transformation of Human Existence," *Review of Politics* 50 (1): 75-96.
Mitchell, Andrew J. (2010), "The Fourfold," in Bret W. David (ed.), *Martin Heidegger: Key Concepts*, 208-18, Durham: Acumen.
Mitchell, Andrew J. (2015), *The Fourfold: Reading the Late Heidegger*, Evanston, IL: Northwestern University Press.
Mitchell, Andrew J., and Peter Trawny, eds. (2017), *Heidegger's Black Notebooks: Responses to Anti-Semitism*, New York: Columbia University Press.
Mohanty, J. N. (1989), *Transcendental Phenomenology: An Analytic Account*, Oxford: Blackwell.
Moran, Dermot (2000), *Introduction to Phenomenology*, London: Routledge.
Moran, Dermot (2007), "Heidegger's Transcendental Phenomenology in the Light of Husserl's Project of First Philosophy," in Steven Crowell and Jeff Malpas (eds.), *Transcendental Heidegger*, 135-50, Stanford, CA: Stanford University Press.
Mulhall, Stephen (1996), *Heidegger and Being and Time*, London: Routledge.
Mulligan, Kevin (1995), "Perception," in Barry Smith and David Woodruff Smith (eds.), *Cambridge Companion to Husserl*, 168-238, Cambridge: Cambridge University Press.
Natorp, Paul (1912), *Allgemeine Psychologie nach kritischer Methode*, Tübingen: J.C.B Mohr.
Nykänen, Hannes (2002), *The "I," the "You" and the Soul: An Ethics of Conscience*, Åbo: Åbo Akademi University Press.
Okrent, Mark (1988), *Heidegger's Pragmatism: Understanding, Being, and the Critique of Metaphysics*, Ithaca, NY: Cornell University Press.
Olafson, Frederick A. (1994a), "Heidegger *à la* Wittgenstein or 'Coping' with Professor Dreyfus," *Inquiry: An Interdisciplinary Journal of Philosophy* 37 (1): 45-64.
Olafson, Frederick A. (1994b), "Individualism, Subjectivity, and Presence: A Response to Taylor Carman," *Inquiry: An Interdisciplinary Journal of Philosophy* 37 (3): 331-7.
Olafson, Frederick A. (2000), "Heidegger's Thought and Nazism," *Inquiry: An Interdisciplinary Journal of Philosophy* 43 (3): 271-88.
Ott, Hugo (1993), *Martin Heidegger: A Political Life*, trans. Allan Blunden, New York: Basic Books.
Oudemans, Theodore C. W. (1990), "Heideggers 'logische Untersuchungen,'" *Heidegger Studies* 6: 85-105.
Overgaard, Søren (2003), "Heidegger's Early Critique of Husserl," *International Journal of Philosophical Studies* 11 (2): 157-75.

Overgaard, Søren (2004), *Husserl and Heidegger on Being in the World*, Dordrecht: Kluwer Academic.
Polt, Richard (2016), "Ponderings II–VI: Black Notebooks 1931–1938," book review, *Notre Dame Philosophical Reviews*. Available online: https://ndpr.nd.edu/news/ponderings-ii-vi-black-notebooks-1931-1938/ (accessed August 28, 2018).
Powell, Jeffrey, ed. (2013), *Heidegger and Language*, Bloomington: Indiana University Press.
Pöggeler, Otto (1989), "Heideggers logische Untersuchungen," in Siegried Blasche, Wolfgang R. Köhler, and Wolfgang Kuhlmann (eds.), *Martin Heidegger: Innen- und Außensichten*, 75–100, Frankfurt am Main: Surhkamp.
Richardson, William J. (1963), *Heidegger: Through Phenomenology to Thought*, The Hague: Martinus Nijhoff.
Richter, Ewald (1989), "Heidegger's These von 'Überspringen der Welt' in traditionellen Wahrheitstheorien und die Fortführung der Wahrheits-frage nach Sein und Zeit," *Heidegger Studies* 5: 47–78.
Rorty, Richard (1999), "On Heidegger's Nazism," in *Philosophy and Social Hope*, 190–7, New York: Penguin Books.
Rosales, Alberto (1970), *Transzendenz und Differenz. Ein Beitrag zum Problem der ontologischen Differenz beim frühen Heidegger*, The Hague: Martinus Nijhoff.
Ruin, Hans (1994), *Enigmatic Origins: Tracing the Theme of Historicity through Heidegger's Works*, Stockholm: Almqvist & Wiksell.
Sadler, Ted (1996), *Heidegger and Aristotle: The Question of Being*, London: Atholone.
Safranski, Rüdiger (1998), *Martin Heidegger: Between Good and Evil*, trans. Ewald Osers, Cambridge, MA: Harvard University Press.
Sallis, John (1978), "Where Does 'Being and Time' Begin? Commentary on Section 1–4," in Frederick Elliston (ed.), *Heidegger's Existential Analytic*, 98–118, The Hague: Mouton.
Sallis, John (1990), *Echoes: After Heidegger*, Bloomington: Indiana University Press.
Scharff, Robert C. (1997), "Heidegger's 'Appropriation' of Dilthey before *Being and Time*," *Journal of the History of Philosophy* 35 (1): 105–28.
Schürmann, Reiner (1990), *Heidegger on Being and Acting: From Principles to Anarchy*, trans. Christine-Marie Gros and Reiner Schürmann, Bloomington: Indiana University Press.
Sellars, Wilfrid (1956), "Empiricism and the Philosophy of Mind," in Herbert Feigl and Michael Scriven (eds.), *Minnesota Studies in the Philosophy of Science, Volume I: The Foundations of Science and the Concepts of Psychology and Psychoanalysis*, 253–329, Minneapolis: University of Minnesota Press.
Sheehan, Thomas (1978), "Heidegger's Interpretation of Aristotle: *Dynamis* and *Ereignis*," *Philosophy Research Archives* 4: 278–314.
Sheehan, Thomas (1981), "Heidegger's Early Years: Fragments for a Philosophical Biography," in Thomas Sheehan (ed.), *Heidegger: The Man and the Thinker*, 3–20, Chicago, IL: Precedent.
Sheehan, Thomas (1984), "Time and Being, 1925–1927," in Robert W. Shahan and J. Mohanty (ed.), *Thinking about Being*, 177–219, Norman: Oklahoma University Press.
Sheehan, Thomas (1988a), "Heidegger's Lehrjahre," in John Sallis, Giuseppina Moneta, and Jacques Taminiaux (eds.), *The Collegium Phaenomenologicum: The First Ten Years*, 77–137, Dordrecht: Kluwer Academic.
Sheehan, Thomas (1988b), "*Hermeneia* and *Apophansis*: The Early Heidegger on Aristotle," in Franco Volpi, Jean-François Mattei, Thomas Sheehan, Jean-François

Courtine, Jacques Taminiaux, John Sallis, Dominique Janicaud, Arion L. Kelkel, Rudolf Bernet, Robert Brisart, Klaus Held, Michel Haar, and Samuel Ijsseling (eds.), *Heidegger et l'idée de la phénoménologie*, 67–80, Dordrecht: Kluwer Academic.
Sheehan, Thomas (1993), "Reading a Life: Heidegger and Hard Times," in Charles Guignon (ed.), *Cambridge Companion to Heidegger*, 70–96, Cambridge: Cambridge University Press.
Sheehan, Thomas (2001a), "A Paradigm Shift in Heidegger Research," *Continental Philosophy Review* 34 (2): 183–202.
Sheehan, Thomas (2001b), "*Kehre* and *Ereignis*: A Prolegomenon to *Introduction to Metaphysics*," in Richard Polt and Gregory Fried, *A Companion to Heidegger's Introduction to Metaphysics*, 3–16, New Haven, CT: Yale University Press.
Sheehan, Thomas (2010), "The Turn," in Bret W. Davis (ed.), *Martin Heidegger: Key Concepts*, 82–101, Durham: Acumen.
Sluga, Hans (1993), *Heidegger's Crisis: Philosophy and Politics in Nazi Germany*, Cambridge, MA: Harvard University Press.
Solomon, Robert (2007), *True to Our Feelings. What Our Emotions Are Really Telling Us*, Oxford: Oxford University Press.
Stapleton, Timothy (1983), *Husserl and Heidegger: The Question of a Phenomenological Beginning*, Albany: State University of New York Press.
Steinmann, Michael (2004), "Der frühe Heidegger und sein Verhältnis zum Neukantianismus," in Alfred Denker, Hans-Helmuth Gander, and Holger Zaborowski (eds.), *Heidegger-Jahrbuch* 1: *Heidegger und die Anfänge seines Denkens*, 259–93, Freiburg: Karl Alber Verlag.
Taminiaux, Jacques (1977), "Heidegger and Husserl's *Logical Investigations*: In Remembrance of Heidegger's Last Seminar (Zähringen, 1973)," *Research in Phenomenology* 7 (1): 58–83.
Taminiaux, Jacques (1991), *Heidegger and the Project of Fundamental Ontology*, ed. and trans. Michael Genre, Albany: State University of New York Press.
Taylor, Charles (1989), *Sources of the Self: The Making of the Modern Identity*, Cambridge: Cambridge University Press.
Taylor, Charles (1995a), "Explanation and Practial Reason," in *Philosophical Arguments*, 34–60, Cambridge, MA: Harvard University Press.
Taylor, Charles (1995b), "Heidegger, Language, and Ecology," in *Philosophical Arguments*, 100–26, Cambridge, MA: Harvard University Press.
Thomson, Iain (2001), "Heidegger on Ontological Education, or: How We Become What We Are," *Inquiry: An Interdisciplinary Journal of Philosophy* 43 (4): 243–68.
Thomson, Iain (2003), "Heidegger and the Politics of the University," *Journal of the History of Philosophy* 41 (4): 515–42.
Thomson, Iain (2005), "Heidegger and National Socialism," in Hubert L. Dreyfus and Mark A. Wrathall (eds.), *A Companion to Heidegger*, 32–48, Oxford: Blackwell.
Trawny, Peter (2015), *Heidegger und der Mythos der jüdischen Weltverschwörung*, 3., überarbeitete und erweiterte Auflage. Frankfurt am Main: Vittorio Klostermann.
Trawny, Peter, and Andrew J. Mitchell, eds. (2015), *Heidegger, die Juden, noch einmal*, Frankfurt am Main: Vittorio Klostermann.
Tugendhat, Ernst ([1969] 1992), "Heidegger's Idea of Truth," in Christopher Macann (ed.), *Martin Heidegger: Critical Assessments, Volume III: Language*, trans. Christopher Macann, 79–92, London: Routledge.
Twain, Mark ([1884] 1994), *Adventures of Huckleberry Finn*, New York: Dover.

Tugendhat, Ernst (1970), *Der Begriff der Wahrheit bei Husserl und Heidegger*, 2nd edition, Berlin: Walter de Gruyter.
van Buren, John (1990), "The Young Heidegger and Phenomenology," *Man and World* 23 (3): 239–72.
van Buren, John (1994a), *The Young Heidegger: Rumor of the Hidden King*, Bloomington: Indiana University Press.
van Buren, John (1994b), "Martin Heidegger, Martin Luther," in Theodore Kisiel and John van Buren (eds.), *Reading Heidegger from the Start: Essays in his Earliest Thought*, 159–74, Albany: State University of New York Press.
van Buren, John (1995), "The Ethics of Formale Anzeige in Heidegger," *American Catholic Philosophical Quarterly* 69 (2): 157–70.
van Dijk, R. J. A. (1991), "Grundbegriffe der Metaphysik. Zur formalanzeigenden Struktur der philosophischen Begriffe bei Heidegger," *Heidegger-Studies* 7: 89–109.
von Herrmann, Friedrich-Wilhelm (1981), *Der Begriff der Phänomenologie bei Husserl und Heidegger*, Frankfurt am Main: Klostermann.
von Herrmann, Friedrich-Wilhelm (1990), *Weg und Methode. Zur hermeneutischen Phänomenologie des seinsgeschichtlichen Denkens*, Frankfurt am Main: Vittorio Klostermann.
von Herrmann, Friedrich-Wilhelm (2000), *Hermeneutik und Reflexion. Der Begriff der Phänomenologie bei Heidegger und Husserl*, Frankfurt am Main: Vittorio Klostermann.
Wanatabe, Jiro (1993), "Categorial Intuition and the Understanding of Being in Husserl and Heidegger," in John Sallis (ed.), *Reading Heidegger: Commemorations*, 109–17, Bloomington: Indiana University Press.
Weigelt, Charlotta (2002), *The Logic of Life: Heidegger's Retrieval of Aristotle's Concept of Logos*, Stockholm: Almqvist & Wiksell.
Westerlund, Fredrik (2010), "Phenomenology as Understanding of Origin: Remarks on Heidegger's First Critique of Husserl," in Friederike Rese (ed.), *Husserl und Heidegger im Vergleich*, 34–56, Frankfurt am Main: Vittorio Klostermann.
Westerlund, Fredrik (2014a), *Heidegger and the Problem of Phenomenality*, doctoral dissertation, University of Helsinki. Available online: https://helda.helsinki.fi/bitstream/handle/10138/45258/Westerlund_vaitoskirja.pdf?sequence=1 (accessed January 31, 2019).
Westerlund, Fredrik (2014b), "What Is a Transcendental Description?," in Sara Heinämaa, Mirja Hartimo, and Timo Miettinen (eds.), *Phenomenology and the Transcendental*, 257–75, London: Routledge.
Westerlund, Fredrik (2019a), "To See Oneself as Seen by Others: A Phenomenological Analysis of the Interpersonal Motives and Structure of Shame," *Journal of Phenomenological Psychology* 50: 60–89.
Westerlund, Fredrik (2019b), "Who Wants to Be Understood? The Desire for Social Affirmation and the Existential Challenge of Self-Understanding," in Joel Backström, Hannes Nykänen, Niklas Toivakainen, and Thomas Wallgren (eds.), *Moral Foundations of Philosophy of Mind*, London: Palgrave Macmillan.
Wittgenstein, Ludwig (1922), *Tractatus Logico-Philosophicus*, trans. C. K. Ogden, London: Routledge.
Wittgenstein, Ludwig (1958), *Philosophical Investigations*, trans. G. E. M. Anscombe, Oxford: Basil Blackwell.
Wolin, Richard (1990), *The Politics of Being: The Political Thought of Martin Heidegger*, Oxford: Oxford University Press.

Wrathall, Mark A. (1999), "Heidegger and Truth as Correspondence," *International Journal of Philosophical Studies* 7 (1): 69–77.
Wrathall, Mark A. (2002), "Heidegger, Truth, and Reference," *Inquiry: An Interdisciplinary Journal of Philosophy* 45 (2): 217–28.
Wrathall, Mark A. (2011), *Heidegger and Unconcealment: Truth, Language, and History*, Cambridge: Cambridge University Press.
Young, Julian (2001), *Heidegger's Philosophy of Art*, Cambridge: Cambridge University Press.
Young, Julian (2002), *Heidegger's Later Philosophy*, Cambridge: Cambridge University Press.
Young, Julian (2006), "The Fourfold," in Charles B. Guignon (ed.), *The Cambridge Companion to Heidegger*, 2nd edition, 373–92, Cambridge: Cambridge University Press.
Zahavi, Dan (2003a), *Husserl's Phenomenology*, Stanford, CA: Standford University Press.
Zahavi, Dan (2003b), "How to Investigate Subjectivity: Natorp and Heidegger on Reflection," *Continental Philosophy Review* 36 (2): 155–76.
Zaner, Richard M. (1973a), "Examples and Possibles: A Criticism of Husserl's Theory of Free- Phantasy Variation," *Research in Phenomenology* 3 (1): 29–43.
Zaner, Richard M. (1973b), "The Art of Free Phantasy Variation in Rigorous Phenomenological Science," in Fred Kersten and Richard Zaner (eds.), *Phenomenology: Continuation and Criticism: Essays in Memory of Dorion Cairns*, 192–219, The Hague: Martinus Nijhoff.
Zimmerman, Michael E. (1990), *Heidegger's Confrontation with Modernity*, Bloomington: Indiana University Press.

INDEX

affirmation; *see* desire for social affirmation
alētheia 139–41, 184
   see also openness of being
anti-Semitism 130, 145, 149–50, 153, 155, 159
anxiety (*Angst*) 104–5, 126–7
Apel, Karl-Otto 59, 229 n.2, 236 n.6
a priori 68, 75, 99, 126, 208–9
Aristotle 7–9, 14, 165, 234 n.1
   ambivalent role for Heidegger 63–4
   exemplary explicator of the historical structure of life 14, 57–9, 63–9, 123, 218, 230 n.4, 232 n.3, 235 n.2
   originator of Western metaphysics 64–6, 79, 123, 139–42, 184, 187–8, 218, 240 n.2
   paradigm of theoretical philosophy 24, 53, 57
   and the scientific revolution 249 n.4
art; *see* work of art
as-structure (*Als-Struktur*) 7, 9, 48, 65, 74, 93–4, 129, 136, 142, 232 n.3
Augustine, Saint 14, 53
Austin, J. L. 1–2
authenticity (*Eigentlichkeit*)
   acknowledgement of groundlessness and finitude 89–90, 104–6
   as the basic existential challenge of life 103, 145–7
   choice of life-possibilities 89–90, 106, 108–12
   condition for ontological understanding 103, 127, 137
   egoism; *see* egoism
   Heidegger's analysis central to the problem of phenomena 61, 103, 134 n.2
   Heidegger's failure to account for the bindingness of life-possibilities; *see* bindingness
   oscillation between subjectivism and collectivism 9, 61, 108–12, 129, 146
   primacy over ethics 146

Backman, Jussi 229 n.2, 234 n.1
Backström, Joel 194, 246 n.2, 250 n.6
Bambach, Charles R. 230 n.5
beginning
   Greek beginning of philosophy 10, 123, 130–1, 139–41, 151, 167, 183, 218–19, 244 n.3
   first beginning vs. other beginning 131, 158–9, 167, 184, 218–19
being
   and beings; *see* ontological difference
   as phenomenality 1, 17–19, 22–6, 28, 44, 80, 82, 87, 97–8, 223
   question of 54, 58, 70, 79–84, 119, 138–9, 232 n.3
   sense of; *see under* sense
   truth of; *see under* truth
   understanding of; *see under* understanding
being-historical thinking (*seynsgeschichtliches Denken*); *see* historical reflection
being-in-the-world (*In-der-Welt-sein*) 58, 83, 85, 96, 99, 120, 126, 234 n.2, 250 n.5
being-with (*Mitsein*) 109, 113–15
Bergson, Henri 14, 53
Bernasconi, Robert 229 n.2, 240 n.1, 243 n.5
Bernet, Rudolf 235 n.3
bindingness of historical being and values
   Heidegger's failure to account for 9, 61, 101, 106–8, 112, 115, 117–18, 129–31, 136–7, 193, 238 n.3
   the question of 6, 9–10, 61, 101, 107, 117–18, 129–31, 137–8, 141–3, 145–8, 151–2, 158–9, 161–4, 166–8,

175, 177, 184, 190, 193–6, 201–5, 241 n.3, 242 n.3, 243 n.4, 245 n.4, 246 n.4, 247 n.5
  see also holy
Black Notebooks 145, 149–50, 155–9, 241 nn.2, 5, 247 n.6
Blochmann, Elisabeth 150
Boedeker, Edgar C. Jr. 7
Brandom, Robert 1
Brogan, Walter 234 n.1
Buber, Martin 157, 194

Campbell, Scott M. 231 n.1
care (*Sorge*) 115
Carman, Taylor 229 n.2, 236 nn.4, 6, 237 n.8, 238 nn.1, 4, 248 n.3
categorial intuition 68, 70–5, 235 nn.4, 7
Cerbone, David 231 n.6
Cézanne, Paul 173
choice; *see under* authenticity
Christianity 14, 53–4, 57, 230 n.5
circumspection (*Umsicht*) 64–5, 87–8, 90–3
  pragmatic meaning of 90–3
  as unthematic skillful coping 91–2
clearing (*Lichtung*) 131, 171–2, 185–90, 193, 217–22, 245 n.4
collectivism 9, 61, 108, 110, 112, 114, 117–18, 129, 146, 154, 159, 196, 198–201, 203–5, 214, 238 n.1, 239 n.7, 241 n.3, 246 n.4, 247 n.5
conscience
  Heidegger's concept of (*Gewissen*) 104–5, 126–7, 157, 239 n.7
  as love 200, 214
Critchley, Simon 235 n.4
Crowe, Benjamin D. 230 n.5
Crowell, Steven 4, 7, 15, 36, 39, 41, 45, 49–50, 60, 132, 179, 183, 190, 229 nn.1, 3, 230 n.5, 231 n.5, 233 n.8, 235 n.4, 238 n.4, 239 n.7, 240 n.1, 241 n.4, 244 n.2, 251 n.1

Dahlstrom, Daniel O. 4, 41–2, 60, 229 n.1, 231 n.5, 232 n.4, 235 nn.3, 6, 7, 236 nn.1, 4, 6
Dasein
  analytic of 58, 80, 85, 90, 103, 124, 126, 179, 234 n.2

  see also being-in-the-world, life-possibilities, authenticity, egoism, understanding
Dastur, Françoise 4, 5, 229 n.2, 235 n.6
Dawkins, Richard 55
death 104, 110–11, 176–7
decisionism 111–12
deconstruction 1, 59, 217, 221–3, 247–8 n.2
Denker, Alfred 229 n.3, 234 n.1, 241 n.5
Derrida, Jacques 1, 59, 217, 219, 221–3, 232 n.5, 247–8 n.2
Descartes, René 68, 97, 124
desire for social affirmation 21, 31–2, 47, 112–17, 146, 159, 196, 197–201, 214, 224, 246 n.2, 246 n.3
destiny (*Geschick*) 2, 10, 45, 48, 110, 131, 141, 146, 150–2, 161, 164, 177, 184, 193, 202, 207–8, 212, 245 n.4
destruction (*Destruktion*)
  from 1922 and in *Being and Time* 63–4, 95, 107–8, 119–27, 218, 229 n.4, 240 n.1
  Heidegger's earliest Freiburg lectures 38, 41–2
diahermeneutics 232 n.5
différance 217, 221–2, 248 n.2
Dilthey, Wilhelm 8, 14, 53, 59, 230 n.5, 233 n.6
discourse (*Rede*) 95–6
disposition (*Befindlichkeit*) 90
divinities 161, 175–7, 191, 243 n.4
  see also god(s)
Donnellan, Keith 208
Dreyfus, Hubert L. 60, 90, 92, 109, 236 n.4, 238 n.1, 239 n.5
dwelling (*Wohnen*) 176–7, 246–7 n.4

earth (*Erde*) 132, 169–77, 185, 187, 202–4, 236 n.1, 243 n.6, 246 n.4
Eckhart, Meister 14, 54
egoism 55, 81
  of Dasein 108, 112–18, 146, 243 n.3
  of the desire for social affirmation 108, 112, 114, 117, 146, 159, 192, 196, 198–201, 246 n.2, 247 nn.4, 5
equipment (*Zeug*) 86–93, 95, 97, 113, 125, 156, 169, 209–11, 236 nn.1, 3

equiprimordiality (*gleichursprünglichkeit*) 85, 128
Ereignis; *see* event
Espinet, David 132, 169–70, 173, 175, 241 n.5, 243 n.6
essentialism 224–5
ethics
  ethical-existential normativity 10, 61, 91, 103, 106–10, 112–13, 115, 117–18, 154, 157, 162, 194–205, 212–13
  primordial ethics 166–7
  superordination of ontology over ethics; *see under* ontology
  see also love
etymology; *see under* historical reflection
event (*Ereignis*) 10, 129, 131, 139, 141–3, 161, 164, 167–77, 179, 184, 186, 188, 193, 202–4, 217–22, 243 n.3
experiential certainty (*Erfahrungsgewißheit*) 51, 54–5

factical life (*das faktische Leben*) 15, 22, 25, 35, 38, 43, 46, 50–4, 57, 66
  see also pretheoretical experience
familiarity (*Vertrautheit*) 44–8, 197, 203–4
Farin, Ingo 241 n. 5
fate (*Schicksal*) 111, 151
Faye, Emmanuel 242 n. 7
Fehér, István M. 230 n.5
Figal, Günter 4, 5, 6, 64, 80, 229 n.2, 233 n.7, 235 n.1, 240 n.1, 242 n.3
finitude
  of Dasein's historical possibilities 90, 101, 103–6, 110–11, 115–16, 127, 146
  of historical being 2, 4–5, 10, 161–2, 164, 171–2, 177, 185, 187, 190, 195, 202, 205, 207, 212, 216, 225, 245 n.4
  of pretheoretical life 25, 37, 45, 47, 52, 54, 65, 69
  of thinking 59, 131, 190, 244 n.3
first-person experience; *see under* phenomenology
fore-structure (*Vor-Struktur*) 94
formal indication (*formale Anzeige*) 41–2, 232 nn.3, 4, 5
for-the-sake-of (*Worumwillen*) 88–9
  see also life-possibilities
Foucault, Michel 1, 59

fourfold (*Geviert*) 132, 168, 173, 175–7, 188, 191–2, 243 n.7, 243–4 n.8, 244 n.9, 246–7 n.4
freedom
  of Dasein's self-choice 90, 111, 146
  of the world-projection 130, 137–8, 146–7, 152, 167, 170
Friedman, Michael 230 n.5
fundamental ontology, project of 5, 14, 60, 137–8, 142, 145–6
  Heidegger's abandonment of 7, 58, 61, 129–30, 136–7, 139, 190
  Heidegger's view of 58, 79–84
  import and necessity of 9, 69, 81–2
  problems and possibilities 9, 82–4

Gadamer, Hans-Georg 1, 4, 5, 59, 215, 229 n.2, 230 n.5, 250 n.7
Gander, Hans-Helmuth 241 n.5
George, Stefan 176, 188
Gethmann, Carl Friedrich 92–3, 229 n.1, 234 n.1, 236 n.6
givenness
  of historical being 98–9, 101, 103, 105, 112, 125, 129, 131, 140–3, 163–5, 169, 171, 193, 202, 210, 212, 245 n.4; *see also* openness of being
  phenomenal givenness 1–2, 8, 17–19, 21–8, 31–3, 36–46, 51–2, 59, 66, 68–72, 74, 80, 86, 100, 120, 122, 181–2, 185, 187, 214–15, 224, 231 n.4, 232 n.2, 235 n.7, 244 n.2; *see also* phenomena
god(s)
  distinction between gods and the god 243 n.4
  flight of the gods 162, 188
  gods 158, 161–5, 167, 171, 176–7, 185–6, 191, 202–5, 212, 242 nn.2, 3, 243 n.4, 245 n.4, 247 n.5
  as holy values 163–4, 176
  see also holy, divinities, bindingness, hero
Goethe, Johann Wolfgang von 187
Gorner, Paul 236 n.2
Greeks; *see under* beginning
Grondin, Jean 240 n.1
groundlessness
  of Dasein's historical possibilities 90, 99, 103–6, 127

of historical being 2, 4–5, 10, 161–2, 164, 202, 205, 207, 212, 238 n.1
of the world-projection 138
Guignon, Charles B. 4, 60, 119–21, 123–4, 229 n.2, 230 n.5, 238 nn.1, 2, 3, 4, 241 n. 3

Habermas, Jürgen 59, 236 n.6, 245 n.1
Hegel, Georg Wilhelm Friedrich 1, 181, 182, 188, 221, 244 n.3
Heinz, Martion 241 n.5
Heraclitus 141, 166, 188
heritage (*Erbe*) 89–90, 103, 105, 107, 112, 121, 123, 125, 136, 143, 146, 174, 185, 193, 202
hermeneutic-deconstructive reading of Heidegger 4–6, 15, 35, 41, 45, 60, 71, 119–21, 132, 169–70, 179, 195, 229 n.2, 233 n.7
hermeneutic intuition 35, 38
hermeneutics 1, 4–6, 14, 59, 64, 120, 122
hero (*Held*) 89–90, 146, 212, 242 n.2
   see also life-possibilities
historical reflection (*geschichtliche Besinnung*)
   Heidegger's conception of 7, 10, 131–2, 139, 179–92, 217–21
   Heidegger's concrete strategies 186–92
   Heidegger's use of etymology 188–90, 219–21, 244 n.3
   problems and limits of 212–21, 224–5
   as true phenomenology 183
historicity
   the event that opens historical being; *see* event
   Heidegger's concept of historicity (*Geschichtlichkeit*) 89–90
   historical structure of phenomena; *see under* phenomena
   historicity of thinking; *see under* destruction, historical reflection
Hitler, Adolph 148–9, 154
Hölderlin, Friedrich 8, 130, 131, 162, 165, 170, 188
holy 145, 158–9, 161–4, 167, 170–1, 176–7, 201–3, 205, 243 nn.3, 4, 246 n.4, 247 n.5
   see also god(s), bindingness
Hopkins, Burt C. 4, 229 n.1
Huckleberry Finn 214–15, 250 n.6

Husserl, Edmund
   categorial intuition; *see* categorial intuition
   eidetics 20–1, 72–4, 77, 230 n.2
   empirical types 76–7
   Heidegger's first Freiburg critique of 27–33, 37–43, 46, 70
   Heidegger's second Marburg critique of 67–77, 121–2, 126–8
   Heidegger's late critique of 180–3
   intentionality 20–1, 44, 68–9, 72, 77, 100
   layer-ontology 30–1, 69, 76, 231 n.7
   natural attitude 18–20, 28, 31
   noema and *noesis* 20, 31, 44, 128
   phenomenological reduction 19–21, 29, 40, 119–20, 128, 181

idealism 69, 97–9, 208
inauthenticity (*Uneigentlichkeit*) 92, 95, 103–6, 108–9, 114, 116, 238 n.1, 239 n.7
Inkpin, Andrew 232 n.4
intentionality; *see under* Husserl
interpretation (*Auslegung, Interpretation*) 64, 70, 93–5, 119–20, 122–7
intuition
   as basic to phenomenology 1–2, 5–6, 8–11, 15, 18, 21, 28, 33, 35–9, 41–2, 45–8, 60–1, 70, 77, 124–8, 132–3, 179, 182, 194, 215, 217–18, 220–1, 223–4, 227, 230 nn.2, 4, 232 n.5, 233 n.8, 240 n.3, 244 n.2
   Heidegger's critique of 6, 9, 59, 64–5, 70–1, 75–7, 94, 99, 122–4, 132, 139, 181–3, 190–4
   transhistorical character of 8, 39, 41–2, 47–8, 77, 182, 125–6, 182, 213–16, 222–5, 233 n.7

Jaspers, Karl 14
Jesus 89, 242 n.2

Kant, Immanuel 1, 13, 14, 53, 68, 124, 137, 188, 230 n.5, 240 n.3, 250 n.1
Kasmier, David 235 n.5
Kellerer, Sidonie 241 n.5
Kierkegaard, Søren 14, 54, 238 n.1, 241 n.6
Kisiel, Theodore 5, 7, 15, 35, 39, 41, 45–6, 48, 50, 60, 67, 229 nn.2, 3, 230 n.5, 231 n.1, 232 n.4

Kockelmans, Joseph J. 243 n.5
Krell, David Farrell 4, 5, 229 n.2, 230 n.5
Kuhn, Thomas 2

Lacan, Jacques 1, 59
lacunae in *Being and Time* 9, 106–8, 112, 125, 137
Lafont, Cristina 10, 194, 207–10, 229 n.2, 236 n.6, 243 n.5, 247 n.1, 248–9 n.3, 249 n.4, 249 n.5
language
 in *Being and Time* 95–6, 165, 209
 Heidegger's later view of 165–6, 176
 see also formal indication, poetry
Lask, Emil 14
Levin, David Michael 235 n.5
Levinas, Emmanuel 10, 21, 113, 157, 194, 196–7, 200, 239 n.7, 246 n.2
Levi-Strauss, Claude 1
life; *see* factical life, pretheoretical experience
life-philosophy 14, 53–4, 230 n.5
life-possibilities
 choice of; *see under* authenticity
 Heidegger's failure to account for the bindingness of; *see* bindingness
 as historical ideals and values 89–90, 106–7, 116–17, 146, 193
 and identity 89, 106–7, 116–17, 146, 193
 as source of ethical-existential significance 61, 89–90, 146, 193, 238 n.1, 239 n.5
 see also authenticity, god(s)
logos 66, 121, 165, 188–9
love
 love for and care about others as source of morality 10, 55, 115–17, 147, 197–202, 214, 246 n.2, 250 n.6
 as primordial attitude of phenomenology 32, 37–9, 70
Löwith, Karl 67, 111
Luther, Martin 14, 54

Maakreel, Rudolf 230 n.5
MacIntyre, Alasdair 215, 250 n.7
Malpas, Jeff 241 n.5, 242 n.8
Marion, Jean-Luc 234–5 n.2, 235 n.1

matter (*Sache*)
 the matter of thinking 135–6, 180–1, 183, 185–9, 219
 the matters themselves 3–4, 17, 46, 67–8, 76, 100, 122, 127, 180–1, 183, 185, 219, 223
 primal matter (*Ur-Sache*) 187
McDowell, John 1
McManus, Denis 236 n.5
McNeill, William 234 n.1
Merleau-Ponty, Maurice 21
metaphysics, Heidegger's later view of 139–42, 147–50, 153–5, 162–4, 166–7, 180–2, 184–5, 187–9, 204–5, 218–21, 243 n.3, 245 n.4, 247 n.6
metapolitics; *see under* politics
metontology 130, 137–9, 240 n.1
Milchman, Alan 241 n.4
Mitchell, Andrew J. 241 n.5
Mohanty, J. N. 235 n.5
Moran, Dermot 4, 7, 229 n.1
Mulhall, Stephen 236 n.2
Mulligan, Kevin 235 n.6
myth of the given 1

naivety
 genuine naivity 52
 supposed naivity of pretheoretical life 9, 13, 22, 25, 49, 51–3, 55
National Socialism
 biographical facts 130, 148–50, 153, 240 n.1
 destiny of the German people 150–4, 220
 Heidegger's anti-Semitism 130, 145, 149–50, 152–3, 155, 159, 247 n.6
 Heidegger's critique of 153–5
 Heidegger's engagement in 8, 130, 145–59, 166–7, 204–5
 the Holocaust 130, 149–50, 154, 247 n.6
 philosophical roots of Heidegger's engagement 146–8, 150–3, 159, 166–7, 204–5
 race 149, 152
 relevance for understanding Heidegger's thinking 8, 159, 241 n.2, 247 n.7, 247 n.8
 spiritual National Socialism 149, 153, 205
 see also Black Notebooks, politics

Natorp, Paul 14, 25, 231–2 n.2
Nazism; *see* National Socialism
necessity 4, 20, 47, 55–7, 61, 63, 73–4, 77, 81–3, 107, 126, 187, 190, 219–20, 224–5, 233 n.8, 245 n.4, 250 n.1, 250–1 n.2
Neo-Kantianism 13–14, 53, 230 n.5
Nietzsche, Friedrich 14, 53, 131, 139, 162, 188
nihilism 130, 147–55, 157, 162–3, 166–7, 184, 204, 241 n.3, 243 n.3, 245 n.4, 246 n.4, 247 n.6
Nykänen, Hannes 194

obligation; *see* bindingness
Okrent, Mark 60, 92, 93
Olafson, Frederick A. 236 n.4, 241 nn.2, 3
ontological difference 7, 9, 55, 65, 79, 81–2, 99, 132, 138, 173–5, 193, 196, 208–13, 234–5 n.2, 247–8 n.2, 248 n.3
ontology
  fundamental ontology; *see* fundamental ontology
  history of 121, 123–4
  metontology; *see* metontology
  non-primacy of 54–6, 82–3, 154–5, 199–201, 226
  and phenomenology 122
  superordination over ethics 81–2, 138, 145–8, 151–3, 166–7, 196–7, 204–5
openness of being 130–1, 139–43, 157–8, 161–2, 164, 166–7, 169, 176, 184, 204, 208, 215, 240 n.2, 242–3 n.3
others
  Heidegger's denial of others as a source of moral normativity 112–18, 146–8, 153–5, 166–7, 193–4, 196, 202–5
  love for others as the source of moral normativity; *see* love
Ott, Hugo 240 n.1
Oudemans, Theodore C. W. 232 n.4
ousia 64–6, 141, 184, 218
Overgaard, Søren 4, 60, 119–20, 126, 128, 229 n.1, 231 nn.5, 7, 235 nn.2, 4, 236 nn.1, 2, 4

Parmenides 141, 245 n.3
Paul, Saint 14, 53, 54
people (*Volk*) 146–7, 150–2, 171

phenomena
  the event that opens up and gives being; *see* event
  Heidegger's appropriation of the term 66
  historical structure of 9–10, 36, 43–8, 57–9, 61, 63–6, 68, 74–6, 79–82, 85–101, 103, 106–8, 112–13, 129, 132, 136–8, 140–3, 165–6, 174–5, 185–6, 193–4, 207–16, 235 n.2, 237 n.7
  problem/question of 1–2, 6–8, 10, 14–15, 22, 35, 57, 59–61, 80, 85, 103, 129–32, 136, 193, 229 n.3, 231 n.4
  as ultimate and irreducible reality 1, 17–19, 22–6, 28, 44, 80, 82, 87, 97–8, 223
phenomenology
  appeal to intuition; *see* intuition
  ethical-existential challenges of 9, 25, 32–3, 37–8, 56, 83, 127, 226–7
  first-person experience 15, 18–19, 22, 25, 28, 81, 122, 128, 179, 192, 217, 223, 227
  Heidegger's early Freiburg phenomenology 21–4, 36–43, 45–8
  Heidegger's view and practice in *Being and Time* 119–28
  Heidegger's view and practice in his later thought 179–83, 190–2, 221
  Husserl's program 17–21
  and ontology 122
  primordial attitude of 37–9
  reflection; *see* reflection
phainomenon 60, 80, 87, 121
philosophy
  end of 180
  ethical-existential task and import of 49–56, 57–8, 65, 79–84, 129–31, 136–9, 145–8, 164–7, 176, 193, 201–5, 226–7
  as self-destruction 52–3
phronesis 64–6
physis 139, 141, 184, 187, 218, 240 n.2, 243 n.6
Plato 24, 53, 139, 140–2, 184, 187, 190, 218, 240 n.2
poetry 132, 147, 151–2, 164–7, 170–1, 176, 185, 202–5
Pöggeler, Otto 59

politics
　apolitical character of *Being and Time*
　　146, 241 n.3
　metapolitics 152
　problems in Heidegger's later
　　thought 204–5
　see also National Socialism
Polt, Richard 158
possibilities of Dasein; *see* life-possibilities
Powell, Jeffrey 243 n.5
pragmatist reading of Heidegger 60, 90,
　92–3, 236 n.4
presence-at-hand (*Vorhandenheit*) 69–70,
　79, 81, 87, 91, 95, 97, 103–4, 107, 113,
　119, 124–5, 168, 209, 218, 236 n.1
pre-Socratics 8, 139, 141, 184, 187–8, 219
pretheoretical experience
　Aristotle's conception of 64–6
　as experience of ethical-existential
　　significance 15, 24, 28–9, 31–3,
　　40, 182
　naivity; *see* naivety
　primacy of 2, 4, 9, 13–16, 22–7, 28–33,
　　40, 50–1, 53, 56–7, 69–70, 182, 209,
　　231 n.6, 234 n.1
　self-sufficiency of 9, 24, 44, 49–57
　structure of 43–7
primal matter (*Ur-Sache*) 187
principle of all principles
　Heidegger's early reinterpretation 37
　Heidegger's late critique of 181
　Husserl's formulation 17–18
primordial science (*Urwissenschaft,
　Ursprungswissenschaft*) 8, 13–14,
　21–4, 31–2, 35–7, 43, 49–54,
　57, 79–80
Putnam, Hilary 194, 208, 249 n.4

readiness-to-hand (*Zuhandenheit*) 87–8,
　93, 97–8, 108, 113, 124–6, 209, 211,
　236 n.1
realism 69, 97, 194, 249 n.4
reality (*Realität*) 96–9
reflection
　historical; *see* historical reflection
　phenomenological 4–6, 9–10, 15,
　　19–22, 28–32, 35–6, 38–40, 42, 45,
　　48, 57, 61, 64, 68, 70, 71, 77, 119–21,
　　125–8, 130, 132, 182–3, 217, 222–3,
　　227, 231–2 n.2, 233 n.8, 235 n.4,
　　240 n.3
relativism 100, 126, 208, 215, 240 n.2, 245
　n.1, 249 n.4
relevance (*Bewandtnis*) 87–9
repetition; *see* retrieval
resoluteness (*Entschlossenheit*) 89, 109–12,
　156, 205
retrieval (*Wiederholung*) 10, 58, 66, 70,
　76, 107–8, 121, 123, 130, 151, 184,
　218–20, 233 n.8, 240 n.2
Richardson, William J. 7, 59, 135, 136,
　143, 229 n.4, 244 n.1
Richter, Ewald 236 n.6
Rickert, Heinrich 14, 46, 233 n.6
Ricoeur, Paul 1
Rorty, Richard 2, 60, 241 n.2
Rosales, Alberto 235 n.2
Rosenberg, Alan 241 n.4
Rubin, Jane 109, 238 n. 1, 239 n.5
Ruin, Hans 4, 5, 22, 66, 229 n.2,
　233 nn.6, 8, 240 n.1

Sadler, Ted 234 n. 1
Safranski, Rüdiger 240 n.1
Sallis, John 4, 5, 60, 229 n.2
Sartre, Jean-Paul 21
Saussure, Ferdinand de 1, 221
Scharff, Robert C. 230 n.5
Scheler, Max 21
Schürmann, Reiner 241 n.2
Schutz, Alfred 21
self-sufficiency; *see under* pretheoretical
　experience
self-world (*Selbstwelt*) 39, 44
Sellars, Wilfrid 1
sense (*Sinn*)
　of being 9–10, 55, 58, 63, 65, 69–70,
　　75, 79–83, 91, 98, 119, 122, 125, 129,
　　136–7, 142, 145, 218, 249 n.5
　content-sense, relation-sense,
　　enactment-sense 43–4
　definition of 82
sense-data 18, 20, 23, 26, 68, 86
shame 20–1, 32, 47, 56, 83, 116–17, 198–9,
　201, 204, 214, 222, 224–6, 246 n.3
Sheehan, Thomas 60, 67, 130, 135–6, 143,
　229 n.3, 234 n.1, 242 n.8
Simmel, Georg 53

skepticism 97, 236 n.5
Sluga, Hans 240 n.1
solicitude (*Fürsorge*) 114–15
Solomon, Robert 251 n.4
spirit of thinking 155–8, 241 n.6
Stapleton, Timothy 229 n.1, 234 n.1
Stein, Edith 21
Steinmann, Michael 230 n.5
Striet, Magnus 241 n.5
strife between world and earth 131, 139, 143, 157, 167–75, 185–7, 202, 221
subjectivism 9, 61, 108–12
sympathy as primordial attitude of phenomenology 32, 37–9, 70
  see also love

taking-notice (*Kenntnisnahme*) 51, 54–5
Taminiaux, Jacques 235 n.4
Taylor, Charles 215, 243 n.5, 250 n.7
temporality (*Zeitlichkeit*) 54, 59, 66, 124, 127, 129, 218, 234 n.2
theoretical philosophy
  Heidegger's early view of 9, 13, 21–5, 49–51, 53–5
  unfeasibility of 24–7, 37–8
they, the (*das Man*) 9, 61, 92, 101, 103–14, 116–18, 129, 157–8, 238 n.1, 238 n.4, 239 nn.5, 7, 247 n.5
thing (*Ding*) 168–9, 175–7
thinking (*Denken*); *see* historical reflection
Thomson, Iain 241 n.4
thrownness (*Geworfenheit*) 89–90, 99, 105, 112, 143, 146, 152, 173
tool; *see* equipment (*Zeug*)
Trakl, Georg 188
transcendence 137–8
transcendental phenomenology 5, 15, 17, 19, 21, 28–31, 35, 49, 59, 119–21, 126, 182–3
transcendental phenomenological reading of Heidegger 4–6, 15, 35–6, 41, 45, 60, 119, 126, 132, 169, 179
transcendental subject 26, 29–31, 35, 39, 69–70, 74, 128, 180–1
Trawny, Peter 241 n.5
truth
  of being 139–42, 184, 208; *see also* openness of being
  as correspondence or correctness 99, 99–101, 124, 139–42, 207, 210–12, 237 nn.7, 8, 250 n.5
  of empirical concepts 76–7, 208–11, 249 n.4
  Heidegger's historicist view of 10–11, 65, 100–1, 124, 140–2, 174, 194, 207–16, 237 nn.7, 8, 249 n.5
  as openness to transhistorical phenomenal realities 10–11, 194, 213–16, 219, 222, 224, 248 n.2
  question of the essence of truth 139–40, 142
turn (*Kehre*) 5, 7, 10, 129–32, 135–43, 179
Tugendhat, Ernst 10, 59, 100, 111, 194, 208, 229 n.2, 236 n.6, 237 nn.7, 8, 239 n.6, 245 n.1, 249 n.5
Twain, Mark 214–15

unconcealedness 140–2, 161, 184, 186, 208; *see also* openness of being
understanding
  of being 48, 52, 55–6, 58, 61, 65–6, 69, 75, 77, 79–84, 90–2, 95, 97–8, 101, 103–4, 107, 113, 119–26, 131, 137–9, 141–2, 147, 154, 180, 183–5, 188, 196, 207–10, 212–13, 218–20, 233 n.7, 234 n.1, 248 n.3, 249 n.4
  circumspection; *see* circumspection
  of life-possibilities 61, 89–93, 95, 101, 104, 106–12, 193; *see also* life-possibilities
  as projection (*Entwurf*) 90
  three dimensions of 90–3, 210–13
  truth of 207–16
universality 4, 15, 25, 35, 39, 41, 45–6, 52, 57, 72, 77, 89, 99, 104, 109, 115, 126, 137, 142, 182, 190, 201, 223–5, 230 n.3, 231 n.2, 233 nn.7, 8, 245 n.4, 246 n.1, 250 n.1

value
  Heidegger's critique of the concept 150, 163–4
  historical values as ultimate source of ethical-existential normativity 10, 89, 106–7, 110, 116–17, 162–4, 171, 174,

176–7, 185–7, 193–203, 205, 207, 210, 212–14, 218, 221, 237 n.8, 242 n.2, 243 nn.3, 4, 245 nn. 1,4, 247 n.5
van Buren, John 4, 5, 15, 35, 39, 41, 45–6, 48–50, 60, 229 nn.2, 3, 230 n.5, 231 n.1, 232 n.4, 235 n.4
van Dijk, R. J. A. 232 n.4
von Herrmann, Friedrich-Wilhelm 229 nn.2, 3, 231 n.5, 235 n.3

Wanatabe, Jiro 235 n.4
Weigelt, Charlotta 234 n.1
Westerlund, Fredrik 20, 229 n.3, 231 n.5, 232 n.2, 237 n.7, 240 nn.1, 2, 3, 246 n.3, 250 n.2, 251 n.3
Wittgenstein, Ludwig 2, 224–5, 234 n.1
Wolin, Richard 239 n.6, 241 n.3
work of art 10, 143, 162–3, 167–76, 185, 202–3
world (*Welt*)
  ontological structure (worldliness) of 85–6, 88–9
  surrounding world (*Umwelt*) 23–4, 44, 86, 113
  see also being-in-the-world, strife between world and earth
world-projection (*Weltentwurf*) 130, 137–9, 146–8, 151–2, 167, 170, 240 n.1
worldview philosophy 21, 46, 230 n.3
Wrathall, Mark A. 186, 229 n.2, 236 n.6, 237 n.8, 242 n.1, 245 n.4, 246 n.4, 248 n.3

Yorck von Wartenburg, Graf Paul 59
Young, Julian 170, 172, 175, 229 n.2, 242 n.1, 242 n.2, 243 nn.4, 7

Zahavi, Dan 15, 19, 36, 39, 45, 229 n.1, 232 n.2
Zaner, Richard M. 235 n.5
Zimmerman, Michael E. 240 n.1

www.ingramcontent.com/pod-product-compliance
Lightning Source LLC
Chambersburg PA
CBHW070021010526
44117CB00011B/1663